MUSLIM WOMEN
REFORMERS

MUSLIM WOMEN
REFORMERS
INSPIRING VOICES AGAINST OPPRESSION

IDA LICHTER

Prometheus Books

59 John Glenn Drive
Amherst, New York 14228–2119

Published 2009 by Prometheus Books

Inquiries should be addressed to
Prometheus Books
59 John Glenn Drive
Amherst, New York 14228–2119
VOICE: 716–691–0133, ext. 210
FAX: 716–691–0137
WWW.PROMETHEUSBOOKS.COM

13 12 11 10 09   5 4 3 2 1

Library of Congress Cataloging-in-Publication Data

Lichter, Ida, 1947–.
    Muslim women reformers : inspiring voices against oppression / by Ida Lichter.
        p. cm.
    Includes bibliographical references.
    ISBN 978–1–59102–716–4(alk. pbk.)
    1. Women human rights workers—Middle East—Biography. 2. Women human rights workers—Islamic countries—Biography. 3. Women human rights workers—Biography. 4. Muslim women—Biography.

HQ1726.5 .L54 2009
323.092/2—dc22

                                                            2009005799

Printed in the United States of America on acid-free paper

All images unless otherwise noted are reprinted by permission and courtesy of
MEMRI (Middle East Media Research Institute), from E. Glass,
"Cartoons in the Arab Press on the Status of Women in the Arab World,"
Inquiry and Analysis Series, no. 397 (October 17, 2007).

Every attempt has been made to trace accurate ownership of copyrighted material
in this book. Errors and omissions will be corrected in subsequent editions,
provided that notification is sent to the publisher.

To the Muslim heroines who fought for reform and died as jihad targets.

Source: *Syria News* (Syria), August 20, 2007.

CONTENTS

ACKNOWLEDGMENTS

I would like to express my grateful appreciation for the assistance of Julian Maclulich, Keren Simons, Rima Kandelaft, and Courteney Powell.

The man is in the spotlight; the woman remains in the dark.
Source: *Syria News* (Syria), July 23, 2007.

INTRODUCTION

I may lose my life during this process, but if I am able to open a door for rights for one woman, then it is worth it.[1]

Since 9/11, the spotlight on fundamentalist Islam has focused mainly on the ideology of suicide terrorism and martyrdom. However, the central demands of this ideology include enforcing shari'ah law on all Muslim women. The extremists have also declared their wish to defeat the United States[2] and their contempt for Western freedoms. Given the opportunity, they would deny all women their rights.

Our media have generally acted as a megaphone for Islamists, rewarding and magnifying their initial 9/11 and subsequent terrorist acts, designed for maximum publicity and recruitment purposes. In contrast, many Muslims with opposing views have not been given a significant voice. There is considerable ignorance of those determined individuals and organizations, particularly in Muslim countries, who are dedicated to the reform of gender discrimination by challenging discriminatory laws and ideology, often at great personal risk. This anthology is dedicated to amplifying their voices.

To liberated women in the West, the reformers would appear to be challenging a medieval environment of cultural restrictions and misogynistic regulations scripted by religious and patriarchal authorities intent on impounding women's lives. According to shari'ah law, women's dress and activity must be restricted. For example, a woman should not leave the house without authorization from her husband or male guardian, and when she is in a public space, she must be entirely covered and walk with her head bowed. In case an unrelated male is nearby, she should remain covered when visiting the house of a female friend. Choice of spouse is not an option, nor can she marry a non-Muslim. She cannot freely divorce her husband, who is encouraged to beat her if she is disobedient and may divorce her with impunity. In the event of rape, she is considered a temptress and may be punished with the lash or stoning to death. If her family believes she has brought them dishonor by dating an unsuitable man or having an affair, her male kin

17

are empowered to take her life. In such societies, oppression of women exemplifies the tension in Islam between tradition and modernity and is superimposed on nongender political and social restrictions.

There is a wide spectrum of views on the meaning of reform and its relationship to political Islam and shari'ah law. In this context, some Muslim women are simply Islamists who advocate "reform" in order to purify the current "degenerate" Islam and reinstate the earliest, undiluted form of the religion. Some are sympathetic to the use of violent means to overthrow governments and reestablish the Islamic caliphate. This type of reform has been excluded from this discussion.

Muslim women reformers are not a homogeneous group and many are still only fledgling media activists and commentators. Some are religious and some are secular. A number of "religious feminists" are in favor of education and political participation for women but against changes to shari'ah-based marriage and family law; however, most demand such reforms. Some argue that discrimination against women is a product of postcolonial oppression but most attribute greater blame to the culture of male-dominated tribalism and religious patriarchy that, in their belief, has distorted authentic Islam in shari'ah-legislated discrimination.

For example, verses that religious authorities use to justify segregation and veiling in order to protect women from sexual assault can be seen as a pretext for the oppression of women and an opportunity for predatory males. Furthermore, many such verses that were relevant to the period of the Prophet in the seventh century may not be appropriate for the twenty-first.

A great many reformers proclaim that the Koran supports gender equality, and they defend demands for women's rights by emphasizing such examples, occasionally utilizing innovative exegesis of Koranic texts. For those who seek changes within Islam through reinterpretation of religious sources, challenges to Islamic regimes and clergy remain largely untested outside Iran. At this interface, creative argument may be insufficient to extract concessions from powerful, reactionary religious authorities, especially those with a grip on the machinery of state.

Reformers are also hampered by governments that are not answerable to the people and prone to vacillate unpredictably between modernizing and traditional outlooks.

Secular feminist activists like Ayaan Hirsi Ali and Wafa Sultan, who insist on the separation of religion and state and argue that misogyny is integral to the Koran and related texts, are branded traitors and Zionist or American agents. In countries like Iran, women reformers with a secular perspective have tactically chosen to behave and dress according to the law in order to gain a better hearing. Speaking out can also invite personal abuse and physical danger. Both Ayaan Hirsi Ali and Wafa Sultan have been subject to death threats. Similarly, Samira Munir, a Norwegian politician of Pakistani origin, was threatened after she supported a ban against headscarves in schools and spoke out against immigrant honor killings, forced marriages, and female genital mutilation. In November 2005, she died under mysterious circumstances.[3]

Muslim women reformers and Western feminists would appear to be natural allies, jointly campaigning against abuses of women's rights by Islamists. However, many women who promote reform within Islam shun overt alliances with Western organizations for fear of becoming identified with occidental values and feminism, viewed by traditional Islamic society as subversive to Muslim culture, identity, and religion. In an Islamic theocracy like Iran, any association with Western organizations could serve as a pretext to increase pressure on dissident groups, curtailing their progress and reducing hard-won gains. However, for many Muslim women reformers, feminist organizations in the West have been particularly disappointing in their silence, which could be construed as political correctness, apathy, fear, or condescension.

On the rare occasion when a non-Muslim feminist like Norway's Hege Storhaug highlights the plight of Muslim women in her country, she is charged with "burkophobia," paranoia, and bigotry by her country's cultural elite.[4] If Western feminists have been demonized and cowed into shutting down any meaningful debate, what is the message for activists in oppressed environments?

Whether reformers believe discrimination against women originates in Koranic injunction, patriarchal society, or a combination of the two, the Muslim women's reform movement challenges some of the cornerstones of the fundamentalist agenda, and reformers' views and activities have become accessible, often via translations on the Internet. Activists in the Muslim world are, however, facing increasing restrictions on the dissemination of their ideas, as some Middle Eastern countries have shut down thousands of Web sites and blogs, purportedly in the national interest.[5]

In reviewing the recent history of Muslim feminists, some sober conclusions can be drawn, particularly regarding promises of women's rights reform. In the two countries that experienced revolutionary upheaval, Algeria and Iran, women joined forces with men to eject regimes perceived as oppressive in favor of more liberal regimes pledging improved women's rights. In both cases, however, betrayal by the new regimes and also by their male compatriots in revolution resulted in regressive, discriminatory legislative restrictions. In Afghanistan, the fall of the Taliban and a new constitution produced some gains but women reformers had been promised much more. It is clear that patriarchal Muslim males can be unreliable allies when it comes to female rights.

I have attempted an overview of Muslim women activists who have challenged ideas, laws, and culture. Also included are a few biographies of veteran reformers and those who risked and lost their lives in the battle against gender discrimination. As I have focused mainly on reformers in Muslim countries, I have omitted many in the West. Their names can be found on some of the reformist Web sites mentioned at the end of this book. Due to the constraints of space and available information, I have also omitted many worthy women reformers in Muslim lands.

In reviewing the reforms, I have limited my assessment to three countries, Afghanistan, Iran, and Saudi Arabia, where the observable dissidents are most striking in number and activity. In the final chapter, I have added several profiles of Muslim men who have consistently supported the rights of women in the Islamic world. In another section, I have included a limited number of transnational organizations that specifically support Muslim women's rights. The names of more may be found among the Web sites at the end of this book.

I was inspired to compile these profiles of Muslim women reformers from around the world when I became aware of their voices and courageous challenges to institutionalized persecution. Freedom for women in Muslim countries would unlock the potential of half their populations and provide a resource for social and economic development. The reformers merit our attention and support, in the same way that Western activists responded to the dissident movement in the former Soviet Union. Moreover, there is scope for working in a grassroots effort with a growing number of Western-based Islamic reform organizations, in contrast to Western governments, which deal primarily with regimes in power. The preservation of hard-earned human rights in the West, and women's rights in particular, could very well depend on ensuring their development in the Muslim world.

1
AFGHANISTAN

BACKGROUND

Women are the property of men from the waist down.[1]

O ppression of women was common in Afghanistan's tribal society, but the situation improved following independence from British rule in 1919, when King Amanullah introduced reforms. He discouraged the veil and polygamy, and he promoted free choice of spouses and education for women, including higher education abroad. The abolition of child marriage increased the minimum age of marriage to twenty-two for men and eighteen for women. However, these reforms were rejected in 1928 by the Loya Jirga (Grand Assembly). In the same year, the mullahs decreed a jihad against the king, and he was overthrown in 1929.

His successor, Habiballah, was a conservative mullah who revoked the king's reforms by closing all girls' schools, banning secular education for boys, and making the veil compulsory, but in 1959, the government of President Daoud recommended the voluntary removal of the veil. At the same time, the number of girls' schools increased, as well as women's employment, and in 1964, a new constitution ratified equal gender rights to education. The Civil Code, introduced in 1977, enacted a statutory marriageable age. Again, conservative mullahs obstructed the reforms endorsed by President Daoud. Instead, they demanded shari'ah law and elimination of gender equality.

When the Soviet army invaded Afghanistan in 1979, some liberal legislation for women was introduced, but it proved unacceptable to traditionalists. After the Soviet troops withdrew in 1989, the Soviet-backed government remained until 1992, eventually deposed by the mujahideen who were committed to restrictions on women's dress, behavior, movement, and education in the name of Islamic shari'ah law. Penalties were widespread and some women were killed.

In 1994, the Taliban took control of Kabul and enforced shari'ah law. In their zeal, the religious leaders authorized the complete subjugation of women by men and openly blamed women's liberty for the country's political corruption and years of conflict. These views were more widely held by the poor in rural areas where illiteracy was high. Traditional mullahs were afraid that female education would undermine religious authority and were in favor of child marriage or marriage at puberty to prevent sexual immorality.

The rationale for male superiority was derived from the Koran, where men were mentioned first, a man's share was deemed twice that of a woman, and, being unable to support themselves, women were dependent on men for protection. Mullahs also opposed the employment of women outside the home, as their primary duty was to the family.

Afghan women were encouraged to believe they were less intelligent than men and that their only right to education was to religious education. Furthermore, a husband's maintenance and sacrifice were considered to impose a debt in perpetuity. Men had every right to punish wives for noncompliance, and the slightest disobedience carried the threat of retribution in hell.

Women are still treated as items of exchange like land or animals. Using women as collateral has been effective in settling disputes and avoiding longlasting blood feuds. For example, women can be traded as compensation for injury or murder committed by a male member of the family. In such cases, mullahs have justified the woman's sacrifice in the name of Islam, because Islam is a "religion of peace" and such exchanges bring "peace between families."[2]

The Karzai government's authority has appeared more willing to compromise, but in spite of Afghanistan's ratification of major human rights treaties[3] and the overthrow of the Taliban regime in 2001, women and young girls are still subject to discrimination and exploitation. In fact, the overthrow of the Taliban did not end the existing constraints on women. Their notions of obedience to husbands and family, acceptance of responsibility for family honor, and acceptance of a subordinate social, legal, economic, and political role had been internalized. It is estimated that 80 percent of marriages still involve betrothal in infancy and coercion by families. Underage marriage, often to much older men, is widespread and culturally entrenched.[4] Mullahs tend to justify child marriage on the basis that one of the Prophet's wives was only nine years old when he married her.

To procure a wife, a prospective husband is required to pay his bride the *mahr*, or "bride price." However, widows are often forced to remarry into their deceased husband's family so that the family can inherit the dowry.

A major problem is the deeply ingrained culture of degradation and violence justified by religion and tradition: for example, the local religious council (*ulema*) can decide to punish a woman with stoning for adultery. The use of domestic violence to control women is common, but wives are usually obliged by their families to tolerate abusive husbands. In any case, there is little access to justice, as police are loath to investigate and there are few female advocates to represent women. Domestic violence is commonplace, especially against child brides, and for wives who contemplate leaving a violent relationship, there are no shelters. Without husbands, women often become beggars in order to feed their children.[5] Rape and abduction are commonplace in areas of armed conflict and are probably underreported. In cases of rape, four adult witnesses are required to testify, otherwise the victim may be accused of *zina*—any sex outside of marriage, including consensual sex, criminalized in the penal code. Women who refuse to marry a husband chosen by male kin, or who transgress sexual mores by even minimal contact with unrelated males, risk punishment in the form of "honor killings," which are not treated as criminal offenses. Vindicated by dishonor to the family name, this summary retribution is meted out by an informal justice system of *jirgas* and *shuras*, community courts and councils composed entirely of men. Furthermore, when Afghan women human rights activists have attempted to initiate reforms for women's protection, they have encountered hostility, derision, intimidation, and violence, including disfiguring acid attacks.[6]

Lack of social support and unbearable family pressures have forced some young women to run away from home, an action classified as an uncodified crime of "running away" and a punishable offense.[7] Even more desperate are the suicides and attempted suicides by self-immolation, mostly associated with violence in the family.[8]

In this tribal, male-dominated society, run by powerful warlords and consumed by perpetual political instability and drug-financed internecine warfare, reforms to criminalize violence against women, let alone to ensure basic women's rights, are considered irrelevant. Women's lives are in danger for other reasons too. At 1,600 deaths per 100,000 live births, maternal mortality is one of the highest in the world.[9]

Segregation of the sexes severely restricts women's opportunities and daily life. Women still fear venturing into the public space without being fully covered, and seclusion inhibits female access to education and the workplace. Illiteracy is particularly high in rural areas; overall literacy, at only 23.5 percent of the population aged fifteen and older, is one of the lowest in the world; and only 12.6 percent of adult women are literate.[10]

Stories of women's oppression rarely make the news as there are only a small number of female journalists. Those few also encounter discrimination and religious restrictions affecting their work as they cannot travel without a guardian or talk to male strangers.[11]

The new constitution, adopted in 2004, is committed to gender equality in principle but does not specify equal rights in family law.[12] In order to enact laws furthering women's rights, activists achieved the 25 percent women's quota for Afghanistan's parliament but the majority of women delegates are under the control of parties of former mujahideen and told how to use the system. For example, some women drafted a bill to enforce mandatory full body covering for women. Others voted against the 25 percent quota and attacked one woman who voted in favor of it.[13]

Lack of security is the major impediment to women's political participation and reinforces seclusion. Women also need to develop the leadership skills required to build productive grassroots networks and eschew tribal tensions, personal rivalries, and dependency on the international community for the bestowal of women's rights. Major opponents for women activists are the warlords who employ private armies, effectively ruling over widespread regions not yet controlled by the central government. Many have histories of flagrant human rights abuses and some are also radical Islamists.[14] They have no compunction in using scare tactics or violence, and their inclusion in the parliament serves as an affront to women activists.

There has also been some resurgence of the Taliban. Together with Pakistani Islamists, and emboldened by government inaction, it set up new restrictions on women in 2008, forbade polio immunization for children, and instituted strict Islamic punishments in accordance with shari'ah law.[15] The terrorizing of women may include acid attacks. An example involved Islamists on motorcycles who poured acid on girls because they were attending school. According to one defiant schoolgirl, "My message for the enemies is that if they do this 100 times, I am still going to continue my studies."[16]

Various projects have been developed to empower Afghan women. For example, the Afghan Rule of Law Project (AROLP),[17] initiated in 2007, promotes women's rights in Islam through increased public awareness and also critical and progressive reinterpretation within the context of Islam. Strategies to ensure success include co-opting Afghan men willing to defend women's rights. Central to the program is a forum for candid discussion between Islamic clerics and Afghan and non-Afghan scholars, without evading particularly sensitive issues like child marriage.

These words were spoken in Kabul by President Hamid Karzai of Afghanistan on International Women's Day, March 8, 2005:

> Today, women play an important role. . . . Of course women in Afghanistan still face challenges. Girls are married in their childhood or married off to resolve disputes. These practices are cruel, against our religion and no longer acceptable.[18]

However, in February 2009, new family laws that "explicitly sanction marital rape" were hurriedly passed for Afghanistan's Shia minority. Refuting the gender equality enshrined in the new constitution, Article 132 enforces sexual intercourse on wives, Article 133 forbids a wife from leaving the house without her husband's permission, and Article 27 sanctions marriage for girls at the age of their first period.[19] Although President Karzai initially decried "the misinterpretation of the law by Western journalists," he subsequently ordered a review.[20]

REVIEW OF REFORMS

The women reformers described in the following pages have been dedicated to overcoming the lifelong plight faced by most of Afghanistan's women, particularly in the rural areas and still evident in spite of the antidiscrimination legislation enshrined in the new constitution.

A selection of eighteen reformers are mentioned here or described in more detail in the following section. Three of them were assassinated. Nearly all have university degrees, including in economics, languages, medical studies, geology, and international studies, and more recently, some of the younger women have studied abroad. Malalai Joya is self-taught in political science and history.

Social reforms at a basic level have been a priority, although hampered by lack of infrastructure. Educational reforms are at the forefront for Fatana

Gailani, Manizha Naderi, Suraya Parlika, Nilofar Sakhi, Sima Samar, and Masuda Sultan, who are convinced that education is the key to women's empowerment and freedom. Gailani believes that the education of women is the "sole means of keeping children from becoming terrorists."[21]

During the Taliban years, teacher and women's rights advocate Safia Amajan and Suraya Parlika, another feminist activist, ran underground schools at great personal risk. Even in 1978, when Parlika was head of the People's Democratic Party of Afghanistan, the authorities objected to her strong advocacy of women's rights and had her thrown into prison for eighteen months and tortured. Amajan was assassinated in 2005 by the Taliban in Kandahar, one of their major strongholds.

Lt-Col Malalai Kakar, head of Kandahar's department of crimes against women and the most senior female police officer in Afghanistan, was also murdered by the Taliban in Kandahar in September 2008. Kakar, a valiant protector of women suffering domestic violence, had been an inspiring reformer who courageously defied recurrent death threats.[22] Another policewoman was killed in Herat Province in the previous June.[23]

Most reformers faced great peril during the Taliban years. Fatana Gailani, who led the charge to establish the Afghanistan Women Council (AWC) and worked tirelessly for the relief and rights of refugees during the Taliban years, received repeated death threats. Shukria Barakzai, journalist and member of parliament, narrowly escaped death when bombs were planted in her bedroom, and in 2007, she was warned that she might become a target for a suicide bomber.

Basic literacy classes for all women and schools for girls were the aims of Amajan, Parlika, Sima Samar, and the organizations Women for Afghan Women (WAW) and the Women Activities and Social Services Association (WASSA), in a country where the female literacy rate is one of the lowest in the world. If women were literate, much more information vital to their legal entitlements and political participation could be imparted.

For those who are literate, women's publications, *Payam-e-Zan* (Women's Message, a newspaper written, published, and distributed by the Revolutionary Association for the Women of Afghanistan—RAWA), and *Aina-e-Zan* (Women's Mirror), by Shukria Barakzai, have facilitated the dissemination of information regarding women's issues.

Six reformers and reformist organizations have been actively involved in the delivery of medical services, including Dr. Sima Samar, who opened the first women's medical center and the RAWA organization, which established medical clinics for refugees in the Pakistani border cities of Peshawar and Quetta. A veteran surgeon, "the General" Suhaila Seddiqi,[24] who remained in Afghanistan during the Taliban period and consistently treated the Taliban with contempt, was legendary for her surgical skills and responsible for organizing the funding and renovation of Kabul's main hospital. She also held a national conference on HIV and oversaw the vaccination of 6 million Afghan children against polio in order to combat one of the highest rates of child mortality in the world. The WASSA organization, run by Nilofar Sakhi, has focused on outreach programs for hygiene, nutrition, pregnancy, childbirth, and childhood illnesses, particularly in rural areas.

Widespread poverty and lack of welfare prompted reformers Amajan and Parlika, and the organizations RAWA, WAW, and WASSA, to initiate training programs for marketable vocational skills like baking, garment making, handicrafts, mobile phone repair, jam and juice works, and other small businesses. In addition, microloans have been made available to women with entrepreneurial capacity so they can provide for their families.

Many refugee families who escaped to Pakistan have also been beneficiaries of an organization set up by Sima Samar. Like RAWA, WAW, and WASSA, Samar's Shuhada organization operates in many areas: education, hygiene, medical treatment, and training and employment for refugees in Pakistan and those living in Afghanistan.

Two organizations deal with the domestic violence that is prevalent in Afghanistan. WAW runs a women's shelter in Kabul and provides family counseling and legal advice. In addition to addressing domestic violence, WASSA also deals with the problems of forced marriage, male domination, and female self-immolation.

Domestic violence is a special research interest of Wazhma Frogh, who concluded that 55 percent of the drug addiction cases among Afghan women were related to gender violence.

Suraya Pakzad, founder of the Voice of Women Organization, is outspoken against forced marriage and child marriage and promotes education about women's rights. Due to worsening security, however, her organization has been forced to abandon many operations.[25]

The type of religious reform advocated is of particular interest. Most of the reformers have not expressed a strong view on Islam although their actions reflect an anti-Islamist position. Four believe that Islam is not inherently sexist and that the Koran contains a message of gender equality if correctly interpreted. According to Nilofar Sakhi, the task of her organization is to co-opt mullahs who are in favor of women's rights in the context of Islam.

Masuda Sultan, Afghan-American writer and human rights campaigner, escaped from Kandahar with her family in 1983. She believes that educating women in Islamic law and history will forge an authentic Muslim identity and raise awareness of their rights. In contrast, Seddiqi, Samar, and Meena Keshwar Kamal, founder of RAWA, openly challenged the Islamists, for which Meena (of RAWA) and her husband paid with their lives. Samar has been a fierce critic of strict shari'ah laws, leading to death threats and prompting Islamist enemies to call her "the Salman Rushdie of Afghanistan."

Women journalists, severely restricted and persecuted under the Taliban, have achieved more autonomy, notwithstanding government censorship. Shafiqa Habibi, who founded the Woman Journalists' Center and heads the New Afghanistan Women Association (the female branch of the Afghan National Journalists' Union), believes her association ensures independence for women journalists campaigning for gender equality.[26] In addition, writing in blogs and online magazines has become a vital means of communicating a message and effecting changes for those who are literate.

With regard to the success of the Afghan women's rights movement, there have been some notable achievements within government. Although Massouda Jalal failed in her run for the presidency, she became minister of women's affairs. Safia Amajan joined the newly formed Department of Women's Affairs in 2001 and rose to become its head. Suraya Parlika entered parliament and in 2003 pushed for the insertion of an article in favor of gender equality into the new constitution. Shukria Barakzai was one of sixty-eight women elected to the lower house, where she spoke out against corruption.

Malalai Joya, elected to represent the province of Farah at the Loya Jirga (Grand Assembly) that assembled to draft the new constitution, spoke out bravely against corruption and warlords in the government. A year later, she was elected to the lower house as its youngest member, with one of the highest numbers of votes. However, she was later suspended for criticizing her colleagues. Sima Samar assumed a cabinet post in the transitional Karzai government in 2001 and became the first director of Afghanistan's Ministry of Women's Affairs. She also introduced the stipulation that 11 percent of the upper house should consist of female representatives. However, Samar was forced to resign after receiving death threats for criticizing shari'ah law, and the office of minister for women's affairs was dropped. On leaving parliament, Samar was offered the position of chair of the first Independent Human Rights Commission in Afghanistan (AIHRC), a position she still holds. The AIHRC educates the people of Afghanistan about human rights and monitors and investigates human rights violations, including extrajudicial killings, forced marriage, rape, torture, and illegal imprisonment.

Many reformers saw the historic opportunity afforded by the new constitution and aimed for dramatic change. Delegates to the conference convened by WAW in Kandahar in 2003 produced an Afghan Women's Bill of Rights but, to their chagrin, the Constitutional Commission included only one item from this bill. Parlika was more successful, working within government.

During the Taliban years, reformers' aims were minimal due to the extreme danger. Amajan, Pakzad, and Parlika ran their educational and training networks clandestinely; Amajan and Pakzad from their own homes, and Parlika in "reciting houses" where bereaved women came to mourn their dead. Similarly, the Golden Needle Sewing School ran underground literary classes, ostensibly forming a sewing circle, in one of the few pursuits for women still acceptable to the Taliban, but actually meeting with a professor from Herat University to discuss literature and the women's own writing.[27]

Overall, progress in educational and health service reforms for women has been impeded by lack of security. Inherent political instability may be increased by military and political upheavals in neighboring countries like Pakistan. Many regional areas are drug-financed battlegrounds for Islamist and warlord territorial strongholds, and are not yet adequately controlled by the government. In these war-torn regions, rape and abduction are commonplace. Adding to these difficulties is the lack of infrastructure, the lack of civil institutions, and the fact that the government is dependent on warlord and tribal alliances. Further threatening the aspirations for reform, many skilled and educated Afghan nationals escaped at the time of the Soviet invasion, leaving a small, albeit heroic, pool of intellectual and administrative talent.

Considering the obstacles and the limited number of women reformers in Afghanistan, they have made great strides; not only as individual activists but in forming cohesive, effective working groups. However, their tasks, requiring leadership and self-reliance, will be ongoing and challenging.

According to Massouda Jalal, the way forward will also require the involvement of men in a process of negotiated power sharing.

An unlikely base for female empowerment, the Afghan police force has attracted recruits, with particular success in Bamyan Province, central Afghanistan, where Habiba Sarabi is the first female governor. Bamyan, which boasts the lowest rate of violence in Afghanistan and has allowed some women to drive, is a model for other regions.[28]

The Afghan diaspora of refugees, mainly in the United States, may provide an increasing source of assistance. Manizha Naderi, herself a child of refugee parents, is now working with WAW in the United States and Afghanistan to assist the integration of Afghan refugees in the United States and develop medical, educational, and vocational services for women required in the rebuilding of Afghanistan. Masuda Sultan, who grew up in the United States and works for a number of outreach projects on behalf of Women for Afghan Women and the Business Council for Peace, founded the Young Afghan–World Alliance (YA–WA) to campaign for humanitarian aid in Afghanistan.[29]

SAFIA AMAJAN

The enemies of Afghanistan are trying to kill those people who are working for the peace and prosperity of Afghanistan. . . . [They] must understand that we have millions of people like [Amajan] who will continue to serve this great nation.[30]

On September 25, 2005, Afghanistan's women lost one of their most devoted champions with the murder of Safia Amajan in Kandahar. Her family name was Warasta but she was nicknamed Amajan, "dear aunt," due to her immense popularity. Amajan was assassinated by the Taliban when she emerged from a taxi outside her house.

The youngest of five sisters, Amajan was born in 1943 to a liberal family with a high respect for education. Her father, a textile merchant from the Baluch minority, decided to give his daughters a good education after the "misfortune" of having five daughters in a row.[31] She could have been married off like her older sisters, but her father died when she was fifteen and she began working as a kindergarten teacher to provide for her family. Later, she became head teacher of Zarghuna Ana High School. An arranged marriage was unacceptable to her, but increased freedom for women during the Communist period gave her the opportunity to select her own husband, a colonel. She gave birth to their only child, a son, when she was in her forties.

During the Taliban era of the 1990s, Amajan was a cautious critic of the regime and its oppression of women. As a Hafiz, a person who had memorized the whole Koran, she was able to hold down one of the few jobs available to females as a women's prayer leader. However, she also ran an underground school for girls from her home, risking execution. Unlike many educated women, she did not flee the country, evoking the love and respect of Afghanistan's women.

After the defeat of the Taliban by NATO forces, Amajan joined the newly formed government Department of Women's Affairs in 2001 and rose to be its head. An inspiring orator, she was able to encourage and motivate women. Her most important projects included organizing donations for the poor, support for women in prison, literacy classes for rural women, and political awareness courses. She opened vocational training schools so that women themselves could generate income, and was particularly active in assisting war widows. Six schools in Kandahar focused on baking and business skills. In tailoring schools, women were taught to make clothes that could be exported. In this way, Amajan helped thousands of women who would otherwise have been ignored by the system and left to fend for themselves without education, skills, or government support.

Working to educate girls and liberate women in Kandahar made her a target in this city, the volatile nest of the Taliban. She requested armored cars or security guards from the government but was refused. When her husband begged her to be careful, she responded, "It's my country, I won't quit my job. I want to do this work for our women, for our country. I want women to be able to work just like men."[32]

Amajan's life was cut short at the age of sixty-three when she was gunned down by two men on motorbicycles during a spate of attacks on hundreds of schools.[33] A regional Taliban commander, Mullah Sadullah, claimed responsibility for the murder. Another Taliban commander, Mullah Hayat Khan, explained, "We have told people again and again that anyone working for the government, and that includes women, will be killed."[34]

SHUKRIA BARAKZAI

I have the power in my hand, the power of the pen.[35]

Shukria Barakzai's campaign slogan when she ran for Afghanistan's parliament in 2005 was typical of the spirited former teacher and journalist turned politician. Barakzai uses word power to denounce violence against women, making her a target for attack by the Taliban and warlords.

She points out that Afghanistan had denied women their rights long before the Taliban's repressive regime forced women out of jobs and exacted penalties for transgressions of traditional roles.

> We grew up with domestic violence without understanding that it is a crime. We respected a husband's right to punish without any understanding that he hasn't got this right.[36]

> Most Afghan men are brutes, so we have to change their mentality; and we have to educate the women.[37]

Shukria Barakzai was born in 1972 in Kabul, where she lives with her husband and three daughters. In 1990, after graduating from high school, she studied geology at Kabul University but was forced to defer her studies two years later when the hard-line Taliban came to power. It was not until they were driven out in 2001 that she returned to university to complete her course.

During the Taliban years, a defining moment occurred when she was ill and forced to leave her house with a female neighbor in order to locate a doctor. Captured by the Taliban, she was humiliated and beaten with a whip for not having a male chaperone. However, the ordeal did not break her spirit. On the contrary, she became defiant, and her audacious initial project was to utilize the Asian Women's Organization as a vehicle for a string of clandestine girls' schools. Had she been discovered, she would have paid with her life.

Shukria firmly believes in a strong, united government to curb the power of the warlords and provide checks on autocratic presidential power.

> Afghanistan could be an example of a new democracy. The existence of 300 free and independent publications, 48 radio stations and 16 television

channels . . . is excellent news. The modern constitution guarantees equal rights for men and women . . . especially for re-establishing the rights and social status of women and their political participation.[38]

Shukria also calls for external support from the international community, which, she maintains, is ignorant of the complex issues:

To begin with, we should educate both men and women about their rights. The situation is different here—we have our own traditions, our own problems. I believe the international community does not know how to address this problem. We know, we Afghan women know.[39]

Unfortunately, the post election scenario seems not to be in favor of women in Afghanistan. Women's development issues have largely been put aside. The international community seems to be busy with Iraq, the Middle East, and reviving relations between U.S. and Europe.[40]

After the fall of the Taliban, Shukria Barakzai's achievements as a reformer were publicly recognized when she was nominated to assist in drafting Afghanistan's new constitution. She was also nominated to sit in the Loya Jirga, or "Grand Assembly," that called for nationwide representatives to adopt the new constitution.[41]

In 2001, she began the first weekly women's magazine, *Aina-e-Zan*, the "Women's Mirror." Distributed as a free women's magazine in the two official languages of Afghanistan, Dari and Pashto, it aspired to unbiased, uncensored reporting to cover social, political, and cultural issues.

The newspaper was conceived with the idea that women may communicate and learn through our shared experiences and our common suffering, and through this communication derive strength and appreciation.[42]

The operation began without a computer and with negligible financial backing. At first, men ridiculed the idea of a women's magazine, but they soon became worried that the concept and content would undermine their authority over women. Confirming her subversive intention, Barakzai retorted, "And of course I would love to whip up our people, particularly women, to fight for their own rights. . . . For strong democracy we need to build a civil society, and media's a part of civil society."[43]

The magazine has gone from strength to strength. Over three thousand copies are distributed each week in more than twelve provinces, a remarkable achievement, as female literacy is only 12.6 percent (in comparison, men's literacy is 32.4 percent).[44]

Making her way as a female journalist was full of obstacles, and as the only woman in a conference room without the backing of a well-known media outfit like the BBC, she was never called upon to ask questions. However, in the past few years, times have changed, and the prime minister has even called upon her to ask the first question.

Her success was acknowledged by the World Press Organization when she was named Editor of the Year in 2004. In her acceptance speech, she raised awareness of the long road ahead:

> My existence as an Afghan woman journalist does not indicate the certainty
> of freedom of speech, the establishment of women's rights, or the indi-
> vidual immunity of Afghan women from violence.[45]

In 2005, Barakzai successfully campaigned for a seat in parliament. Her aims were to improve the position of women and to "create a cultural revolution in Afghanistan."[46] In an election that proved to be a huge breakthrough for female politicians, she was one of sixty-eight women elected to the Wolesi Jirga, the lower house of the national parliament, where about a quarter of the seats are allocated to women. Three women were also elected to the cabinet but only to symbolic positions as ministers for women's affairs, martyrs and the disabled, and youth affairs.[47]

When necessary, Barakzai was quick to defend fellow women members of parliament. After Malalai Joya spoke out against corruption in the government and male MPs shouted insults at her, Barakzai fervently condemned the rabble-rousers.

She has experienced personal setbacks, too. In 2003, her husband took a second wife without consulting her, but she turned her humiliation into a positive experience, empathizing with the thousands of women in her position and encouraging them to join her call for freedom.

> Our patriarchal society does not like to hear this voice, it's a voice that even
> Afghan politicians want to silence. But despite these problems, I and mil-
> lions of other Afghan women have been successful through our tireless

efforts to open a small glimpse of hope, for the future generations and for the children of Afghanistan.[48]

I will fight for equality. . . . I am talking about equal rights for access to education, for self-confidence, equal rights to choose a husband, to be more independent, to be more active, to be what we want to be in the future.[49]

Afghan women are the humblest creatures of the 21st century—women still regarded as second-class humans, yet daily striving to improve their place in society. They deserve the respect and support of women everywhere.[50]

Being a high-profile woman is dangerous. On two occasions, Barakzai narrowly escaped death when bombs were planted in her bedroom. In 2007, she received a letter from government intelligence informing her she might be the target for a suicide bomber.

When I leave home these days on work, I am not quite sure whether I will be back [alive]. Life has become so insecure. I am not planning to leave the country yet, but I do have to think about my kids.[51]

WAZHMA FROGH

Mullah, give me five minutes, I will tell you something, and after that if you want to say I am an infidel and I am a threat to you, just kill me.[52]

In 2002, Wazhma Frogh was visiting Badakhshan Province in the remote northeast to start a local literacy program, when she overheard the village mullah preaching a fatwa demanding that the community carry out a death sentence on her. Summoning up courage, she strode through the mosque in a large black chador to challenge the mullah, making a statement that asked him for "five minutes." In Arabic and the regional Dari language, she recited five verses from the Koran praising tolerance, nonaggression, and the benefits of education, and then she roundly denounced the prevailing culture that endorsed child marriage, wife beating, and the exclusion of women from education. To everyone's surprise, the mullah backed off, put his hand on her head, and said, "God bless you, my daughter," thereby giving her tacit approval for her literacy project.

Frogh was born in Afghanistan in 1980. As a child, she learned the importance of gaining men's respect in order to change their perceptions of women. When her family escaped from Afghanistan and went to Pakistan in the 1990s, her father, a former army officer, had difficulty finding work to support the family. Even though she was only in the eighth grade, Wazhma took the initiative of becoming a tutor for the landlord's children in exchange for rent reduction. She also taught herself English at night, studying by the bathroom light so as not to disturb the rest of her family in their meager living quarters. Her father, who had never thought of women as breadwinners, was impressed and began seeking her opinion on many family matters.

During her early years, Frogh became aware of discrimination against women when she saw them forced to eat in the kitchen while the men ate in the dining room and saw the girls sweep out the courtyards where only boys were allowed to play.[53] However, it was after experiencing the life of an Afghan refugee and observing the life of other refugees in Pakistan during the civil war that she decided to dedicate herself to conflict resolution and to helping fellow refugees. A gender specialist, social activist, and researcher, she has worked for ten years in relief and development programs with women and children in Afghanistan and Pakistan. Her expertise lies in the areas of literacy, civil society, and organizational development, and she is particularly interested in research into women's issues in Afghanistan and their participation in reconstruction.

> Arguments based on principles of universal human rights or on what international conventions say don't persuade many Afghans to support reforms. . . . Only religious arguments hold sway.[54]

Wazhma Frogh believes authentic Islam is not sexist. On the contrary, she maintains the Koran contains verses that justify gender equality and that these provide compelling religious arguments that are crucial weapons for debating with mullahs, many of whom have only learned the Koran by rote and don't have a deep understanding of the texts.

> The literacy rate is very low in the country and when a preacher preaches for his own benefit, a man who cannot read or write will believe . . . that this is the real religion and then applies all those self-made rules [in] his home. As a result all the weak members of the family become victims of his ignorance.[55]

Her fluency in Arabic and erudite arguments based on Islamic jurisprudence can outdo the local mullahs and she is convinced that these arguments constitute the best tactics in the battle to persuade regional religious authorities, tribal leaders, and even government to endorse reforms. She believes they might even sway Islamist radicals to relinquish violence but is well aware that taking on the religious and tribal leadership could mean risking her life.

Wazhma is also adamant about the importance of separating politics from religion to foster tolerance of all religions and stop Shia versus Sunni bloodletting. To gain wide cultural acceptance of these views, she maintains that they must be part of the education curriculum in which an authentic Islam is taught without the accretions of patriarchy.[56]

After conducting research in centers where Afghan women were being treated for drug addiction, she concluded that 55 percent of cases were related to gender violence.

> We all know that drugs usage is prohibited in Islam, our religion and also the addicted person is [hated] in that society too. Therefore, if we want a society cleaned up of all the drugs, we should all work towards building a peaceful and advanced society to eliminate every kind of gender based violence.[57]

She described the case of a young girl she met in one of the centers, an orphanage. The girl was fourteen years old when her father forced her to marry a member of the Taliban after the latter threatened to kill her brother. As girls have little worth compared with boys, her father said he had no alternative. Subsequently, she realized her husband was addicted to heroin, as were several other women who lived in the house and who were regularly beaten by him. The other women in the house were using hashish and heroin to escape their sorrows and she joined them, stealing from her husband to pay for the drugs. When she became pregnant, her husband threatened to kill her if she bore a daughter, declaring he hated girls. As soon as the baby was born and he discovered it was a girl, he was about to kill his wife but, instead, smothered his newborn daughter. Sometime later, during the coalition's raids on the Taliban, the house was bombed and the young woman was the only survivor.[58]

While researching women's issues in a southeastern province, where early and forced marriage is common practice, Frogh learned that 90 percent of the families sold their daughters in marriage for about $300 to avoid "problems and burdens in future." Some of these girls were as young as three years old.[59] "Many fathers said a woman has no value at all and if we can get some $300 [for] a daughter then this is the best opportunity for an income."[60]

Frogh maintains these values are spread by Muslim preachers and embraced by males in communities that are 85 percent illiterate.[61] The aid organizations and the international community, which tend to focus on the educated urban population, should recognize the importance of the rural communities, she says, as these represent over 80 percent of the population in Afghanistan. In addition, the international community needs to be aware that the tribal courts, which have historically dispensed customary law, enjoy rural support and have the power and influence to thwart and overrule Western ideas imposed by any nongovernmental organization (NGO) or indeed the central government in Kabul.[62] In spite of millions of dollars in aid, "girls are still given in exchange for a fighting dog or to settle disputes between families."[63]

Deteriorating security has intensified violence against women and Frogh has warned about the risks for young girls. "Rapes in the country have been growing tremendously, particularly child rapes within the ages of 9, 8, 7, even [younger] than that."[64]

In the period after the fall of the Taliban, the hope for women's emancipation now appears tenuous. In February 2008, when Wazhma met President Bush during a meeting on women and security in Washington, she expressed her great disappointment at the return and omnipresence of the Taliban and the number of former human rights abusers in the Karzai government.[65]

Wazhma's articles on women's rights, politics, religion, and early and forced marriage are published on her own blog, at http://www.wazhmafrogh .blogspot.com, and also in *Development Activism* at www.devactivism.org and *Persian Mirror* at www.persianmirror.com. Wazhma is director of the Afghanistan office of the international human rights advocacy group Global Rights: Partners for Justice.

MASSOUDA JALAL

> *My hands are empty but I want to prove that a woman with empty hands can do a lot. It will be a lesson for all the women of*

*Afghanistan. Already five thousand years, we women have waited for
our turn. We cannot wait another century.*[66]

Massouda Jalal has made it her life's work to empower Afghanistan's women.
She was the first woman in the nation's history to run for president and later
became minister of women's affairs.

Declared equal under the post-Taliban constitution, women still face
enormous restrictions, especially in public life. By attacking the conven-
tional image of women, Jalal became a pioneer for those women who wish to
make a difference by taking on leadership positions in Afghanistan.

Women's leadership has to be bought with a clear vision, fired by commitment, nourished by credibility, galvanized by performance, and cradled
incessantly in the bosom of power.[67]

Massouda Jalal's goal is the creation of a culture in Afghanistan that will support women's leadership. She would like to see women work on all the difficult issues but this entails mobilization and mutual support: "They need a
source of nourishment . . . a source of energy when they are lost in the dark
and are running out of strength."[68]

Jalal believes women need to work toward negotiated power sharing
with men. However, their lives are so shackled by men in the public and private space that no reforms are possible without male support and men would
be reluctant to give up their domination. Her solution is to involve men:
"They say that the best way to win a war is not by defeating your enemies,
but by winning them to your side. . . . We need a men's movement for
gender equality. And we need it now."[69] She also believes the Koran contains
arguments in favor of gender reform if properly interpreted.

Massouda Jalal was born to a middle-class Tajik family on January 5,
1962. One of seven children, she grew up in a liberal family that valued education. Her father, an administrator with an international textile company,
had more worldly views than most Afghans and instilled personal ambition
and determination in his children: "I never had the feeling that as a girl or
as a woman I was less competent, never! I had three brothers, but I was usually better than them. And in medical school I enjoyed competing with the
male students in my class."[70]

She moved to Kabul to attend high school and university, where she qualified as a doctor and psychiatrist but changed to pediatrics when the mental health department was closed in the 1990s during the Afghan civil war. She was a member of the university faculty and worked in several hospitals. Aged thirty, she married a law professor at Kabul University, with whom she had three children.

When the Taliban arrived in Kabul, she was fired from her job but then secretly employed by the United Nations between 1996 and 2001 to work on a women's project within the World Food Programme. The work was extremely dangerous and before she started, she was made to sign a disclaimer exempting the UN from liability for her safety. When the Taliban learned she was working, they had her imprisoned for two days. Undeterred, she organized health and education programs and a bread-baking business for women. A car-pool scheme was essential as women were unable to leave home without a male relative as chaperone.

After US forces removed the Taliban government in 2001, Jalal was invited, together with two hundred other women, to attend the Loya Jirga, or the Grand Assembly, convened to determine the interim president.

"During the loya jirga the warlords came into the tent and dictated to delegates they [should] vote for (Hamid) Karzai."[71] Not intimidated, Jalal decided to challenge Karzai and put herself forward as interim president. She received only 171 out of the 1,575 votes, coming a distant second. "I wanted to make a record and I wanted to challenge, whether I won or not,"[72] she said.

President Karzai offered her a position as vice president but she turned it down as she is fiercely critical of his governance, accusing him of neglecting women's rights and making deals with warlords for political gain.

Her personal integrity and refusal to compromise won her respect and many supporters from different tribes and regions. Consequently, she decided to run in the 2004 election. Her campaign, however, faced major setbacks. There was very little money and her headquarters, a borrowed apartment in a Russian-built block, was run down and bullet ridden. Jalal's husband, who was also her campaign manager, was jeered and humiliated. As a woman, she was forbidden to speak at mosques. She had no media coverage because the stations were owned by rivals. Some newspapers disregarded her name, referring to her only as "a woman." On two occasions, the Afghan Supreme Court's Religious Order Department condemned her candidacy as "illegal and un-Islamic."[73] Unable to contest the presidency with the advantages of her opponents, she campaigned in the women's bakeries she had founded during the Taliban era.

In addition, she received countless death threats. If attacked, she would have been virtually defenseless, as she had no bodyguards and refused to arm anyone. "If I show weakness some men will say 'look, she is not brave.' They will say 'there is another woman who gave up.' . . . I have dug a hole and buried all my fears."[74]

Jalal stood on a prodemocracy, anticorruption platform.

> I can win on October 9th because I am a woman, and in Afghanistan it is only women who have no blood on their hands.[75]

Jalal promised to change the face of Afghan politics by providing a democratic government to serve the people and one that excluded warlords and former generals. On the publicity trail, she wore the traditional Islamic veil and campaigned alongside her husband. "I am one of you," she promised, "I will listen to you; my door will be open even when I am president. My hands are clean and I will work hard to make your lives better."[76]

Jalal came sixth out of the twenty-three candidates; she was elected to the cabinet as minister of women's affairs, and in this capacity has made significant improvements in the lives of Afghan women. At the head of a large ministry staff in Kabul and the outer regions, she is responsible for health and gender issues and monitors compliance with international treaties.

She would like the Ministry of Women's Affairs to tackle the high incidence of mental disability among Afghans, due primarily to intermarriage among first cousins. Although most families are aware of the risk of consanguinity, they tend to marry off children within the family to avoid paying large dowries.

Jalal has also expanded her international profile. In 2005, she held a conference in New York on women's leadership in Afghanistan's reconstruction.

> I have had an impact. If I do not become president, the girls of this country will. I created honor and values for the women of Afghanistan. They are not nothing anymore.[77]

MALALAI JOYA

> *They will kill me but they will not kill my voice, because it is the voice of all Afghan women. You can cut the flower, but you cannot stop the coming of spring.*[78]

> *Through my voice, the suffering women of a repressed nation sang the long-forgotten song of freedom, a patriotic melody conducted by the sorrows and grievances felt by women all throughout Afghanistan.*[79]

Malalai Joya wears a burqa to hide her identity and does not sleep in the same house for more than one or two nights in a row. The president of Afghanistan has given her several AK-47 assault rifles and the UN provides her with full-time armed guards. She has survived four attempts on her life, her house has been bombed, her clinic and orphanage have been attacked, and she receives frequent death threats and threats of suicide attacks against her family. She is a heroine to most Afghan people and an inspiration all over the world, but powerful warlords, men with their own armies and prisons, seek to have her silenced.[80]

Malalai Joya was born on April 25, 1979, and raised in Farah, a province in Western Afghanistan on the Iranian border. Her father was a medical student who lost his foot fighting the Soviets; her mother is uneducated and suffers from depression. Joya has three brothers and six sisters and is married to a student of agriculture.[81] Self-taught in literature, political science, and history, Joya hopes one day to study literature at university. She wants to write books about the Afghan people, having kept a journal of her experiences and the individuals she has met.

When she graduated from high school she chose not to go on to university because she wanted to help educate other Afghans.[82] Instead, from the age of eighteen, Joya worked in the Herat and Peshawar refugee camps for four years, teaching Afghan women to read and write. In 1998, after the Soviets had withdrawn and when Afghanistan was in the grip of the Taliban, she returned from the camps and established an orphanage and a health clinic in Kabul. She continued the literacy classes, but this time in secret and at the risk of death, because the Islamists forbade women to be educated.

After the fall of the Taliban, Joya was elected to represent the province of Farah, and in December 2003 she went as a delegate to the Loya Jirga that was assembled to draft the new constitution for Afghanistan.[83] At the assembly, Joya, then only twenty-five years old, protested that the individuals being appointed to head government committees were ex-mujahideen fighters who had brought Afghanistan to its present ravaged state through years of civil war.

> [They were] those who turned our country into the nucleus of national and international wars. They were the most anti-women people in the society . . . who brought our country to this state and they intend to do the same again.
>
> If they are forgiven by our people, the bare-footed Afghan people, our history will never forgive them. They are all recorded in the history of our country.[84]

They included war criminals, drug traffickers, and misogynists who should face trial rather than be rewarded with influential positions in government; their presence confirmed the whispered misgivings of the people and called into question the legitimacy of the Loya Jirga itself.[85]

> After she spoke, there was a moment of stunned silence. Then there was uproar. The mujahideen, some who literally had guns at their feet, rushed towards her, shouting. She was brought under the protection of UN security forces.[86]

On January 4, 2004, Joya again publicly denounced the influence of the warlords over the political process, asserting that the people of Afghanistan were like "pigeons who have been freed from Taliban cages, but whose wings have been cut off and who are in the claws of vampires who suck their blood." Most of those vampires, she added, were to be found in the parliament itself. She also took the American president to task for supporting the "extremist warlords, the Northern Alliance criminals."[87]

In September 2004, Joya and a delegation of village elders, armed with evidence of human-rights abuses, persuaded President Hamid Karzai to dismiss the governor of Farah, who had been a Taliban commander.[88]

Joya was elected to the 249-seat Wolesi Jirga, the House of Representatives, or lower house of parliament, as its youngest member, in Afghanistan's 2005 parliamentary elections. She had one of the highest numbers of votes, competing against men in her own right, rather than being elected to the seats reserved for women.

In February 2007, during a rally to support a proposed amnesty for Afghans suspected of war crimes, thousands of former mujahideen fighters shouted "Death to Malalai Joya!"[89]

In May 2007, Joya criticized the parliament in an interview with a private Afghan TV station, Tolo TV, for failing to provide for the Afghan people, comparing it unfavorably with a stable. At least "a cattle house is full of animals, like a cow giving milk, a donkey carrying something, a dog that's loyal." This parliament, she said, was more like "a stable or zoo."[90]

In the same month, having watched a record of the interview, a majority of the members of the lower house of the Afghan parliament moved to suspend Joya for the remainder of her five-year term. She was found guilty of violating Article 70 of the legislature's rules of procedure, an article that forbids lawmakers from criticizing one another. Specifically, she was declared to have insulted the institution of parliament. Several members also called for her to be prosecuted in a court of law.[91] Joya believes that her suspension was the result of a political conspiracy and that Article 70 was written specifically for her.[92]

Protests against Joya's suspension were organized in Afghan provinces including Farah, Jalalabad, Takhar, and Kabul and, on June 21, 2007, supporters in Rome, New York, Barcelona, Milan, Bologna, Viareggio, Vancouver, Melbourne, and other cities declared an International Action Day, calling on the Afghan government to reinstate her.[93]

Joya filed a complaint about her suspension, but no action was taken. Since her suspension, Joya's life has become even more precarious but she continues to criticize the warlords in the Afghan parliament,[94]

I have seen too many sorrows and I have no fear in my soul anymore.[95]

I know that if not today, then probably tomorrow, I will be physically annihilated, but the voice of protest will continue, because it is the voice of the people of my country.[96]

Awards

"Malalai of Maiwand" awarded to Malalai Joya for her speech in the Loya Jirga, by the Cultural Union of Afghans in Europe, January 2004

International Women of the Year Award 2004, Valle d'Aosta province of Italy, December 2004

1,000 Women for the Nobel Peace Prize 2005

Certificate of Honor for "ongoing work on behalf of human rights," awarded by Mr. Tom Bates, mayor of Berkeley, California, March 15, 2006

Gwangju Award for Human Rights 2006, May 18th Foundation, South Korea, March 2006

Women of Peace Award 2006, Women's PeacePower Foundation, August 2006

Young Global Leader for 2007, World Economic Forum

Golden Fleur-de-Lis (Giglio d'Oro), Region of Toscana of Italy, July 23, 2007

Sakharov Prize for Freedom of Thought, European Parliament, September 11, 2007

Anna Politkovskaya Award 2008

MEENA KESHWAR KAMAL AND RAWA

> *Whenever fundamentalists exist as a military and political force in our injured land, the problem of Afghanistan will not be solved. . . . The sworn enemies of human rights, democracy and secularism have gripped their claws over our country and attempt to restore their religious fascism on our people.*[97]

Meena Keshwar Kamal was born in Kabul on February 27, 1956. Like many teenagers growing up in the seventies, she believed in challenging oppression by speaking out and empowering people through education. At the age of twenty, she left university to devote herself to establishing the rights of women through education and political awareness.

In 1977, aged twenty-one, Meena founded the first association in Afghanistan for the promotion of women's rights: the Revolutionary Association for the Women of Afghanistan (RAWA). Its goals were the restoration of democracy in Afghanistan, equality for men and women, and the separation of religion and state.

In 1979, Meena established medical facilities, orphanages, and schools for refugee children and their mothers. The schools ran courses in literacy and practical skills and were the first to offer young Afghan women the opportunity to improve their lives. Meena also campaigned and organized meetings to encourage resistance to the Soviet invasion of Afghanistan.

Meena launched a feminist magazine in 1981. *Payam-e-Zan* (Women's Message) was published in Persian and Pashto to "give voice to the silent and oppressed women of Afghanistan."[98]

She visited several European countries to protest against Islamic extremism and the Soviet-backed government in Afghanistan. In 1981, Meena was invited to France by the French government to represent the Afghan resistance movement at the Socialist Party Congress. The Soviet delegation at the congress left the hall when she gave the victory sign and participants cheered her.[99]

Meena was married to Afghanistan Liberation Organization leader Faiz Ahmad, who was murdered by agents of the mujahideen leader Gulbuddin Hekmatyar on November 12, 1986. Meena herself and two RAWA colleagues were murdered on February 4, 1987, in Quetta, Pakistan, close to the Afghan border, during the Soviet occupation. She had three children, but their whereabouts are unknown. Two Afghans, who were found guilty and executed in 2002, were associated with Gulbuddin Hekmatyar's Hezb-i-Islami and Khad, the intelligence branch of the then Communist Afghan regime.[100]

Time magazine, November 13, 2006, acknowledged Meena's contribution to human rights: "Although she was only 30 when she died, Meena had already planted the seeds of an Afghan women's rights movement based on the power of knowledge."[101]

The Revolutionary Association of the Women of Afghanistan (RAWA)[102]

RAWA's first political campaigns were directed against the Communist Afghan government that took over in 1978, and against the Soviet occupation from 1979, when RAWA members distributed anti-Soviet leaflets, staged demonstrations and strikes, and encouraged women to assist the resistance movement in whatever way they could.

RAWA members' demonstrations against the Soviet invaders made them a target for the Russians and local Communist supporters, and their calls for a democratic, secular government and championing of human rights, particularly those of women, made them enemies of Islamic fundamentalists. After the overthrow of the Soviet-backed regime in 1992, RAWA continued to protest human rights violations, especially those against women committed by Islamic extremists and the Taliban.

The military intervention by the United States in October 2001 officially ended Taliban control of Afghanistan. However, according to the RAWA Web site,

> by reinstalling the warlords in power in Afghanistan, the US administration [replaced] one fundamentalist regime with another. The US government and Mr. Karzai mostly rely on Northern Alliance criminal leaders who are as brutal and misogynist as the Taliban.

RAWA asserts that as long as Islamic fundamentalists remain a military and political force in Afghanistan, the oppression of Afghan individuals, particularly women and children, will continue.

In Afghanistan, RAWA's main program consists of providing support to female victims of war or atrocities committed by Islamic radicals. The organization also helps women who are tortured or mistreated by their husbands, relatives, or in-laws, providing shelter, medical treatment, and counseling as needed.

RAWA maintains contact with the families of people who have been imprisoned by the authorities in Afghanistan or by the Pakistani police and in some cases provides them with legal aid. RAWA members help traumatized families to leave war zones and transport them to safer places, supplying basic living needs and medical treatment. They also trace missing females, reunite them with family members, and run nine orphanages in Peshawar, Islamabad, Rawalpindi, and Quetta.

Much of RAWA members' work consists of documenting and drawing international attention to human rights violations through press statements and printed publications. They give interviews to the media and assist journalists in their coverage of Afghanistan and the refugee camps in Pakistan.

Their Web site also maintains extensive coverage of human rights violations and persecution of women.

RAWA established the Malalai Hospital in Peshawar and the Malalai Clinic in Quetta, which provides free medical care to Afghan women and children. In addition, RAWA runs mobile health teams in eight provinces of Afghanistan, providing medical aid, conducting first aid courses, and giving polio vaccinations.

To combat one of the world's lowest national literacy rates, RAWA runs fifteen primary and secondary schools for women and children and provides teachers and materials for numerous literacy courses in the refugee camps and in twelve provinces in Afghanistan.

RAWA helps women feed their families by running workshops and providing microloans for businesses like chicken and fish farms, manufacture of handicrafts, carpets and garments, and jam and pickle production. The organization also holds numerous discussion groups for women and girls to raise awareness about democracy and civic freedom and the need to resist fundamentalist regimes.

RAWA receives some income from the products of the workshops and small businesses it supports and from the sale of publications, audiocassettes, and posters. For the most part, however, the organization relies on membership fees and donations from supporters around the world.

Awards Presented to RAWA[103]

The French Republic's "Liberty, Equality, Fraternity Human Rights Prize"
    to RAWA
    Islamabad, April 15, 2000
Emma Humphries Memorial Prize 2001
    London, October 6, 2001
The sixth "Asian Human Rights Award 2001" to RAWA
    Tokyo, December 7, 2001
University of Antwerp awards RAWA an honorary doctorate
    for outstanding nonacademic achievements
    Antwerp, Belgium, May 16, 2003
Certificate of Honor from the Region Lombardia (Italy)
    Lombardia, 2003

The "20th International Alfonso Comín Award"
  Barcelona, Spain, November 25, 2003
Certificate of Special Congressional Recognition from the US Congress
  Santa Barbara, California, May 2, 2004
Soroptimist International of Santa Barbara "Advancing the Status of
  Women" Award
  Santa Barbara, California, May 2, 2004
A Certificate of Recognition from the California Legislature Assembly
  Santa Barbara, California, May 2, 2004
Honorary award to RAWA presented by Dr. Karan Singh
  New Delhi, India, April 22, 2007

MANIZHA NADERI AND WAW (AFGHANISTAN/USA)

How would you feel . . . if we brought Osama Bin Laden and made him mayor of New York City? . . . That's how the Afghans feel about the warlord governors.[104]

Manizha Naderi left a comfortable life in New York for the turmoil and unrest of a war-torn country in order to direct the Afghanistan branch of WAW:

I am an Afghan woman. I wanted to help my Afghan sisters who have suffered for so long. . . . I will not rest until every Afghan woman is free of oppression.[105]

Manizha Naderi was born in Kabul in 1975. Her family fled to Pakistan in 1980 after the Soviet invasion of Afghanistan. In 1984, they immigrated to the United States, where Manizha was brought up in New York and New Jersey. She is fluent in English and German and speaks both of Afghanistan's national languages, Pashto and Dari.

In college, she gained a BA and after graduating, became a member of the Queens General Assembly in New York, an organization that provides a forum for delegates of diverse ethnicities to discuss community issues, exchange ideas, and report back to their neighborhoods. She also became the

New York manager of the Business Council for Peace project (BPeace), a non-profit organization assisting women in war-torn countries and operating in Afghanistan since 2003.

In 2003, Naderi joined WAW as a volunteer and soon became the organization's first full-time staff member, managing the office, organizing fundraising events, and liaising with other feminist groups and Afghan organizations.

Women for Afghan Women (WAW) (Afghanistan/USA)

WAW was founded in 2001 in New York City in order to help the unas-similated resident Afghans. Between 300,000 and 400,000 native Afghans live in New York, mostly isolated from outside society, uneducated, poor, and pursuing traditional ways of life. In New York City, Manizha Naderi initiated and built a community outreach program, which holds English, girls' leadership, and vocational classes. It also assists with legal referrals, provides a domestic violence referral service, and provides assistance for children with problems at school. The program won the Union Square Award in 2003 for its work with the Afghan community.

> WAW promotes the agency of local Afghan women through the creation
> of safe forums where Afghan women can network, develop programs to
> meet their specific needs, and participate in human rights advocacy in the
> international sphere.[106]

WAW's main domain, however, is in Afghanistan itself, where the NGO runs programs in literacy, English language, and computer skills as well as vocational training and empowerment seminars for women. It also arranges microloans for business-minded women.

In spite of equal rights being granted in the 2002 constitution, Afghan women lead lives of quiet desperation. Activities that Western women take for granted, such as choice of dress or leaving home without a male relative as chaperone, can make them targets for intimidation, violence, and even murder.

WAW addresses the immense problem of domestic violence, accepted as a social norm, and also rape, which is not an offense under the criminal code. The perpetrators are rarely, if ever, penalized and if they are, a "revolving door" prison system operates for their benefit. The victims, however, can be punished, beaten, and killed, with negligible consequences, and the same judges who sentenced women to death by stoning for minor crimes under the Taliban regime are still operating today.

> In a country where the foundations of civil law are in ruins, perpetrators of abuse are rarely punished; more often, women are revictimized for the abuses they have suffered at the hands of men.[107]

Many women feel the situation is hopeless and turn to drastic measures. According to Manizha Naderi, "Young girls are burning themselves up. They are putting gasoline on themselves and burning themselves up because they can't take it anymore."[108]

WAW tries to intervene when women are in dangerous family settings, and provides counseling for all family members. It has built safe houses and family guidance centers for women who are victims of domestic violence or have just been released from prison after committing a "moral crime." WAW also campaigns for the release of such women prisoners.

In order to give women a strong community voice, WAW has established women's councils (*shuras*) and holds conferences to educate the international community about the dire situation for women in Afghanistan. It also raises funds for the reconstruction of villages, schools, and medical clinics. WAW has opened schools in refugee camps and started an orphan-sponsoring program.

One of WAW's main achievements was the Family Guidance Center in Kabul. Initiated by Manizha Naderi, the center is a safe house for women victims of severe, chronic domestic violence, and provides counselors, legal assistance for the victims, and classes on women's affairs held by progressive Islamist scholars. Reeducation is directed at the male perpetrators of domestic violence. Together with other organizations working to protect women and children, WAW is building up a databank to evaluate and manage domestic violence.

WAW has held two annual conferences in New York. At its third conference, in 2003, held defiantly in the old Taliban stronghold, Kandahar, WAW took advantage of the timing of discussions on the new Afghanistan constitution, which was to determine women' rights. The conference "awoke a representative group of Afghan women to their potential power as a united body and allowed them to articulate their demands in the public arena."[109]

Working together for the first time, forty-five ethnically diverse female activists of varying ages and levels of education (some illiterate) produced the Afghan Women's Bill of Rights (reproduced below), which was presented to the Constitutional Commission, Minister of Women's Affairs Habiba Sorabi, and President Karzai for consideration and ratification. The document was also distributed throughout the country.

The Bill of Rights demanded equality, freedom, and security for women among other things, and the Constitutional Commission led WAW to believe that all but one item of the Women's Bill of Rights would be incorporated in the constitution. However, the final draft notably avoided women's rights.

> The constitutional commission promised us that every single right, except one, which [specified] the minimum age that girls could get married . . . was included in the constitution. And so we believed them. Why wouldn't we believe them?
>
> . . . And we waited for the draft of the constitution to come out. And when it did, not even one single point was in the constitution.[110]

In one article, the draft constitution stated: "The citizens of Afghanistan—whether man or woman—have equal rights and duties before the law," but another article asserted: "No law can be contrary to the beliefs and provisions of the sacred religion of Islam,"[111] thereby leaving the field open to misogynistic interpretations.

To make matters worse, the chair of the constitutional Loya Jirga remarked, "Even God has not given you equal rights because under his decision two women are counted as equal to one man."[112]

A disillusioned Naderi remarked: "It seems impossible to read it [the Bill of Rights] without realizing that it is a cry for liberation on the part of women who have endured brutal suppression but whose collective will remains unbroken. . . . Now that the draft of the Constitution has been released, failing to mention specific rights for women, we know that this cry fell on deaf ears."[113]

For Naderi and the women who created the Bill of Rights, the battle is not over. Afghanistan's women, who refuse to be silenced or beaten, "are those who move the cradle with one hand, and the world with the other."[114]

The Afghan Women's Bill of Rights
(reproduced by permission of WAW)

On September 5, 2003, in the historic city of Kandahar, we, the Afghan Muslim participants in the conference, "Women and the Constitution: Kandahar 2003," from Kabul, Mazar-e-Sharif, Kandahar, Herat, Wardak, Jousjan, Badakhshan, Samangan, Farah, Logar, Gardez, Kapisa, Uruzgan, Paktia, Helmand, Baghlan, Sar-e-Pul, having considered the issues of the constitution that affect the futures of ourselves, our children, and our society, make the following demands on behalf of the women of Afghanistan. Moreover, as representatives of all of Afghan women, we demand that these rights are not only secured in the constitution but implemented.

1. Mandatory education for women through secondary school and opportunities for all women for higher education.
2. Provision of up-to-date health services for women with special attention to reproductive rights.
3. Protection and security for women: the prevention and criminalization of sexual harassment against women publicly and in the home, of sexual abuse of women and children, of domestic violence, and of "bad blood-price" (the use of women as compensation for crimes by one family against another).
4. Reduction of the time before women can remarry after their husbands have disappeared, and mandatory government support of women during that time.
5. Freedom of speech.
6. Freedom to vote and run for election to office.
7. Rights to marry and divorce according to Islam.
8. Equal pay for equal work.
9. Right to financial independence and ownership of property.
10. Right to participate fully and to the highest levels in the economic and commercial life of the country.
11. Mandatory provision of economic opportunities for women.
12. Equal representation of women in the Loya Jirga and Parliament.
13. Full inclusion of women in the judiciary system.
14. Minimum marriageable age set at 18 years.

15. Guarantee of all constitutional rights to widows, disabled women, and orphans.
16. Full rights of inheritance.

Additional demands affecting the lives of women:

1. Disarmament and national security.
2. Trials of war criminals in international criminal courts and the disempowerment of warlords.
3. A strong central government.
4. A commitment to end government corruption.
5. Decisive action against foreign invasion and protection of the sovereignty of Afghanistan.

SURAYA PARLIKA

I will continue my activities until Afghanistan has democracy, peace, equality between women and men, social development and the involvement of women in political, economic and social affairs.[115]

Suraya Parlika has a long history of courageous activism on behalf of Afghan women's rights. During the political turmoil of the Soviet era, the civil war, and the Taliban regime, she has narrowly missed assassination and suffered imprisonment and torture.

Parlika was born to an intellectual Tajik family in 1944 in Kamari village of Afghanistan's Bagrami district. Both her father and uncle had high positions in the Communist party. She completed high school in 1962, received her undergraduate degree in economics from Kabul University in 1966, then worked in the housing department. Five years later, she took up an administrative position in the international relations department of the university and, like many other Communists, traveled to the USSR. There she spent four years in Kiev studying for a master's in international economics, obtaining the degree in 1977. When she returned to Afghanistan, she worked in the international relations department again.

She also joined the leftist People's Democratic Party of Afghanistan

(PDPA) and became a high-profile feminist activist. She was appointed head of the women's branch of the PDPA in 1978 after the PDPA overthrew the government of Mohammed Daoud Khan in the "Saur Revolution." However, several months later, the authorities objected to her strong advocacy of women's rights and she was incarcerated in the Pol-e-Charkhi prison for eighteen months: "They took every opportunity [to torture me] by burning me with cigarette butts, pulling out my nails and burning parts of [my] body. I still bear the scars from the burns."[116]

Parlika was released following another coup, when the ruling Khalq faction of the PDPA was deposed by the Parcham faction with Soviet backing. Undeterred by her prison ordeal, she resumed her previous position as head of the PDPA women's division and organized an international conference to raise awareness of the plight of Afghanistan's women.

In 1986 she was elected president and secretary-general of the Afghan Red Crescent. One of her major projects was the dispatch of war-injured Afghan children to the United States for treatment. In the same year, Parlika was elected to the Loya Jirga, which had gathered to settle the affairs of the nation.

In 1992, after the Taliban mujahideen ousted the Najibullah government and fired women from all jobs except menial ones, women became virtual prisoners in their own homes. In protest, Parlika started the All Afghan Women's Union (AAWU) in Kabul to provide training centers for women, but most of the meetings had to be held clandestinely in "reciting houses" where bereaved women came to mourn their dead.[117]

When the Taliban entered Kabul in 1996, Parlika refused to leave and continued the AAWU movement underground, moving constantly between safe houses to avoid capture and execution: "When I am threatened, I just keep running my campaign. I am not afraid for even one moment."[118]

Since the fall of the Taliban in 2001, some intimidation and attacks have continued. However, the AAWU has persistently run classes for hundreds of women in literacy, basic English, information technology, and commerce as well as workshops on parliamentary democracy.

Parlika is also an entrepreneur and a strong believer in financial independence as the key to improvement in women's status: "Business people are the ambassadors of peace in the world. If we've got women entrepreneurs, other women will feel that business can help them make a better life."[119]

Parlika's revolutionary women's training centers, together with microcredit assistance, have given beggars, orphans, and widows hope for financial independence. Apart from setting up bakeries and garment-making businesses, they have started mobile phone repair shops, together with handicrafts and jam and juice works, avoiding the traditional carpet making, as earnings from this were usually received by male kin, bypassing the women. The new businesses not only give women economic independence but also provide social interaction for many women depressed by enforced segregation at home. However, Parlika's business ventures have put her at risk and she has escaped assassination twice.[120]

Her main battle, she admits, is the struggle against the ingrained attitudes of men:

> Girls are married very young, sometimes when still in their mother's womb, sometimes to very old men. Before she can breathe the air, she's a prisoner. To marry by her will is considered immoral, like prostitution.[121]

Parlika likes to emphasize that women weren't always so repressed. Prior to the Taliban, women were truck drivers, construction workers, and academics. "But now our political, educational and all social institutions are razed to the ground."[122]

After 9/11, she founded the Afghan Peace Circle, a cog in the global network of Peacexpeace women's circles, and she has successfully distributed microloans received from an American chapter.

In 2002 in the aftermath of the US invasion, Parlika joined a commission of eighteen men and three women to create guidelines for elections and determine how an elected government would be run. This led to the setting up of a new Loya Jirga, to which she was nominated with more votes than any other member. In recognition of her achievement, President Hamid Karzai awarded Parlika a medal of honor.

Her role in the government gave her a new platform to bring about constitutional change: "I look with pride at the Afghan women's participation in the presidential elections. This is an indication that our decades-long efforts have not been brought to naught."[123]

In 2003, she pushed for the insertion of an article into the country's constitution ensuring gender equality. The bill demanded mandatory education for girls, freedom of speech for women, freedom to vote in elections and run for office, equal representation in parliament, equal pay for equal work, and the rights to financial independence and property ownership. It also called for criminal charges to be brought against men guilty of violence toward women and a ban on the bartering of women by families in exchange for debts. Finally, it included an increase in the minimum marriageable age to eighteen years and the right to marry and divorce in accordance with the laws of Islam.

Despite her success in the public sphere, astonishing for a woman and particularly an unmarried woman in Afghanistan, Parlika believes there is much more that needs to be done:

> Provincial warlords continue to impose restrictions on women, and women who work, go out without a burqa, or advocate for women's rights endure constant threats.[124]

She also warns that the warlords' militias must be controlled if there is to be any long-term political stability.[125]

Parlika was nominated for the 2005 Nobel Peace Prize by the 1,000 Women for Peace.[126]

NILOFAR SAKHI

> *In almost all Islamic countries there is ongoing struggle in separating religion from politics and the struggle for secular government is based on the fact that Sharia law won't allow any other system to be implemented.*[127]

Nilofor Sakhi conducts workshops and seminars in Afghanistan on women's rights, the Convention for the Elimination of Discrimination against Women (CEDAW), and gender development.

She was cofounder and executive director of the Women Activities and Social Services Association (WASSA) based in Herat, Afghanistan. WASSA educates women and builds networks among women's groups in Afghanistan and internationally. The association is active in the four western provinces, Herat, Badghis, Ghowr, and Farah, and focuses primarily on rural areas.

A year and a half after WASSA had established a literacy program in one of the remote villages, Sakhi returned to find seventy-eight women who could read and write where previously there were none. The women who had attended the literacy programs had, in turn, taught others. In each village where the association sets up literacy centers, it must first win the approval of the local elders and mullahs. While many still disapprove of women's education, WASSA does find a few strong allies among them:

> Those mullahs who were won over incorporated verses from the Quran that proclaimed women's equal rights in rallies for democracy in the villages as well as in radio and television programs.[128]

Afghanistan has one of the world's highest rates of death in childbirth and child mortality in infancy, and alongside the literacy programs, WASSA arranges discussions of nutrition, pregnancy, childbirth, and disease prevention.

Forced marriages and the lack of education and employment lead some Afghan women to commit suicide, often by setting themselves on fire. In Herat alone, more than a hundred such incidents were reported in 2003. Domestic violence also remains an entrenched problem. WASSA does what it can, providing an avenue for abused, threatened, or distressed women to seek help and referring them to local government, the Afghan Independent Human Rights Commission, or family counseling services. To open up employment and income-generating possibilities for women, WASSA offers vocational training in embroidery, quilt making, and carpet weaving.

The organization also strives to make women aware of their legal rights, holding workshops for female candidates and voters during elections and conducting campaigns with posters and leaflets to encourage women to vote. WASSA helped to establish Radio Sahar (Dawn) in Herat in October 2003, for the promotion of female participation in the 2004 and 2005 elections.

> At first, even the educated women of Herat city could not express what their legal rights were, but after a year and a half of these workshops, even uneducated women from the provinces spoke up about [them].[129]

Sakhi was awarded a Fulbright Scholarship at the Center for Justice and Peace Building, Eastern Mennonite University, Virginia, and completed a master's degree in conflict transformation and peace building in the United States in 2007. She hopes to obtain funding to open offices for WASSA in Kabul and Kandahar when the security situation permits.

Afghan women have made substantial progress since the Taliban government was removed in 2001, but their society is still dominated by patriarchal concepts and tribal customs. Empowerment of women in Afghanistan, Sakhi says, will require a long-term commitment. In relation to women's rights, she points out that they take a secondary place to shari'ah law in Islamic societies:

> In Islam, God is the only sovereign and ultimate source of legitimate law. How, then, can a democratic conception of the people's authority be reconciled with an Islamic understanding of God's authority?[130]

Individual rights, equality before the law, and freedom of expression must be defended, as Sakhi puts it, within "the complex relationship between Shari'ah law . . . and the administrative practices of the state." As in Turkey, democratic evolution will be gradual and "very challenging."[131]

SIMA SAMAR AND SHUHADA

> *I believe that women's rights are human rights, and everyone believes that. But this is, in a way, put aside . . . because they try to say that we must respect the traditions and culture and religion in the country. But we do not have to respect traditions that oppress women and violate human rights.*[132]

Sima Samar was born on February 4, 1957, in Jaghori, Afghanistan. She is a Hazara, one of an ethnic minority composing around 17 percent of the population of Afghanistan and subject to some of the fiercest sectarian persecution. She married aged eighteen and began studying medicine at Kabul University, becoming the first Hazara woman medical graduate. Initially she worked at a government hospital in Kabul, where she saw women die in pregnancy and childbirth every day for lack of medicine and equipment.[133]

When the Soviet army reached Kabul, Samar returned to Jaghori, where she provided medical services in rural areas, including the treatment of mujahideen fighters during their resistance to the invasion. In 1984, when her husband was arrested and subsequently disappeared, Samar fled the Russians once more, this time going to Pakistan, together with her young son.

She began working in the refugee camp at the Mission Hospital in Quetta on the border. In 1987, she established the first medical center for women in Quetta and two years later, the Shuhada Organization, the first agency to provide desperately needed health and education services for Afghan women and girls.

After seventeen years of exile, Dr. Samar returned to Afghanistan in November 2001, after the United States deposed the Taliban. A transitional government was installed and Samar assumed a cabinet post in President Karzai's administration. From December 22, 2001, until June 22, 2002, she was the elected vice president, and one of only two women in the cabinet.

Under her direction, the first Afghanistan Ministry of Women's Affairs was established to provide advocacy, training, and service programs to help restore the rights of women and improve their economic, political, legal, and social status. Among other accomplishments, Dr. Samar oversaw the reentry of girls to education and won the right for female government employees to return to their jobs and keep their seniority; the ministry also introduced the stipulation that 11 percent of the Loya Jirga should consist of female representatives.[134]

However, Samar's concern for women, her demands for equality and justice, and her criticism of conservative Islamic laws, particularly shari'ah, made her powerful enemies. She spoke out publicly against purdah, the seclusion of women, and the requirement for women to wear the burqa, which aggravates conditions such as osteomalacia (a softening of the bones caused by a deficiency of vitamin D, which is usually derived from sunlight). In 2003, when the Loya Jirga convened to create a new constitution for Afghanistan, religious conservatives referred ominously to Dr. Samar's precarious situation, calling her "the Salman Rushdie of Afghanistan."[135] She was taunted by male colleagues, she received death threats, and her role in government quickly became untenable.

In September 2006, the murder of Safia Amajan, Dr. Samar's provincial counterpart and director of the Ministry of Women's Affairs in Kandahar, was a stark demonstration of the real and immediate threat to women who take on political roles in Afghanistan.[136] As an outspoken champion of women's rights, Samar has always faced danger when moving around Afghanistan.[137]

When Samar relinquished her governmental position, the office of minister for women's affairs was not filled. On leaving parliament she was offered the position of chair of the first Independent Human Rights Commission in Afghanistan (AIHRC), a position she still holds.

In 2005, Samar was appointed the United Nations special rapporteur on human rights in the Sudan, particularly Darfur. She is part of the international network called Women Living under Muslim Laws (WLUML), which has links in forty countries and a powerful presence at the United Nations.

Samar believes that peace will never be achieved in Afghanistan by force but that the ruthless exploitation of religious and ethnic divisions in Afghanistan will continue until the general population is educated enough to see beyond these divisions.

Discussing the current state of Afghanistan, she explained that when the Russians left and the Taliban took over, human rights violations occurred daily. The United States no longer had a strategic interest in the country and wanted little to do with a fundamentalist government, that is, until September 11. Even after American intervention, she maintains, conditions did not improve for the people. During the transitional period, while an Afghan government was being established, there was no rule of law or judicial system.

> We were fighting for accountability and justice. We believed no peace would be sustained without justice.[138]

Regarding the democratic elections in Afghanistan, Samar believes they were rushed, and with no screening of contenders, parliament became filled with warlords who had the money to run for office.

> Yes, we have a lot of girls going to school, but no one actually looks at the quality of schools.[139]

Promises to improve the education system have also not been kept, Samar observes. Despite the efforts of the Shuhada Organization, many schools still lack books, furniture, and even buildings, and there are new privations, she adds. In 1975, electricity was always available, but now it is accessible only every other night for three or four hours. Samar believes, however, despite the problems, that there is still hope, and she stresses the role of the next generation in asserting human rights globally, encouraging students to care about these issues and take action.

It is important to remember, she cautions, that human rights, especially women's rights, take precedence over traditions and culture.

> [Since] the fall of the Taliban government, we have not achieved much on human rights on the ground. One of the reasons is . . . that we cannot bring democracy and human rights through military activities only. . . . At least we had [an] election, we had [a] constitution. But the reality is that we keep losing the ground to the Taliban and Talibanization in the country.[140]

The Shuhada Organization

Shuhada is a Dari word, which translates as "martyrs." It was adopted as the title of the Shuhada Organization (SO) in recognition of the thousands of lives sacrificed during the conflict in Afghanistan. The symbol of the organization is a pair of hands holding a trough in which a tulip in full bloom stands. A flame and a snake also decorate the emblem. The pair of hands represents the ideal of unity while the tulip signifies the *shuhada*. The flame symbolizes the commitment of the organization to education, while the snake signifies its activities in the health sector.[141]

Sima Samar is the founder and director of the Shuhada Organization, which is a nonprofit NGO created for the protection and empowerment of Afghan women and children. It provides health services, education, medical training, and employment programs in Afghanistan and for Afghan refugees in Pakistan. The organization is also responsible for four hospitals and twelve clinics in Afghanistan, sixty schools for more than twenty thousand students, and a hospital and school for a thousand girls in Quetta. It distributes food and disseminates information on hygiene and family planning, and it supplies medical outreach workers and mobile health services. The organization opened a science institute in Pakistan in 2001 to train young women and men as physicians' assistants, science teachers, and emergency medical technicians. These endeavors reflect Samar's conviction that education is essential for the self-determination and political freedom of the Afghan population.[142]

Awards for Sima Samar

Community Leadership Award from Roman Magsaysay Award Foundation in the Philippines, 1994

Global Leader for Tomorrow Award from World Economic Forum in Switzerland, 1995

100 Heroines Award in the United States, 1998

Best Social Worker Award, Mailo Trust Foundation, Quetta, Pakistan, March 2001

Paul Grunninger Human Rights Award, Paul Grunninger Foundation, Switzerland, March 2001

Voices of Courage Award, Women's Commission for Refugee Women and Children, New York, June 2001

John Humphrey Freedom Award, Rights and Democracy, Montreal, Canada, December 2001

Ms. magazine, Women of the Year, on behalf of Afghan Women, United States, December 2001

Women of the Month, Toronto, Canada, December 2001

International Human Rights Award, International Human Rights Law Group, Washington, DC, April 2002

Freedom Award, Women's Association for Freedom and Democracy, Barcelona, July 2002

Lawyers Committee for Human Rights, New York, October 2002

Perdita Huston Human Rights Award, 2003

JFK Library Profile in Courage Award, 2004

Named as one of A Different View's 15 Champions of World Democracy in January 2008

2

ALGERIA

BACKGROUND

In 1962, Algeria gained independence after a bloody war (1954–62) costing hundreds of thousands of lives. During the anticolonial rebellion against France, Algerian women, subject to long-term patriarchal restraints, were active and courageous participants. They fought side by side with men on all revolutionary fronts, not only in the cause of national liberation but in the expectation of concomitant full enfranchisement. However, most Algerian men did not support women's emancipation, and soon after independence, they often betrayed their compatriot wives by divorcing them for younger, "more presentable" women.[1]

Ahmed Ben Bella was elected first president of Algeria, but he was deposed by Houari Boumedienne in 1965. In the battle for succession after Boumedienne's death in 1978, the Islamo-Ba'thist clan, a minority group in the ruling National Liberation Front Party (FLN), put forward Colonel Chedli Bendjedid for president. In order to realize their objective of implementing shari'ah law, they would require a combined assault on women, education, and the legal system, the three pillars of shari'ah.[2]

Bendjedid suspended the 1963 postrevolution constitution, which conferred equal rights on men and women and stipulated a clear division between the secular state and private choice of religion. The Socialist-military FLN introduced laws hostile to women, broke away from French traditions, replaced French with Arabic in schools, and chose Islamic and Arab identity over secularism. Moreover, the new constitution, which declared Islam to be the state religion, meant that women were forbidden to travel without a chaperone and were relegated in perpetuity to the control of husbands or male relatives. Husbands could vote in place of their wives, and divorce and inheritance laws were rewritten in favor of men.

During the struggle for full citizenship, feminists were active in opposing the Family Code, which incorporated discriminatory elements of shari'ah law. After the first draft was released in 1979, two hundred university women demanded changes, calling for monogamy, unencumbered rights for women to seek employment, equal division of family property, identical conditions for divorce, and effective protection of abandoned children.

In October 1981, women activists took to the streets to protest against the government's decision to debate the Family Code in secret and two weeks later brought a petition with over ten thousand signatures to the National Assembly. In the event, they were outmaneuvered by the assembly leaders. The demonstrators were joined by women war veterans on December 23, 1981, and their placards read "No to Silence, Yes to Democracy!" and "No to the betrayal of the ideals of November 1, 1954!"[3]

However, the Family Code became law in 1984, a disappointment for the secular feminists who felt betrayed by the FLN's concessions to Islamic fundamentalists. According to the code, women were (and still are) considered minors, their roles restricted to those of wives, daughters, or mothers. Worse, the code legitimized state-sanctioned violence against women who defied Islamist rules. Women warned that although they were the first targets of the Islamists, the violence would soon reach men too. However, the ruling FLN took no heed, made little effort to protect women, and was in fact colluding with the Islamists to stay in power. One debate in the early 1980s even centered on the length of the stick with which husbands were allowed to beat their wives. In addition, the FLN conspired with the Islamists by relinquishing control over the education system, resulting in a radical influence on youth.[4]

After hundreds of young people were killed in the riots of 1988 while protesting against loss of freedoms, corruption, and economic mismanagement, the FLN amended the constitution to allow a multiparty parliamentary system. Initially, the Islamic organizations, supported by Arab states, gained popularity by providing welfare for the poor via mosques and ideologically offering religious certainty and a simplified world order.

In 1991, the Islamic Salvation Front (FIS) received 41 percent of the votes in the first round of elections. At that point, the army canceled the second round, in fear of the Islamists installing a theocratic state along Iranian lines. The FIS responded with escalating violence by armed factions like the Islamic Army of Salvation (AIS) and the Armed Islamic Group (GIA), which were allied to the FIS.

Ex-military chief Mohammed Boudiaf became president in 1992 and in the same year was gunned down while making a public speech. Subsequent retaliation by the army caused the deaths of tens of thousands of people. At the same time, radical Islam grew and used terrorism as a tactic to gain power. The result was a civil conflict with the loss of over 100,000 lives, 80 percent of them women and children. Women who refused to wear the *hijab* were murdered; all unveiled women were designated potential military targets, with lists of condemned women fixed to mosque entrances. In 1996, Nabile Diahnine, president of the feminist group Cri de Femmes, was assassinated on her way to work. Targeted women were decapitated and teenage girls gunned down. Horrifying gang rape was common, often following kidnapping and sometimes involving girls under twelve. There were reports of women who had been kidnapped, made sexual slaves, and then murdered. These rape victims faced further ignomity, as families, feeling shamed and dishonored, kept silent and disowned them.[5] Moreover, few authorities were prepared to condemn and punish organized rape as a serious crime or recognize the victims' need for counseling. Massacres were followed by vast internal displacement. There was some protest from the military but it did not lead to protection for women. In fact men, on the whole, remained silent, as if paralyzed by fear. Apart from the violence, the effect on families was severe, as Islamism turned children against parents, encouraging them to spy on and denounce family members who drank alcohol, smoked, or watched television.

Algerian feminists did their best to bring international attention to the atrocities, although the US administration and many European governments supported the fundamentalists, who adeptly understood how to manipulate the Western media by using human rights language and portraying themselves as political victims.[6]

Numbed by revolution, people lost faith in a government bedeviled by corruption and the inability to prevent Islamist suicide bombings or even provide basic services.

More recently, women have taken advantage of the educational opportunities that are available and have emerged as an economic and political force, providing 70 percent of lawyers, 60 percent of judges, and 60 percent of university students. At the same time, Algerian women have become more religious, with a larger number praying in mosques and wearing the *hijab*, which, they maintain, gives them immunity from moral criticism by men and allows for more freedom to move in the public space.

In a population where 70 percent are under thirty years of age, women drive taxis and buses, police the traffic, dominate the media, and generally earn more than men. While they represent only 20 percent of the workforce, this percentage is twice as large as in previous generations. If these trends continue and women demand a greater political presence, they could eventually claim a role in state power, which is still dominated by men. This quiet, steady progress has gone unnoticed, with the spotlight on Islamist radicals struggling for power and the conservative clergy still solidly opposed to women's emancipation. Islamist propaganda continued to blame women for the unemployment of men in the early 1990s, even though women only held 1 percent of jobs at the time.

In spite of religious pressure against women's freedoms, changes are also manifest in reduced birth rates and a delayed marriage age, which was previously seventeen or eighteen years of age. The current average age of marriage for women is twenty-nine.[7] In contrast to aspiring females, young males tend to leave school early, often to work as lowly street traders commonly known as *hittistes*, literally "people who hold up the walls" in French Arabic.[8]

Women's Rights[9]

Algerian cartoonist Ali Dilem, of Kabyle origin, has worked for the French-language Algerian independent daily *Liberté* since 1997. He attracted international acclaim for criticizing Algerian Islamists, the FLN Party, and the role of the military. In 2006, he was sentenced to one year's imprisonment and a fine of 50,000 dinars ($660) for defaming Algerian president Abdelaziz Bouteflika.

During the civil war, Dilem provoked the wrath of Algerian Islamists, resulting in death threats. A fatwa that was issued against him was endorsed by Algerian minister of religious affairs Boulem Ghoulamallah.

KHALIDA MESSAOUDI

We are dealing with an influential fundamentalist international that has a clear strategy. In order to secure women's rights, we need a democratic international of women—otherwise we have absolutely

Source: Ali Dilem, *Liberté*, November 27, 2005

Source: Ali Dilem, *Liberté*, October 3, 2005

no chance of conquering this beast. Not only Algerian, but Sudanese Iranian and Afghani women know what I am talking about. They know the horror of "God's State" all too well. But alone, without your support, without the women's and human rights movement of the countries of the West, we are losing this battle of life and death.[10]

Messaoudi believes the West is not only misinformed about the global intentions of Islamist movements but also misguidedly accepts misogyny in the name of multiculturalism:

> Even the members of the United Nations appear deep down to believe that the suppression of Algerian women is founded on the culture of our country—and under the pretext of "respect for other cultures" one simply has to respect and accept the suppression of women.
>
> We Algerian women call that a "cultural trap." All the countries of the west have fallen into this trap. They believe that suppression is a cultural question—and do not want to understand that it is a purely political question.
>
> We would at least like the people of the Western world to learn about our history before [they] judge us. We suffer from the racist view that universality is subject to geographic borders and is not valid all over the world. . . . Of course it cannot be a solution for the victims of Islamic fundamentalism to ask the west to deal with the matter on our behalf. But we need the help and support of the countries of Europe in our fight against the suppression of women in Islamic countries.
>
> . . . [During the civil war, 1990–98] 2,084 women have been abducted without one international committee protesting against it. Even worse: an Algerian woman has no right to political asylum in Germany if she is being persecuted by the GIA, the armed "Warriors of God," because she is not being threatened by the state. In contrast, her torturers are given asylum, because they are threatened by the death sentence after all the crimes they have committed in their home country.
>
> But it does not stop there: even women who are persecuted in an established "state of God" are refused political asylum; also under the pretext that the persecution is cultural and not political.[11]

Khalida Messaoudi was born in 1958 into a Kabyle (Berber) family. She grew up with four siblings in the tolerant environment of many Kabyle families, with respect for individual choice of religion and disdain for compulsion.

Her father, a civil servant, sent her to a well-known girls' high school where he believed she would have the best education available. Here she was confronted with the Arabization and Islamization policies of the ruling Socialist-military unified party, the National Liberation Front (FLN). These policies were in full swing and integral to the FLN's educational program.

Messaoudi began her career as a mathematics teacher in 1982, and campaigned for international standards in secular education rather than the emphasis on Arabization and Islamization. Around the same time, she joined with feminists, Communists, and former women partisans (the Moudjahidates) from the time of the war of independence from the French to collect 10,000 signatures protesting new Islamist laws that discriminated against women. One of these laws prevented women from traveling without a chaperone. Due to the support of the Moudjahidates, the petition was influential in repealing the travel law, but the shari'ah-based family law bills were quickly ratified in 1984 before much opposition reemerged.

In 1985, Messaoudi founded the first group of independent women, the Association for the Equality of Men and Women in the Face of the Law, and in 1985, she became a founding member and vice president of the first Algerian league of human rights. Her sympathies also extended to the Kabyle people, who were fighting for recognition of their own language and culture.

Messaoudi is one of Algeria's most passionate feminists and, in 1990, was a founding member of the Association Indépendant pour le Triomphe des Droits de Femme (AITDF; Independent Association for the Triumph of Women's Rights). When President Boudiaf came to power, Messaoudi worked on his advisory committee. Boudiaf had been a founding member of the FLN, but he formed a clandestine party in opposition to the dictatorship of Ben Bella after independence, and this action led to an exile of twenty-seven years before he was installed as president by the military government in 1992. In the same year, he was assassinated by his bodyguard in full view of cameras. For many in the West, the assassination was difficult to comprehend, but Messaoudi explained it was a consequence of the power struggle within the Algerian Army in which a republican faction opposed to the FIS had challenged the old guard, which was willing to make deals with the FIS in order to stay in power. It was this old guard that arranged the execution.[12]

During the eight years of brutal civil war that started in 1990, about eighty people a day were being killed by Islamist militias. Messaoudi spoke out courageously:

They concentrate on journalists because writers symbolize freedom of expression, which the fundamentalists find intolerable. Intellectuals, teachers, writers, thinkers—these are the people killed because it is they who defend traditional notions of liberty. But sometimes simple citizens are killed too, randomly, just for the purpose of terror. One day ordinary people may decide to say "No" to the fundamentalists' ambitions and they want to avoid that happening. They kill women who oppose their views of how we should behave. They cannot allow difference. That is why they insist on veils to cover the difference. They are fascists who claim Allah is on their side and that they are marching under the banner of righteousness.[13]

According to Messaoudi, the growth in Algerian Islamism was a direct consequence of the policy of Arabization introduced by the FLN dictatorship during its one-party rule from 1962 to 1992, and also its scheming with the major Islamist organization, the FIS. She maintains that the Socialist FLN and the Islamists were simply two sides of the same coin:

People in the West do not understand. The Islamic movement is not an opposition to the Government; it is in fact the best way for the one-party state to reconstitute itself. This is not to say that the fundamentalists don't have a popular base. After years of one-party rule people are desperate and many feel the FIS will make a difference. But when you examine their program, there is nothing new. They just want to be the new dictatorship. If necessary they will compromise and absorb members of the FLN Government into their ranks. But it will simply be the old one-party state with a new face.[14]

A regrettable feature of the civil war was the silence of Algerian men in the face of the atrocities suffered by the women: "Men were painfully absent from our struggle. This reinforced my conviction that Algerian women could expect salvation only from themselves."[15]

On June 12, 1993, Khalida Messaoudi was condemned to death in a fatwa issued by the Islamic Salvation Front (FIS):

The soldiers of God, the trustees of the power of God, inform the aides of the tyrants, the trustees of the power of Satan, of the following: . . . We consider you to be criminals. The movement for the State of Islam is more powerful than ever before. It is capable of finding all criminals and all traitors, who refuse to submit to Islam, anywhere, whether inside or outside the country. We will find you and kill you, wherever you are hiding and wherever you have barricaded yourselves in, even when you go to Mecca and cling to the curtains of the Kaaba! [The fatwa bore the signature and stamp of the organization Action for the Islamic State.][16]

Unlike others in a similar predicament, Messaoudi opted to remain in Algeria, but was forced to go into hiding, changing location every day. In the process, she had to give up her work as a teacher and narrowly survived several attempts on her life. When asked how she coped, she answered:

How do I live? It's not a question of how I live but of how I survive. When you are condemned to death your first objective is to stay alive . . . not only physically but as a symbol. You must be constantly on the move with no fixed points—no house, no regular work. I have developed the habit of not having any habits.[17]

In spite of the death threats, Messaoudi became vice president of the Mouvement pour la République (MPR) in 1993, and in 1997, she was voted into parliament as a representative of the RCD Party, a small secular opposition party. She then devoted herself to collecting "A Million Signatures," in a campaign aimed at removing the misogynistic aspects of shari'ah law from the Algerian Family Code.

For her declaration of solidarity with the Berbers' protests, Messaoudi was ostracized by her party, but she ascribed this expulsion as actually being due to her campaign for women's rights:

the fact that I can be elected does not mean I possess even the most elementary of human rights. Because according to the ruling law—which was not made by the fundamentalists, but by the Algerian Republic—I am not of age as a woman. The Algerian parliament passed the new family law in 1984. . . . According to it I am able to participate in making laws in parliament, but in my private life I am still a minor. Polygamy is allowed by law, and a man is still in the position to cast off his wife. If I wanted to marry, I would not be allowed to make the decision myself, but my 74 year old father must do it for me. If he were no longer alive, a brother or uncle or even a son would decide; also, with regard to whether I can travel abroad or not.[18]

She was joint founder of the Association SOS Femmes en Détresse, an association to promote women's rights, and, in 2000 and 2001, vice president of the Commission Nationale de Réforme du Système Educatif (CNRSE). In 2003, Messaoudi was appointed minister of communication and culture.

Always in the vanguard of the secularist feminist and democratic movements in Algeria, she fought hard on two fronts: against Islamist extremism and for women's emancipation, including rights to tertiary education, the professions, independent work, divorce, and freedom from compulsion to wear the *hijab* head covering.

One of her major regrets was allowing herself to be "taken in" by the Islamic Revolution and she castigates herself: "Didn't you subscribe to a Marxist reading of that event, which suited you just as it suited everyone else? Didn't you prefer the comfort of your intellectual interpretation? I see my own cowardice in a certain number of people from the West and from the Maghreb whose support I now seek but fail to get."[19]

Awards

1999 Recipient of the Hellman-Hammett grant
1997 Albert Langer Prize

Published Work

Messaoudi, Khalida. *Unbowed: An Algerian Woman Confronts Islamic Fundamentalism*. Interviewed by Elisabeth Schemla. Translated by Anne C. Vila. Philadelphia: University of Pennsylvania Press, 1998.

BAHRAIN

BACKGROUND

Bahraini women's personal status is defined by Islamic law. Differences exist in the personal status code for Sunni and Shi'a women.[1]

Personal status is set by Islamic law, but women in Bahrain can travel freely and dress as they please. Shia women receive preferential treatment compared with Sunni women in relation to divorce and inheritance, probably reflecting the demographics, as the majority of Bahraini Muslims are Shia.

The Bahrain constitution provides for equality of the sexes in terms of healthcare, welfare, education, and employment, and the Supreme Council for Women acts as an advisory board for the government. However, these laws are not enforced and the impact of religious attitudes acts as a means of maintaining the patriarchal social system.

Statistically, women make up a substantial sector of the population and have made considerable progress relative to other countries in the region. Female youth literacy (females aged 15–24) is almost 100 percent.[2] Notable appointments of women have included Dr. Nada Haffaz as minister of health in 2004 and Dr. Fatima Al-Blushi to the Ministry of Social Affairs in January 2005. Significant progress was made in the judiciary when the first female judge was appointed in June 2006 and Doha Al-Zayyani became the first female judge in the constitutional court in April 2007. In 2005, parliament approved a law to establish a women's university.

Women have advanced in the private sector, particularly in banking, where a woman became general manager of the National Bank of Commerce and others took up managerial positions in banking, insurance, and investment institutions.

In 2000, the upper house of Bahrain's bicameral legislature, the Consultative Council of 40 members, was opened to women and the emir appointed 6 women. The political changes in 2000 also gave women the right to vote and run for office, and 34 women registered from among 320 candidates in the 2002 municipal elections and 8 from among 174 candidates in the parliamentary elections. Although no women won any seats in these elections, 19 women out of 206 candidates contested the parliamentary elections held in 2006 and one female candidate, Latifa Al-Quood, won a seat. She became the first elected female deputy in Bahrain. Dr. Nada Haffaz was appointed minister of health in 2004, and Dr. Fatema Al-Blushi, dean of the College of Education at the University of Bahrain, was appointed minister of social affairs in 2005 during a cabinet reshuffle.

The Supreme Council for Women in Bahrain was founded by Emir Sheikh Hamad bin Issa Al-Khalifa in 2001 and is chaired by his wife Sheikha Sabika bint Ibrahim Al-Khalifa. In March 2005, the council announced a "national strategy for advancement of Bahraini women," committed to the advancement of women by eliminating all discrimination, achieving women's full participation in the public and private workforce, and enabling them to occupy leadership positions.

Bahrain is also a signatory to the Convention on the Elimination of All Forms of Discrimination against Women (CEDAW). Like other signatory nations, Bahrain made reservations with regard to areas that may conflict with Islamic law.

WAJEEHA AL-BAHARNA

> *Change is contagious. When an Arab State sees that another has reformed its nationality law for example, it is immediately encouraged to do the same. Thus, it is a great opportunity to discuss obstacles and challenges with regional partners, draw attention to common issues and possible course of action, as well as being informed on relevant changes and solutions adopted in other countries, such as Algeria, Egypt, and Morocco.[3]*

In Bahrain, male citizens married to foreign wives can transmit their nationality to their wives after five years of marriage and automatically to all children born inside or outside the kingdom. However, Bahraini women married to foreigners were denied similar rights until recently. Treated as foreigners, these husbands and children suffered discrimination unknown to children of Bahraini men married to non-Bahraini women. Exploitation of marriage to Bahraini women simply to gain nationality was cited by government authorities to justify objections to amendments of the nationality laws.

The foreign status of these husbands and children meant they were disadvantaged with respect to healthcare, jobs, and educational opportunities, and in spite of being born in Bahrain, the children required annually renewed residency permits and could not be included in their parents' passports. Although statistics were not available, a sizable population was affected, as many women in Bahrain were married to Egyptian, Algerian, Palestinian, Pakistani, and Indian men.

> Many of the families affected are poor and cannot afford the fees for residency permits, healthcare, and education.
> Children have no job security. Employment is difficult. If they go to hospitals or medical centers, they have to pay—it is free only for citizens. When they apply to university they are considered foreigners, and priority is given to Bahraini citizens.[4]

Wajeeha Al-Baharna, president of the Bahrain Women's Society, is a social activist dedicated to reform of the nationality laws in Bahrain. Compelled to act against these injustices, she accepted the assistance of a Beirut-based organization, the Collective for Research and Training on Development—Action (CRTD-A),[5] in a regional cooperative to change nationality laws. "Our campaign is very purposive and seeks specifically to modify one phrase in the law in order to give both men and women the right to pass on their nationality to their offspring."[6]

The drive for reform in Bahrain started in May 2005 with workshops to increase public awareness and seminars aimed at women's organizations, journalists, and members of parliament.

> We had a meeting with Bahraini women married to non-nationals and the outcome was astounding. In one day, 140 women came to our offices and we listened to their sad and painful accounts. This meeting was covered by the local newspapers and has made a big difference in the community.

Everyone was talking about it, saying they didn't know how much these women were suffering.[7]

Based on the data, a register of individual case studies was established. The plight of these women, including the large number involved, was taken up by the media, generating national publicity. Various parliamentary groups were lobbied by Al-Baharna and the Bahrain Women's Society, including the Islamic, Economic, and Democratic blocs, the Shura Council (the Committee for Women and Children), and the undersecretary for passports and immigration of the Ministry of the Interior. In all cases, the response was positive and encouraging. Surprising support also came from Islamic clergy, who, although opposed to changes in religious family law, were in favor of amendments to nationality law.

The campaign faced some predictable obstacles. Many of the disadvantaged women expected an immediate transformation of the laws. Although pitiful and angry, they were unwilling to face the media with their grievances, and the media were inconsistent and largely preoccupied with issues of government.

In September 2006, concrete progress was achieved when Bahrain's Emir Sheikh Hamad bin Issa Al-Khalifa granted citizenship to three hundred children of foreign fathers married to Bahraini mothers.

GHADA JAMSHEER

Even in mosques they accuse me of heresy. So what? You think that if they accuse me of heresy, it affects me? . . . Allah will decide whether I go to Paradise or Hell, not them.[8]

Ghada Jamsheer has been accused of being unpatriotic, anti-Islam, and a heretic, but she stands firm in her battle for justice. A Sunni Muslim, in a majority Sunni state, she is president of the Committee of Women's Petition in Bahrain and has been fighting to raise awareness of the inequality between the sexes in the Gulf region.

Compared with women of other countries in the region, Bahraini women appear to have much more freedom. Jamsheer herself is feisty and outspoken;

she travels freely and refuses to wear a headscarf. While acknowledging the progress and development taking place, she says it is not enough. Women, she says, are prisoners in their own homes, forced into domestic duties and submission to their families, forbidden to marry as they please, and, in many cases, brutally circumcised. She holds scathing views on male-invented Muslim forms of marriage in both the Shiite and Sunni sects. The Shiite shari'ah law authorizes temporary *muta* marriages and, she claims, pedophilia: "Is it conceivable for a grown man to have sex with an infant girl?" she asks, "and you people tell me that the Islamic Sharia authorises this?"[9] In Sunni *misyar* marriages, a man is permitted to marry a woman from another town and visit her once a month, which, says Jamsheer, "diminishes the woman's honor as a human being."[10]

> We have no family planning in Bahrain. . . . They bring multitudes of children into the world, without thinking, who grow up in the streets.
>
> It's accepted for a man to marry a Filipino woman, a Bahraini woman, and a third woman from Iran, and then he takes two or three women in mut'ah marriage. . . . How many children will he have?![11]

Bahraini women have little respite from unhappy marriages, a fact Jamsheer blames on the government and family law system. The government, she claims, uses the family law issue as a bargaining tool with opposition Islamic groups, many of which actively support the oppression of women:

> Women have become victims of the power struggle, sectarian differences, mismanagement of the government, and unfair distribution of national wealth and resources.[12]

The Women's Petition Committee, of which Jamsheer is president, campaigns for the reform of shari'ah courts and the adoption of a family law system that promotes women's and children's rights:

> In Bahrain, thousands of women and children are under the mercy of an incompetent judicial system and the unwritten family laws, struggling for years to get a divorce or child custody, and living under social rejection and hardships.
>
> These were the reasons behind starting the [Women's] Petition Committee six years ago. The committee has had a non-stop campaign calling

for reforming sharia courts and adopting a family law that promotes women and children's rights. The response from the authority was to dismiss seven incompetent judges, but to appoint others based on political affiliation rather than competence.[13]

Jamsheer has filed hundreds of stories about women denied justice in shari'ah courts. She believes there is an urgent need for civil courts to replace the shari'ah system because judges abuse their power through arbitrary interpretations of the Koran.[14] In addition, she has faced charges over her outspoken criticism of laws and corrupt Bahraini judges.[15]

She urges oppressed and persecuted women to request asylum in another country such as Spain in order to live freely and be protected.

> If a woman cannot get any protection in her country, cannot get any protection from the courts, cannot get any protection in the marital home— where will she go? Where will she go?[16]

Jamsheer also calls for equal representation for women in parliament. She says the National Assembly has failed women:

> partially because the assembly was under the control of the government. In regard to the new assembly, and as a result of government manipulation of elections, the majority of the new House of Representatives are members of Islamist groups who have other priorities than women's rights.[17]

Jamsheer contrasted the positive spin with the reality: only one female candidate was elected to government uncontested, but only because the government had arranged for her to be the only candidate from a sparsely populated region. Ten women were appointed to the Shura Council, but only because of their loyalty to the ruling family.[18]

Jamsheer has shown no fear in castigating the ruling elites and criticized the government-appointed Supreme Women's Council, which, she demanded, should be dismissed:

> The Council is under the control of the women of the royal family, some women of tribal families, and in addition women of families loyal to the royal family in return for positions and in their self interest. . . . The work of the Council is based on the discrimination among women of society, for

women of the royal family are not subject to the rulings of the shariah courts like all other women in this country.[19]

Her outspoken criticism of the government may have prompted surveillance, which is allegedly employed by the government to curtail the activities of activists like herself and the members of her Women's Petition Committee. According to the Bahraini Center for Human Rights, "a Bahraini man was offered a large sum of money by [a] Public Security official in exchange for information on, and access to, the home of Women's Petition Committee head Ghada Jamsheer."[20]

On the cage: "Some of [Our] Customs and Traditions."
Source: *Al-Yawm* (Saudi Arabia), July 30, 2007.

BANGLADESH

BACKGROUND

Giving women the same opportunities as men gives them a better chance of leading fulfilling and productive lives; when equality prevents women from realizing their potential, not only individuals but the country itself stands to suffer.[1]

When independence was achieved in 1971, the Bangladesh constitution guaranteed equality to men and women in all spheres of public life as a fundamental right. However, in 1977, the constitution was amended to make "absolute trust and faith in the Almighty Allah a fundamental principle of state policy and the basis of all actions."[2] This meant that in private spheres such as marriage, divorce, custody of children, and inheritance, personal laws that discriminated against women prevailed. Furthermore, even the constitutional guarantee of equality in public life was not upheld in practice. The National Policy for the Advancement of Women, originally formulated in 1997 following the UN Beijing Women's Conference, was highly acclaimed, but in 2005, the government changed some of the equality principles surreptitiously without consulting any of the women's groups.[3] Women activists suspected the involvement of Islamist groups like Jamaat-i-Islami, Bangladesh, a religious political party in the ruling coalition.

The new policy in 2005 eliminated equality in areas of assets and inheritance and no longer encouraged the women's rights movement and NGOs. Clauses in favor of placing women in senior posts, including the Foreign Service and the judiciary, were deleted. Women were to be employed in "appropriate" professions. On violence against women, the 1997 policy expressed concern about state or police violence and community edicts subjecting women to public lashing, stoning, and even burning to death, but the 2005 policy did not mention these issues. The revisions, which tightened control over women's employment, economic independence, and sexuality, were congruent with growing Islamist politics including suicide bombings. The tension between Islamist forces and the women's movement was probably intensified by the work of NGO schools, which marginalized the *madrassas* (Islamic schools) and constituted a threat to local mullahs.[4]

According to Professor Sadeka Halim of Dhaka University, "The new policy contradicts the government's millennium development goals (MDGs) and its strategy for meeting those. As for us women, the original policy was like a protective shield and an excellent instrument for empowerment. I would say we were one step ahead but will now be thrown two steps back."[5]

Bangladesh had ratified CEDAW in 1984 with reservations on core provisions dealing with marriage and divorce, but from 2005, there was little hope that any previous pledges to withdraw the reservations would be honored.

There are no formal barriers to women's participation in political office in Bangladesh; indeed, there have been two female prime ministers. But patriarchal attitudes have seen women's representation at the ministerial level never rise above 3 percent.[6] Aside from the office of prime minister, ministerial roles, such as those of culture, social welfare, and women have reflected gender stereotypes.[7] In 2005, among the three hundred general seats in the legislature, women held only seven.[8] Since 1976, the government has instituted, and consistently met, a 10 percent quota for women officers in all government ministries, directorates, and autonomous bodies. However, meeting only the minimal requirement, which is very low by international standards, does not demonstrate leadership from the government on employment equity, and very few women hold senior positions.[9]

For most Bangladeshi women, the greatest challenges are extreme poverty and related health problems. These are particularly pronounced in rural areas, where more than 75 percent of the country's 150 million inhabitants live. According to UNICEF'S 2008 *State of the World's Children Report*, Bangladesh has the highest maternal mortality rate in South Asia,[10] and the 2007 *Demographic and Health Survey* showed that 21,000 mothers die annually of pregnancy and childbirth-related causes. The Bangladeshi government's budget for health is 5.9 percent of the overall national budget, of which safe delivery services represent only a small fraction.[11]

Women in the rural districts have been at risk of seriously disfiguring terror attacks in the form of acid throwing. Between January and July 2008, 112 such attacks, mainly related to property and family disputes, claimed 148 victims.

The hydrochloric or sulphuric acid damage can leave victims with blindness and facial scarring down to the bone, and the resulting social ostracism has dire consequences for marriage and employment of women survivors.[12]

In Bangladesh, such attacks occur every two days, prompting the enactment of two new government laws in 2002 that restricted the availability and use of corrosive substances and facilitated the prosecution of offenders. However, few attackers have been punished.[13]

In order to increase awareness of acid violence and related issues, the Acid Survivors Foundation (ASF) was established to coordinate medical and legal assistance to survivors and increase public awareness in Bangladesh.[14]

TASLIMA NASREEN

With the fundamentalists in power, there will be no political stability, no democracy, nor human rights. They rely on blind faith and not reason; they insist on laws which they believe divine. They are against individualism; they prefer to sacrifice the individual in favor of group loyalty and the rights of the Muslim community; and they advocate hatred and violence. They do not want women to work, and if 50 percent of the population is inactive, how can there be development?

For their own political purposes, not only the Middle Eastern leaders but also the Western ones have made compromises with the fundamentalists—to get votes or to fight communism. Both have given the fundamentalists a sort of legitimacy.[15]

Taslima Nasreen (also known as Taslima Nasrin) is a Bangladeshi doctor, writer, radical feminist, human rights activist, secularist, long-term exile, and foremost, a courageous defender of women's rights from the oppression of religious fundamentalism. She has instigated vigorous debate and exposed controversial issues through her feminist writings, and the violent response of Islamic militants has driven her into the international spotlight.

Nasreen was born in August 1962 to a middle-class Muslim family in Mymensingh, East Pakistan, which was later granted independence and became known as Bangladesh, one of the poorest and most densely populated nations on earth. Although her home life was highly restrictive and conservative, she received a liberal education and developed a passion for both science and writing.

At school she was exposed to the teachings of the Islamic religion and first began to question the inequalities advocated in the Koran:

> Men are superior to women . . . men have the right to beat women. . . . In the matter of inheritance, women are not equal with men, and the testimony of women in a court of law is worth half that of men. In the Qur'an, it is written that men can have four wives. It is impossible to think that this is equality. I don't believe any positive interpretation of these verses is possible.[16]

> In marriage, Islam protects the rights of men and men only. Once the marriage is consummated, women have no rights whatsoever in this field. The Koran gave total freedom to men saying, "Your women are as your field, go unto them as you will (2.223)."[17]

> Men will be rewarded with wine, food, and 72 virgins in Paradise, including their wives on earth. And what is the reward for a pious woman? Nothing. Nothing but the same old husband, the same man who caused her suffering while they were on earth. It became clear to me that the male of the species had written the holy Quran for its own interest, its own comfort, its own fun.[18]

Furthermore, "Repeatedly indoctrinated with such teaching, the self-confidence of women gets crushed. They do not unite, protest, oppose. Women not only remain silent against this anti-female society, there are women who actually hold it in high esteem and celebrate it."[19]

Following in her father's footsteps, she studied medicine and received her degree at the age of twenty-three. She began her work as a doctor in the poorer parts of her country, and later worked in public hospitals in the capital, Dhaka. In this role she witnessed how inequality impacted the lives of Bangladeshi women to the extent that even basic access to healthcare was not guaranteed, and women were not usually taken to hospitals until terminally ill.[20]

While working as a physician, she began to write in earnest, as a newspaper columnist and a best-selling author of novels and poetry. In her newspaper column, which she started in 1989, Nasreen took up the plight of women in her male-dominated country, causing Islamists in Bangladesh to take notice:

The fundamentalists organized demonstrations and processions against me from 1990 on; they attacked and sacked the newspaper office where I used to write my columns.[21]

Why shouldn't I write about what I've seen? I'm a doctor, remember! Do you know [what it's] like to see a woman crying out in the delivery room when she gives birth to a girl, terrified that her husband will divorce her? To see the ruptured vaginas of women who've been raped? The six- and seven-year-olds who have been violated by their fathers, brothers and uncles—by their own families? No, I will not keep quiet. I will continue to speak out about these women's wretched lives.[22]

However, it was her 1991 book, *Nirbachito Kolam* (English translation, *Selected Columns*, 2004), a selection of her newspaper articles and columns, that first attracted the animosity of influential Muslim figures. In her book she described the atrocities she had seen, like a twenty-one-year-old woman being buried up to the waist and stoned to death when a Muslim cleric condemned her second marriage. The book catalyzed the first fatwa against Nasreen, and Zainal Abedin Babul, a mullah, supported by other clerics, declared a $5,000 bounty on her head. Her passport was revoked by the Bangladeshi authorities and she was ordered to cease writing or lose her job as a doctor.

In spite of threats, Nasreen remained steadfast in her opposition to the religiously sanctioned subjugation of women. She continued to write and describe the suffering of women and religious minorities in Bangladesh and elsewhere in the name of faith. While most political organizations avoided endorsing her, she enjoyed mass public support from women and men who continued to read her work and support her views.

It is not a question of a conflict between the West and the East, or between Christianity and Islam. It is, rather, a fight between tradition and innovation, antimodernism and modernity . . . between those who value freedom and those who do not. In this fight, it bears noting, some Muslims defend modern ways.[23]

In 1994, Nasreen published her second book, entitled *Lajja* (Shame), which described how Hindus had been subject to Islamist abuse in Bangladesh. Babul filed a case against her, claiming she had insulted Islam.

The government of Bangladesh banned her book, and in July 1994, she was misquoted in an Indian newspaper, the *Statesman*, as saying the Koran should be revised to accommodate women's rights. She was charged with blasphemy, even though there were no such laws. At the same time, mass protests were organized, calling for her arrest and execution.

> Unfortunately, the newspaper misquoted me as saying . . . "the Qur'an should be revised thoroughly." But as I do not believe in the Qur'an, there is no reason for me to say it should be revised. . . . Nothing will be gained by reforming the Qur'an; instead, what is needed is a uniform civil code of laws that is not based on religious dogmas, and . . . equally applicable to men and women.[24]

Nasreen was forced to go into hiding and then flee Bangladesh, seeking refuge in Sweden, under constant police guard. However, she also came to the attention of the West, where her courageous stand was acclaimed.

> Through my writings, I tried to encourage women to fight for their rights and freedom. My voice gave women the chance to think differently.[25]

She has been particularly outspoken against purdah, the covering of women's entire bodies except for their eyes, wrists, and feet for modesty and to hide their beauty:

> Why are women covered? Because they are sex objects. Because when men see them, they are roused. Why should women have to be penalized for men's sexual problems?
> What should women do? . . . They should snatch from the men their freedom and their rights. They should throw away this apparel of discrimination and burn their burqas.[26]

Nasreen believes strongly in the importance of separating religion from the law. "I want civil laws that give equality and justice for women. . . . I don't want any law based on religion."[27]

During a trip to London in December 1994, Nasreen urged the British government to abolish its blasphemy law, which she said promotes intolerance of religious freedom and provides a poor example to countries such as Bangladesh. The blasphemy law in the United Kingdom was eventually abolished on May 8, 2008.

In 1998, she returned to her homeland when her mother was diagnosed with terminal cancer. Although disguised, she was recognized at the airport and word leaked that she was in the country. Nasreen was brought before the High Court, her property was seized, and the Islamic United Alliance demanded that she be killed according to shari'ah law. When she was declared a target by the Islamic terror group Harkatul Jihad-al-Aslami, she fled once more to Sweden and then to France.

Despite her absence, the Bangladeshi government was not appeased. One member declared, "We still demand her death that will warn all murtads [infidels] that they cannot escape the gallows."[28]

In April 2002, Nasreen requested asylum in India, which was denied for fear of offending India's Islamists. However, she was granted leave to remain in Kolkota, West Bengal State, culturally associated with Bangladesh (which was formerly East Bengal).

More fatwas were issued against her by Muslim Indian clerics. In 2007, Muslim leader Taqi Raza Khan offered 500,000 rupees to anyone who would decapitate Nasreen. She was attacked at a book launch, where chairs were thrown and she was slapped in the face. During mass demonstrations, effigies of her were burned. However, when ordered to leave India, Nasreen was defiant.

> Why should I stop attending any public function? That is the platform to express my mind. And, one sure thing is that by disrupting public function the way they did recently or by issuing Fatwa against me they cannot shun my voice. . . . I would keep my struggle against injustice alive.[29]

> What is my crime? My crime is that I have found that Islam does not consider woman a separate human being.[30]

Despite support from international organizations for freedom of expression, Nasreen's life was in constant danger. Imams issued fatwas against her, and the price on her head became increasingly high. Her attackers remained unchecked by the authorities in Kolkota, and her potential assassins were not apprehended. The strength of the violent demonstrations, fatwas, and threats forced her to leave India. She was smuggled out of Kolkota to Jaipur and subsequently returned to Europe, where she continues to live in exile. On July 7, 2008, she was granted honorary citizenship of Paris, where she currently resides.

Despite a life of uncertainty and the danger of continued threats of violence, Nasreen continues to speak out:

> Come what may, I will continue my fight for equality and justice without any compromise until my death. Come what may, I will never be silenced.[31]

> For centuries, women have been taught that they must not speak out against their abusers. . . . My voice gave women the chance to think differently.[32]

Accordingly, Nasreen has been recognized by the international community, has received many awards and honors, and has spoken at countless events. She is aware, however, of the tendency in the West to uphold and exonerate cultures:

> I have been attacked in Europe for criticizing Islam. They tell me that not all traditions in the Islamic world are harmful to women. Imagine, I have been told that the position of women in Bangladesh is very good. They even consider harems not necessarily bad for women!
> If customs are bad for Western women, they are also bad for Eastern women. If education is good for Western women, surely it must also be good for Eastern ones. Muslim women urgently need a modern, secular education, as the rate of illiteracy among them is very high; education would give them some kind of economic independence, and finally would help to liberate them.[33]

Awards

Ananda Award, India, 1992

Natyasava Award, Bangladesh, 1992

Hellman-Hammett grant from Human Rights Watch, United States, 1994

Humanist Award from Human-Etisk Forbund, Norway, 1994

Human Rights Award from the Government of France, 1994

Feminist of the Year from Feminist Majority Foundation, United States, 1994

Kurt Tucholsky Prize, Swedish PEN, Sweden, 1994

Sakharov Prize for Freedom of Thought from the European Parliament, 1994

Honorary doctorate from Ghent University, Belgium, 1995

Monismanien Prize from Uppsala University, Sweden, 1995

Scholarship from the German Academic Exchange Service, Germany, 1995

Distinguished Humanist Award from International Humanist and Ethical Union, Great Britain, 1996

Humanist Laureate from International Academy for Humanism, United States, 1996

Ananda Award, India, 2000

Global Leader for Tomorrow, World Economic Forum, 2000

Erwin Fischer Award, International League of Non-religious and Atheists (IBKA), Germany, 2002

Free-Thought Heroine Award, Freedom from Religion Foundation, United States, 2002

Fellowship at Carr Center for Human Rights Policy, John F. Kennedy School of Government, Harvard University, United States, 2003

UNESCO–Madanjeet Singh Prize for the Promotion of Tolerance and Non-violence, 2004

Honorary Doctorate from American University of Paris, France, 2005

Grand Prix International Condorcet-Aron, from the French Parliament, in Belgium, 2005

Feminist School of Iran Prize, November 22, 2008

Published Works

Poetry

Shikore Bipul Khudha (Hunger in the Roots), 1986

Nirbashito Bahire Ontore (Banished Without and Within), 1989

Amar Kichu Jay Ashe Ne (I Couldn't Care Less), 1990

Atole Ontorin (Captive in the Abyss), 1991

Balikar Gollachut (Game of the Girls), 1992

Behula Eka Bhashiyechilo Bhela (Behula Floated the Raft Alone), 1993

Ay Kosto Jhepe, Jibon Debo Mepe (Pain Come Roaring Down, I'll Measure Out My Life for You), 1994

The Game in Reverse: Poems and Essays by Taslima Nasrin, 1995

Nirbashito Narir Kobita (Poems from Exile), 1996

Jolopodyo (Waterlilies), 2000

Khali Khali Lage (Feeling Empty), 2004

Kicchukhan Thako (Stay for a While), 2005

Essay Collections

Jabo na Keno? Jabo (Why Shouldn't I Go? I Will Go), 1992
Nosto Meyer Nosto Godyo (Fallen Prose of a Fallen Woman), 1992
Choto Choto Dukkho Kotha (Little Bites of Agony), 1994
Selected Columns (English translation of *Nirbashito Kolam*, 2004)

Novels

Oporpokkho (The Opponent), 1992
Shodh (Revenge), 1992
Nimontron (Invitation), 1993
Phera (Return), 1993
Bhromor Koio Gia (Tell Him the Secret), 1994
Forashi Premik (French Lover), 2002
Lajja (Shame), 2003

Autobiography

Amar Meyebela (My Girlhood), 1999
Utal Hawa (Wild Wind), 2002
Dwikhondito (Split Up in Two), 2003
Ka (Speak Up), 2003
Sei Sob Andhokar (All That Darkness), 2004
Meyebela, My Bengali Girlhood—A Memoir of Growing Up Female in a Muslim World, 2002
Ami Bhalo Nei, Tumi Bhalo Theko Priyo Desh (I Am Not Okay, but You Stay Well My Beloved Homeland), 2006

5

CANADA

IRSHAD MANJI (UGANDA/CANADA)

*We Muslims, including moderates living here in the West, are rou-
tinely raised to believe that the Koran is the final and therefore perfect manifesto of God's will, untouched and immutable.*

*This is a supremacy complex. It's dangerous because it inhibits
moderates from asking hard questions about what happens when
faith becomes dogma. To avoid the discomfort, we sanitize.*[1]

Irshad Manji was born into an Egyptian/Indian family in 1968 in Ugan-
da. Her family was prosperous and ran a Mercedes dealership, but her
father was autocratic and abusive.[2] When Idi Amin expelled non-Africans from
the country, her family moved to Vancouver, Canada, in 1972. Manji attended
the local Islamic school, or *madrassa*, as she grew up, but at the age of fourteen
she walked out, having enraged the teacher by asking too many questions. She
continued to study Islam through her own reading and with Arabic tutors.[3]

In 1990, Manji completed an honors degree in the history of ideas from
the University of British Columbia and was awarded the Governor-General's
Medal for the highest academic achievement in the humanities.[4]

Manji worked successively as a legislative aide in the Canadian parliament, a press secretary in the Ontario government, and a speechwriter for the
leader of the New Democratic Party. At twenty-four, she became the national
affairs editor for the *Ottawa Citizen*. She has hosted and produced several
public affairs programs on television, including *QT: QueerTelevision*, which
documented the experiences of gay people in the Muslim world.[5]

As well as working in television production, Manji writes for a number
of news media including the *New York Times*, the *Times* (London), the *Wall
Street Journal*, Canada's *Globe and Mail*, and several Web sites including Al-
Arabiya.net.[6]

In 2003, Manji published *The Trouble with Islam: A Wake-Up Call for Honesty and Change* (Random House, Canada); the book is an open letter to her fellow Muslims, which asks them to question and challenge for themselves aspects of Islam such as the attitudes it promotes toward women, homosexuals, and ethnic groups. She argues that these antipathies have been imposed on the faith by those authorities who have traditionally interpreted the Koran, and she calls for Muslims to liberalize, personalize, and contemporize their faith in the same way as Christians and Jews.[7]

> From the emerging generation, I continually hear this question: "Is there a way to reconcile our faith with freedom of thought?"
>
> Yes, there is. The Qur'an contains three times as many verses calling on us to think than verses that tell us what is forbidden or acceptable. In that sense, re-interpretation—which means re-thinking Qur'anic passages, not re-writing them—is an Islamic responsibility.[8]

In *The Trouble with Islam*, Manji uses the term *ijtihad*, normally a technical and legal term used to describe the practice of jurists in interpreting the Koran in its application to modern life, in a looser sense, to signify the right of the individual to independent thought within the faith. She sees *ijtihad* as the "Islamic tradition of independent reasoning which . . . allowed every Muslim, female or male, straight or gay, old or young, to update his or her religious practice in light of contemporary circumstances."[9]

> Dogma is hobbling our faith, because we Muslims have forgotten Islam's own tradition of independent thinking: ijtihad.
>
> From the 8th to the 12th centuries, the "gates of ijtihad"—of discussion, debate and dissent—remained open. At the twilight of the 12th century, however, the gates of ijtihad closed. Not coincidentally, that is when Islamic civilization led the world in ingenuity. . . . Why? The fragile Islamic empire, stretching from Iraq in the east to Spain in the west, began to experience internal convulsions. Dissident denominations cropped up and declared their own governments.
>
> For hundreds of years since, three equations have informed mainstream Islamic practice. First, unity equals uniformity. . . . Second, debate equals division. . . . Third, division equals heresy.[10]
>
> Which, in turn, means that the spirit of ijtihad must be suppressed.
>
> It is a pattern that persists to this very day. Not long ago, my mother's

imam in Vancouver preached that I am a bigger "criminal" than Osama bin Laden because my views on religious reform have caused more "division" among Muslims than al Qaeda's terrorism has. Apparently, he did not detect the irony in proclaiming that debate is worse than terrorism.[11]

The good news is that the gates of ijtihad were shut not for spiritual or theological reasons but for entirely political ones. This means there is no blasphemy in seeking to resuscitate Islam's tradition of independent thinking.[12]

Manji began writing *The Trouble with Islam* in 2002, while serving as a visiting fellow at Yale University and journalist-in-residence at the University of Toronto. The book has been published in almost thirty countries, including Pakistan, India, Lebanon, and Indonesia, and the foreign language versions provided on the Web site for citizens of countries where the book is banned have been downloaded more than 500,000 times.[13]

Conservative Muslims and Islamic authorities are not impressed by the fact that Manji is an opinionated lesbian, a product of Western academia and culture, that she questions the infallibility of the Koran, and that she expresses pro-Israeli sentiments. Because of death threats that she has received in response to her opinions, she has installed bulletproof glass in her house, employs a bodyguard, maintains ongoing communication with the Canadian police, and doesn't use a mobile phone because it could be used to track her movements. Parallels have been drawn between Irshad Manji and Salman Rushdie, who encouraged Manji to write her book, saying that the reformation of Islam would begin with people like her.[14]

A number of critics view Manji's scholarship as amateurish and lowbrow, and they accuse her of dismissing the tolerant period of Ottoman rule,[15] "the thousands of books, texts, and articles written that question, analyse, and interpret the Koran, written over fourteen hundred years by Muslim scholars from around the world" and of a "deep disdain and disrespect for the psychology and sensibilities of Muslims."[16]

The *New York Times* has referred to her as "a crown jewel in the history of the modern women's movement" who promotes an "Islamic Reformation," although probably disqualified as a lesbian.[17] The American Society for the Advancement of Muslims has chosen Irshad as a Muslim Leader of Tomorrow.[18] The *Times of India* said that Manji's courage is to be commended in her defiance of fatwas against her life.[19]

In order to further the aims of her book, Manji started Operation Ijtihad, a global campaign, largely Internet based, to popularize critical thinking within, and about, modern Islam. In recognition of Operation Ijtihad, the World Economic Forum nominated Manji as a Young Global Leader in 2006.[20]

An expert in media production, Manji uses new media such as the social networks MySpace, Facebook, AuthorNation, YouTube, Digg, Squidoo, and online discussion boards to facilitate discussion about Muslim reform and moral courage.[21] She has also produced a PBS documentary, *Faith without Fear* (2007), which follows her journey through the Middle East, Western Europe, and North America addressing issues such as human rights, in an exploration of the application of Islam in the twenty-first century.[22] The documentary was nominated for Canada's most prestigious media award, the Gemini, in 2007 and was given a gold award at the New York Television Festival in 2008.

Since January 2008, Manji has been the director of the Moral Courage Project at New York University. Students enrolled in the project take courses in management, finance, and policy and gain work experience in urban communities. The aim of the project is to produce leaders in the public service field who are capable of effecting positive change.[23] Manji was a visiting fellow with the International Security Studies Program at Yale from 2005 to 2006, and is a senior fellow of the European Foundation for Democracy in Brussels.[24]

Manji was awarded Oprah Winfrey's first annual Chutzpah Award for "audacity, nerve, boldness and conviction." *Ms.* magazine named her a "Feminist for the 21st Century," and Immigration Equality gave her its Global Vision Prize. In May 2008, she received an honorary doctorate from the University of Puget Sound.[25]

6
EGYPT

BACKGROUND

All secular-oriented women activists have experienced a whole range of legal, cultural and political restrictions ... unfortunately, many feminists reproduce the very same discourses as fundamentalist and conservative nationalist voices in Egypt. However, a small number of activists dare to challenge points of reference.[1]

Women in the Republic of Egypt have seen some improvement in their status; however, there are still numerous significant issues and difficulties to be overcome. Moreover, "In all cases, real decisions in the Arab world are, at all levels, in the hands of men."[2]

Feminism in Egypt has been part of the nation's development since the nineteenth century, and opportunities were provided by the twentieth century and its various developments:

As the twentieth century unfolded, a new awareness about what it meant to be "female" took root. The story of Egyptian feminism is the story of feminism in a nationalist century.... The first half of the century was marked by a fierce nationalist struggle.... During the course of the century, women have given shape to a newer, modern identity.... Women articulated feminism within the discourses of both Islamic modernism and secular nationalism.[3]

Even in the pre–World War I years, Egyptian feminists were making demands for reform. At the Nationalist Congress of 1911, "Malak Hifni Nasif seized the opportunity to issue the first set of feminist demands. These included women's right and access to all forms and levels of education, the right to work in the occupations and professions of their choice and their right to participate in congregational prayer in mosques."[4]

Despite continuing efforts, women did not gain the right to vote and run for political office in Egypt until 1956. The first female parliamentarian soon followed: in 1957, Rawya Attiya became the first woman to be elected to parliament. Throughout the first half of the twentieth century, women's interests were represented by groups such as the Wafdist Women's Central Committee and the Egyptian Feminist Union; the latter was forced to close in 1956 but was permitted to reopen as a social service organization under the name Huda Sha'rawi Association.[5]

Progress was made gradually, including changes in access to higher positions in various professions. For example, in March 2007, thirty women took an oath before the Supreme Judicial Council to take their positions as judges:

> Human rights and women's associations welcomed their appointment, while some male judges and Islamist activists objected to this appointment [on] the pretext that Islam does not allow women to preside over the judiciary. However, Egyptian constitution and law do not prohibit women from occupying judicial positions.[6]

Conservative and traditional attitudes are also evident in the contentious issues of female genital mutilation and honor killings. The latter have been a source of debate as part of a broader problem of domestic violence.

> According to a report issued by the United Nations Children's Fund (UNICEF) in 2002, 35 per cent of Egyptian women have been beaten by their husbands. A 2002 study reported by the All Party Parliamentary Group on Population and Development found that 47 per cent of all homicides with female victims were cases of "honor killing" in which relatives murder a woman suspected of sexual impropriety, which includes being raped, in order to rid the family name of the perceived slur.[7]

Female genital mutilation has continued, despite government efforts to end the practice by banning the procedure and closing clinics. Suzanne Mubarak, wife of President Hosni Mubarak, and head of the National Council for Motherhood and Childhood (NCMC), has been in the forefront of the movement to amend the law in order to criminalize female genital mutilation (FGM). The law was passed in June 2008 but not without the Muslim Brotherhood hurling accusations. They claimed that "outlawing FGM was tantamount to promoting vice" and that the NCMC was pandering to Western influence.[8]

The Ministry of Religious Affairs . . . issued a booklet explaining why the practice was not called for in Islam; Egypt's grand mufti, Ali [Guma], declared it haram, or prohibited by Islam. . . .

But . . . widespread social change in Egypt comes slowly, very slowly. This country is conservative, religious, and for many, guided largely by traditions, even when those traditions do not adhere to the tenets of their faith, be it Christianity or Islam.[9]

As in other Arab countries, blogs and Web journals, indifferent to gender, mushroomed freely. Egypt's bloggers in the vanguard of this movement have developed the Internet as a tool of political dissent, harassing a regime in control of the print media.[10]

Despite detention and prosecution faced by bloggers, Egyptian woman blogger Nora Younis received the 2008 Human Rights First annual award.[11]

EKBAL BARAKA

Women make up 51 percent of Egypt's population, but only two percent in parliament, in the government and all the elected councils. We have to fight to regain our rights. I say regain because the Egyptian woman was the first in history to have all the rights, and to be a ruler and a queen before her husband and before her brother.[12]

Ekbal Baraka was born on April 1, 1942, in Cairo. She graduated from Alexandria University with an honors degree in English language and literature in 1962 and obtained a diploma in drama from the same department in 1964.[13] She has worked as an English teacher in Kuwait, a radio speaker, an editor for the Egyptian weeklies *Sabah el Kheir* and *Rosel Yousef*, and a freelance writer for various Egyptian and Arabic newspapers.[14] In 1979, Baraka gained a second BA, in Arabic language and literature, from Cairo University. This involved the study of the Koran, the hadith, Arabic language and rhetoric, Arab-Muslim history, philosophy, poetry, and prose.[15]

Baraka has become one of the best-known and most influential feminists in the Arab world. She was the editor-in-chief of *HAWAA*, the first and most popular women's magazine in the Arab region, from June 1993 to June 2007. Every week she appears on a television current affairs program, and she also lectures on women, Islam, and Arab culture at universities and conferences.[16]

She has published twenty books on travel, literature, literary criticism, and politics, including four on Islam, six novels, and two collections of short stories. Many of her novels and short stories have been adapted for Egyptian television or film and, in 2000, Baraka started to write her own radio and TV plays. She is president of the Egyptian Pen Center.[17]

Baraka has written a number of articles and spoken on television deploring what she sees as the current "reactionary wave that threatens to take Arabs back to the Middle Ages," and she is critical of polygamy, temporary marriage, and religious justifications for domestic violence.[18]

Baraka seeks to reconcile her feminist convictions with her religious faith and to that end, has come to believe that discrimination against women is not an essential part of Islam, but rather a result of a particular interpretation of its provisions. She also believes that religion should not be imposed upon people by the state.[19]

Her book *The Veil: A Modern Viewpoint*[20] argues that the custom of wearing the veil, which has seen a resurgence among young Egyptian Muslim women, is demeaning, predates Islam, and is not stipulated by the Koran or the hadith.[21] *The Veil* sold well and was printed in three editions, including one brought out by the Syrian publishing house Dar Kiwan. In 2004, the Muslim Brotherhood sued Baraka, among other parties, over the book and demanded she should be prevented from writing in Egypt. However, she managed to avoid conviction and a possible jail sentence. The mufti, Egypt's leading religious authority, attempted to ban *The Veil* in November 2006.[22] In publicly challenging Islamism, Baraka risks her life because the disapproval of the mufti and the Muslim Brotherhood might be interpreted as the equivalent of a fatwa.

Her latest books, *Muslim Women in the Conflict of Fez versus Hat* and *The New Woman*, look at the history of modern Egypt from the perspective of the women's movement, from the nineteenth century to the foundation of the Egyptian Women's Union in 1923.[23]

NONIE DARWISH (EGYPT/USA)

Israel is the only non-Muslim state in the Middle East. That's why it's a target; many Muslims want the Middle East to be exclusively under

> *Muslim control. Isn't it enough that Muslims have been blessed with fifty-five Muslim states extending from Morocco to South East Asia? Why do they feel compelled to destroy a nation so small you can hardly find it on the map?*
>
> *And this obsession has gone beyond the question of Jewish sovereignty. Many Muslims want to make the Middle East Jew-free. Every decent Muslim and Arab must say no to this, not only because Israel has every right to exist as a nation and is an asset in the region, but also because hatred and terrorism are destroying the moral fabric and goodness within their own societies.*[24]

Nonie Darwish, an Egyptian American writer and convert to Christianity, is the founder of Arabs for Israel.[25]

Darwish grew up in Cairo, the daughter of a high-ranking intelligence officer in the Egyptian army. The author of *Now They Call Me Infidel: Why I Renounced Jihad for America, Israel, and the War on Terror*, Darwish details the cultural indoctrination of her childhood and her journey away from this mind-set.[26]

In 1950s Egypt, Darwish was immersed in a "culture of hatred against the Jews." She was taught that Jews were "monsters" who killed Arab children to drink their blood, and they were described as "dogs," "pigs,'" and "devils."[27] Martyrdom was romanticized, and all of society's ills, such as poverty, were blamed on Jews. Hatred of Israel was incorporated into every subject to ensure that it reached the students, who took from this the message that peace between Israel and Arabs would lead to a loss in pride.

> Close to 900,000 Jews were driven from Arab countries, a terrible loss. I know from personal experience that the culture of Egypt was never the same.[28]

At the same time, the politics of the Arab world dictated that the Palestinian refugees should live in poverty, as Darwish had witnessed when she lived in Gaza. Thus, none of the Arab countries were prepared to extend their land and resources or grant nationality to the refugees. When her father was killed by a bomb in Gaza, he was glorified as a hero, and her mother received a visit from President Nasser to give her the country's highest military reward.[29]

After the Arab defeat by Israel in the 1967 war, Darwish writes, Israel was portrayed as the aggressor and Egypt as the victim rather than as the perpetrator of the war. Lies and distortions were fed to the people to explain their defeat, but Darwish argues that the defeat was in fact caused by the lack of motivation of an army consisting of impoverished peasants who had no incentive to fight against Israel. Their true oppressors were their superiors in the army, whereas Israel was fighting for its survival.

While she was studying sociology and anthropology at the American University in Cairo, Darwish began to compare the ethos of tolerance and respect at that university with the opposite nature of her upbringing mired in hatred. She began to question and analyze the beliefs of Islamic suprema-cism, Judeophobia, and the demonization of Israel. Simultaneously, she was witnessing the exclusion from society of her mother as a widow. Friends no longer wanted to be in contact with her, viewing her as a threat to their own marriages, leaving her with no support system on which to lean. Being a widow also carried extra restrictions on her behavior so as not to disrespect her dead husband's memory, such as no longer being able to swim at the beach with her children.

Darwish also became aware of other situations involving attitudes to women. A new maid who came to work at their home had been raped by her former boss and turned out of the house, pregnant with his child. Fearful of what might happen if her male relatives found out and blamed her for the rape, she went to a government home. Darwish later learned the girl was murdered, most likely by her own family to retain their honor.

The honor of a man, says Darwish, is bound to the sexual status of his female relatives, and the legacy of slavery has meant that domestic servants are treated as if they are "owned" by their employers, resulting in many instances of rape. Honor killings are condoned and physical abuse is common and unquestioned, even depicted as normal in television shows. Men have easy access to divorce, whereas women may be refused that right and severely punished if they engage in extramarital relations, even if they have been abandoned by their husbands.

> The husband according to Islamic law has the right to divide his loyalty between four women. . . . Islam asks men to be fair and just among the wives and to treat them all equally. In practice, when the inevitable conflicts of mar-riage occur, many Moslem men resort to a second wife (or threat thereof) as their "solution" instead of working out the problem with the first.[30]

Muslim scholars often claim that Muslim women have more rights than Western women because they have the right to keep their property separate from that of their husbands; that is true, says Darwish, but they don't tell you why:

> The right in question has developed so as to protect a wife's property inherited from her family from going to the second, third or fourth wife. Polygamy thus totally changes the dynamics of the relationship between husband and wife or wives. The loyalty unit is no longer husband/wife, but wife and male members of her own family and later wife and her first born son who will protect her interests if the husband gets another wife.[31]

Darwish points out that younger Muslim men are often deprived in the bridal stakes. Financially advantaged, old Egyptian men have a better chance procuring a bride than poorer, younger men, leaving young unmarried men in a prime position for recruitment by Islamist extremists. According to Darwish, Muslim men who marry non-Muslim women are rewarded for spreading the faith; however, Muslim women who do the equivalent do so at great risk to their lives.

A central mission for Darwish is to caution the West about Islamist hatred:

> The notion that Islam teaches only peace and tolerance is ridiculous. If you heard, as I have, the anti-American and anti-Jewish hate that is being preached in many mosques and on Arab TV, you'd think you were in Nazi Germany, except that the commands are coming from Allah instead of Hitler.

She believes the ultimate goal of radical Islamists is Muslim imperialism:

> They want to conquer the world for Islam, to usher in a Caliphate—that is, a supreme totalitarian Islamic government that would forcibly impose sharia law on everyone.[32]

> Many Westerners do not realize that World War Three has already begun. Many thousands of Muslims have been bred to be suicide bombers ready to give up their lives in service of jihad. That is why we must not let ourselves be lulled into thinking that jihad is about self-improvement.[33]

Darwish promotes several proposals for reform, including changing the law against conversion from Islam, preventing radical clerics from taking over mosques, and ending the inclination to blame Israel and America for every problem the Arab world experiences.

> At a time when most religions struggle to explain evil in the world, Radical Islam found the answer, without hesitation, they say it is the Jews. Just listen to most Friday sermons in mosques all around the Muslim world. In these sermons week after week, there is one theme that keeps repeating itself: The Jews are responsible for all that is wrong in Arab society and Arabs are not responsible for their failures.[34]

> When I first started speaking out I received many e-mails from Arabs who said they supported me but were afraid of retaliation. Many said, "Please do not use my name," and I honored that. Yet I felt there needed to be a forum for them to speak out; that was the original impetus for www.ArabsFor Israel.com.[35]

Published Work

Now They Call Me Infidel: Why I Renounced Jihad for America, Israel, and the War on Terror (New York: Sentinel, 2006)
Cruel and Usual Punishment (Nashville: Thomas Nelson, 2008)

AIDA SEIF EL-DAWLA

> *More people come to us for assistance, but they also wanted to take their torturers to court. Those who came to us were people who reached a point where they don't think anything worse could happen to them. That there's nothing worse than your son being tortured and hanged upside down from his feet, or that your daughter is held in a prison cell full of men. When everything is violated there is nothing to fear.[36]*

In 1989, Dr. Aida Seif El-Dawla decided the situation had to change in her homeland, Egypt, and along with a few colleagues, she began documenting violations against human rights. In 1993, she cofounded the El Nadim Center for the Psychological Rehabilitation of Victims of Violence, the only clinic dedicated to providing assistance to torture survivors and survivors of domestic violence, as well as the Task Force against Female Circumcision.

Since it was established, El Nadim has expanded from assisting victims of torture to publishing and disseminating their testimonies. Since March 2002, more than a dozen people have died as a result of torture by Egyptian police and security forces and thousands of men, women, and children live with the physical and psychological scars. El-Dawla's pioneering work provides not only solace and care for torture victims but also the tools for obtaining justice.

> At first people came and were afraid, and we were afraid, too. We had decided to help the victims only and not do any campaigns. We thought we knew what was happening; we thought we could monitor the places where torture occurred. But we discovered that torture happens everywhere and anywhere and is systemic—it's supported by the state.[37]

In addition, El-Dawla found that becoming more active in campaigning and publishing testimonies encouraged more people to come forward for assistance.

Although left-wing and outspoken, El-Dawla is not a member of any political party. Born into a politically active family, she came of age at a time when the Egyptian government was pursuing limited economic and social reforms while severely restricting civil and political rights. Her father was arrested twice for his opposition to President Anwar Sadat:

> Before I entered university I had seen my father arrested twice, and two other family members arrested as well, all for the unforgivable "crime" of thinking differently and expressing what they thought and believed.[38]

While studying psychiatry at university in the 1970s, she was an active member of the Egyptian student movement, addressing social, political, and gender-based injustices.

As a founding member of the New Women Research Center, Dr. El-Dawla has played a key role in the development of strategies challenging the obstacles to women's liberation posed by government policy. She has also fought religious fundamentalists' efforts to force women back to a veiled society and is an advocate against female genital mutilation:

> Between 85% to 95% of Egyptian women are exposed to female genital mutilation (FGM). . . . this violation is practiced by parties who are powerful socially and hence their anger should be avoided. [Women] are not told that it is their right not to be mutilated, for eventually they may challenge their violators.[39]

Unsurprisingly, her work has made her few friends in the political arena or among the male elite. Her campaign against moral rigidity has seen her speak out publicly about the ways in which Egypt has responded to Western-inspired modernity in the areas of industrialization, liberalism, and socialism since the mid-nineteenth century. Instead of dealing with these problematic issues, she laments, millions have chosen to focus on sex and morality as a cure for their woes. Female morality and sexuality is often presented as posing more danger to society than political corruption or war.[40]

On November 4, 2003, El-Dawla received the highest honor of the Human Rights Watch for her work against torture in Egypt; she donated her award to the El Nadim Center.

> Although there is no protection from torture or arrest, international relations make a difference when something does happen because the world gets to know.[41]

> I realize that civil activism alone cannot change the world. Civil action has to be politicized.[42]

RABAB EL-MAHDI

> *There is discrimination against women in all areas—only 1% of elected MPs are women, and family and labour laws are stacked against women.*[43]

> *I'm concerned with attempts to focus on sexual liberation. . . . Priorities have to be decided locally. . . . The obsession in the West with Muslim women is Eurocentric, condescending and patronising.*[44]

Rabab El-Mahdi was born in 1975 and grew up in Cairo in an academic family. She gained her PhD from McGill University in Montreal with a dissertation on the impact of neoliberal economic reconstruction on the changing patterns of state-civil society relations in Egypt and Bolivia.[45] She has worked for several NGOs, the Canadian International Development Agency, and the United Nations.[46]

In 2005, she returned to Egypt to participate in the presidential election campaigns and took a position as an assistant professor of political science at the American University in Cairo. She thought 2005 was a good time to push for social change, but the elections were widely reported to have been stage-managed and were marked by suppression of opposition by President Mubarak's security forces. An alternative media outlet was provided by Egyptian bloggers: "My friends overseas all followed what happened through the blogs, because they have more credibility than the mainstream media."[47]

El-Mahdi attended weekly rallies and protests and was subjected to intimidation and physical and sexual assault at the hands of the riot police.[48]

She campaigned on behalf of the independent Revolutionary Socialists and Kifaya (Enough), the opposition group, which both call for democratic reform in Egypt. Rabab is also a leading member of the Women for Democracy movement, which operates under the slogan "The street is ours."[49]

Academics have been increasingly at risk in Egypt. They have been subject to intimidation and violence from both government officials and Islamist militants and risk detention and torture if they research or speak about sensitive issues.[50] "What kind of academic freedom do we aspire to when you have this kind of knife on your neck all the time?"[51]

El-Mahdi, however, has written about modern Egyptian society, the policies of the current regime, the protest movements, and the women's movement in Egypt. She is the author of *Egypt's Feminist Movement: Different or Non-Existent?* and coeditor of *Egypt: The Moment of Change*. The latter examines the effects on Egyptian society of the imposition of neoliberal economic policies, the impact of Islamism, and the influence of opposition groups. Many of the contributors to the book are Egyptian academics and activists.[52]

Regarding Islamic dress, El-Mahdi objects to the way that women's sexual status and the growing popularity of the *hijab* has been singled out as an issue by Western commentators. Although she would prefer to see the hijab discarded, she believes that veiling has actually brought women more freedom in the public space.[53] She sees it as one aspect of the overall socioeconomic and political picture and not necessarily the most important one:

I don't think the sexual status of women has lagged behind other areas. There is discrimination against women in all areas—only 1% of elected MPs are women, and family and labour laws are stacked against women.[54]

NAWAL EL-SAADAWI

Danger has been a part of my life ever since I picked up a pen and wrote. Nothing is more perilous than truth in a world that lies. Nothing is more perilous than knowledge in a world that has considered knowledge a sin since Adam and Eve.[55]

Dr. Nawal El-Saadawi is an Egyptian psychiatrist, author, and activist who has become an internationally respected authority on women's issues. She has published more than forty works of fiction and nonfiction, which focus on the sociological and legal status of women, particularly in Egypt. Her works have been translated into more than twenty languages, but many of them are considered a threat to society in Egypt and have been banned there. She has been a lifelong left-wing critic of oppressive religious and political discourses, despite the loss of her medical career, imprisonment, exile, and death threats.

El-Saadawi was born on October 27, 1931, in Kafr Tahla, a small village outside Cairo on the banks of the Nile. Her father was a civil servant in the Ministry of Education and went to great lengths to ensure that Saadawi, and her three brothers and five younger sisters, were well educated. She was taught to think for herself and to speak her mind. At the age of six, however, she was subjected to traditional genital mutilation.[56]

El-Saadawi did well at school and went on to study medicine at Cairo University, graduating in 1955. She practiced at the university and for two years at the rural health clinic at Kafr Tahla, but she was called back to Cairo after she attempted to rescue a patient from domestic violence. She was successively promoted, becoming the director general of the Department of Education in Egypt's Ministry of Health in 1966. In 1968, she became the secretary-general of the Medical Association in Cairo and started and edited *Health Magazine* on the association's behalf.

El-Saadawi's first work of nonfiction, *Women and Sex*, was published in 1972. Her discussion of the taboo subject, and her criticism of the practice of genital mutilation, angered religious and political authorities. Her book was banned, the Ministry of Health dismissed her, *Health Magazine* was closed down, and she was prevented from practicing as a doctor.[57] From 1973 to 1976, with government positions no longer available. El-Saadawi researched women and neurosis in the Faculty of Medicine at Ain Shams University. Her research, which included twenty in-depth case studies of women in prisons and hospitals, was published in *Women and Neurosis* in 1976 and inspired her novel *Woman at Point Zero*.[58]

In 1977, she published her most famous work, *The Naked Face of Woman*, which explores topics including female genital mutilation and aggression against female children, prostitution, sexual relationships, marriage, divorce, and Islamic fundamentalism. From 1979 to 1980, El-Saadawi was the United Nations advisor for the Women's Program in Africa and the Middle East.

In September 1981, El-Saadawi was imprisoned by President Anwar Sadat for her criticism of his policies. She was released in 1982, a month after his assassination. After her release, Saadawi continued to speak out against the repressive nature of the Egyptian government. In the afterword to her next book, *Memoirs from a Women's Prison* (1983), El-Saadawi noted the corrupt nature of her country's government, the dangers of publishing under such authoritarian conditions, and her determination to continue to write the truth:

> When I came out of prison there were two routes I could have taken. I could have become one of those slaves to the ruling institution, thereby acquiring security, prosperity, the state prize, and the title of "great writer;" I could have seen my picture in the newspapers and on television. Or I could continue on the difficult path, the one that had led me to prison.[59]

In 1982, 120 women formed the Arab Women's Solidarity Association (AWSA), with Dr. El-Saadawi as president. The society was established with the foundational belief that the liberation of Arab women is inseparable from the struggle for the liberation of Arabs in general from economic, cultural, and media domination. An international nonprofit organization, AWSA hosted international conferences and promoted Arab women's active participation in social, economic, cultural, and political life.[60]

In January 1991, the Egyptian government closed down the association's magazine, *Noon*, because of its criticism of US involvement in the first Gulf War. Six months later, the government banned the association and redistributed its funds.

El-Saadawi had been receiving death threats from radical religious groups since the publication of her novel *The Fall of the Imam* in 1987, and, in 1991, having lived with armed guards outside her house in Gaza for several years, she left Egypt and became a visiting professor in North American universities. From 1993 to 1996 she was a writer-in-residence at Duke University's Asian and African Languages Department and she lectured at Washington State. After five years of exile she returned to Egypt in 1996, because she felt that she could not fight for an improvement in conditions there from outside the country.

In 2001, El-Saadawi was accused of apostasy and of insulting Islam; had she been convicted in the Egyptian Personal Law Courts, she would have been forcibly divorced from her husband of thirty-seven years, the novelist and activist Dr. Sherif Hetata, and would have faced a term of three years in prison. During an interview with the Egyptian weekly *Al Maydan*, she had referred to the fact that some elements of the hajj (the annual pilgrimage to Mecca all Muslims are expected to make at least once in their lifetime), such as kissing the black stone, predated Islam and were of pagan origin. She had expressed these opinions before, but the political climate in Egypt had become more repressive and her comments made sensational headlines. She successfully defended her action, however, and the charges were dropped.[61]

She came into conflict with the Egyptian authorities again in 2006 when she supported her daughter, Dr. Mona Helmi, in her view that children could be named according to their maternal, rather than solely their paternal, lineage.

El-Saadawi declared: "We must change the law so that a father will not be the exclusive custodian of the children . . . where a husband leaves, the mother will have exclusive custody of the children . . . the mother's name will be given the same honor as the father's name and the children will be able to have their mother's name and not just their father's name."[62]

According to the Islamists, she was an "enemy of the religion" or "enemy of the veil" who deserved to die.[63] The popular religious authority Yusuf Al-Qaradawi came to Saadawi's aid, saying that naming a child after the father was simply "a custom that existed all over the world" and not an Islamic ruling. However, his views did not placate the extremists, who considered El-Saadawi's remarks to be heretical.[64]

In March 2007, the Islamic Research Council agreed to present a petition to the general prosecutor against El-Saadawi for insulting Islam in her play *God Resigns at the Summit Meeting*. Five of her books, including the play, had been banned in Cairo two months earlier. Her publisher withdrew the play from circulation and destroyed the copies in his possession in the presence of security police.[65]

In March 2007, with the case filed against her for supporting her daughter still pending, Dr. El-Saadawi left Egypt for Belgium, where she applied for a long-term visa for the United States. Once again, her name was appearing on the death lists of fundamentalist groups, and she felt that she was in serious danger.[66]

SUZANNE MUBARAK AND SMWIPM

We cannot afford to ignore the gender dimension—for women are an integral part of the solution. They are the custodians of the environment and its primary victims. . . . They play a decisive part in poverty alleviation, economic growth, human development and of course human security.[67]

The Suzanne Mubarak Women's International Peace Movement (SMWIPM),[68] a nonprofit, self-funding NGO based in Cairo, was established in 2003 to empower women through cross-cultural dialogue, human rights, reconciliation, and peace building using both existing infrastructure and new initiatives. The organization hosts regional, national, and international meetings.

Suzanne Mubarak, wife of Egyptian president Hosni Mubarak, was born in 1941, the daughter of an Egyptian surgeon and a Welsh nurse. She has a bachelor's degree in political science from the American University in Cairo and a master's in sociology of education. The founder and chairperson of numerous women's committees and children's educational projects in Egypt, she has made a significant contribution to regional and international organizations and conferences on the status of women, children, peace, health, and the environment.

Many organizations have been established under the umbrella of SMWIPM, including a youth network, and media and communications, events and fundraising sections, all aimed at the promotion of peace initiatives through seminars, conferences, and exhibitions.

During the launching of the movement in 2003, Mubarak put forward her goal of harnessing women as resilient and motivated activists determined to avoid the calamities of war. She also asserted the importance of implementing UN Resolution 1325 of October 31, 2000, which called for increased representation of women in relation to conflict resolution. Further meetings dealing with this issue included a seminar in Cairo in 2006, when fifty-two delegates from fourteen Arab countries examined the place of Arab women in the context of UNSC 1325 and the peace discourse.[69]

In 2003, Mubarak formed the global Arab Women Organization (AWO) to raise knowledge of existing Arab women's rights and further their empowerment. The foundation is based in Cairo under the auspices of the Arab League.[70]

At the Bibliotheca Alexandrina, she established the Arab Institute for Peace Studies in 2006. This organization used a resource developed by the Geneva Center for the Democratic Control of Armed Forces (DCAF)[71] to fight against human trafficking and child labor by integrating trafficked children into schools, compensating their families, and punishing the perpetrators.

Mubarak's educational programs include the Arab Reading for All project,[72] the Girls Education Initiative and the Susan Mubarak Science Exploration Centre in Cairo.[73]

In line with her vision of teaching principles of peace to future generations, the forum titled "The Power of Youth for Peace (Youth Speak—We Listen!)," brought together eight hundred young people from over a hundred countries and was later reinforced with the Cyber Peace Initiative information technology program.[74] The WOMATHON for Peace Event in Cairo, 2007, was a tribute to sport as an effective tool to promote women's health and the development of tolerant attitudes. The participants, who ran a four-kilometer race, included eight thousand women and girls of all ages from the twenty-six governorates of Egypt.[75] Cultural diversity was the theme for the "One World" Peace Festival, Cairo, May 8, 2008. The one-day festival, organized and run by a team of youngsters, attracted thirty thousand people to the acts and exhibitions presented.[76]

Suzanne Mubarak's many international awards include the Maurice Pate Award, 1989, in recognition of her efforts to ensure child survival, protection, and development; an honorary Fulbright award for her work in child development and education; a Paul Harris Fellowship from Rotary International; the WHO Health for All Gold Medal; the International Book Award, 1995, from the International Book Committee for promoting reading in Egypt; the Avicenne Medal from UNESCO; the Prize of Tolerance from the European Academy of Sciences and Arts, Salzburg, 1998; honorary doctorates from

Westminster College, New Wilmington, Pennsylvania; Iwa University, Seoul, Korea; and the American University in Spain; and the Culture Ministry's Prize, Athens, 2007, for the regeneration of the library in Alexandria and Mubarak's local and international work with children and women for peace.

> Women are the peace activists representing the source of power and hope for their children and societies. . . . They are the unknown soldiers . . . with many achievements.[77]

DALIA ZIADA

> *Amer's incarceration—for writing on a Web site . . . comes as the future of the Middle East hangs in the balance. While recent years have witnessed a surge in young voices challenging the status quo, powerful forces are trying to close down that window of greater liberty.*
>
> *The technology that has empowered unknown students in closed societies to speak to the world also gives readers everywhere the ability to rally together to protect free expression.*[78]

Civil rights activist Ziada and her colleague, Esraa Al-Shafei, have campaigned in support of twenty-two-year-old blogger Abdul Kareem Nabeel Suleiman Amer, the first Egyptian jailed for articles published on his own blog.[79] Amer, who had been a student at Al-Azhar, the leading Islamic university, became disillusioned about the discrimination against women and bigotry toward non-Muslims. After criticizing Al-Azhar and calling Egyptian president Hosni Mubarak a dictator, Amer was arrested and sentenced to three years in prison for "contempt of religion" and one year for "defaming the President of Egypt."[80] He also enraged political Islamists when he discredited the earliest Muslims as inappropriate examples for the contemporary world and provoked local authorities by exposing the damage and looting in the name of Islam during riots in 2005.[81]

Although a faithful Muslim, Ziada firmly believes in the individual's right to choose his or her faith:

Above all, it is Kareem's absolute choice to be a Muslim, a Christian, . . . Jewish or even an atheist. Freedom of belief is one of the basic rights given to all humans.[82]

A poem titled "Prisoner," which Ziada wrote in support of Amer, was what initially caught the attention of Egypt's State Security Service. Ziada has been accused of spying for the CIA,[83] and her blog was added to a list of fifty Web sites that Amer's appeals judge, Abdul Fattah Murad, wanted banned.[84] In response to the judge, she wrote: "I am a Muslim and I am proud of this. However, I will never agree with your shameful practices against my friend Kareem Amer. Clear?"[85]

Dalia Ziada was born in 1982 and raised in Egypt. Her father was an engineer lieutenant colonel in the Egyptian army and her mother is an Arabic language teacher and headmistress of an Egyptian government school. Her career in activism began in high school, when she felt compelled to protest against female circumcision, having been a victim of it herself.[86]

After graduating from the faculty of English and American Language and Literature at Ain Shams University in 2002, she joined women's groups and started volunteer work. Her work with the Arab Network for Human Rights Information (ANHRI) prompted her to become a human rights activist, political and social blogger,[87] writer, and translator. She is the regional coordinator of the Tharwa Foundation in Egypt and director of the American Islamic Congress Office in Cairo. She is also the founder and executive director of the Softcopy Translation Center for Non-Government Organizations (STC), a Web-based Arabic/English translation company that provides a free service for NGOs across the globe in the belief that human rights reform can be stimulated by the removal of language barriers. In 2006, Ziada translated "Implacable Adversaries: Arab Governments and the Internet," an ANHRI report covering eighteen Arab countries and their governments' treatment of the Internet.[88] (Judge Abdul Fattah Murad, Kareem Amer's appeals judge and chief judge of the appeals court in Alexandria, was accused of plagiarizing many pages of the 2006 report in his book *The Scientific and Legal Fundamentals of Internet Blogs*.)[89]

Ziada's essay on women's rights in Egypt earned her an honorable mention from the Hands across the Mideast Support Alliance (HAMSA). "In my world women are as many as raindrops. Yet they have no noteworthy impact on their societies. . . . The day will come for us to be noted in the books of history as 'the oppressed majority' of the millennium, or probably of all ages."[90]

According to Ziada, the major goals for Egypt and the wider Arab world are freedom of expression and women's rights. "Validate women and you validate the whole society."[91] Achieving reform, however, will require changing the mentality of Arab women.[92] Western activists, Ziada says, could help raise the morale of their Egyptian counterparts by putting international pressure on the Egyptian regime.[93]

The woman says to her daughter: "You will marry him and that's that. Your father gave him his word!"
Source: Ahmed Toughan, *Al-Gumhouriyya* (Egypt), September 19, 2007.

FRANCE

FADELA AMARA AND NI PUTES NI SOUMISES (ALGERIA/FRANCE)

The burka is a prison; it's a straitjacket.

It is not a religious insignia but the insignia of a totalitarian political project that advocates inequality between the sexes and which is totally devoid of democracy.

The veil and the burka are the same thing. . . . We have to fight against this obscurantist practice which endangers equality between men and women.[1]

Fadela Amara was born near Clermont-Ferrand, France, to Muslim parents who came to France from Kabylie, Algeria, in 1955. She was brought up with four sisters, six brothers, and other relatives in a small apartment in a temporary housing project.[2] Most of the residents of the project were Muslim immigrants from the Maghreb.[3] Amara's father was an illiterate construction worker with a job in the markets, and her mother was a housewife.[4]

In 1978, when Amara was fourteen, her youngest brother, five-year-old Malik, was run down by a drunk driver. Amara was shocked to witness the police siding with the driver, intimidating her father, and physically shaking her distraught mother. When she remonstrated with the officer, he just said, "These *bougnoules* [Arabs] piss me off." The boy died from his injuries later that night.[5]

> I saw how the cops were able to mistreat people just because they were Arabs. . . . It was like an electroshock.[6]

The circumstances of her brother's death ignited a passion in Amara that has fueled her battle against injustice, discrimination, and racism ever since. She did not complete high school and has never had a career beyond office work, but Amara's determined campaigning for various allied causes has led her to positions of influence in successive French governments.[7]

In 1980, at the age of sixteen, Amara successfully campaigned against and defeated the Clermont-Ferrand council's plan to tear down the estate where her family lived.[8] At seventeen, she organized a march of 400 young people to register to vote.[9] In 1983, she took part in a march by second-generation North African immigrants against discrimination and for equality in French society.[10] In 1986, she joined SOS Racisme, a French antiracism organization, and in 1988, she helped to create the National Federation of Solidarity Houses to campaign for equality for women in housing projects. In 2000, she became president of the National Federation,[11] which today encompasses nearly 300 neighborhood associations.

In January 2002, Amara organized an Assembly of Young Women from the Ghettos at the Sorbonne. About 300 young women from all over France met to compare experiences and debate issues of violence against women and the deployment of cultural traditions to subjugate them. The assembly started a petition that was eventually sent, with 20,000 signatures, to presidential candidates in the 2002 election.[12]

On October 4, 2002, a twenty-three-year-old gang leader, Jamal Derrar, murdered a seventeen-year-old French Arab woman, Sohane Benziane, by pouring gasoline over her and setting her alight.[13] A memorial to Benziane was desecrated, and when police took the murderer back to the murder scene to reenact the crime, he was cheered by other young men.[14]

The incident shocked France, but it was just one more manifestation of the tragic cultural interface in the ghettos, where young Arab men live in poverty with low rates of employment, segregated from mainstream French culture. They mix urban gang culture and Islamic tradition and express their impotence and frustration through the complete domination of the lives of females in their society.

> Daughters, sisters, cousins, female neighbors must either act like submissive but virtuous vassals, or be treated like cheap whores. Any sign of independence or femininity is viewed as a challenge and provocation.[15]

In these communities, gang rape has become such a common punishment for women who transgress, by wearing skirts or makeup, for example, that it is simply referred to as *tournante*, or "take your turn." The number of incidents of *tournante* has dramatically increased in Europe in the last twenty years, and as well as debasing women within Muslim communities, it increasingly involves premeditated attacks on non-Arab women as well.[16]

In response to the death of Sohane Benziane, Amara joined a silent march with 2,000 others and subsequently organized a series of gatherings at which women could talk about the acts of violence in their districts. In February 2003, she organized a March of Women from the Suburbs, which visited twenty-three cities and drew the nation's attention to the predicament of young women in the ghettos. Throughout the march, at public meetings, marchers were heckled by Islamic extremists.

A slogan from the march for Sohane Benziane, "Neither Whores nor Doormats," became the name for a new movement, Ni Putes Ni Soumises (Neither Whores Nor Doormats; NPNS), with Amara as its founder and president.[17] The NPNS produced a free *How to Respect* guide, which was later sold for one euro and featured on France's best seller list for months. NPNS has set up a national network of shelters for victims of sexual assault in the projects, and Amara has recruited psychologists and lawyers to work with victims of oppression and abuse.[18] The organization now has more than 6,000 members and sixty branches in Europe, Lebanon, and Saudi Arabia.[19] As president of NPNS, Amara has received numerous death threats.[20]

In August 2004, Amara was appointed a member of France's Consultative Committee for Human Rights by the then prime minister, Jean-Pierre Raffarin. In that year, the French government passed controversial legislation banning headscarves in schools in order to promote better integration into French society. Many French feminists regarded this prohibition of a particular ethnic practice as a form of cultural imperialism. Amara, however, saw the headscarf "as a visible symbol of the subjugation of women"[21] that is part of a "political use of Islam."[22] Amara spoke in support of the new legislation to the Stasi Commission in October 2003. She considered the refusal of feminists to condemn particular cultural practices as a failure to fight discrimination:

> They won't denounce forced marriages or female genital mutilation, because, they say, it's tradition. It's nothing more than neo-colonialism.[23]

> Immigrants must be given a strong message of respect for women and put an end to their subjugation and the fundamentalists' manipulation of the silent majority of immigrants.[24]

In 2005, as a consequence of what she perceived to be the failure of French feminists to extend the advances they had won to the women of the ghettos, and also their valuation of cultural relativity over women's rights, she took the NPNS out of the collective Comité National des Femmes, the coalition of women's rights organizations in France.[25]

In the same year, Amara was made a member of the High Authority for the Fight against Discrimination by President Jacques Chirac.[26] In June 2007, President Sarkozy appointed her secretary of state for urban policy.[27]

Although an avowed secularist, Amara is proud to be a Muslim and she cautions against conflating the Islamic religion with the political and sociological goals of Islamic activists:

> Islam, as a religion and a faith, should not be confused with the Islamic activists who make use of it to promote their political program. I'm a Muslim who is fighting the Islamists, but not Islam. To me, it's not a problem that Islam—like most other religions—is trying to recruit more believers. The problem occurs when the religion becomes a political project with fascist tendencies. That's something I won't consent to—either on the European continent or in my home, in France.[28]

Fadela Amara and Sylvia Zappi's book, titled *Breaking the Silence: French Women's Voices from the Ghetto*, was released in 2006.[29]

SAMIRA BELLIL (ALGERIA/FRANCE)

I never considered being anonymous. I had to be credible. There are so many young women who have been suffering, who need to open their mouths. They are so isolated. I want to give them some hope. God, they need it.[30]

Samira Bellil was born in November 27, 1972, to Algerian parents in Algiers but grew up in the Parisian suburb of Seine-Saint-Denis. Soon after the family arrived in France, Bellil's father went to prison for what Samira later dismissed as "stupidities," and she was sent to a good foster family in Belgium. Five years later, she was brought back to France and to a father who was distant and violent.[31]

Seine-Saint-Denis is one of twenty housing estates situated around Paris. Known variously as *banlieues*, *cités*, or *quartiers*, these are high-density public housing areas and they exist outside most major cities in France. They were created by the French government in the postwar years to provide cheap housing for immigrants from the former French colonies in ethnic, largely Muslim, communities.[32]

Over the years, the *banlieues* have degenerated into lawless concrete wastelands, where police seldom venture. A combination of high unemployment, gang culture, and Islamism has created a culture that is repressive and hostile, particularly to females. Women are expected to be submissive to men, cover themselves, and stay at home. Any young woman who does not conform to strict standards of modesty becomes a target for abuse, assault, and rape. Gang rapes have been increasing by 15 to 20 percent each year in the *banlieues* and there has been a series of shocking murders of young women.[33]

According to Bellil, "It's about what happens when a Muslim culture rubs up against a western one, and the worst of both remain. . . . A gap between home where boys are treated like kings, as is commonplace in North African and African cultures, and outside where they are delinquents and scum. A gap between boys and girls at school, where girls do better and leave boys behind. . . . Girls who are known to them—sisters or cousins of friends—are off limits, because of the honour code."[34]

Dozens of cases of gang rape go before the courts at any one time, and the crime accounts for up to a fifth of all serious juvenile offences, which are often downgraded to "sexual assault," with perpetrators receiving only a suspended sentence.[35]

> People listen more to what the perpetrators say instead of demanding justice for the victim.[36]

As a young girl, Bellil defied the conventions of the *banlieues* by socializing, dressing like an ordinary French teenager, and having a boyfriend. In the late 1980s, when she was fourteen, her "boyfriend" handed her over to three of his friends who beat her and kept her overnight, raping her for hours:

> I was gang raped by three people I knew, and I couldn't say anything, because in my culture, your family is dishonored if you lose your virginity.

> So I kept quiet, and the rapes continued. The next time, I was pulled off a commuter train and no one lifted a finger to help me. . . . Everybody turned their head away. They were all looking out the window.[37]

K, the most violent of the rapists, had dragged her out of the train by her hair and she was gang raped again.[38]

As a rape victim, Bellil knew that her parents and her community would believe she had brought shame upon her family. Fearful that any member of the family might be attacked in revenge if she spoke out, she observed the law of silence that rules the ghettos. When two of her friends told her they had also been raped by K, however, Samira decided to talk to the police and to press charges against her attackers. As a result, K served two years in prison, but Samira was disowned by her family and rejected by her friends and neighbors.[39]

> The shame caused by any sexual assault can be crippling: both Islam and machismo prize girls' virginity. Reprisals are a real threat: apartments have been burned down; little sisters are threatened.[40]

Over the following years, Bellil lived in foster homes and then in squats or on the street in a miserable state of drug addiction and despair. In time, however, she started to see a psychotherapist and, after several years of counseling, began to write about her experiences as an inspiration to her "sisters in hell" in the *quartiers*.

In November 2002, Bellil's autobiography, *Dans l'enfer des tournantes* (In the Hell of the *tournantes*),[41] was published. She used her real name in the book, and at the suggestion of her editor, her picture appeared on the cover, even though she was living in the same housing estate as her attackers.[42] Her book is directed to the women of the *banlieues*:

> It's to tell girls that they can survive and see justice done. And also to urge mothers to break with this infernal vicious cycle of the all-powerful male. It drives me crazy to still hear women say, "Ah, that girl went looking for it. . . ." Your reputation is important in the projects. It follows you everywhere. A girl can be branded easy or a little slut even if she does nothing wrong.[43]

A month before the book was released, on October 4, 2002, Sohane Benziane was burned to death in the *banlieue* at Vitry-sur-Seine. Sohane's murder and

Bellil's book brought the reality of life for young women in the ghettos to the attention of the public and the government of France.[44]

> When the fact of the gang rapes came out, no one protested, because of fatalism, because . . . the racial component is too risky to touch.[45]

Bellil also helped initiate the women's rights reform movement, referred to above, Ni Putes Ni Soumises.

> Before, they would rape us. Now, they're burning us alive. Sohane [Benziane] can't speak anymore, so I'm gonna do the talking.[46]

Bellil led demonstrations and marches across France, speaking out about the culture of violence against women in the *banlieues*, and she also spoke about her experiences in an interview for CBS's *60 Minutes*.[47]

Bellil was eventually reconciled with her mother and became close to her two sisters. She gave up thoughts of revenge, saying, "I can't carry all that violence forever,"[48] and moved back to her original neighborhood, working with youth and also in drama, which was her passion. On September 4, 2004, however, she died of stomach cancer.[49]

Samira Bellil was chosen as one of thirteen "faces of France," known as the Mariannes. Her portrait was displayed outside the French National Assembly on Bastille Day, July 14, 2003, and two years later, a school in l'Île-Saint-Denis was named École Samira Bellil in her honor.[50]

> My life is not the same life today; before, it was terrible, it was terrible. But I fight very hard to be what I am now today. And I win, and for me, it's wonderful, and now I smile.[51]

On the woman's folder: "University Graduate." The sign on the right says "Job";
the sign on the left says "Further Studies." All the paths lead to the sign saying "Marriage."
Source: Sultan Alsubaie, *Al-Madina* (Saudi Arabia), May 27, 2007.

8

INDONESIA

BACKGROUND

Women have their rights, and Indonesia has recognized them. It's just that the country hasn't completely respected and fulfilled women's rights yet.[1]

Prior to 1945, the Dutch ruled in Indonesia. The colonial government was largely supportive of the Indonesian women's movement, which emerged early in the twentieth century. The movement was sparked by forces such as socioeconomic growth, urbanization, modern education, improved communications, and exposure to Western ideas. Women began to form organizations to pursue their own interests. The most notable exponent of this early feminism was Raden Ayu Kartini, who promoted the right of women to receive education and espoused gender equality.

The first Indonesian women's congress, Kowani, was held in 1928. Still in existence, Kowani is now a federation of seventy nationwide voluntary women's organizations, with a total of 25 million members.[2]

Islam was first adopted by Indonesians through the influence of traders and became the country's dominant religion by the sixteenth century. Indonesia is currently the most populous Muslim country in the world, with approximately 240 million people, of whom 86 percent identify as Muslim.[3]

Women are unequal to men in terms of rights and opportunities. In this subordinate role, the woman is often a victim of domestic violence and political, sexual, and economic discrimination.

In the 1930s, the most radical women's organization of the day, Isteri Sedar,[4] advocated greater equality in marriage for Islamic women, in particular, opposing practices approved by the Islamic courts such as child marriage, arbitrary divorce of wives, and polygamy. Kartini questioned why memorizing and reciting the Koran in Arabic was required, without any obligation to understand the words. However, the women's congress chose to downplay such issues in order to pacify religious groups that opposed any changes they regarded as undermining Islamic family law.

In 1949, following independence from Dutch rule and Japanese wartime occupation, the democratic government of the new Republic of Indonesia granted women the right to vote and equal pay in the civil service. From the start, the constitution and national guidelines on state policy that were issued from time to time explicitly guaranteed women's rights to equality. Yet, the reality was very different. Further, the main objective of the women's movement, a marriage act that overrode the Islamic marriage laws, was ignored by the government, which feared arousing the wrath of Islamic parties.

Gerwani was one of the largest women's organizations operating in the newly independent Indonesian state. Closely aligned with the Communist Party of Indonesia (PKI), Gerwani was formed in 1950 as a mouthpiece for women's and children's rights and democracy. The organization had a peak of about 1.5 million members in 1965, but in the same year, following an aborted military coup during which it was estimated that a million people were killed, Gerwani was banned along with most other left-leaning groups when Suharto seized power from Sukarno. The army alleged that Gerwani members had helped to kill the generals. Thousands of Gerwani members were raped or killed as part of an anti-Communist purge by Suharto.[5]

Feminism was stifled under the oppressive "New Order" administration of Suharto, who embarked upon an ambitious program of socioeconomic development and opened Indonesia up to foreign investment. Women became the prime workforce for factories set up by multinationals, working for relatively low wages.

However, in this period and under the successive governments of B. J. Habibie and Wahid, international human rights treaties were ratified and legislation was enacted to protect the rights of women. In 1974, the Marriage Act offered women more legal protection and certainty in marriage than previously afforded under the male-run Islamic system. The act, which is still seen by many as an unsatisfactory solution, states that a husband can marry another woman if the wife agrees and if she cannot have children or fulfill her obligations. Indonesia ratified the Convention on the Elimination of All Forms of Discrimination against Women (CEDAW)[6] in 1974. The Indonesian Five Year Plan (1996–2000) also sought to improve women's status in society and enhance their role in development.

The National Plan of Action for Women (2000–2004) identified the need to improve and raise awareness of gender equality in everyday life and politics and abolish domestic violence.[7]

Despite these affirmative acts, Indonesian women, particularly at the lower end of the socioeconomic and political scale, are still subject to violence and sexual discrimination.

Approximately 2.6 million females are domestic workers, some as young as twelve or thirteen years old.[8] They are susceptible to economic exploitation and physical, psychological, and sexual violence. Protection is almost nonexistent, as they are excluded from the 2003 Manpower Act, which enforced legal rights pertaining to maximum hours of work and a minimum wage. Poorly trained domestic workers often have little understanding of the terms of their employment, leaving them open to forced labor, debt bondage, and human trafficking. In 2008, the Human Trafficking Criminal Actions Eradication Draft Bill became law, providing a definition of sexual exploitation and legal provisions regarding trafficking for the purposes of labor and prostitution.

Indonesia has one of the highest rates of maternal mortality in Southeast Asia. An estimated 230–310 women die each year for every 100,000 births.[9] The main causes identified by the World Health Organization are female genital mutilation, early marriages, lack of access to information regarding services for sexual and reproductive health, pregnancy and childbirth, sexually transmitted disease, and the high incidence of unsafe abortions.[10] In 2006, the number of female genital mutilation cases increased,[11] and the government has now forbidden health workers from carrying out the procedure. One in three women has experienced domestic violence,[12] which is widely perceived to be a private matter and not the government's concern. In 2006, the National Commission on Violence against Women sought to amend the Criminal Code procedures that required female rape victims to prove penetration.

In 1994, the government also established a nine-year compulsory education program to fight illiteracy, which is higher among women than men.

Despite the enactment of the Marriage Act of 1974, polygamy is widely prevalent, particularly in rural areas. In 1983, when the government banned civil servants from taking a second wife, it came under considerable attack, but women's groups continue to lobby for the banning of polygamy.

According to the Legal Aid Foundation of the Indonesian Women's Association for Justice, the incidence of polygamy has been rising. However, the number of divorces has also grown, many due to polygamy and an increasing number ascribed to "conflict over political issues." Nasaruddin Umar, director general for Islamic guidance at the Religious Affairs Ministry, believes "women [are] becoming increasingly aware of their rights thanks to the efforts of NGOs and women activists."[13]

Indonesian women are generally excluded from the political decision-making process and occupy only 9 percent of the seats in the Legislative Assembly,[14] hampering efforts to change discriminatory laws. However, in 2001, Indonesia voted into office its first female president, Megawati Sukarnoputri.

A former general, Susilo Bambang Yudhoyono, assumed office in 2004 with a pledge to undertake reforms. In 2006, Indonesia acceded to the International Covenant on Civil and Political Rights and the International Covenant on Economic, Social, and Cultural Rights.

In general, however, the political transition has not resulted in significant improvement in female political participation.[15] Women are facing new threats to their personal freedoms and dignity. An upsurge of "politicized Islam" in some parts of Indonesia has been prompting the adoption of shari'ah law in violation of Indonesia's secular constitution.[16] Women have been arrested or caned and paraded by Islamic paramilitary groups for failing to wear the headscarf. Islamist members of the paramilitaries increasingly "hijack" the traditionally "peaceful" Islam of Indonesia, claiming they are the true defenders of the faith.[17]

Following decades of uprisings by rebels in the province of Aceh, partial shari'ah law, sanctioned by the Indonesian government, has been rigorously enforced since the tsunami in 2004. Although it was initially popular due to promises to reduce violence and lawlessness, locals have turned against the public whippings and enforced Islamic dress.[18] The pressure on religious minorities in Padang, capital of the province of West Sumatra, has increased since the expansion of shari'ah laws in more than nineteen districts. Female students, who are harassed by Islamists for not wearing the mandatory headscarf and often suspended from school, keep silent due to fear of reprisals.[19] Human rights groups have lobbied the government to revoke these unconstitutional laws but the government, while promising action, has shown reluctance to act against Muslim extremists.

RAHIMA

> *As a result of growing pressure from ultraconservative Islamists, parts of Sharia have already been implemented in 16 of the 32 provinces of Indonesia. In Aceh or in the city of Tangerang, west of Jakarta, Islamicization is on the advance.*
>
> *The fundamentalists are meeting with such resonance not only because of their ideas and practices, but because they have undertaken much that the communities were sorely lacking. They offered economic assistance and medical care for free.*[20]

Rahima is an Islamic nongovernmental organization based in Jakarta that promotes the equality of women in Indonesian society. Founded in 2000 by young Islamic scholars closely associated with Indonesia's largest Muslim organization, Nahdlatul Ulama (NU), Rahima is attempting to change the way women are treated within the Islamic framework. The organization rejects the authoritarian, patriarchal interpretation of shari'ah or Islamic law, in the belief that inequality is a result of the misinterpretation of religious teachings. Instead, they advocate a moderate, democratic, and progressive interpretation of shari'ah and the Koran. Activists often rely on quotations from the Koran to refute the hard-line ideology of conservative Muslims.

The Indonesian situation has been unique among Muslim countries. Although the development of the women's movement is still very much in a transitional stage, Indonesia has thousands of institutions where women can study to become specialists in Islamic studies and exercise powerful religious influence.

One such influential woman is Rahima's director, Aditiana Dewi Erdani. She believes that the current economic and political upheavals in Indonesia have stimulated a pious religious fervor, making hard-line Islamist ideologies like Saudi Arabia's Wahhabi Islam more attractive. Erdani rejects the patriarchal nature of Islamic law:

> Of course, Sharia is part of the Islamic self-image, but . . . Rahima is . . . opposed to patriarchal discourse, and this is the reason why we reject Sharia laws in Indonesia—because they do not represent the real Islamic Sharia, but only a politically instrumentalized Sharia.[21]

Erdani took over as director of Rahima from Farha Ciciek in 2007. Born in 1967 in Jakarta, she studied law at Diponegoro University in Semarang and graduated in 1991. Until 2001, she worked for the Indonesian Society for Pesantren and Community Development before moving to Rahima in 2007.

Rahima seeks to implement its ideas of democracy and equality at a grassroots level by traveling to remote villages, particularly in the rural districts of central Java, to advocate a change in attitudes to domestic violence and gender equality in education and community decision making. Rahima activists conduct training sessions for teachers and students at Islamic boarding schools (pesantrens) with the aim of integrating gender equality into education and developing a core of teachers who advocate women's rights. Despite initial resistance, Rahima has succeeded in building up a network of progressive pesantrens that endorse a moderate message. In its magazine, Rahima promotes articles that condemn domestic violence, denounce polygamy, and campaign for better representation of women in politics.[22]

The organization works with other NGOs, both Muslim and non-Muslim, such as the National Commission for Women, the Voluntary Team for Humanity, and the Wahid Institute, named after the country's former president and probably best-known Islamic scholar.

9
IRAN

BACKGROUND

Iran is a country in which women have had a long and rich history of influence that can be traced back thousands of years,[1] but Iran's current policies toward women seem incompatible with that history. Ever since 1984, there have been patrols on the streets of Iran entirely dedicated to policing women's dress.[2] In court, a woman's testimony is equivalent to half that of a man's,[3] and progressive activists are routinely harassed and imprisoned by the state.[4] Among all this discrimination, a thriving women's movement has flourished, carrying on the legacy of Iranian women organizing to fight for their rights.[5]

Prerevolution Iran was dominated by pro-Western, secular elites. In the 1940s and 1950s, women's groups formulated criticism of practices such as polygamy, agitated for democratic reform and electoral rights, and campaigned for the implementation of health, education, and social strategies.[6] By 1978, the Organization of Iranian Women addressed women's welfare in 349 branches, 113 centers, and 55 other organizations, which were used by over a million women.[7] The revolution in the following year spelled destruction for these centers.[8] Under US-supported Reza Shah, European clothes and unveiling were made compulsory for all citizens.[9] A huge number of women and men fought together against this creeping Westernization and erasure of their own culture and supported the Islamic Revolution in 1979.[10] However, many women later felt betrayed by the ideals of the revolution, which left them behind. One of Ayatollah Khomeini's first acts was to dismiss women judges like Shirin Ebadi,[11] later a recipient of the Nobel Peace Prize. The wearing of the *hijab* for women was enforced, and demonstrators protesting against this and other activities were attacked in the streets.[12]

Other gains that women had achieved were reversed, and they found themselves far worse off than before. The legal rights of Iranian women were rewritten, and under these laws, women were relegated to a low position in society and the rights afforded to them corresponded to this downgrade. The historic Iranian movement for women's rights and all its victories were lost, aside from the right to vote. Iranian women were denied access to the university faculties of law, and all female judges were removed from their positions after Article 163 of the Islamic constitution prohibited their employment in such a significant role. In the courtroom, the testimony of a woman was deemed to be untrue, and a punishable offense unless it could be upheld by a man.[13] In this event, the woman's evidence was no longer recognized.

Patriarchal norms were fortified and legalized. Article 115 of the Islamic constitution specified that the president and leader of the Iranian nation was required to be male. A wife could not be given employment without the formal consent of her husband, who was guaranteed child custody in the event of divorce. Children were deemed to be the property of their father, to the extent that he was entitled to decide whether they could live or die. If a father murdered his child, the only penalty was to pay blood money to the inheritors.[14] Because there is no fixed blood money for children, fathers who murder their children have only to pay themselves the blood money.[15]

The murder of a man was regarded as a capital offense, whereas the killing of a woman was not afforded the same serious status.[16] The punishments for murderers were divided according to the sex of the perpetrator. Execution was the inevitable end for a female killer, whereas a male murderer was given the alternative of paying *diyya* (blood money) to the next of kin of his victim.[17] If the victim of a male murderer is a female relative killed on the pretext of adultery/fornication, there is no stipulated punishment. The maiming or injury of a woman, or the violent attack on her is punishable only if and when the male perpetrator is paid mutilation money.[18] Female assailants were not granted this luxury.[19]

The education of women was not valued by the Islamic Republic, which barred women from studying 54 percent of subjects in higher education, reducing female students to only 10 percent of the student population in 1983.[20] Iranian women, however, were not universally passive in their acceptance of these sanctions, and by 1991, women had won the right to specific quotas within certain subjects (although they were still barred from ninety-seven academic areas). Most notably, women were granted access to study medicine, and in Qum, they could study at a purpose-built, all-female medical faculty. In 1994, a nationwide quota was introduced by the government, which aimed to fill 25 percent of places in certain medical fields with female students.[21]

The judicial process does not protect women and sentences them more harshly, as in the case where a sixteen-year-old girl, Atefah Rahjabi, thought to be mentally incompetent, was publicly hanged for comitting adultery while her alleged male partner received only a hundred lashes.[22] Unveiled women have been blamed by a top Shia cleric for being "sources of all that is bad in society"[23] and accused of inviting men to rape them.[24] Iranian law does not recognize marital rape or "emotional violence" as criminal; nor does it provide any shelter for victims of domestic violence, the leading cause of female suicide in Iran.[25] The only recourse for such women is to enter brothels or to return home to their abusers.[26]

Many political dissidents have turned to the virtual world of the Internet as an important outlet for expression and to connect with each other. Farsi has become the fourth most popular language on the Internet, in a community known as "Weblogestan."[27] The government has cracked down on Internet usage in Iran, inexplicably arresting certain bloggers for "undermining National Security through cultural activity"[28] and blocking women's rights Web sites.[29] In July 2008, a new law was passed allowing the death penalty for "online crimes," effectively making it even harder for dissidents to mobilize.[30] The leading reformist women's magazine, *Zanan*, which had covered women's issues for sixteen years, was shut down in January 2008, for "portraying a negative image of women in Iran."[31]

Although there are women who have been appointed into positions of political power, they tend to hold the same views as the ruling majority.[32] In May 2006, Zohreh Tabibzadeh Nouri, who was appointed the head of the Iranian Center for Women and Family Affairs, spoke of the Iranian refusal to sign human rights charters: "As long as I live and remain in charge of this center, I will not let anyone sign international charters [or] declarations of international conferences on women's rights, since we can [fix] the gaps and existing problems through the Islamic faith. I see no reason to follow the unsuccessful Western model."[33]

The sixth Majlis (Islamic Consultative Assembly) of Iran currently has 12 female deputies out of 290 and has rejected calls to promote gender equality.[34] The government's employment of women in certain spheres has been criticized by feminists for being a cynical ploy designed to make it appear as if women are fully involved in society. For example, the inclusion of women in the police force has been touted by the government as evidence of its progressive policies; however, these policewomen are used against the female civilian population. They violently break up women's rights demonstrations, beating the protestors with clubs and sticks.[35] The use of women by the government to oppress other women removes men—those with the real power and responsibility—from the equation and also serves to undermine the protests by apparently showing that not all women are unhappy with the discrimination against them.

The female population of Iran has not easily submitted to these intimidations. Iranian feminism is a diverse movement encompassing ideology derived from both secular and Islamic models. Though these elements have sometimes clashed, they have worked together and supported each other several times. In June 2006, a demonstration calling for equality under the law was attended by thousands of women, who were violently dispersed by the police.[36] Women demonstrators at other rallies have been arrested and sentenced to lashings, a punishment that has always been a target of their criticisms.[37] Routinely, women's rights activists are arrested in their homes and imprisoned.[38] An important collaborative initiative is the One Million Signatures Demanding Change to Discriminatory Laws Campaign. This grassroots drive often sees women going door to door to collect signatures. It aims to raise awareness, promote education about the injustices perpetrated against Iranian women, and demand changes to the law[39] that can "give hope to women that together they can accomplish anything."[40] Many of the signatories and authors of this campaign have been arrested.[41] Similar campaigns exist in Iran against "honor killings" and stoning to death, which still occur.[42] Kobra Najjar was a victim of domestic violence at the hands of her heroin-addicted husband, who forced her into prostitution to pay for his drug habit. In July 2008, she was sentenced to death by stoning for adultery (via her prostitution).[43] As of July 2008, seven women and one man were awaiting death by stoning for the crime of adultery.[44]

When Mohammad Khatami served as fifth president of Iran from August 2, 1997, to August 2, 2005, the women who voted for him and helped bring him to power were hopeful he would institute reforms to improve their status and change laws that discriminated against women, for example, those involving marriage and divorce. However, Khatami did not introduce any bills making a significant difference to women or indeed to democratization. Instead, he was occupied with local political crises, and women's issues, ranking lowest in the patriarchal Iranian culture, were forgotten.[45]

President Ahmadinejad has introduced three policies that limit women's participation outside the home. The Program for Social Safety gives the special Guidance Police the authority to apprehend and detain any woman not wearing appropriate Islamic clothing, and repeat offenders may be fined and sentenced to flogging. The Family Protection Act legitimizes polygamy, marriage at the age of thirteen, temporary marriages, and a tax on bride price. In another intervention to limit women's participation in public life, the organization dealing with admissions to university has introduced a gender-based policy to decrease the female quota and increase the male quota in some fields of study. In the past, the female acceptance rate at university was about 65 percent.[46]

REVIEW OF REFORMS

The women's movement in Iran, depicted in the following profiles of activists, developed during the reform period of President Khatami and resulted in the strengthening of collaborative projects and the formation of over six hundred registered NGOs. Following a year of discussion and planning, the first protest took place in front of Tehran University in June 2005, carried out by women demanding changes to discriminatory laws. During a similar protest on March 8, 2006, to coincide with International Women's Day, police attacked the protesters and beat them with batons. In June of that year, another peaceful protest was violently broken up by the police and seventy protesters were arrested; this time, an additional contingent of female police officers was used in the attack. Although most protesters were released within a week, it was clear that a major crackdown had been launched.

In the next phase, the women's movement, in the greatest unified bloc since the revolution, formulated the One Million Signatures Campaign. Initiated in August 2006, it aimed to raise awareness of gender discrimination and prepare a petition to parliament for the reform of gender-biased laws including polygamy, custody of children given to men in cases of divorce, a woman's entitlement to only half the inheritance of a man, and a woman's testimony in court carrying only half the weight of a man's. Other legislative demands included changes in favor of freedom of dress, equal marriage rights, the abolition of quotas for females at universities, and equal compensation in the event of injury.

A selection of fifty-six reformers are mentioned here or profiled in the following section. About half are writers and journalists. The rest include lawyers, students, academics, and filmmakers, with ages ranging from twenty-one to sixty-eight. Many women and a few men associated with the protests were arrested on a variety of charges. "Acting against national security" was the most common, followed by "participating in an illegal gathering" and "propaganda against the state." Other charges included "insulting Islam," "disturbing public order," "violating the observance of the *hijab*," "immoral behavior," and "abnormal movements" (that resemble dancing).[47]

The dissenters represent a much larger number of women activists (and a few men) who have participated in this campaign and the women's rights movement over many years, for example, the Iranian writer and publisher Shahla Lahiji, who was arrested, along with eighteen other reformers, for participating in an academic and cultural conference in Berlin on April 7–9, 2000, at which political and social reform in Iran were debated in public.

During the demonstration against discriminatory Islamic law in Hafte Tir Square, Tehran, on June 12, 2006, more than seventy protesters were arrested and beaten, often by female police officers, in spite of the protesters' insistence that their protest was not in opposition to religion or the Iranian political system. Delaram Ali, a sociology student who was severely beaten during the protest and had her arm broken, was detained on security charges and sentenced to a prison term of two years and ten months, with ten lashes, later revoked. According to eyewitness accounts, police officers attacked the women, broke their placards, and threatened they would be "hanged from trees" if the demonstration was not halted.[48] Another student protester, Azadeh Forghani, was arrested, charged with "acting against national security," and given a two-year suspended sentence. Women's rights activist Fariba Mohajer was sentenced to four years in prison, suspended for three years.[49]

Noushin Khorasani, an Iranian scholar and journalist charged with "conspiracy and disrupting national security,"[50] was sentenced to a three-year prison term, including six months of mandatory imprisonment, under article 610 of the Islamic penal code. Women's rights defender Alieh Aghdam-Doust was detained and sentenced to three years in prison.[51]

Broadcast journalist Parvin Ardalan, journalist Noushin Khorasani, activists Sussan Tahmasebi and Fariba Mohajer, and social worker Shahla Entesari were summoned to court for organizing the demonstration on June 12, 2006. Mohajer, who was abroad, was represented by her lawyer. On

March 4, 2007, the day of their trial, many of their colleagues came to protest outside the courthouse and over thirty people were detained and charged with illegal assembly and intention to disrupt national security and public order. When police started arresting the protesters, the women who had been summoned and Entesari's lawyer, Shadi Sadr, left the courtroom and were then arrested.

Nahid Jafari, a member of the One Million Signatures Campaign, was arrested during this protest and charged with illegal gathering and collusion intended to disrupt national security, disruption of public order, and refusal to adhere to the orders of the police. Others arrested at the same protest included women's rights activists Nasrin Afzali, Marzieh Mortazi, Elnaz Ansari, Parastoo Dokoohaki, Niloofar Golkar, and Sussan Tahmasebi, journalists Mahboubeh Abbasgholizadeh, Jila Baniyaghoub, Maryam Hosseinkhah, and Mahboubeh Hosseinzadeh, students Azadeh Forghani and Zeinab Peyghambarzadeh, and sociologists Jelveh Javaheri and Nahid Keshavarz.[52]

For convening activist meetings in her home, the Revolutionary Court charged Khadijeh Moghaddam with acting against national security, disrupting public opinion, and spreading propaganda against the state, and she was detained for seven days in solitary confinement.

Many were arrested while collecting signatures as part of the nationwide One Million Signatures Campaign. Zeinab Peyghambarzadeh, a student activist, was the first to be arrested, on December 15, 2006, for collecting signatures on the Tehran Metro underground railway, and was charged with "acting against national security."[53] Mahboubeh Hosseinzadeh and Nahid Keshavarz were arrested while collecting signatures in Laleh Park, charged with "acting against national security," and detained in Evin prison.[54] Activists Nasim Sarabandi and Fatemeh Dehdashti were charged with "acting against national security" and sentenced to a six-month term in prison, suspended for two years. Ehteram Shadfar, aged sixty-two, was arrested on June 10, 2007, while collecting signatures and received a similar sentence.

Journalist Mahboubeh Karami, a member of the One Million Signatures Campaign and Campaign for Equality, was one of about eighty women arrested and detained on June 13, 2008, and charged with actions against national security in connection with a protest on behalf of Abbas Palizdar in Mellat Square, Tehran. Palizdar had been arrested after he accused several senior Iranian officials of financial corruption. Karami, however, denied any association with the demonstration.[55] After almost seventy days in Evin prison, which included rough interrogation, she was released on bail of 100 million tomans, approximately $100,000.[56]

On January 30, 2009, women's rights activist Nafiseh Azad was arrested whilst trying to convince police not to arrest two other members of the One Million Signatures Campaign who were collecting signatures in the Tochal Mountains north of Tehran. She was detained for six days and charged with "actions against national security, through the spreading of propaganda against the state."[57]

Women's movement lawyer Nasrin Sotudeh, who has also campaigned against the execution of child offenders, represented many members of the One Million Signatures Campaign. In July 2008, she appeared before the Revolutionary Court, charged with acting against Iran's "national security" by having unauthorized dealings with "Iranians outside the country."[58]

A number of activist writers and cyber journalists were rounded up by government officials. Mahboubeh Abbasgholizadeh and Fereshteh Ghazi were arrested and Ghazi was beaten and kept in solitary confinement. Jelveh Javaheri and Maryam Hosseinkhah were arrested and charged with acting against national security and publication of lies. They were also accused of disturbing public opinion and of publishing articles on the Web sites of the One Million Signatures Campaign, Change for Equality, and the Women's Cultural Center, Zanestan. Their bail was set at 50 million tomans and 100 million tomans, respectively, sums that neither of their families could afford. Javaheri and Hosseinkhah were released after some weeks when the bail amount was reduced.

Parvin Ardalan was summoned to court on April 5, 2008, and charged with acting against national security in relation to her work for the Change for Equality and Zanestan Web sites.[59] The Change for Equality Web site was blocked for the eighteenth time on December 7, 2008, together with the Feminist School Web site and the personal blog of Jila Baniyaghoub.[60] Baniyaghoub was arrested by Iran's security forces on June 12, 2006, while reporting on the women's demonstration at Hafte Tir Square, and several times after 2006 for covering demonstrations that called for the end of the "sexual apartheid" laws affecting women. Badrossadat Mofidi, secretary of the Association of Iranian Journalists, believes the pressures are becoming intolerable. Journalists have been detained and in some cases, efforts to trace their whereabouts have proved futile.[61]

Mehrnoush Najafi, a reformer with political aspirations, was one of forty-six women who won seats in the city council elections held throughout Iran in January 2007. A human rights lawyer, blogger,[62] and women's rights activist, she contested and won a seat in Hamedan province.

Of a group of six women who demanded additional reforms in government, four were in favor of secular government and the separation of religion and state; all these women live outside Iran. The fifth in this group, award-winning film producer and director Manijeh Hekmat,[63] resident in Iran, organized a petition signed by 170 leaders of the Iranian film industry. The wording spoke of transformation by peaceful, democratic means and avoided any radical demands. Even so, some of the signatories were threatened with dismissal by Iranian TV networks if they refused to recant. Another distinguished female film director and screenwriter, Tamineh Milani,[64] who consistently tackled controversial issues, from women's struggles in a male-dominated society to misconceptions about the 1979 Islamic Revolution, was charged with "supporting factions waging war against God, and misusing the arts in support of counter-revolutionary and opposition groups."[65]

In contrast to most women activists in Afghanistan, those in Iran have not focused on reforms in education, health services, or cultural matters. Although improvements in these areas could be beneficial, the vast majority of women in Iran are literate and the dire state of women's education and health in Afghanistan is not comparable to that in Iran. In contrast to Afghanistan, Iranian women have challenged their second-class status by demanding reform of discriminatory legislation and by taking to the streets in peaceful demonstrations.

Saudi Arabia's closed society does not have the rich history of Iranian women's organizations or the open trading, educational, and cultural exchanges that characterized Iran prior to the revolution. Nor was there a period of relative freedom in Saudi Arabia, as there was in Iran during the presidency of Khatami, which gave activists time and opportunity to devise their most advantageous strategies.

Like Muslim women dissidents elsewhere, women reformers living in Iran, including those with secular views, conform to the legislated Islamic dress and behavior in order to establish their religious credentials and avoid exclusion. It is very unlikely that any reformer who adopted a secular position would be included in the debate.

As emphasized by activist journalist Nahid Tavasoli, the aim of the women's movement is not to remove the Islamic regime but to work from within to change discriminatory legislation.[66] Confining debate to the Islamic context prevents the government from accusations that the members of the movement are acting on behalf of Western interests. Issues of gender equality are therefore best demonstrated by reference to the Koran and the edicts of Islam. To this end, reformers have reiterated that they have no wish to impose secular rule and have affirmed that the reforms they advocate are consistent with Islamic principles.

Unlike a similar enterprise in Morocco, which received government support, the drive for women's rights reform in Iran has been severely hampered by the regime's response. The threat perceived by the government has caused the authorities to adopt a position of suspicion and defensive hostility, for despite protestations to the contrary, the demands by women reformers shake the patriarchal if not the theological foundations of the Islamic Republic.

The betrayal by reformist President Khatami was bitter, even though Shirin Ebadi attempted to sweeten the blow by granting him the excuse of preoccupation with internal divisions. In any case, women activists cannot rely on support from men in power, even if they are ideological allies, as their priority is usually democracy first and women's rights second. The UN, too, is no reliable ally, struggling to reach consensus on sanctions against Iran for refusing to suspend uranium enrichment, rather than agreement on motions to penalize the regime for human rights violations against women dissidents.

Overall, the agitation and sacrifices of the activists have not produced major legislative changes. On the contrary, President Ahmadinejad has enforced a crackdown since succeeding to the presidency in 2005, bringing state power to bear in the form of police violence, arbitrary arrests, and increased censorship.

Censorship extends to the print media: on January 28, 2008, the feminist monthly *Zanan* (Women), a long-time supporter of the One Million Signatures Campaign, was banned by the Secretariat of the Press Oversight Council. Government has particularly targeted media activists like Parnaz Azima and other cyber journalists who use the Internet as a means of disseminating uncensored information. Accusations of collusion and conspiracy with the West also give the regime a pretext for increasing pressure on the women's movement and serve to hinder the women's progress. In addition, those who are arrested cannot expect to have a fair trial, as the many discrepancies in sentencing point to inherent deficiencies in the integrity of the Iranian courts and judiciary.

There is substantial support for Muslim women's rights in the Iranian diaspora, from a diverse group of Iranian-born women, including Maryam Rajavi, president-elect of the National Council of Resistance of Iran (NCRI), Manda Zand-Ervin and Banafsheh Zand-Bonazzi, mother and daughter founders of the Alliance of Iranian Women (AIW), the lawyer and writer Mehrangiz Kar, writer Azar Majedi, broadcast journalist Maryam Namazie, writer Azam Kamguian, and activist Homa Arjomand. All have spoken against the tyranny of the Iranian Republic and Arjomand lobbied success-fully to remove a separate system of shari'ah courts in Ontario, Canada. How-ever, such activity has produced few tangible results for those reformers who live in Iran. The movement is also disadvantaged by the departure of the intellectual and financial elite at the time of the revolution.

In spite of the dearth of tangible reforms, activists like Parvin Ardalan believe the contribution of women to public life has momentum and will eventually be followed by laws that will undo the entrenched legal discrim-ination that has made women second-class citizens.

The Iranian dissenters are also resourceful, well educated, determined, and aspirational, motivated by love and knowledge of their culture and familiarity with their country's prerevolutionary and ancient history as a rich, intellectual civilization and a regional power. There are some signs of hope. In September 2008, the reformers triumphed when the Iranian parliament denied the passage of a bill that would have required divorced women to pay taxes on their alimony and facilitated polygamy by allowing men to take a second wife without the consent of the first as previously mandated.[67] Other small achievements include raising the minimum usual age for marriage for girls from nine to thirteen (although the age for boys is fifteen), and allowing divorced mothers longer custody of children.[68]

There is also evidence of progress elsewhere: a growth of feminist groups at universities and colleges, collaboration between various women's organiza-tions in spite of ideological differences, and strengthened communication within and outside Iran via the Internet, notwithstanding determined measures by the regime to block Web sites. Undoubtedly, a great deal of the strength of the women's movement is derived from intelligent use of the Inter-net and blogging, skills that have facilitated communication in the restricted public space and in the absence of freedom of association. Another initiative for reform, the Campaign to Stop Stoning Forever, launched in 2006, has saved people from stoning to death for offenses such as adultery and has assisted others in obtaining a stay of execution.

Although activists do not have an appetite for another revolution that could repeat the betrayal and disappointments of Khomeini's Islamic Republic, there are signs of rebellion against the repressive theocracy. Among the youth, who account for two-thirds of the urban population, dissent is being expressed in sexual exploits[69] and an embrace of Western fashions.[70]

In February 2009, marking the thirty-year anniversary of the Islamic Revolution, Amnesty International USA declared that "women continue to face discrimination—both in law and practice. Impunity for human rights abuses is widespread."[71]

WEBLOGESTAN: THE IRANIAN BLOGOSPHERE

Iran's blogosphere mirrors the erratic, fickle and often startling qualities of life in the Islamic republic itself. The rules of what is permissible fluctuate with maddening imprecision, so people test the limits.[72]

The seemingly endless possibilities of the Internet present a number of problems for both bloggers and governments attempting to control free speech. Sites can be established as quickly as authorities try to shut them down, while bloggers themselves are repeatedly put in the position of having to find ways around restrictions placed on Internet service providers (ISPs). These situations are clearly exemplified by the actions of the Iranian government.

Hossein Derakhshan, an Iranian technician-journalist living in Canada, has been described as "the spiritual father of the bloggers in Iran."[73] With his Internet posting of a user-friendly "How to Blog" manual in Farsi, he initiated the vast proliferation of blogs in that language since 2000.[74] The number of blogs in Iran is estimated at 700,000, of which 40,000 to 110,000 are active.[75] These exclude blogs listed on international servers like Google.

With more than half the 70-million-strong population aged under 30, Iran has one of the highest number of bloggers in the world.[76]

The range of sites in Iran is quite broad, dealing with issues and opportunities as wide-ranging as social networking and news sites. Free expression is the main concern for the Iranian authorities but their clampdown on the reformist press in 2000 resulted in the rapid growth of Web logs.[77]

Women bloggers are mostly university students, journalists, and social activists based in Tehran, attracted by the Internet and anxious to express themselves freely and speedily in a society where the public forum has been suppressed.

Dissident views have brought various bloggers to the attention of the authorities and illegal Web sites have been identified by a government committee. A target list contained those who did not espouse "hard-line Muslim attitudes to women and people who might tell jokes about the government."[78] According to a Human Rights Watch report in 2005, many people who worked at sites critical of the government were arrested and some were tortured.

> The right to free expression is enshrined in the Iranian constitution and in international human rights treaties ratified by Iran. Article 23 of the Iranian constitution holds that "the investigation of individuals' beliefs is forbidden, and no one may be molested or taken to task simply for holding a certain belief." . . . Iran's leaders have rhetorically upheld these commitments. . . . In practice, vaguely worded Iranian laws and regulations restrict the exercise of the rights to free expression and to access information. Article 500 of the country's Penal Code states that "anyone who undertakes any form of propaganda against the state . . . will be sentenced to between three months and one year in prison," and leaves "propaganda" undefined.
>
> On December 1, 2002, journalist Sina Motalebi posted an article on his blog about the trial of Hashem Aghajari, a university professor who was sentenced to death in November 2002 after he criticized aspects of Iran's clerical rule. . . .
>
> The judiciary agents told him that his postings amounted to "disturbing the public opinion" and "propaganda against the judiciary. . . ."
>
> Arash Sigarchi, former editor of the daily *Gilan Emrouz*, maintains a blog called Panjareh Eltehab ("Window of Anguish"). . . . Agents of the Ministry of Intelligence arrested him.
>
> After his release, Sigarchi told reporters that the only evidence presented against him was "a few selected postings from my blog, selected transcripts of my interviews with Radio Farda reporters, and a few of my journalistic writings. . . ."
>
> Sigarchi's trial violated international standards for fair trials. It was held behind closed doors and in the absence of his lawyer—indeed, he was not allowed to meet with his lawyer for months after his arrest.[79]

A study conducted by Harvard Law School's Berkman Center, as part of broader research looking at sixty countries in total, notes that many Iranians can use blogs to express critical viewpoints. It shows that less than a quarter of the blogs seeking change have been blocked, but this could simply be a means for the government to maintain a semblance of freedom of expression.[80] The situation is difficult to assess as "Iran's filtering policy and techniques remain opaque."[81]

Reformist bloggers take these opportunities because, in the opinion of a blogger named Inharfha, it is better than "sitting back and watching how our country is being taken back to the ruins of Medieval times."[82] Some bloggers continue to hope that the sites will provide an opportunity for change, albeit slow. Iranian dissident Mehrangiz Kar believes it "will bring change within certain limits."[83]

Progovernment bloggers, or those who are simply very careful, have not faced the fate of individuals who raise opposition from organizations such as the Passdaran Revolutionary Guards. This organization published a report on July 9, 2007, calling for monitoring and control of blogs. The report coincided with an ongoing case against four journalists and raised issues of threats to national security: "web bloggs [sic] can be the field where spying can take place and where measures against the national security and Islamic state can be pursued."[84]

The Passdaran Revolutionary Guards Corps has consistently attacked the Internet as a subversive instrument of "Internet Imperialism" and accused the US government of instigating a "velvet revolution" to overthrow Iran's regime. The Dutch parliament, they claim, also undermines the Islamic republic via media and Web logs.[85] These views have been supported by Islamists in parliament: "the Internet is like a rabid dog that has been let loose but now we are trying to control it."[86]

MAHBOUBEH ABBASGHOLIZADEH AND FERESHTEH GHAZI

Two years ago, after repeated acts of torture and cruelty were committed, Ayatollah Shahrudi (head of Iran's Judiciary Branch) dismissed my mother's case, as he did the case belonging to the web-

bloggers. But some authorities keep returning to the same methods in order to accomplish what they could not attain in the previous incident.[87]

The Iranian government's control of the media has become part of a much wider global debate regarding the rights of journalists.

Agence France-Presse reported that "on 11 October 2004, the head of the judiciary, Ayatollah Mahmoud Hashemi Shahrudi, declared new 'cyber crimes' laws, stating that 'Anyone who disseminates information aimed at disturbing the public mind through computer systems or telecommunications . . . would be punished in accordance with the crime of disseminating lies.'"[88]

This was not only applied to printed newspapers and journals; the focus was on blocked Web sites, blogs, and the arrest of various cyber journalists and activists like Mahboubeh Abbasgholizadeh and Fereshteh Ghazi, who had been using the Internet as a free press. Arrested in late 2004, these women have had to deal with the authorities more than once and have given evidence on the mistreatment of prisoners.

Like other similar arrests, these were based on vague laws, with charges rarely made public. Another common feature of many cases is the lack of access to legal representation; those who take on the cases are often faced with difficulties at the most basic levels, including access to their clients and their files.

Abbasgholizadeh has been editor of *Farzaneh* and *Zanan*, publications dealing with women's issues. She is also the director of the Non-Government Organization Training Center. Fereshteh Ghazi worked on the daily newspaper *Etemad*, Internet Web sites, and various online journals, including *Emrooz*, which was shut down in 2003. A specific offense was her "letter in support of a woman who had been sentenced to death for killing a senior official whom the woman accused of trying to rape her."[89]

Both women experienced hardships while detained in the infamous Ward 209 in Evin prison. "Fereshteh Ghazi provided details of her treatment by interrogators, including severe beatings that resulted in a broken nose during one interrogation session. The detainees were kept under lengthy solitary confinement in a secret detention center and were repeatedly subjected to psychological and physical torture."[90]

Abbasgholizadeh's daughter Maryam raised issues about the judicial process in her mother's case:

> Initially there were three charges made against her, the same ones that were made against all thirty-one arrested women. But in his meeting with the defense lawyers, Judge Haddad added two new charges, which according to the defense attorneys are illegal. One of them is that interrogations begin on the assumption of guilt. During interrogations, they try to fish for other charges to be made against my mother.[91]

In the case of Fereshteh Ghazi, Iranian authorities were quick to charge her with "immoral behavior," a charge predicted by Reporters without Borders, which claimed it "had received reports that the woman would be accused of having illicit sex with five other journalists arrested last month."[92]

The 2004 arrests of Abbasgholizadeh and Ghazi coincided with protests by Canada in the United Nations and Canada's resolution on November 5, 2004, expressing concern regarding human rights in Iran. "Relations between Canada and Iran have been strained since the beating [to] death of Iranian-Canadian photographer Zahra Kazemi in July 2003 while she was in detention."[93]

> Iran has failed to adequately cooperate with visits made by United Nations human rights representatives. The recommendations made by, for example, the UN Working Group on Arbitrary Detention (WGAD), following its February 2003 visit appear to have been ignored.[94]

HANA ABDI AND RONAK SAFARZADEH

In October 2007, two women's rights activists from the city of Sanandaj in Kurdistan province, Hana Abdi and Ronak Safarzadeh, were collecting signatures in support of the One Million Signatures Campaign. Shortly afterward, they were arrested, their houses ransacked, and their computers and campaign literature confiscated. Both women were refused bail. During their incarceration they were interrogated by Intelligence Ministry officials.

Abdi and Safarzadeh, both twenty-one years old at the time, have been active in the women's movement. Abdi is a psychology student at Payam Noor University in Birjand and Safarzadeh is a graphic artist. Abdi is also a member of Azar Mehr Women's NGO in Kurdistan.

Safarzadeh was charged with security violations and Abdi was charged with gathering and collusion with the intent of committing a crime against national security. On June 18, 2008, Abdi's case was heard by Judge Tayari of the Revolutionary Court in Sanandaj. She was sentenced to five years in exile, for the prison where she is held, in the city of Jolfa in West Azarbaijan province, is far from the province of Kurdistan, where she has her home. Her sentence, one of the harshest handed down to a women's rights activist, is the maximum allowed in such cases.

Abdi has been in detention since November 6, 2007, and she spent two months of that time in solitary confinement. According to her lawyer, Dr. Mohammad Sharif, "This sentence is seriously inappropriate given the nature of the case against my client. . . . I absolutely did not expect such a sentence. . . . I had predicted that she would be sentenced to 2 years prison term, in a city close to . . . her family, not in a border province so far away. . . . Our prisons are not segregated, meaning that she will probably have to spend these 5 years in prison with ordinary criminals. I am very concerned about this issue."[95]

NASRIN AFZALI

Nasrin Afzali was arrested during a peaceful protest outside the Revolutionary Court in March 2007. She was one of a group of thirty-two activists who were demonstrating in solidarity with five other women activists who had been charged with offenses. Afzali was charged with illegal assembly, complicity to threaten national security, disruption of public order, and disregard for police orders. Despite the fact that the court acquitted her of the charges of illegal assembly and disregard for police orders, Afzali still received a prison sentence of six months and ten lashes. She found the actions of the court illogical: "How can someone be acquitted on charges of illegal assembly and disregard for police orders while be[ing] sentenced for disrupting public order at the same time?"[96]

Since 2005, Nasrin Afzali has been part of an ingenious protest by Iranian feminists, highlighting the treatment of women as second-class citizens through the medium of sport. In Iran, women are not permitted to enter stadiums to watch live football (soccer) matches for religious reasons (although there are no restrictions on televised games). The first time the women attempted to enter Azadi[97] stadium, the largest in Tehran, they were physically abused by guards and police, and on the second occasion their bus was driven in the opposite direction. On the third instance, the women were armed with new "placards"—their veils:

> In Iran wearing a scarf is obligatory and all women have to wear them and not wearing a scarf will sentenced by jail. So this time football lovers and women's rights activists . . . write their motto "Woman's share is half of the Freedom" on their scarfs.[98]

The women involved in these protests are not risking their freedom and physical security for the love of football. As Afzali explained, "I hate soccer! But the segregation of the sexes is one of the core policies of the Islamic regime. We thought that one of the best symbols to represent our opposition is the stadium. It also allowed us to rally adolescents, who are not particularly concerned about the rights of women, but love soccer."[99]

DELARAM ALI

In November 2007, twenty-four-year-old sociology student Delaram Ali was given a sentence of two and a half years in jail and a ten-lash flogging for her involvement in the June 12, 2006, protest in Tehran's Hafte Tir Square in support of women's rights. The decision was met with widespread condemnation by international human rights groups. A joint statement from Amnesty International, Equality Now, the International Federation for Human Rights, Front Line, Human Rights First, Women Living under Muslim Laws, and the World Organization against Torture stated they would regard Ali's imprisonment "as a gross violation of her rights to freedom of expression and association."[100]

Ali was originally tried in May 2007, when she faced charges of "participation in an illegal gathering," "propaganda against the system," and "disrupting public order and peace." However, according to Nobel laureate Shirin Ebadi, "Women who are put on trial are accused of undermining national security and conspiring to overthrow the regime because they voice their human needs. Iranian courts do not have the courage to admit that they are convicting a woman who is willing to stand up and say I have rights as a person. Thus they label her as a conspirator against national security."[101]

Delaram Ali's case made international headlines for several reasons. The

BBC noted that she was "not a well-known leader of Iran's feminist movement who has repeatedly challenged the government," and therefore her sentence served as a "chilling warning to anyone thinking of dabbling with politics."[102]

Ali was the first of the women arrested to have her sentence implemented, and her case showed little regard for the rule of law in Iran. The charges against the police, who beat Ali and broke her hand, were dismissed. Her trial, with summons and court orders issued verbally, did not follow standard procedure and she was subject to harassment and intimidation throughout.

Delaram Ali accepted her fate with dignity:

> Since the government is threatened by our movement, prison is part of that struggle. . . . This movement . . . will not be silenced because one or two people are in prison; actually, women's rights activists will become more passionate and determined.[103]

NOUSHABEH AMIRI

The Iranian journalist Noushabeh Amiri is a reporter for *Rooz online*, an independent Iranian news site based in France. In 2003, Amiri left Iran for Paris with her husband, also a journalist, who was detained in Iran from 1982 to 1988.

Amiri founded *Rooz* in 2005. It currently has more than 300,000 viewers. Previously, she had been fired from the *Kayhan* newspaper for an interview with Ayatollah Khomeini about women (never published). After the more moderate cleric Mohammad Khatami came to power, Amiri worked for newspapers such as *Toos* and *Neshat*, and together with her husband, started a film magazine:

> Again we were harassed and threatened, even blacklisted. The fundamentalists working closely with the Intelligence Ministry continued to interrogate us regularly, and finally the magazine was closed down.[104]

Speaking about the state of journalism in Iran under Ahmadinejad, Amiri cautioned:

Things have been bleak. During Khatami, though we encountered many obstacles, and journalists were scrutinized and some arrested, there was relative freedom of the press and I was able to function as a journalist. Now the situation has drastically changed for the worse. . . . With Ahmadinejad's ascendance to the presidency, the idea that a woman's place is in the house, and that she should be obedient and that her role is to be a good mother and a wife, is widely promoted. Nonetheless, with women being active on all fronts, it is not going to happen. . . . We have tremendous human potential, a generation that is bright, eager and willing to learn. I think that change will be forthcoming though it will not happen immediately or even quickly.[105]

Amiri wrote an article condemning Ahmadinejad's oppression of criticism by various sectors of Iranian society, including students who were unhappy with the government's security operatives running their universities. The students had also called for the release of fellow students from prison.

And what happened to them? One by one they were rounded up by the state and put into that lovely prison, which the Iranian officials claim to be "the best prison in the world." Yes, we are talking about none other than Evin prison. . . . Ward 209 of the prison is now a famous world spot for anyone who demonstrates.[106]

PARVIN ARDALAN

Currently hordes of women and men are targeted, harassed and arrested by morality police across our country because of their dress. This program is implemented under the guise of a government program intended to protect the social security of citizens.

We state that in our society, culture outpaces the law. Women's high rates in university-level education and their active struggle for a continued presence in the social, political and cultural spheres attest to these claims, and reaffirm that we cannot sustain a situation where laws lag behind our culture.[107]

Ardalan's adult life has been dominated by police intimidation due to her activism on behalf of Iranian women's rights. As a journalist committed to women's rights and unable to publish her work freely in Iran, Ardalan turned to the Internet and became editor of the immensely popular Feminist Tribune of Iran Web site. Here, she wrote articles and garnered support for meetings and workshops. However, the government led by President Mahmoud Ahmadinejad was intent on abolishing thousands of Web sites and blogs without warning, particularly those critical of the government. In Parvin's case, she was unaware her site had been removed until a friend informed her by e-mail. "We lost one of our greatest tools. It's hindered our work, which I suppose was the goal."[108]

For most Iranian activist women, young and reliant on the Internet, an important line of communication was lost when this feminist Web site was shut down.

Parvin Ardalan was also editor-in-chief of the Women's Cultural Center's online journal, *Zanestan*, before the organizations were shut down by government authorities in 2007.[109] The Women's Cultural Center, an NGO in Tehran, had helped to organize the June 12, 2005, sit-in for women's rights at the University of Tehran. Representatives from more than ninety women's groups were included, making this the largest women's coalition to emerge since the revolution.[110]

Ardalan was also a founding member of Change for Equality,[111] which, in August 2006, initiated the One Million Signatures Campaign to petition for changes in laws discriminating against women. The campaign was inspired by women activists in Morocco, but unlike the Moroccan enterprise, which had received the support of government, One Million Signatures aimed for grassroots endorsement. Activists insisted they had "nothing against religion or the Iranian political system."[112] However, this declaration did not prevent dozens of women and some men, who collected signatures from all over the country or wrote for the Web site, from being arrested and charged with antistate propaganda.

Even if it has not yielded any changes in legislation, Ardalan believes the campaign encouraged discussion and increased awareness of the priority of women's rights in the pursuit of democratic freedoms and a civil society.

On March 4, 2007, Ardalan was among thirty-three protestors who were harassed, apprehended by police, and charged with "endangering national security, propaganda against the state and taking part in an illegal gathering."[113] They were protesting outside a revolutionary court where five women were on trial for previously demonstrating against misogynistic

Islamic laws, in a protest that had ended with police violence and the arrest of seventy people. Ardalan and her colleagues held up placards saying, "We have the right to hold peaceful protests."[114] Like the women on trial, they also campaigned against polygamy and prejudicial custody laws.

In recognition of her bold social activism for human rights and women's rights in Iran and her increasing influence outside her own country, Ardalan was awarded the 2007 Olof Palme Prize. The prize, in honor of Swedish prime minister Olof Palme, who was assassinated in 1986, is awarded annually to outstanding individuals for their promotion of peace and equality.[115]

On March 3, 2008, Ardalan was prevented from traveling to Stockholm to accept the prize of $75,000, which was accepted on her behalf by her sister. She was not notified about the travel ban until she had boarded an Air France plane to Stockholm. Officials later confiscated her passport.

In her speech, relayed by video during the award ceremony, Ardalan said:

> Iranian women's demands have been pursued and supported by social movements, activists and human rights organizations across the world. The continuation of our struggle and movement relies heavily on supporters inside and outside Iran.[116]

She also acknowledged the collective work of Iranian women human rights defenders and the price they have paid for demanding basic rights such as freedom of dress, equal marriage rights, repudiation of polygamy, abolition of female quotas at universities, and equal compensation in the event of injury. "We ask why our laws recognize men as full human beings, setting them as the standard, and value women at half the male standard, and sometimes even less."

> As women's rights activists, we have exposed the negative impact of laws on our lives, through the employment of a variety of civil strategies. Criticizing and opposing these violent laws, we have demanded reform and change. But in response to our peaceful and civil objections, the government has charged us with security crimes, such as acting against the state or spreading propaganda against the state.[117]

Women activists like herself have consistently campaigned against the execution of children convicted of criminal offenses, also honor crimes, stoning, and laws that forbid women from passing on their nationality to their children.

Although gains for women were renounced by Iran's Islamic government following the revolution, Ardalan believes the educational achievements and contributions of women to the cultural and political life of the country are unstoppable and eventually laws in favor of women's rights will follow. She referred to the contempt of the Iranian government for the UN Covenant on Civil and Political Rights, the International Covenant on Economic, Social, and Cultural Rights, and other international human rights conventions that they ratified but never implemented. Furthermore, she said, the Iranian government, in the name of national security, employs religious police to hound and intimidate women who don't fully abide by the regulation dress code and imprisons members of students', teachers', and workers' groups that dare to provide any opposition.[118]

> At the heart of this movement are the mothers of activists who have become active in support of the Campaign and their children. These mothers support younger activists when they are arrested, they follow-up on their cases and push for their release. . . . The entrance of mothers, fathers, and other family members of activists, into the equal rights movements and peace movements, has expanded the reach of our effort and has strengthened the bond between different movements in Iran.[119]

HOMA ARJOMAND (IRAN/CANADA)

> *I'd like to emphasize the presence of two forces operating within the Canadian Muslim community. One tries to implement Shari'a law with its repressive measures against women, while the other relies on modernism and secularism to resist such attempts. . . . Only the secular movement which is already present in our society can effectively counter political Islam.*[120]

> *Only a secular state and a secular society that respects human rights can ensure women's liberation.*[121]

In order to prevent the emergence of segregated communities, Homa Arjomand, campaign coordinator of the International Campaign against Shari'a Court in Canada,[122] lobbied to remove the legitimacy of religious courts that were already operating in Ontario.[123]

Iranian-born Arjomand became an activist against the Islamic regime when she was seventeen years old. After a period of study in the United Kingdom, she returned to Iran, where she worked as a university lecturer. While living in Iran, she experienced the impact of political Islam institutionalized as state ideology and law: "anti-freedom, anti-women and anti-secularism." She also witnessed stoning and the execution of fellow activists in the women's movement.[124]

Threatened by the Islamic regime for her dissident activities, Arjomand fled from Iran in 1989, together with her husband and two children, and assisted by smugglers, they rode through the mountains to Turkey.[125] After settling in Canada in 1990, Arjomand worked as a counselor for immigrant women.

Under Ontario's Arbitration Act of 1991, shari'ah courts were established to arbitrate marriage, family, and business disputes.[126] Strong arguments in favor of the courts had included the right to choose religious practice and the education of children without government intrusion.[127] The process was voluntary but the decisions of the court were binding.[128]

In 2003, at the launching of an organization titled the Islamic Institute of Civil Justice, the president of the Canadian Society of Muslims, Syed Mumtaz Ali, went a step further by proclaiming that being a "good Muslim" meant using only shari'ah courts and not Canadian law to settle disputes.[129] The Islamic Institute also wanted to start its own shari'ah-based tribunals under the Arbitration Act.[130]

Arjomand was well aware of shari'ah court decisions in Canada that had discriminated against women in matters of marriage, divorce, and custody. As a result, domestic violence had gone unpunished, financial support and access to children after divorce were minimal, and children were sent to family members in the home countries, where underage girls were forcibly married.

If a completely separate system of arbitration within shari'ah were to be instituted, Arjomand feared that a "state within a state" would be created, inevitably violating the freedoms that Muslim women were entitled to enjoy as Canadian citizens.[131] Although the national law was not bound to endorse the decisions of shari'ah courts, she felt certain that Muslim women would be too fearful to pose a challenge. In addition, she believed the Islamic Institute of Civil Justice was attacking "secularism, modernism and women's rights" under the pretext of accepting multicultural differences and minority rights.[132]

Having fled "political Islam" and its application of shari'ah law in Iran, Arjomand believed that the new Islamic Institute of Civil Justice typified the drive and reach of this Islamist movement. According to Arjomand, political

Islam, a global movement characterized by theocratic ambitions and misogyny, was considerably strengthened after Western governments used Islamist organizations to fight the cold war.[133] The movement, with links to "Iran, Algeria, Nigeria and Saudi Arabia . . . encourages honor killing . . . stones women to death for adultery and in places where it has state power, exposes a nine year old girl to rape under the name of marriage."[134] "Under political Islam women are second-class citizens who are denied their full legal rights."[135]

Moreover, Arjomand holds political Islam accountable for creating "little Irans, Afghanistans, Somalias and Pakistans" in Canada.[136] In 2003, starting with a few supporters, she initiated the International Campaign against Shari'a Court in Canada and built up an alliance of a thousand activists from 183 organizations in fourteen countries.[137]

During a 2004 review of Ontario's 1991 Arbitration Act, she accused the Islamic movement of attacking secular society and attempting to coerce Muslim women to accept shari'ah law, thereby denying them "the Canadian values of equality and gender justice" inherent in Canadian law.[138]

As a result of Arjomand's intensive campaign to counter faith-based courts, the then premier of Ontario, Dalton McGuinty, banned all religious arbitrations, and new legislation was passed mandating the sole use of Canadian law in the province.[139]

With regard to the Western feminist movement, Arjomand asserts that it tends to justify the multicultural pretensions of Islamists instead of joining activists like herself in opposing honor killings,[140] religious schools, female circumcision, and the imposition of archaic shari'ah jurisdictions: "cultural relativism . . . is more important to them than the universal rights of women and children."[141]

Arjomand was named Woman of the Year by the *Gazette Des Femmes* in 2005, and in 2006, she received the annual Toronto Humanist of the Year Award and the Humanist Association of Canada (HAC) Humanist of the Year Award.[142]

PARNAZ AZIMA

The interrogation was about everything, about my own life. . . . What was I doing before leaving Iran 25 years ago. What I was doing in my life before coming to Radio Free Europe. And then about what was I

doing in Radio Free Europe. And they were always insisting that if I
cooperated with them, everything would be closed.[143]

Azima, aged fifty-nine, who holds dual Iranian American nationality, is one of Iran's best-known literary translators and works for Radio Farda, the American-funded Persian-language broadcasting service of Radio Free Europe/Radio Liberty. Produced in Washington and Prague, Radio Free Europe provides uncensored news to countries where a free press is either banned by the government or not fully established. Among other stories, Farda reported on the expulsion of Bahai students from Iranian universities and analyzed the crackdown on women's dress code violations. It also reported the protests over the government's gas-rationing policies and the story about "dog prisons." Pet dogs are viewed negatively in Islam and police are under pressure to arrest children walking their dogs in the park.[144]

Azima traveled to Tehran in January 2007 to visit her ninety-five-year-old mother, who was ill. Her passport was confiscated upon her arrival at Tehran airport. She was forbidden to leave the country for seven months, charged with security-related violations, and released on bail. She managed to escape from Iran on September 18.

In March 2008, Azima was convicted by Tehran's 13th Revolutionary Court for the crime of spreading propaganda and working for the "anti-revolutionary" Radio Farda. She said the Iranian government had threatened to seize her mother's home if she did not return to serve the sentence.[145] She noted that officials particularly urged her to avoid covering sensitive issues like human rights[146] and tried to discourage her from returning to Farda.[147]

The Iranian regime, which tries to jam Farda's signal and block its Web site, has intensified pressure on activists at home and also on the United States, which supports Farda. Intelligence officers in Tehran have interrogated and threatened family members of Farda staffers, including a journalist who was summoned by an Iranian court to face charges of conducting "activities against national security."[148]

PARVIN DARABI

Equality does not take precedence over justice. Justice does not
mean that all laws must be the same for men and women. One of the

mistakes the Westerners make is to forget this. The difference in the stature, vitality, voice, development, muscular quality and physical strength of men and women show that men are stronger and more capable in all fields. Men's brains are bigger so men are more inclined to fight and women are more excitable.[149]

Following the suicide of her sister Homa by self-immolation in protest against the compulsory veiling of Iranian women in 1994, electronics engineer Parvin Darabi established the Dr. Homa Darabi Foundation in her honor.[150]

Women did not remain silent. They launched campaigns in the major cities of the country. In the Summer [of] 1981, however, wearing the Islamic outfit in the government offices and ministries became mandatory.

Once more, women marched in protest. This time, however, the Islamic Republic was well established and the media were fully under its control. The Revolutionary Council threatened those women who ignored the Islamic outfit with dismissal.

When the Islamic Republic was established in Iran in 1979, the country experienced a dramatic return to the dark ages. Women were the first victims of the regression. More than 130 years of struggle was repudiated by the medieval religious rulers.

In March 1979, Khomeini employed the hijab as a symbol of struggle against imperialism and corruption. He declared that "women should not enter the ministries of the Islamic Republic bare-headed. They may keep on working provided that they wear the hijab."[151]

The Dr. Homa Darabi Foundation is also a voice of dissent, not only against the Islamic Republic of Iran, but also against Islam.

I am a Moslem woman. I have no face. I have no identity. At age 9, based on lunar year . . . I am considered an adult. Being an adult means that I have to adhere [to] Islamic laws. . . .

I have to pray five times a day, fast one month out of the year and cover myself from head to toe in yards of black fabric. I am eligible to be married and can be punished for any wrong doing. I can be incarcerated and, if needed, executed for my crimes, even political ones.

I am not allowed to swim . . . or any other sport. I am not even permitted to watch men play sports. . . .

From age 7, I am segregated from all males in and out of my extended family.

I have to study under female teachers and professors. However, since women of prior generations were not allowed to go to school, there are not that many qualified women teachers and professors. Male professors must teach me from behind a wall.

I am to be treated by female doctors. Go to female dentists. And if there are none, then I have to go without or I must be examined through some sort of divider.

I am not allowed to practice birth control or have abortions, even if carrying or having a child means I have to die.

I cannot get custody of my children. Even if their father dies. In the case of divorce or death I have to surrender my children to their father and/or his family.

I will get arrested, beaten, and sometimes even executed if I wear make-up, nylons, bright colors and specifically the color of red.

. . . I am supposed to be seen outside of my home three times in my life. When I am born, when I get married and when I die.

. . . if I am arrested for wearing make-up, the guards will force me to clean my face with cotton balls rubbed in pieces of glass.

In Islam, if a 6 or 7 year old girl is raped by an adult man, she will be the one that gets punished. It is her fault because she provoked it. The parents then will burn or kill her because she has dishonored the family.

In 1991, the Prosecutor-General of Iran, declared that "anyone who rejects the principle of hijab is an apostate and the punishment for an apostate under Islamic law is death."[152]

Darabi's objections to the Iranian government's treatment of women stem from the Islamic Retribution Bill, 1982, in which "the value of woman is considered only half as much as the value of man. . . . The worth of a man's life is equal to the market value of 100 camels or 200 cows and that of a woman is equal to half of the man's, 50 camels or 100 cows."[153]

Discriminatory laws regarding marriage, polygamy, inheritance, divorce, and custody of children reinforce the status of women as second-class citizens. "Women never reach the age of majority" and therefore will never be entitled to the custody of their children. "That is why in Saudi Arabia women are not given a birth certificate or an identification card. Just recently the Islamic government of Saudi Arabia allowed women to carry an identification card only if their guardian would allow. Just the fact that women need guardians is an insult."[154]

Women's everyday lives are tightly controlled. They cannot engage in sport, study particular subjects, leave the house without permission, or even express their femininity through their clothing[155] and makeup.

Darabi highlights the beliefs and practices that stem from Islamic teachings about men and women: "Islam believes and promotes only one relationship between male and female and that is the relation of lust."[156]

> I cannot choose my mate and am not permitted to divorce him if things did not work out.
>
> According to Khomeini, "The most suitable time for a girl to get married is the time when the girl can have her first menstrual period in her husband's house rather than her father's."
>
> My husband can divorce me without my knowledge and by the Islamic law he is required to support me for only 100 days. And if he dies, I am entitled to 1/8 of his Estate.
>
> Polygamy is legal in Islam. A man may marry "four Permanent" and as many "Provisional" or temporary wives as he desires.
>
> As a political prisoner I will be used as a concubine for the revolutionary guards. In case I am condemned to death I will not undergo the sentence as long as I am a virgin. Thus I will be systematically raped before the sentence is executed. Mullahs believe that virgin girls who die go to heaven but politically inclined girls are ungodly creatures and they do not deserve to go to heaven, therefore they are raped so that the Mullahs can be sure that they indeed will be sent to hell.[157]

> I have to meet all my husband's desires including the sexual ones. And if I refuse he has the right to deny me food, shelter, and all of life's necessities. I have to say yes every time he wants to have sex.[158]

Hojatoleslam Imani, a religious leader in Iran, instructed, "A woman should endure any violence or torture imposed on her by her husband for she is fully at his disposal. Without his permission she may not leave her house even for a good action. Otherwise her prayers and devotions will not be accepted by God and curses of heaven and earth will fall upon her."[159]

Darabi expressed shock and disappointment when a CNN reporter of Iranian origin, Christiane Amanpour, said Iranian women were better off since the 1979 revolution. In an open letter of January 29, 2009, Darabi accused Amanpour of justifying the imprisonment and executions of hundreds of women and ignoring prerevolutionary women's freedoms such as the right to vote, divorce, obtaining custody of children, travel without restrictions, and also the ban on polygamy.[160]

SHIRIN EBADI

The Nobel Prize gave me advantages outside Iran, but inside the country nothing has changed.
*   But abroad things were different and I was allowed to publicize my opinions loud and clear.*[161]

Shirin Ebadi is the first female Iranian judge, a human rights activist, and founder of the Center for the Defense of Human Rights.[162] In 2003, she received the Nobel Prize for Peace in honor of her work. She advocates the use of nonviolent, democratic methods in order to achieve reform and believes that reform must be carried out within the existing institutional framework to be legitimate.[163] In order to showcase this, she wears the veil when in Iran because it is mandatory, but she would prefer to change the law because "it is not the state's business to tell women whether to cover their heads or not."[164]

Attempts on Ebadi's life, death threats, and imprisonment have left her scarred with fear; but she "refuses to be silenced."[165]

After the Islamic Revolution in 1979, female judges were forced to resign, and Ebadi and forty of her female colleagues were removed from their positions.[166] Her protests using peaceful means over thirteen years helped restore women judges in Iran.[167] In 1988, she represented the families of dissident writers and intellectuals whose assassinations could be traced back to the government. She was arrested on the charge of videotaping her clients' confessions, which had implicated some members of the government. In January 2000, she lost her license to practice law, was arrested and kept in solitary confinement, and is still at risk from forces within and outside the government.[168]

Despite being called a "treacherous Granny"[169] by hardline newspaper *Kayhan*, Ebadi sees herself as a true Iranian patriot. Clearly, she maintains a strong bond with her home country, explaining that "without the connection to Iran, my life has no meaning."[170] She is involved in the campaign against corporate schemes that have signed away the care of Iranian historic sites, almost certainly spelling out their destruction or erosion.[171] Her motivation for restructuring the country comes out of a sincere love for the Iranian people and land, and also out of anger directed at those who, in her view, have appropriated Islam for political means.[172] "People must stop exploiting Islam. They talk of an 'Islamic' mentality so that they can assert that women are weak and unstable and . . . of an 'Islamic' economy so that they will be able to justify their exploitation of the nation's resources . . . of 'Islamic' education so that they can justify their policy of brainwashing children and young people."[173]

She has clearly stated that she does not oppose Islam itself but that she does oppose the misogynistic, patriarchal justification for the oppression of women based on arguments about their biological difference from men.[174]

> Why is the situation of women in the Muslim world so deplorable? The answer is because the dominant culture in Islamic countries is patriarchal. This culture interprets religion according to its own interests. I will give you an example. In Iran, there is a law stipulating that the financial compensation, or diya, for accidentally killing a woman is half that for killing a man.[175]

> If a man kills a woman, the family of the victim must even pay a few million Tomans [Iranian currency; equivalent to a few thousand dollars] . . . as retribution in order for the judicial system to punish the murderer.[176]

Religion is all about interpretation, and today's Islam, in Ebadi's opinion, has been corrupted by adherence to ancient interpretations:

> We need an interpretation that suits the needs of our time and place. Interpretations made 600 years ago are no longer satisfactory. Contemporary problems call for contemporary solutions. The world cannot be governed by ancient perspectives.[177]

Ebadi espouses a separation between religion and the state, which, she believes, is compatible with Shi'ite traditions:

> What we have in Iran today is not a religious regime, but a regime in which the people holding the power exploit religion in order to remain in power. If the current regime does not mend its ways and begin to reflect the will of the people, it will fail even if it adopts a secular path. I support separation of religion and state because the political arena is open to an unlimited number of interests. This position [i.e., separation of religion and state] is in effect supported by the leading religious authorities, and it corresponds with Shi'ite tradition.[178]

The human rights violations experienced almost universally throughout Islamic countries should not, Ebadi argues, be linked with Islam and used to argue that the religion is incompatible with human rights, for these inequalities are political as opposed to religious.[179] The assertion that these laws stem from Islam is also used against women to keep them in a subordinate position in which they are considered too incompetent to be included in the decision-making process.[180]

Her message for Muslim women is not to blindly follow the instructions of the clerics:

> Do not believe that you are condemned to inferior status. Look carefully in the Koran so that the oppressors will not succeed in misleading you with their commentary and their selective quotes. Do not let people masquerading as clerics claim that they have a monopoly on understanding Islam.[181]

Ebadi also advocates education for women not based on religion or women's roles as wives and mothers. "Instead of telling women to cover their heads, we should tell them to use their heads."[182]

She sees the situation of women in the Muslim world as different depending on the country—Saudi Arabia being the most oppressive, but others like Bangladesh and Pakistan less so, as women in these countries have become political leaders.[183]

Ebadi argues that rights for women should be seen in the context of social justice and not as an exclusively feminist issue.[184] She calls on the government to abide by the international covenants it has signed on human rights and social justice, including the Covenant of Civil and Political Rights, the Covenant of Economic and Social Rights, and the Universal Declaration of Human Rights.[185]

Ebadi condemns Iran's democratic deficit caused by the fact that all candidates for president are screened by the Guardians Council.[186] She argues that people in Iran have turned against the idea of violent revolution because of their experiences in 1979 and would therefore be more attracted to electoral reform.

At a rally in August 2007, held to protest the imprisonment of three student journalists, Ebadi criticized the lack of freedom of speech in Iran: "Had these students pointed guns at the people? We always have this problem that people are imprisoned because there is no freedom of speech."[187]

Earlier that year, she represented a group of writers and publishers objecting to the increased censorship practiced by the government and argued that it was unconstitutional.[188] Speaking to a journalist for *Rooz*, Ebadi condemned Iran's exaggerated focus on becoming a nuclear power: "How can they even attain nuclear energy without the freedom of expression?"[189]

Women who engage in peaceful protests against the regime, such as Delaram Ali, are frequently arrested for the crime of "undermining national security." Ebadi has added her voice to the opposition to the manner in which Ali's case was handled and asserts that the Iranian government is obviously afraid of women who agitate for their rights.[190]

The One Million Signatures Campaign for gender equality in Iran adheres totally to Ebadi's policy of initiating reform within the existing institutional framework, however much the women involved are subject to harassment by government officials.[191] Ebadi identifies as false the charge of undermining national security, for which some have been arrested. As she points out, the only security they could possibly be undermining is the existence of the patriarchal order.[192]

She perceives Iran as being a better democracy than other countries in the region, but believes it must make huge strides in order to satisfy the aspirations of the people. In this process, it must be the responsibility of the Iranians themselves to improve their situation; she does not condone foreign intervention or attacks, although she finds it frustrating that dissenters in Iran are branded as foreign agents.[193] Economic sanctions should not be used, says Ebadi, as they serve only to punish the Iranian people.[194] Ebadi believes the United States was selective and hypocritical in targeting only Saddam Hussein's regime, which she takes as evidence that the Iraq war was really fought over oil.[195]

In August 2008, Iran's official state media outlet, the Islamic Republic

News Agency, published articles accusing Ebadi's daughter, Nargess Tavasso-lian, a student at McGill University, of having converted to the Bahai faith. Such an action is regarded as apostasy and carries a death sentence. In the arti-cles, the attacks on Ebadi included alleged associations with Bahais and the CIA, her defense of homosexuals, and her criticism of shari'ah punishments. According to human rights activist Mehrangiz Kar, "In light of such laws, it is obvious that they are setting the stage for Shirin Ebadi's elimination."[196]

Ebadi's office, the Center for the Defense of Human Rights in Tehran, was forcibly closed by Iranian government authorities in December 2008, after her organization assisted the United Nations in preparing a report cen-suring Iran's human rights violations. The center, which defends many women activists and political prisoners and is financed by Ebadi's Nobel Peace Prize money, was accused of circulating propaganda against Iran.[197]

HALEH ESFANDIARI (IRAN/USA)

How did I end up a political prisoner? . . . The charge seemed ludicrous. I, a 67-year-old grandmother, was being accused of threatening the security of the most populous and powerful country in the Middle East because I had organized conferences in Washington on Iran and other states of the region. But the implications were frightening.[198]

The Iranian-born academic Haleh Esfandiari is director of the Middle East Program at the Woodrow Wilson International Center for Scholars, where her work raises questions, encourages debate, and attempts to resolve cross-cultural and political issues. As she holds both US and Iranian passports, her detention in Iran aroused comment from US officials, including Secretary of State Condoleezza Rice.

Esfandiari, who has lived in Potomac, in the United States since 1980, regularly visited Iran to see her mother.

In the 1960s she worked as a journalist at Iran's *Kayhan* newspaper and held the position of deputy secretary-general of the Women's Organization of Iran. She earned her PhD at the University of Vienna.

With tensions increasing in Iran at the time of the Iranian Revolution, Esfandiari moved to Britain with her husband, Shaul Bakhash, and daughter. Her husband received an offer from Princeton University and Esfandiari took up a position at the same university teaching Persian literature, holding this position from 1980 to 1994. Esfandiari became a fellow of the Wilson Center in 1995 and she is also an advisor to the RAND Corporation.

The rights of women in the Middle East are one of her major areas of expertise. According to Rola Dashti in Kuwait, Esfandiari was "instrumental in engaging women to take part in public life."[199] In April 2005, she contributed "Iranian Woman, Please Stand Up" to *Foreign Policy* magazine. In the article, she focused on Shahla Sherkat and her feminist mission as editor of the Iranian reformist women's magazine *Zanan*.[200]

Esfandiari's detention, which was to become the subject of international media attention and was compared to the 1980s hostage crisis, began with a robbery in December 2006. She was in Tehran to visit her mother when she was robbed at knifepoint, losing her baggage and passports. This resulted in the necessity to apply for new documents, but instead of receiving a new passport, she found herself facing interrogation for up to eight hours a day. Essentially under house arrest, she was questioned regularly about her own activities and those of the Wilson Center until "pressured to make a false confession or to falsely implicate the Wilson Center in activities in which it had no part."[201]

On May 8, 2007, she found herself under arrest and imprisoned in the notorious Ward 209 of Evin prison in Tehran, where she was constantly questioned by Iranian Intelligence. On May 21, she was charged with attempting to topple Iran's Islamic regime.

The interrogations Esfandiari continued to face while in prison all dealt with the same issues and appeared to be based on the assumption that the United States was engaged in a "velvet" revolution

> like the peaceful ones that occurred in Georgia and Ukraine. To achieve this end, it uses think tanks, foundations and even universities to organize workshops for Iranian women, to invite Iranian opinion-makers and scholars to conferences and to offer them fellowships . . . to create a network of like-minded people in Iran who are intent on regime change.[202]

In the early stages of her incarceration in Ward 209, Esfandiari was denied visitors, including her ninety-three-year-old mother, who attempted to see her soon after she was arrested. Eventually, her mother was given permission to visit her in prison and Esfandiari was also allowed to call her family. However, her solicitor, Shirin Ebadi, observed that telephone conversations with her mother had to be conducted in Farsi rather than in her mother's native German, so that they could be monitored by prison officials.[203] Ebadi was also concerned with the failure of authorities to present the court with Esfandiari's file once the investigative phase was over.

Those in the Wilson Center, along with her family, worked zealously for her release, but Esfandiari admitted there were low points when she wondered if she would be forgotten by the world. Even when she was eventually permitted access to newspapers, she was "unaware of the media attention . . . of the campaign that my family and supporters had set in motion to secure my freedom."[204] A significant part of that campaign was the communication between Lee Hamilton, president of the Wilson Center, and various Iranian political and spiritual leaders.

Esfandiari's release came on August 21, after more than three months in prison. She was able to return to her mother's home when $333,000 bail had been raised. Following her ordeal, she wrote as follows:

> According to the Intelligence Ministry, the Iranians invited abroad are handpicked for their potential as political activists rather than for their scholarly achievement. They are part of a foreign plot to create networks of like-minded Iranians who will then push for a change of regime through peaceful means.
>
> That line of thinking explains official Iranian suspicion of the grant-giving programs of American foundations, universities, and think tanks. . . . The idea that wealthy families set up foundations for philanthropic and scholarly purposes is a concept alien to the Iranian regime. In its view, all of these institutions carry out a mandate set for them by the U.S. government.[205]

Published Work

Reconstructed Lives: Women and Iran's Islamic Revolution. Baltimore: Johns Hopkins University Press, 1997

AZAM KAMGUIAN (IRAN/UK)

The very statement that an Islamic republic exists somewhere means that brutal violence exists within it.[206]

Azam Kamguian is an Iranian writer and women's rights activist. She was born in Iran in 1958. At the age of twelve, she began to question her belief in Islam, and at fifteen, she relinquished it.[207] She became a political activist two years later.

> I would have given a lot to be able to believe. But in the end I had to tread the rocky and non-comforting path of atheism. I gave up the shelter of a divine shadow—but I gained a life that could question and explore life and human existence.[208]

While Kamguian was studying medicine in prerevolutionary Iran, she was arrested for organizing student protests and imprisoned for a year. When the Islamic Republic of Iran took power in 1979, Kamguian was again imprisoned because of her political activities. She was kept in solitary confinement and tortured but managed to keep her identity a secret, for fear that if her history as an activist was discovered, she would be executed.[209]

> I, along with thousands of political prisoners, was tortured by order of the representative of Allah and Sharia; tortured, while the verses of the Koran about non-believers were played in the torture chambers. The voice reading the Koran mixed with our cries of pain from lashes and other brutal forms of torture. They raped women political prisoners for the sake of Allah and in expectation of his reward. They prayed before raping them. Thousands were shot to death by execution squads while Koranic verses were recited. Prisoners were awakened every day at dawn to the sound of gunshots aimed at their friends and cellmates. From the numbers of shots you could work out how many had been murdered that day. The killing machine did not stop for a minute. The fathers and mothers, husbands and wives who received the bloody clothes of their loved ones had to pay for the bullets. They created an Islamic Auschwitz. Many of the best, the most passionate and progressive people were massacred. The dimensions of the horror are beyond imagining.[210]

When she was released in 1983, Kamguian went to Kurdistan for eight years, where she continued the struggle against political Islam in Iran. In 1991, she went to the United States, and later she moved to the United Kingdom.[211]

Kamguian started writing in 1979 and her books include the following:

Islam, Women, Challenges and Perspectives; Feminism, Socialism and Human Nature; On Religion, Women's Liberation and Political Processes in the Middle East; Islam and Women's Rights; Iranian Women's Movement for Equality; Godlessness, Freedom from Religion and Human Happiness; and *Unveiling Islam and Multiculturalism: In Defence of Secularism and Universal Women's Rights.*[212]

Kamguian has organized campaigns for women's rights in the Middle East and advocated for secularism at national and international conferences. She has also written numerous articles, given interviews, and spoken at conferences on Islam, women's rights, and human rights issues.[213]

The founder and chairperson of the Committee to Defend Women's Rights in the Middle East, Kamguian is also the editor of its bulletin, *Women in the Middle East.* She is a representative of the Worker-Communist Party of Iran, a contributor to the party's journal, *WPI Briefing*, and a member of the editorial staff of *Medusa*, the Farsi journal of the Center for Women and Socialism.[214]

The three decades since the Iranian Revolution, she says, "have been some of the darkest in the memory of Iranian people. The Islamic regime, the first established government of political Islam in the Middle East, brought nothing but repression, torture, and death."[215] However, Kamguian points out that "the post-revolutionary period in Iran has also seen extraordinary gender and cultural awareness among Iranian women," and that resistance has been constant:

> Women's resistance against Islamic laws has been a daily fact of life. The penalty for breaking the rules of segregation and Hijab has been insult, cash fines, expulsion, and deprivation from education, arrest, imprisonment, beating, and flogging. Tens of thousands of women, the great majority born after the establishment of the Islamic Republic, have defied the rules and have been attacked by Islamic moral squads with fists, knives, cutters, and acid.[216]

Kamguian argues that there is a "massive social hatred of Islam" in Iran and that Islam "should and will"[217] suffer a major defeat:

> The movement against Islam primarily will be a mass popular movement against the political and social expression of Islam. The fact is that Iranian society has changed dramatically and deeply since 1979. The movement for secularism and atheism, for modern ideas and culture, for individual

freedom, for women's liberation and civil liberties has been widespread and deep. Women and the youth are the champions of this battle—a battle that threatens the basic pillars of the Islamic system. The most hopeful signs and the most remarkable stimulus for change continue to come directly from Iranian women and youth both in Iran and in exile. Any change in Iran will not only affect the lives of people living in Iran, but will have a significant impact on the region and worldwide. For the first time in the history of humanity in the Middle East, there will be a movement . . . to criticize Islam, and a movement to push religion back to where it belongs.[218]

Kamguian does not believe in attempts to reform Islam or in the possibility of a positive reinterpretation of the Koran, because of what she calls Islam's "intrinsic animosity . . . to equality between the sexes and to women's rights and their role in society."[219]

Essentially, Islam is a set of beliefs and rules that militate against human prosperity, happiness, welfare, freedom, equality and knowledge. Islam and a full human life are contradictory concepts, opposed to each other. Islam, under any kind of interpretation, is and always has been, a strong force against secularism, modernism, egalitarianism and women's rights. Political Islam, however, is a political movement that has come to the fore against secular and progressive movements for liberation, and against cultural and intellectual advances. Violence and disregard for human dignity are inherent in the manifestos of political Islamic groups.[220]

Kamguian argues that the insistence among intellectuals and the media in the West that the enemy is fundamentalism, not Islam, is a "shameful" product of a self-centered, postcolonial guilt complex:

For people like me, first-hand victims of the Islamic Holocaust, it was suffocating to listen to and to have to refute endless tales to justify this terror, atrocity and misogyny. . . . What we have seen [in Iran] is the reality of Islam in power. . . . The aftermath of September 11 exposed some of the reality of what is happening to people living under the constant terror of Islam. It exposed something of the tragedy that befell women under the Taliban. It revealed, to some extent, the true substance of Islam. But it became plain to see that this carnage is Islamic. It became evident that it is all about Islam.[221]

The only solution, Kamguian asserts, is to "get rid of political Islam as a pre-condition to any improvements in the status of women in the Middle East." "The social system," she argues, "is based on Islamic misogyny and backwardness, and Middle Eastern women will have no cause to regret its passing. The 21st Century must be the century that rids itself of political Islam."[222] She believes this will be achieved by the women and the younger generation in Iran, and she calls for global support:

> The people of the world must rise up and support our struggle to eradicate this right wing, active, genocidal and murderous Islamic movement, and support our battle for the Enlightenment in the Middle East. I call you and all atheists, secularists and freethinkers to join our camp and strengthen our movement to free ourselves and Iranian society from political Islam, to get rid of Islam, and to abolish it from the state, education and public life.[223]

Committee to Defend Women's Rights in the Middle East (CDWRME)[224]

The organization was formed in 2001 by women's rights activists from Jordan, Lebanon, and Iran and coordinated by Azam Kamguian. Its credo forcefully declares that the argument of cultural relativism cannot be used to excuse misogyny and the oppression of women. It calls for the abolition of shari'ah-based legal codes and their replacement with secular, egalitarian family law.

CDWRME campaigns for the recognition of "honor killing" as murder and for the exacting of appropriate punishment for offenders. In addition, it believes that abuse, intimidation, and violence perpetrated by male relatives on women and girls should be criminalized.

In the political sphere, the committee demands full enfranchisement of women, their right to be elected to any political office, and their right to form sociopolitical organizations without restriction or harassment.

MEHRANGIZ KAR (IRAN/USA)

> *The political debate in Iran follows two key schools of thought. One is that by reforming the religion, we can solve the political problems*

and satisfy human rights. The other view is that we need a total separation of religion and state. This last group would not even enter the debate on the compatibility of Islam, human rights, and women's rights. I follow the latter; I believe that it is not possible to combine these two together.[225]

Mehrangiz Kar was born in 1944 in Ahvaz, a city in the south of Iran. She went to school there and graduated from Tehran University in 1967 with a degree in law and political science. She then started working in the Institute of Social Security.[226]

In 1969, Kar married Siamak Pourzand, an Iranian journalist, who later became a noted cultural commentator and film critic. She has two daughters with him. In the 1970s, Kar gained a reputation as a distinguished author and feminist, writing numerous articles for Iran's leading publications, including *Kayhan*, *Ferdowsi*, and *Zanan*.[227] She was the editor of the *Zan* literary review, which is now banned, and she is the author of numerous books on human rights and social issues in Iran.[228] Kar passed the bar exam in 1979, the year the shah was overthrown and Iran became an Islamic Republic.

From the early days of the revolution, many Iranians became disenchanted with the apparent contradiction between revolutionary ideals and brutal reality. Many revolutionaries and radicals militated against the reactionary structure of the new constitution. They aimed at eradicating the forces of reaction with revolutionary zeal and speed. But the judiciary, utilizing the defense of Islam as a justification, promptly suppressed the opposition. The eight-year war with Iraq provided the regime with the perfect excuse to increase the level of violence that led to the horrific mass executions of the political prisoners.[229]

The new Islamic regime was far less tolerant of professional women; female judges were forced to resign and female lawyers were sidelined into bureaucratic positions. Kar adapted to the situation, working pro bono for the community for three years and gaining the respect of the shari'ah judges. Initially cautious, she began writing again, particularly about human rights issues under Islamic law.[230]

Kar's legal career spanned twenty-two years, during which she worked as a public defender in Iran's civil and criminal courts. She defended numerous clients accused of crimes under the Islamic penal code, in cases that ranged from adultery and divorce to human rights abuses by state officials.[231]

Her reputation as a feminist activist, writer, and thinker, however, was to cost her dearly. Before the revolution, she was often pictured in magazines, with short hair and without the *hijab* or veil, which later became mandatory. When the Islamic Republic was established, she observed the dress rules and codes of behavior that the new regime demanded, but, due to her history and published opinions, she was considered by the authorities as a person who promoted Western ideas and morality.

> My writings, while they were not in agreement with the previous political system, did not promote religious ideas. My social appearance and behavior also supported the fact that I did not have any religious tendency. . . . I had no problem until I restarted to express my opinion, which did not directly attack the government. But, even that was too much, for some media began to introduce me as anti-revolution or as one in support of the previous regime. I fought and continued because the pressure did not succeed in silencing me.[232]

She sought permission several times to start various support agencies for women, but permission was refused.[233]

> In Iran, government permission is required to form any organization; in other words, the law allows the government to stop legal formation of any organization whether it is political or civil, without even giving a reason. This is the key legislation preventing the secular belief from having official activity or freedom to express itself.
>
> . . . extremists have never had any problems. They have many women's groups and organizations. Most of these groups have a very close connection to the government. . . . They are effective in charity work . . . but they are incapable when it comes to legal issues. They cannot promote women's rights in any way.[234]

In April 2000, Kar attended a conference at the Heinrich Böll Institute in Berlin titled "Iran after the Elections." At the conference, she spoke about the need for constitutional reform and the importance of a secular future for Iran. On her return to Iran, she was arrested, together with most of the other Iranian journalists who had attended the conference.[235]

She was taken to Evin prison on April 3, 2000, and charged with "acting against the internal security of the State" and "disparaging the sacred order of the Islamic Republic of Iran." She was denied legal counsel and medicine and held for two months in solitary confinement.[236]

On June 29, 2000, Kar was freed on bail equivalent to $60,000. She had been diagnosed with breast cancer and asked for permission to go abroad for treatment, but permission was refused. She had a mastectomy and underwent a course of chemotherapy in Iran.[237] On January 13, 2001, the Islamic Revolutionary Court sentenced her to four years in prison. However, in autumn of that year, through the intercession of agencies in the Netherlands, she was finally permitted to leave Iran for medical treatment abroad.[238]

Mehrangiz Kar's appeal against her sentence was heard in November 2001, and the verdict was announced in February 2002, when she was already in the United States. Her sentence was commuted to "time already served" and a fine. Three further charges, for which she can still be arrested if she returns to Iran, have been filed in the Iranian Public Court: "violating the observance of *hijab*," "denying the instructions of the Koran," and "insulting Islam."[239]

After Kar had left for the United States, her husband, Siamak Pourzand, then seventy-one years old, was arrested on November 24, 2001. He was kept in solitary confinement and the authorities would not divulge his whereabouts. He was made to phone Mehrangiz and their daughters several times to pass on the message that they should not talk to the media about his arrest. He was also accused of working for the former shah of Iran, spying for the United States, and channeling US funds to the reformist press. Tried in a closed court in June 2002, he was sentenced to eight years in prison.[240]

On July 9, 2002, Pourzand's sentence was upheld in the Tehran Court of Appeal,[241] and later that month, he was forced to admit publicly to the charges against him on state television and to implicate other activists and intellectuals, including his wife. In the televised interrogation he appeared "gaunt, ill, and obviously under enormous psychological pressure."[242]

Pourzand's health has seriously deteriorated since his arrest and he has had recurrent heart attacks. He has been held for months at a time in solitary confinement and his family and several human rights organizations allege he has been subjected to physical and psychological torture.[243] While he has been allowed to leave prison for medical treatment, such as a spinal operation to avoid becoming paralyzed, most of the time he has been neglected. When his sister was permitted to visit him, she reported that he was "totally devastated physically and psychologically" and had been "denied the simplest means of healthcare and personal hygiene." Today, he is out of Evin on regulated medical leave, alternating between the hospital and his home, but his prison sentence still stands.[244]

Kar's writing is no longer published in Iran, and she is banned from appearing in the media. Since she arrived in the United States, she has written a memoir, and she continues to write, lecture, and give interviews on human rights issues in Iran. She has served as a fellow at the National Endowment for Democracy, the Woodrow Wilson Center, the American University, Washington, DC, the University of Virginia, Charlottesville, and Columbia University.

From 2005 to 2006 she was a Radcliffe Fellow at Harvard, based at the Carr Center for Human Rights Policy, and from 2007 to 2008, she was a Newhouse Fellow in residence at the Newhouse Center for the Humanities, Wellesley College, with the support of the Scholars at Risk network.[245]

> I have sent three letters to President Hatami asking him, "Please give me safe passage to Iran to visit my husband." He has never replied, but he sent a verbal message through an intermediary that said, "I can't do anything for you."[246]

Awards

2000 PEN/NOVIB Award of PEN Clube (Netherlands), for writers who have lost their liberty for political and ideological reasons

2000 Donna Dell'anno Award of the Conseil De Lavallee Consiglio Regionale Della Valle D'aosta (Italy), for persevering in the fight for freedom and the defense of women's rights

2000 Latifeh Yarshater Award of the Society for Iranian Studies (United States), for the best book on Iranian women

2001 Vasyl Stus Freedom-to-Write Award of PEN New England (Massachusetts), for a writer who has struggled in the face of oppression and brutality to make her voice heard

2002 Ludovic Trarieux International Human Rights Prize (France), for a lawyer working to promote women's human rights, Human Rights Institute of the Bar of Bordeaux and the European Lawyers Union

2002 Democracy Award of the National Endowment for Democracy (US), for advancing human rights and democracy

2002 Hellman/Hammett Grant from Human Rights Watch (International), for a writer who is a target of political persecution

2004 Human Rights Award, Human Rights First (formerly Lawyers Committee for Human Rights)

Honorary Member of the Pen Club in the United States, Canada, and the United Kingdom. Kar ran the Pen Club in Iran in the year before her arrest (1999–2000), despite the arrest and murder of intellectuals at that time

Selected Published Works

The Angel of Justice and Patches of Hell. Tehran: Roshangaran, 1991.

The Quest for Identity: Iranian Women in History and Pre-History. With Shahla Lahji. Tehran: Roshangaran, 1992.

Women in the Labour Market of Iran. Tehran: Roshangaran, 1994.

Children of Addiction. Tehran: Roshangaran, 1996. Second edition.

Women's Political Rights in Iran. Tehran: Roshangaran, 1997.

Legal Structure of the Family System in Iran. Tehran: Roshangaran, 1999.

Elimination of Gender Discrimination: A Comparison of the Convention on Elimination of All Forms of Discrimination against Women (CEDAW) and Iran's Contemporary Laws. Iran: Qatreh, 1999.

Violence against Women in Iran. Tehran: Roshangaran, 2000.

The Burned Palms. Tehran: Roshangaran, 2001.

Legal Obstacles against Political Development in Iran. Iran: Qatreh, 2001.

Women's Participation in Politics: Obstacles and Possibilities. Tehran: Roshangaran, 2001.

NAHID KESHAVARZ AND MAHBOUBEH HOSSEINZADEH

On April 2, 2007, women's rights activists Nahid Keshavarz and Mahboubeh Hosseinzadeh were arrested at Laleh Park, Tehran, while collecting signatures in support of the One Million Signatures Campaign.

During the thirteen days of their detention, their attorney, Nasrin

Sotudeh, was denied access to their files. Family members were prevented from posting bail on their behalf. Sadigheh Keshavarz, Nahid's sister, said: "I went to the court in an effort to post bail for my sister. But court officials instead asked me why I had come. They said that the case against my sister was no concern of mine."[247]

During the interrogations, the women were asked to sign a statement agreeing to end their activities in the campaign. Refusing to do so, the two women were charged with "actions against national security."[248] They were told that the demands of the campaign with respect to equal rights to inheritance for women, equal value of testimony of men and women, equal financial remuneration for bodily injury or death, and the elimination of polygamy were in contradiction with the tenets of Islam.[249]

Keshavarz, a sociologist and journalist, is a member of the Women's Cultural Center, a leading women's NGO in Tehran. Hosseinzadeh, a journalist, is a member of the Iran Civil Society Organizations Training and Research Center, which has been shut down by security forces.

The women were released on April 15, 2007, with a surety of $20,000 to be paid if they flee. Both are still awaiting trial.

AZAR MAJEDI (IRAN/UK)

> Women are the first victims of political Islam and Islamic terrorist gangs. Sexual apartheid, stoning, compulsory Islamic veil and covering and stripping women of all rights are the fruits of this reactionary and fascistic movement. Political Islam has committed countless crimes both where they are in power, like the Islamic Republic in Iran, the Mujahedin and the Taliban in Afghanistan, in the Sudan and Saudi Arabia, and where they are in opposition, as in Algeria. . . . Terrorising the population is the policy and strategy of this force for seizing power.[250]

Azar Majedi is known for her defense of women's rights and egalitarian ideas. As founder of the Organization for Women's Liberation—Iran,[251] she has worked tirelessly for the advancement of women and in response to the need to challenge what she sees as political Islam.

Born in Iran, Majedi completed her university education abroad. When she returned to Iran in 1978, she began to work against the dictatorial regime in her homeland. Since her university days, she has been active in the defense of women's rights and was responsible for the celebration of International Women's Day in Iran in 1979. She has also written many articles and pamphlets, has a long association with the Left, and has been the subject of interviews in various media, including *Time* magazine and the *International Herald Tribune*.

In 1979, while establishing herself as an ardent activist, she also began her life with Mansoor Hikmat. He, like Majedi, was politically active and came from an educated, secular, left-wing family. According to Majedi, theirs was "a beautiful life."[252] Following the revolution in Iran, left-wing parties and opposition groups were faced with increasing pressure from the authorities.

> In 1982 when the Islamic Republic had begun brutal attacks against all the left and opposition groups, torturing and killing thousands, she and her husband were forced to escape from the security forces and left for Kurdistan.[253]

It was after they decided to flee that Hikmat established the Communist Party of Iran (CPI). Majedi and her husband moved to Europe in 1984 and she continued to work for women's rights. She now lives in the United Kingdom. Her political activities have included working with the International Campaign for the Defense of Women's Rights in Iran, as well as cofounding the Center for Women and Socialism.

In 1991, Hikmat and Majedi both left the CPI, and Hikmat became one of the founders of the Worker-Communist Party of Iran (WPI). Majedi, along with other members of the CPI, followed him in establishing this new communist party at the time of the collapse of the USSR. She is still a member of the WPI leadership and is active in raising awareness of various issues, including sexual apartheid:

> When we talk about sexual apartheid in Iran, we are in fact pointing to its similarity with the racial apartheid of South Africa. In Iran, women and men are segregated from each other and women are deprived of their rights. This segregation is the very same apartheid. We began calling the Islamic Republic of Iran a system of sexual apartheid in our literature over 15 years ago.[254]

Iranian women have lived under sexual apartheid, with almost no rights. At the same time, a strong struggle led by both the women themselves and opposition forces fighting for freedom and equality of sexual rights is underway.[255]

Majedi has organized a number of international conferences dealing with political Islam and women's rights, making sure that female activists who support the Islamic constitution have not been invited to speak:

We shall never allow pawns of the regime, those who are [an] integral part of the system's machine of violence, of murder, of executions, of dictatorship to come outside and put on a liberal and democratic mask to better whitewash the Islamic Republic.[256]

Shirin Ebadi was permitted to attend a conference, but Majedi has been cautious about inviting such activists to her conferences, as it could suit the regime's agenda:

I think the balance of forces has changed in Iran. . . . The change has taken place not because the Islamic Republic has become more liberal, more democratic, but because the people have forced it to yield, to accept compromise. The other reason is that the regime can also take some advantages by authorising these ladies to come, claiming that it is not as dictatorial as portrayed.[257]

Majedi's assessment of life in Iran has been critical of both the Islamic Republic and the shah:

Look at the history of Iran. The last 20 years have been some of the darkest in people's lives, especially women's. The Islamic regime has brought nothing but repression, death, torture, lack of rights and dark reaction. Things weren't [much] better before either. The truth is that the situation of women in Iran is so bad today that some people forget—or want to forget—how it was under the Shah's regime. . . . Even at that time Islamic laws were in force against women. Women were not free. . . . At that time too the political system was one of repression, torture and persecution.[258]

However, Majedi does make a distinction between political Islam, that is, the Islam of the Republic, and that of prerevolutionary Iran:

One of the [worst] stumbling blocks against the freedom of women in Iran is the ruling theocracy. The difference [between] this Islam [and] the one before the revolution is that this one is political, with its police, armies, prisons, revolutionary guards, justice, [and] hezbollah militia that suppresses people. This is a different Islam. As a result, we fight this regime on two fronts: political and religious. . . . Our struggle is not against the Muslims . . . but against a political regime based on religion. There can't be compromises with a regime that has made sexual apartheid, humiliation of women, its own identity.[259]

She also believes that the Iranian people were "duped" by the Islamic regime. Iranians had aspired to more rights but not to a repressive theocracy:

An Islamic regime came to power after the revolution with freedom and justice on its agenda, but it . . . [organized] a very brutal oppression of the whole population, in order to establish the kind of regime we witness today.[260]

In her book *Women's Rights vs. Political Islam*, Majedi develops many of her central ideas. She has also published a journal titled *Reflections*, and is the editor of *Medusa*,[261] a publication dealing with women's issues. From 1999 until 2002, she was director of Radio International, which broadcasts into Iran, and has appeared on ITV, Voice of America, and the BBC.

In 2002, Majedi was chairperson of the Organization for Women's Liberation—Iran (OWL)—which campaigns against stoning, political executions, gender discrimination, and women's rights violations. During the international conference titled "Why Is Secularism Necessary?" held by OWL on the occasion of International Women's Day, March 8, 2009, Azar Majedi presented resolutions condemning the Islamic Republic of Iran for suppression of women and gender apartheid and advocating "the necessity of building an international secularist movement for women's liberation."[262]

Women were the first social strata of the society to be suppressed by the Islamic regime. The imposition of Islamic laws, such as the compulsory veil, gender segregation in public places, negation of the right to divorce or custody of children for women, and the subsequent punishments for defying these laws, such as arrests, imprisonment, stoning and execution, have all made life a hell for millions of women in Iran.

However, what we are witnessing is the growing women's movement to combat women's suppression and humiliation. Women in Iran demand freedom, equality, separation of religion from state, and an end to sexual apartheid. OWL belongs to this movement. We regard political Islam as one of the main obstacles in the path of women's movement for change, especially in the Middle Eastern countries.[263]

ZIBA MIR-HOSSEINI (IRAN/UK)

Both in Paris and later in Iran, [Ayatollah Khomeini] repeatedly assured women that "Islam" had the best program for the advancement of women and protection of their rights. This was in line with the belief of the masses of women from the so-called traditional classes who gave their whole-hearted support to the revolution. For them, like other Muslim women, Islam had always been associated with justice and human dignity.[264]

Ziba Mir-Hosseini obtained her BA in sociology from Tehran University in 1974 and her PhD in social anthropology from the University of Cambridge in 1980. She supported the Iranian Revolution of 1979, and she returned there, having gained her doctorate, in 1980. Her Western academic training, however, did not endear her to the new regime and she was considered too "young and modern" to become a lecturer at Tehran University.[265] Mir-Hosseini believes that the sense of betrayal she experienced was one that many Iranian women felt after the revolution:

Women felt that the very men they loved—their fathers, brothers and husbands—had tacitly colluded with the state in depriving them of what they considered to be their rights. What made the matter more painful for believing women activists was that religion gave these men the authority and legitimacy to do this. It was then that the seeds of a new dissent were planted.[266]

In 1984, Mir-Hosseini divorced her husband and left Iran for the United Kingdom. Eventually she achieved her ambition: to lecture at the School of Oriental and African Studies (SOAS) at the University of London. She is a research associate in the Department of Social Anthropology at the University of Cambridge and a senior research associate at the Middle East Institute at SOAS. She also works as a freelance researcher and independent consultant on Islam and law, gender, family relations, and development issues.[267]

Mir-Hosseini has held numerous research fellowships and several appointments including Hauser Global Law Visiting Professor at the School of Law, New York University (2002, 2004, 2006). Her published books include *Marriage on Trial: A Study of Family Law in Iran and Morocco*,[268] which she researched in the Tehran family law courts and in Morocco; *Feminism and the Islamic Republic: Dialogues with the Ulema*;[269] *Islam and Gender: The Religious Debate in Contemporary Islam*;[270] and, with Richard Tapper, *Islam and Democracy in Iran: Eshkevari and the Quest for Reform*.[271] Mir-Hosseini has also codirected two award-winning documentaries: *Divorce Iranian Style* (1998) and *Runaway* (2001).[272]

Mir-Hosseini's books and films do not gloss over the harsh realities of life for women in Iran or the injustice of their treatment in the family courts, but she does see grounds for optimism. She considers herself a representative of a new Iranian feminist movement committed to reconciling the Muslim faith with democracy and gender equality. She doesn't see Islamic law as revealed, sacred, and fixed; rather, she argues, it is human, local, and multiple. Most important, she points out, it has reacted historically to social practice and human experience and therefore, she believes, it can incorporate feminist values.[273]

She believes that egalitarianism is inherent in shari'ah law and is compatible with women's rights, but the situation will not improve until women participate in the production of knowledge in Islamic law.[274] "Women's legal rights," she says, "must now be raised and addressed within a religious framework, where the jurisprudential construction of gender can be reexamined and gender inequality can be redressed."[275] This inequality, she believes, is the major issue that faces Iran in its domestic policy, and educated, proactive women who "have mastered religious speech and traditional discourse" have now begun "to use their mastery to secure their rights."[276]

Feminist Islamic scholarship is trying to unearth the facts that were there. We can't be afraid to look at legal tradition critically.[277]

Reform in favor of Muslim women's rights is inevitable and will be powerful, Mir-Hosseini believes: "There's so much tension and energy there now. It will be a flood."[278]

AZAR NAFISI (IRAN/USA)

I felt . . . from [the] late 1980's, that this illusion with the revolution began with the youth who had been very revolutionary, who were even hostage takers, they were quoting Imam Khomeini before, and now, they're quoting Hannah Arendt, and Karl Popper, and going to jail for it. They understand . . . the price of individual freedom the way my generation could never understand.[279]

Azar Nafisi was born in Tehran in December 1955, the daughter of Ahmad Nafisi, a former mayor of Tehran, who was imprisoned by the shah in the 1970s, and Nezhat Nafisi, one of the first six women to be elected to the Iranian parliament in 1963. Azar grew up in Iran but was sent to school in Lancaster, United Kingdom, when she was thirteen, completed her last year of high school in the United States, and went on to gain a PhD in English and American literature from the University of Oklahoma and a fellowship from Oxford University.[280]

> No wonder when Ayatollah Khomeini came in, the most important thing for him was to change the women's situation. The men in these countries become very scared when women become conscious.[281]

In 1979, the year Iran became an Islamic republic, Nafisi returned and took up the post of professor of English literature at the University of Tehran, "where she became known for advocating on behalf of Iran's intellectuals, youth and especially young women." However, she was dismissed from the university in 1981, having chosen to stay at home rather than wear the Islamic veil.[282]

> The regime used the idea of the veil, the fact that women's hair is supposed to tempt men . . . as an ideology . . . a tool of control. Because you would all look alike. And you would all look the way that the guy who was ruling

your country told you to look. This was extreme form of control. And you see it in all totalitarian states.[283]

For Nafisi, the imposition of mandatory veiling for women was a usurpation of Islam,

> changing what had been a freely chosen expression of religious faith into a rote act imposed on them by the state.
>
> My grandmother was . . . [an] intensely religious woman who never parted with her chador, she was nonetheless outraged at those who had defiled her religion by using violence to impose their interpretation of it on her grandchildren. "This is not Islam!" she would insist.

Nafisi extended this argument to point out that the regime in Iran was acting against the values of the faith by legislating to coerce religious observance.[284] She observed, however, that life "in those societies is not dangerous because you know . . . this is against the law, and this is not. The most dangerous thing about ordinary people living in these countries is the arbitrary nature of the law. . . . It is based on the will of the individuals who decide at one moment or another what to do."[285]

Nafisi did not return to teaching until 1987, when she lectured briefly at the Free Islamic University and Shahid Beheshti University, then for a number of years at Allameh Tabatabai University. However, in 1995, constant harassment by the authorities made it impossible for her to conduct classes properly. She gave up her teaching position and, for the next two years, held weekly study meetings in her own home with seven of her most committed female students. The group studied literary works including *Lolita*, *Madame Bovary*, *The Great Gatsby*, and the novels of Henry James and Jane Austen. The meetings were conducted in secret because such works had been banned in Iran since the revolution.[286]

After eighteen years in Iran, Nafisi moved back to the United States in June 1997, where she wrote *Reading* Lolita *in Tehran: A Memoir in Books*.[287] The narrative revisits the days of Nafisi's secret study group and is an exploration of literary works against the backdrop of life in postrevolutionary Iran. The central theme is that literature has the power to create meaning, space, and identity even for those within the iron grip of a totalitarian regime. As a metaphor, Nafisi chose Nabokov's novel:

The desperate truth of Lolita's story is . . . the confiscation of one individual's life by another. The parallel to women's lives is clear: we had become the figment of someone else's dreams. A stern ayatollah, a self-proclaimed philosopher-king, had come to rule our land. . . . And he now wanted to re-create us.[288]

Reading Lolita was received enthusiastically by both readers and critics; it was on the *New York Times* best seller list for more than two years and has been translated into more than thirty languages. It received the 2004 Non-fiction Book of the Year Award from Booksense, the Frederic W. Ness Book Award, the 2004 Latifeh Yarsheter Book Award, and an Achievement Award from the American Immigration Law Foundation; and it was a finalist for the 2004 PEN/Martha Albrand Award for the Art of the Memoir. In 2006, Nafisi won a Persian Golden Lioness Award for literature, presented by the World Academy of Arts, Literature, and Media.[289]

The most notorious and adverse response to *Reading* Lolita was that of Hamid Dabashi, professor of Iranian studies and comparative literature at Columbia University. In April 2006, Dabashi, alarmed at Seymour Hirsh's report that the Pentagon was considering the use of nuclear weapons against Iran, sent his review of *Reading* Lolita, which he had written three years earlier, to the Egyptian newspaper *Al-Ahram*. On August 4, 2006, he gave an interview to *Znet* magazine, reiterating and expanding his original comments.[290]

Dabashi sees *Reading* Lolita *in Tehran* as a prime example of "the body of mémoire by people from an Islamic background that has over the last half a decade, ever since the commencement of its 'War on Terrorism,' flooded the US market":

This body of literature . . . ordinarily points to legitimate concerns about the plight of Muslim women in the Islamic world and yet puts that predicament squarely at the service of the US ideological psy-op. . . . The US is now engaged in a prolonged and open-ended war with terrorism. This terrorism has an ostensibly "Islamic" disposition and provenance. "Islam" in this particular reading is vile, violent, and above all abusive of women—and thus fighting against Islamic terrorism, ipso facto, is also to save Muslim women from the evil of their men.[291]

Dabashi accused Nafisi of being a "comprador intellectual," a collaborator in the service of US imperialism in its efforts to create an intellectual atmosphere conducive to US aggression against Iran. Dabashi was also incensed that Nafisi chose to ignore Iranian literature and to favor "Western classics," which, he argues, is both dismissive of Iranian literature and a blow to the struggle for the inclusion of multicultural and postcolonial perspectives in the contemporary academic curriculum.[292]

Dabashi's review is considered extreme, not least because of its scathing tone and ad hominem approach. The consensus in the field is that Nafisi is "not a willing agent of American imperial ambition." She did not support the war in Iraq, she is no longer with the Benador agency, and she numbers more radicals among her friends than conservatives.[293]

Nafisi has written for numerous publications, including the *New York Times*, the *Washington Post*, the *Wall Street Journal*, the *Los Angeles Times*, the *Baltimore Sun*, and the *New Republic*. Her published works include *Anti-Terra: A Critical Study of Vladimir Nabokov's Novels* (1994); and chapters in *Eye of the Storm: Women in Post-Revolutionary Iran* (1992), *Muslim Women and Politics of Participation* (1997), *Religious Fundamentalisms and the Human Rights of Women* (1999), and *Republic of the Imagination* (2006).

She is a visiting professor and director of the Dialogue Project at the Foreign Policy Institute of Johns Hopkins University's School of Advanced International Studies in Washington, DC, where she lectures in aesthetics, culture, and literature. She is also a trustee of the Foundation for Iranian Studies and of Freedom House.[294]

MARYAM NAMAZIE (IRAN/UK)

My parents are Muslims and they are nice people. There are plenty— the majority—of Muslims who are nice people. But political Islam is not nice. It routinely takes away the rights of women and children, and it threatens and terrorises those who will not come into line with its ideology.[295]

People in Iran have for decades been massacred, annihilated and beheaded for insulting and offending Islam—whether by improper veiling, for their sexual relations and sexuality, political opposition to god's rule on earth, demands for basic rights, and even for simply

*dancing, laughing, [and] listening to music. . . . [T]his political move-
ment has to be challenged and stopped.*[296]

Maryam Namazie was born in 1968 in Tehran. Her grandfather was a mullah
and her father, a journalist, was brought up as a strict Muslim. Namazie left
Iran, however, at the age of thirteen with her mother when the Islamic
Republic was established in 1979. "There were beatings, acid was thrown in
women's faces, and there were executions on television every day."[297] At first,
they lived in Delhi, India, and when her father and younger sister joined
them, they moved to the United Kingdom. Finally, the family settled in the
United States, where Namazie went to university.[298]

After graduating, she worked with Ethiopian refugees in the Sudan as
part of the United Nations Development Programme. When an Islamic government took power in the Sudan, Namazie started a clandestine human
rights network to document government activities, but was discovered and
threatened by Sudan's security services. The UN then arranged for her to
leave the country.[299]

On her return to the United States in 1991, she established the Committee
for Humanitarian Assistance to Iranian Refugees. Namazie was then elected
executive director of the International Federation of Iranian Refugees (IFIR),
which now has more than forty branches in a number of countries.[300] IFIR campaigns against the deportation of Iranian refugees to Iran and has successfully
lobbied the governments of Germany, Sweden, Turkey, and Canada on various
refugee and human rights issues.[301] In 1994, Namazie produced a documentary
on the situation of Iranian refugees in Turkey and successfully campaigned for
an extension to the period in which asylum seekers can apply for asylum.

In 2005, Namazie won the UK National Secular Society's "Secularist of
the Year" award, which raised her international profile.[302] In 2006, together
with Salman Rushdie and Irshad Manji, she was one of twelve signatories to
a letter published in response to the "Muhammad cartoons" controversy.
Titled "Manifesto: Together Facing the New Totalitarianism," the document
is a declaration of the need to fight for secular values and personal freedom
in the face of Islamic totalitarianism.[303]

Namazie's most prominent role is head of the Council of Ex-Muslims of
Britain (CEMB), which represents former Muslims whose renunciation of
Islam has put them in danger from Islamists. CEMB was launched in the
United Kingdom on June 22, 2007. The council demands the freedom to

criticize religion, calls for the separation of religion from the state, and the protection of children from religious indoctrination. It opposes the death sentence that exists under shari'ah law for apostates and calls for an end to all forms of religious intimidation. The council is sponsored by the British Humanist Association and the National Secular Society, and many members of the organization are Iranian exiles:

> We are quite certain we represent a majority in Europe and a vast secular and humanist protest movement in countries like Iran.[304]

CEMB believes that concern for political correctness in liberal democracies is causing them to respect minority and religious rights above human rights: "'Every human is equal' does not mean that every belief is equal."[305]

Namazie refers to Islam as "a reactionary right wing movement" to which violence and oppression are intrinsic. In the UK and in Canada, she has campaigned successfully against the introduction of shari'ah law, which she considers to be "fundamentally discriminatory and misogynist."[306]

She is a member of the Central Committee of the Worker-Communist Party of Iran (WPI), the secretary of the International Relations Committee of the party, and the editor of its English newspaper, *WPI Briefing*. The Worker-Communist Party seeks to replace the Islamic Republic of Iran with a socialist republic.[307]

A leading activist within the Organization for Women's Liberation (OWL), Namazie hosts a weekly program, *TV International/English*, which is broadcast via satellite to the Middle East and Europe, and on the Internet. She is also the spokesperson of Equal Rights Now, an organization that campaigns against discrimination of women in Iran and is involved in the Third Camp, which opposes both the use of military power by the United States and also Islamic terrorism.[308]

LILI POURZAND (IRAN/CANADA)

> *The Iranian policewomen usually [come] from sectors that experience all the problems [faced by] women in a patriarchal society. [So] how could they [use] their clubs to silence the peaceful outcry of the Iranian women who went out to the streets to demonstrate and*

demand the restoration of their rights? How could they [beat them]
till they bled and [then] lead them like born criminals, handcuffed, to
unfamiliar and frightening detention facilities?[309]

In 2006, Pourzand highlighted the Iranian government's new method of
exploiting women under the pretense of "involving them in society" when
she wrote about the use of the women-only police force to break up demonstrations of women activists:

> The Iranian authorities have presented this activity as an innovation within
> the male-dominated system that controls the Iranian security forces, and
> have carried out an intensive propaganda campaign as evidence of the
> inclusive nature of the Iranian security forces.[310]

Pourzand was shocked at images of chador-clad women beating peaceful protestors with clubs and sticks and incredulous at their lack of insight and
empathy with the women activists.

> How can we believe that none among the Iranian policewomen object to
> being forced to live with their husbands because it is impossible for them
> to sue for divorce? . . . that their hearts are not bleeding because they have
> no right to custody of their children in case of divorce or separation? Should
> one of their daughters be murdered by a man, how can we believe that the
> mother would be happy that the blood-price paid for the murder of her
> daughter is half the sum paid for [the murder of] a man? And if she
> demands that the murderer of her daughter be punished, [will she happily
> accept the fact] that the law requires her to pay the murderer's family a
> double [sum] for her daughter's blood (that is, a sum equivalent to the full
> blood-price for a man)? How can we believe that the Iranian policewoman
> is happy to inherit only an eighth of her deceased husband's property?[311]

Journalist Lili Pourzand, a member of the Ontario Iranian Women's Association, has written articles and given interviews about the discrimination suffered by Iranian women, which she believes stems from inherent flaws in the
country's political and legal systems that demote women to the status of
second-class citizens. For example, women will be stoned to death if found
guilty of adultery, whereas men will never be charged with adultery because
the law allows them to take "temporary" wives.[312]

In the last two decades, many, many Iranian women inside and outside Iran [have] started different kinds of movements to get more rights for Iranian women and to be able to participate more in political and social positions. And these movements are from different kinds of points of view. Some of them are secular. Some of them are religious and some of them are reformist. But, no matter what is their point of view, the most important thing is that they all know the current legislation and legal system of Iran doesn't work for Iranian women.[313]

Activists like Lili Pourzand face frustration in trying to overturn the discriminatory laws:

We are trapped in a circle in our legislation system because anything that needs to be approved from the Parliament has to go to another supreme parliament . . . the Guardian Council. And the Guardian Council's duty is to approve the laws according to Sharia. And most of the time it's not getting approved from that. So, really our way is blocked.[314]

MARYAM RAJAVI (IRAN/FRANCE)

Let there be no doubt that the peddlers of religion who rule Iran in the name of Islam, but shed blood, suppress the people and advocate export of fundamentalism and terrorism, are themselves the worst enemies of Islam and Muslims.[315]

Born to a middle-class family in Tehran in 1953, Maryam Rajavi has a degree in metallurgy and was a university student leader during the anti-shah movement. One of her sisters was executed by the shah's regime. Another died under torture while eight months pregnant during Khomeini's era and her husband was also executed during Khomeini's rule.[316]

Since 1993, Maryam Rajavi has been the president-elect of the National Council of Resistance of Iran (NCRI), a self-styled parliament in exile based in France and dedicated to a future secular parliamentary democracy in Iran. The NCRI poses a serious oppositional challenge to the ruling clerics of Iran. Their platform affirms women's rights to elect and be elected, their freedom to choose any occupation or public office, including the presidency, equal pay for equal work, free choice of clothing, freedom to choose their husbands, equal rights in divorce, prohibition of polygamy, elimination of legal discrimination in court testimony, guardianship, custody, and inheritance, and free choice of clothing.[317] This pro-women philosophy is displayed clearly within the NCRI, where women make up half the members and hold senior positions of responsibility.

The armed wing of the NCRI, the People's Mojahedin Organization of Iran (PMOI),[318] was established in the 1960s. Professing an Islamist and Marxist ideology, the PMOI helped overthrow the shah in the 1979 revolution.[319] However, the group rapidly turned against the theocratic regime. During the Iran-Iraq war in the 1980s, the group allied with Saddam Hussein.[320]

Members of the PMOI are based in Iran and Iraq and have provided intelligence about Iran's nuclear program and assistance to the Iraqi insurgency. The movement, however, was charged with terrorist involvement in Iran and Europe, and its political headquarters outside Paris were raided in 2003.[321] The PMOI was designated as a terrorist organization by the United States, Canada, and various European countries, a listing the group fought to overturn after renouncing terrorism.[322] On January 26, 2009, to the chagrin of Iran, the European Union announced the delisting of the PMOI as a terrorist organization.[323]

Maryam Rajavi has spoken out against the 2008 elections held in Iran, declaring them "nothing but a farce."[324] The PMOI monitored 25,000 out of 45,000 polling stations and found that about 95 percent of eligible voters boycotted the elections.[325]

Rajavi firmly believes that the NCRI is the only organization capable of harnessing the enormous antiregime potential within Iran as the antithesis to Islamic fundamentalism: "one cannot fight fundamentalism with an anti-Islamic culture. The only way to confront it is to offer a modern and lenient Islam."[326]

SHADI SADR

My grandmother wasn't allowed the life she wanted. I was lucky. I achieved everything but the struggle was still hard. I don't want the dearest person in my life—my daughter—to have the same obstacles.[327]

In a country like Iran, generally, being a woman is hard. What's harder is being a social activist, and in particular if you're an advocate of women's rights. For the publication of my articles regarding women, not only do I have trouble with the traditionalists, but also with people who consider themselves modern. The former don't recognize equal rights for men and women, the latter believe that women's rights are not a priority, that our concern must be democracy first, women's rights second. I've never been to jail, but I have a criminal file because my crime is that I spoke out at the Ghazvin University against polygamy. Because of this they said my speech was blasphemous.[328]

Shadi Sadr was born in Tehran in 1974. At the age of fifteen, she won a writing competition run by a youth magazine, *Sorush-e-Nojavan* (Youth Call), and was invited to contribute articles to the magazine. Sadr went on to write for various reformist publications throughout her twenties, but despite being promoted within several news organizations, she was not eligible, as a woman, to become an executive editor or to join an editorial board. In order to write without censure, she started the Women in Iran Web site in 2001 to document and discuss Iranian women's issues.

In 2003, when she discovered that the authorities were filtering the Web site, she investigated the matter and confronted the Ministry of Communications and Information Technology. When the ministry denied filtering, Sadr found a journalist who was also a member of parliament to assist her, and they proved to other parliamentarians that her site was indeed inaccessible and had not been publishing antigovernment or sexually explicit material. Shortly afterward, the restrictions were lifted.[329] Sadr is editor-in-chief of the Meydaan (Women's Field) Web site,[330] which, in May 2008, was reported as having been blocked by government authorities.[331]

Sadr gained a master's degree in law and political science from Tehran University. In 2003, she passed her bar exams and cofounded the Rahi Legal Center to give affordable advice to women and NGOs on human rights issues (the center was closed on March 15, 2007). The center, staffed by volunteers, defended numerous controversial cases on a pro bono basis,[332] and Sadr secured the release of eight women condemned to death for adultery.[333] She has frequently been subjected to interrogation by Iran's security forces, but in spite of the dangers, she has defended, and brought to world attention, human rights cases no one else would accept.[334]

Alongside her legal work, Sadr continued to write articles for newspapers, magazines, and journals and to speak on women's and human rights issues in Iran and internationally. In 2004, she traveled to New York to receive the Ida B. Wells Award for Bravery in Journalism.[335] In her acceptance speech, she outlined some of the developments in the struggle for Iranian women's rights:

> [First,] we can now observe a rapid growth of various feminist groups at the universities and colleges throughout the country.
>
> Second, women organizations, despite their ideological differences, have just begun the process of forming national consulting networks based on common goals and objectives.
>
> Third, thanks to the Internet, Web sites and Weblogs, new bridges between Iranian women in Diaspora and those inside Iran are built and old ones are strengthened.[336]

In 2005, the Iranian government refused to renew Sadr's passport, so as to prevent her from traveling abroad.

Sadr helped launch the Stop Stoning Forever campaign in October 2006. A resolution against stoning was passed by the European Parliament six weeks later.[337] Largely made up of lawyers, journalists, and academics, the Stop Stoning Forever organization is determined to put an end to the practice of stoning people to death for offenses such as adultery. Stoning is legal in Afghanistan, Iran, Iraq, Pakistan, Saudi Arabia, Sudan, the United Arab Emirates, and parts of Nigeria. Many Muslim nations, including Malaysia, Indonesia, Tunisia, and Algeria, have banned the practice. In Pakistan and Iraq, stonings are usually carried out by communities. State-sanctioned stonings have mostly occurred in Iran, where, under the Islamic penal code, stoning is a punishment for adultery and similar transgressions. The ancient custom was revived by the authorities after the Islamic Revolution in 1979.

Most of those killed by stoning are women. Under Iranian law, a man can divorce his wife easily, can take more than one wife, and can even have "temporary" wives. A woman in Iran, however, does not have the same rights as a man to divorce or claim custody of children. Girls can be forced into arranged marriages from the age of thirteen, and for women, there is little hope of escape from a marriage, however abusive the husband might be. If a woman is raped, moreover, she may be perceived as having brought dishonor upon her family and be considered immoral and deserving of punishment. The laws against moral transgressions, already heavily prejudiced against women, are imposed by male judges with a standard of proof "within the judge's knowledge."[338]

When people are to be stoned, they are ritually washed, dressed in a white kaftan, and buried up to the neck in the ground. The stones are thrown by a crowd of people from the community, which may include the family and in-laws of the victim. Regulations require that the stones be neither too small, so that they inflict too little damage, nor so large that the ordeal is over too quickly.

> The parliament and the judiciary have the power to change the law. The only thing that we can do is to show that public stoning sentences continue to be issued and executions by public stonings continue to be carried out across the country. For example . . . two women were stoned in Mashad, and that news of their execution was published on the internet in a matter of hours. The reaction of the international community to that news forced the Iranian government to stop public stonings for two years. If lawmakers and judges continue to face that type of opposition and pressure, there are enough human rights and international laws that they can use to change these type[s] of laws completely.[339]

In 2002, when the Stop Stoning Forever campaign started to draw world-wide attention to the issue, the head of Iran's judiciary announced a ban on stoning. Campaign activists then formed a commission (Iran's Stoning Fact Finding Commission) to investigate and protest the stoning sentences that are, in fact, still being carried out, although the judiciary officially denies that the practice continues. Members of the campaign stress that this punishment is a form of torture, imposed for moral offenses rather than actual crimes, and that it contravenes Iran's international commitments to human rights.[340] Since the campaign was launched, six people have been saved from stoning, others have been granted stays of execution, and some cases are being reviewed or retried.[341] More recently, the campaign has confined its activities to individual cases in Iran and merged with the Global Campaign to Stop Killing and Stoning Women, which is coordinated by Women Living under Muslim Laws (WLUML).[342]

Sadr and other Iranian lawyers believe the campaign has made Iran's judges more sensitive to public opinion on stonings and executions,[343] but Dr. Mohammad Javad Larijani, secretary general of Iran's Human Rights Committee, stated recently that the Iranian authorities are not ashamed of retaining stoning as a sentencing option in Iranian law.[344] Dr. Larijani considers the protests against stoning to be part of a political campaign against Iran mounted by Western nations over the past thirty years, and he reserves the right of Iran to interpret international human rights agreements in the context of its societal values. He asserts that state-sanctioned stoning practically never occurs in Iran, but he considers it to be appropriate retribution for the "atrocity" of adultery and points out that it is considered a lesser punishment than the death sentence, because "in stoning, the defendant has a chance to survive."[345]

On March 4, 2007, Sadr was one of thirty-three women arrested in Tehran while protesting the prosecution of several women involved in a peaceful demonstration for gender equality. While the other women were released, Sadr was held with one other activist until March 19, before being released on $225,000 bail.[346] While Sadr was interned in Evin prison in Tehran, her legal offices were searched. Her practice was officially closed by agents of the Tehran Court of Revolution, allegedly because of international funding sources.[347] The Iranian government has been targeting NGOs for investigation and closure since the American and Dutch governments made funds available for dissenting political groups, including feminist organizations, in Iran.[348]

Sadr was summoned to court in August 2007 and charged with illegal assembly, collusion against national security, disruption of public order, and refusing to obey police orders at the time of her arrest. No verdict has yet been issued. Some of the women who were arrested with her have had the charges against them dropped, but others have been sentenced to flogging and suspended prison sentences.[349]

MAHSA SHEKARLOO

The laws in Iran are so horrific, that women here are basically rendered incapable of doing anything.[350]

Tehran-based feminist journalist Mahsa Shekarloo aims to provide a platform for women in Iran via her online magazine, *Badjens*.

Shekarloo, who came to Iran from the United States in 2000, created *Badjens* (meaning disreputable or sly) as a vehicle to discuss gender inequalities in Iran.

I wanted to see what women were doing, and I realized that they were doing a lot more than I knew, and I was very surprised how active they were. . . . Badjens had many goals, but one of the main goals is not only to bring information outside of Iran, but also . . . help women in Iran come out of [their] particular kind of isolation.[351]

Badjens has reported on topics such as the Islamist attitude toward the rise of prostitution in Iran and the case of Saeed Hanei. Hanei claimed that his murder of sixteen prostitutes in the city of Mashad in 2000 to 2002 was justified according to Islamic law, as he was only destroying corruption in Iranian society. Conservative newspapers sprang to his defense. According to Shekarloo, he was "heralded as a religious do-gooder who had committed necessary killings sanctioned by Islam."[352] When it was discovered that Hanei had had sex with his victims, he lost conservative support and was executed in 2002.

For Shekarloo, the episode exposed the hypocrisy on which Iranian society's sexual politics is based. "Hanei highlighted Iranian society's increasing failure to regulate sexual practices and norms of morality."[353]

Despite the fact that the case sparked a national scandal, the women's movement was largely silent:

Zanan magazine covered the story, but only by way of examining Hanei. . . . Prostitution as sexual institution or economic market was never discussed.[354]

Shekarloo is a signatory to the One Million Signatures Campaign and a founder of the Women's Cultural Center, an NGO in Tehran that helped to organize the June 12, 2005, sit-in for women's rights in front of the University of Tehran. In the largest female coalition since the Islamic Revolution of 1979, more than two thousand women attended, representing over ninety women's groups:

The sit-in was a declaration that the system's fundamental legal structure precludes the possibility of realizing women's full rights, and by extension, meaningful democracy.

In the words of a slogan repeatedly chanted at the sit-in: "Equal rights is our minimum demand."[355]

Male reformers believe the struggle for democracy has priority over women's rights. In response, the women who organized the sit-in stated: "Democracy cannot be achieved without freedom and equal rights."[356]

Women activists are mostly middle class and university educated. According to Shekarloo, the alliance includes both pious and secular women: religious women who avoid the term feminist; "Islamic feminists" who insist that women's rights can be provided within the framework of Islamic law; "Muslim feminists" who come from religious backgrounds but do not promote Islamic law; and feminists who advocate a secular republic in Iran.[357]

SHAHLA SHERKAT AND *ZANAN* MAGAZINE

> *I keep careful track of all the unfair things legislators say about women. And then, when they run for office, I publish all the quotes alongside their pictures so women will know not to vote for them.*[358]

Shahla Sherkat was born on March 30, 1956, in Isfahan, Iran. She gained a degree in psychology from Tehran University and a certificate in journalism from the Keyhan Institute Iran, and she worked as a journalist for over twenty years.[359]

From 1979 to 1980, Sherkat was the assistant editor of *Rah-e Zeynab* (Zeynab's Path), a weekly, government-owned women's magazine. From 1980 to 1982, she worked in the publishing department of the production company Kanoon-e Parvaresh Fekri. From 1982 to 1990, she edited *Zan-e-ruz* (Today's Woman). This was a state-funded publication, and after several disagreements over the magazine's conservative coverage of women's issues, Sherkat was dismissed.[360]

Before she left, however, Sherkat got permission from the authorities to establish a new magazine, *Zanan*, meaning "women" in Farsi.[361] The monthly magazine was established in 1992, with a staff of five, and over the next sixteen years it became the most widely read and influential publication on women's issues in the country.[362]

Many commentators have noted that *Zanan* lasted so long and remained true to its purpose because of Sherkat's intelligence and subtlety in dealing with issues to which religious and political authorities might object. Sherkat is a devout Muslim and her staff scrupulously complied with dress codes and, for the most part, with government mandates. The publication generally took a moderate line and avoided politics unless they directly affected women's rights. Over the years, *Zanan* explored numerous sensitive topics including Iran's divorce and custody laws, polygamy, prostitution, a feminist exegesis of shari'ah, the government's inadequate response to HIV/AIDS, domestic abuse, child abuse, women in prison, gender discrimination in the university system, and international women's issues.[363] The magazine gained many thousands of subscribers in Iran and among expatriate communities.

> *Zanan* has provided a pluralist forum for women's voices from diverse ide-
> ological and cultural backgrounds. *Zanan*'s license holder, editor and man-
> ager, Shahla Sherkat has represented a gradual shift among numerous
> Muslim women activists from radical Islamism to a liberal spiritualism and
> egalitarian reformism and pragmatic feminism. . . . each issue includes
> enlightening sections on social problems and contentious issues.[364]

Zanan was credited with helping to get President Khatami elected in 1997, when he was interviewed in the magazine and featured on the cover, while the three other candidates declined to be interviewed. Khatami was voted in by an overwhelming proportion of women as well as by the younger generation. He attempted to make democratic and progressive reforms, but could not overcome the antipathy of the hardline religious authorities. Even while he was in power, the conservatives caused many journalists to be arrested and numerous pro-Khatami publications to be closed down.[365]

When President Mahmoud Ahmadinejad came to power in 2005, there was even less tolerance for dissent, and in 2008, Sherkat's application to renew her license to publish *Zanan* was refused. On January 28, Sherkat was informed by the Commission for Press Authorization and Surveillance that *Zanan* presented "a grim picture of the situation of women in the Islamic Republic" and that the publication "compromised the mental health of its readers by providing morally questionable information."[366]

The refusal to renew *Zanan's* license was probably related to the January 2008 issue, which featured an investigative article on the martyrdom movement, titled "Dying in Order to Kill":

> The Behesht-e Zahara Cemetery in Tehran [hosts] the ceremony of the mar-
> tyrdom-seekers [istishhadiyoun] . . . who have come to declare that even
> when there is no war they are willing to seek martyrdom.

> The Al-Usra Choir from Lebanon takes the stage and sings in Arabic:
> The sword writes in letters of blood—muqawama [resistance].
> Become one with this dead body that has the power to destroy.
>
> Among the militant-looking masculine martyrdom seekers [stands] a small woman. In 1979, she was [among those] who scaled the wall of the "nest of spies" [i.e., the US embassy] in Tehran. Today she is the leader of the martyrdom seekers. . . . [Her name is] Firooz Rajai-Far. . . .
>
> According to Rajai-Far, of the 55,000 Iranians who have volunteered for martyrdom operations, a third of them—that is, about 20,000—are women. . . . Martyrdom operations are intended for the day [Iran] is occupied or [the day] the official forces of the regime collapse. . . .
>
> Rajai-Far stresses: "One of the tasks that [the volunteer must perform] in order to carry out a martyrdom operation is to rid himself of his fear of death."
>
> "Another part of the training [program] is concerned with preparation for guerilla warfare. . . . We have experts who plan the operations, prepare the necessary gear, pick out the route [of advance], and, within two or three hours, train a suitable individual for the mission. . . . Even a child can carry out such a mission. . . ."
>
> "All fatwas state that defense [of the homeland] is a religious duty . . . and [consequently] there is no need for permission from the father or husband. . . . Among [our] recruits are many married women. . . . We have [entire] families that have proudly signed up [for martyrdom operations]—from the seven-year-old child to the 70-year-old grandmother—wishing to walk the path [of the martyrs] as a family."[367]

Sherkat was also accused of "weakening military and revolutionary institutions," which was taken to be a reference to the story on women who sign up to become martyrs[368] and to an article concerning the alleged rape of a woman by two members of the Basij Resistance Force, a paramilitary militia subordinate to the Iranian Revolutionary Guard.[369]

While the closure can be linked to specific recent articles, it is remarkable that *Zanan* survived sixteen years and 152 issues in a country that Reporters without Borders has called "the biggest prison for journalists in the Middle East."[370] Sherkat was frequently summoned to Iran's Press Court to defend her decision to run various articles. In 1987, she faced charges for printing a story about a girl at a Caspian beach who was beaten and arrested by police for not completely covering her hair. She was also charged over an article written by Shirin Ebadi, the Nobel Peace Prize winner, and again for a series of articles on Islamic law and women by women's rights attorney Mehrangiz Kar and Islamic cleric Mohsen Saidzadeh. Each of these cases was eventually dropped.[371]

In January 2001, Sherkat was fined and sentenced to four months in prison by the Revolutionary Court on charges of anti-Islamic activities after she attended a conference in Berlin titled "The Future of Reform in Iran." During the conference, Sherkat had said that the Islamic dress code should be encouraged but should not be mandatory. On appeal, the prison sentence was dropped, but Sherkat still had to pay a heavy fine. Several other journalists who attended the conference received jail terms ranging from four months to nine years.[372]

Zanan also faced the continuing financial difficulties that beset any independent magazine owner. Most of the journal's revenue came from advertisements for cosmetics and other women's products.[373]

Commentators have noted that *Zanan* was closed at a time when the government in Iran was cracking down on feminist activity. Authorities were responding harshly to the One Million Signatures Campaign for women's legal equality, and the Ministry of Culture advised the media not to publish news about the women's movement or the arrest of its members. Instead, the public prosecutor ordered the dissemination of "positive and encouraging" news to show that there were no serious internal problems in Iran.[374]

Shahla Sherkat was awarded the Courage in Journalism Award by the International Women's Media Foundation in 2004. For her "dangerous and challenging work as the publisher of *Zanan*," she received the Louis Lyons Award from the Nieman Foundation for Journalism at Harvard University in 2005.

Zanan's news and views spun around cyberspace so fast it was clear it was onto something: gender equality and gender justice within Islam—exactly where much of the world thought it was missing.[375]

SUSSAN TAHMASEBI

The [One Million Signatures] Campaign is not an opposition group or opposed to the government. It seeks to work within the existing system to create change and to express the demands of a major segment of

> *the Iranian population to the government. From the start of the Campaign we have faced resistance from some segments of the Iranian government, particularly security forces. . . . Our efforts to secure public seminar space for conferences addressing women's rights, or meetings for Campaign members have been systematically denied. Our Web site has been systematically blocked and filtered (over ten times). . . . Our members have been arrested, despite the fact that our work is peaceful and civic and there is no law that bans the collection of signatures in support of petitions directed at the Parliament.*[376]

Sussan Tahmasebi is a spokesperson for the One Million Signatures Campaign, which aims to collect a million signatures in support of a petition addressed to the Iranian parliament. The petition asks for the reform of current laws that discriminate against women and was officially launched on August 27, 2006.

One of the main aims of the campaign is to educate citizens of Iran, particularly women, about the negative impact of these discriminatory laws on their lives and on society as a whole. Those who agree with the aims of the campaign can support it by signing the petition. About a thousand activists have become involved and taken the training course on the relevant laws and the method of collecting signatures in over fifteen provinces. Apart from qualified collectors, many volunteers have downloaded the petition from the campaign Web site and begun their own search for signatures.

The movement's educational booklet, "Effect of Laws on Women's Lives," discusses some of the legal changes that the campaign seeks, such as equal rights for women in marriage, equal rights to divorce for women, an end to polygamy and temporary marriage, an increase in the age of criminal responsibility to eighteen for both girls and boys, the right for women to pass on their nationality to their children, equal *diyya* (compensation for bodily injury or death) for both women and men, equal inheritance rights, reform of laws that reduce punishment for offenders in cases of honor killings, equal testimony rights for men and women in court, and the reform of other laws that discriminate against women.

While the Campaign seeks to bring Iranian law addressing women's status in line with international human rights standards, these demands are in no way in contradiction to Islam.

Shiite Islam, on which the interpretations of Sharia rely with respect to Iranian law, claims to be dynamic and responsive to the specific needs of people and time.

We ask that the laws come in line with international human rights standards and recognize the important role that religious scholars can play in facilitating our demand . . .

It was decided, and the Campaign stands firm on this issue to this day, that no funding support from international organizations, foundations or governments whether overt or covert would be accepted.[377]

Prominent activist Sussan Tahmasebi was charged with colluding with intent to harm national security after she was arrested, together with thirty-two other women, on March 4, 2007. For her part in organizing a previous demonstration against legalized gender discriminations in June 2006, she was convicted of acting against national security.[378]

On one aspect of discriminatory law, however, Tahmasebi is hopeful about legislative changes. *Diyya*, or "blood money," paid as compensation for injury or death rather than retribution, is deemed to be twice the value for men as for women. In relation to "blood money," the government has already modified the laws to allow non-Muslim men equal status with Muslim men. According to Tahmasebi, "It was a lost opportunity to do the same for women. It got a lot of women, even conservative women, upset."[379] As conservative women strongly supported equivalent gender legislation, Tahmasebi believes future parliaments may act more favorably.[380]

10
IRAQ

BACKGROUND

Despite efforts being made by some members of the interim Iraqi administration, there is strong opposition from many religious leaders to the creation of a society in which women play their full part. The contribution of every Iraqi woman will be vital in the massive task of reconstruction following the years of bloody dictatorship and war, exacerbated by economic sanctions.[1]

H istorically, women in Iraq have experienced uncertainty not merely because of religious influences but also due to changes in administrations and the impact of sanctions and war.

The Code of Personal Status was first promulgated in 1959 under the regime of Abdal-Karim Qasim, which took power after the overthrow of the Hashemite monarchy in July 1958. Until that time, family laws were based on tradition or customary law and had never been codified. Qasim was executed in 1963 and many of the family law reforms he had implemented were reversed by the successive rulers under religious pressure.[2]

Prior to the coup d'état in 1968, an active civil society existed, but after the Ba'ath Party seized power, the women's organizations were disbanded and replaced with the General Federation of Iraqi Women (GFIW).

In the years between 1970 and 1991, women in Iraq played a significant role in both political and economic developments.

Prior to the first Gulf War, the government passed laws mandating the education of both sexes. Laws requiring the eradication of illiteracy were passed by the end of the 1970s. The GFIW ran literacy centers with mandatory attendance.[3] It also played a part in various areas of women's progress, helping establish and run 250 rural and urban community centers that were designed to aid in job training, education, and social programs but were also used by the regime to promote propaganda. The effectiveness of the GFIW in women's reform remains controversial. It played a role in lobbying for changes to the personal code, but some Iraqi women believe the role of the GFIW was more destructive and "did not reflect or represent the struggle of millions of oppressed Iraqi women."[4]

In 1976, the Iraqi Bureau of Statistics reported significant advances: "women constituted approximately 38.5 percent of those in the education profession, 31 percent of the medical profession, 25 percent of lab technicians, 15 percent of accountants and 15 percent of civil servants."[5]

Like other countries in the region, Iraq became a signatory to the Convention on the Elimination of All Forms of Discrimination against Women (CEDAW). However, Iraq declared reservations related to the conferring of nationality, a right belonging solely to the father, and reservations on matters related to marriage and family relations.[6]

Advances for women were not maintained following the first Gulf War in 1990, and the sanctions and conflict from 2003 onward have also proved a hindrance to women in Iraq. As conditions worsened after 1991, women suffered a decrease in access to education, due in some cases to economic difficulties: for example, families kept girls at home instead of sending them to school and female literacy was substantially reduced.

The most significant factor, however, was the Saddam regime's desire to use Islamic and tribal traditions to its advantage. As a result, the influence of religious views in social policy was considerably increased. "In collusion with conservative religious groups and tribal leaders, the government issued numerous decrees and introduced legislation negatively impacting women's legal status in the labor code, criminal justice system, and personal status laws."[7] For example, a decree issued in 1990 exempted men from punishment if they killed or assaulted female members of the family in defense of family honor. Consequently, the number of "honor killings" increased markedly.[8]

Following the second Iraq conflict and the fall of the Saddam regime, the women of Iraq have recognized that they need to play an important role to ensure the development of their country:

> We actually have the example of Iraq/Kurdistan, the Kurdish Experiment, where we have women parliamentarians, we have women judges, women ministers, and we're hoping . . . that would carry on into the rest of Iraq.[9]

HOUZAN MAHMOUD (KURDISTAN)

> *Women are less than commodities in Kurdish society. The patriarchal and tribal nature of the authorities in this region has created a climate where violence and degradation against women are almost accepted daily practices. Civil and individual freedoms cannot exist when one's gender means that one has no right to live as an autonomous human being, when one is not an individual in a community, but the chattel of others, a symbol of male "honor," that can be soiled and disposed of, like a rag.*[10]

Kurdish feminist and labor activist Houzan Mahmoud was born in 1973 in the town of Sulaymaniyah, northern Iraq. A self-described "full time activist," she is the representative abroad of the Organization of Women's Freedom in Iraq (OWFI; an organization described in the section on Yanar Mohammed) and the Iraqi Freedom Congress (IFC). The IFC is a civil, secular, resistance movement, aiming to develop a democratic, secular, and progressive alternative to both the US occupation and political Islam in Iraq. Mahmoud has written many articles for UK publications such as the *Guardian*, the *Independent*, and the *New Statesman* about the situation of women in Iraq, Kurdistan, and the Middle East. She has also led international campaigns against the rape and abduction of women in Iraq and the imposition of shari'ah law in the Iraqi constitution.

Houzan Mahmoud acknowledges that while women's rights were routinely violated during the years of the Saddam regime, perhaps best personified by Uday Hussein's summoning of young virgins to his palace for pleasure, she believes the current situation is worse. US occupation was supposed to bring "liberation," yet violence against women has escalated, with girls and women reduced to a "cheap commodity to be traded in post-Saddam Iraq."[11] Beheadings, rapes, beatings, suicides through self-immolation, genital mutilation, trafficking, and child abuse masquerading as the marriage of girls as young as nine are all on the increase.[12] A 2007 UN report on human rights in Iraq revealed that in the province of Erbil, rapes quadrupled between 2003 and 2006, while in the (comparatively) "peaceful and orderly" northern area of Kurdistan, more than forty honor killings occurred in three months.[13] The so-called crimes of women are often merely to have dressed "inappropriately." For example, in Basra alone, police acknowledge that fifteen women a month are murdered for breaking Islamic dress codes. Women who had previously worn Western clothes and had moved about freely all their lives have been terrorized into wearing the *abaya* and staying inside unless accompanied by male relatives.

As a powerful example, Mahmoud points to the move by the Iraqi Governing Council (IGC) to change the date of International Women's Day from March 8 to August 18, the birth date of Fatima Zahra, the Prophet Muhammad's daughter. "This had nothing to do with women's rights, and everything to do with subordinating women to religious rules."[14]

> Just recently Iraq's central government passed a law denying women the
> right to apply for passports without the consent of a male relative. This has
> all the appearance of treating women as somehow inferiors, or even minors,
> who need to be "looked after" by "responsible" males.[15]

The religious and cultural "ownership" of women's bodies is played out perhaps most tragically in honor killings:

> The idea that a woman represents family "honor" is becoming central to
> Iraqi culture, and protecting that honor has cost many women their lives
> in recent months. Rape is considered so shaming to the family's honor that
> death—by suicide or murder—is needed to expunge it.[16]

In her role within OWFI, Mahmoud has brought to the world's attention the plight of many of the victims, such as Doa Khalil Aswad, who, at just seventeen years of age, was brutally stoned to death while up to a thousand local men, including police officers, watched and filmed the murder on their mobile phones . . . her "crime"? She fell in love with a young Arab Muslim, someone outside her tribal group and religious sect.

> The stories of thousands of women who have been brutally killed in this
> region over a period of years are salutary examples. They crossed a line. . . .
> They even had the temerity to choose a sexual partner according to their
> own desires. I condemn these brutalities against women and have dedicated
> my life to fight for their liberation. I feel a great bitterness that many of
> those young women who wanted to rebel and protest against tribal, reli-
> gious and patriarchal barriers are now dead.[17]

Mahmoud's solution to the violence against women is a secular constitution, "based on full equality of men and women, as well as the complete separation of religion from the state and education system."[18] Implicit is her opposition to the inclusion of shari'ah law in the Iraqi constitution, which Mahmoud views as "the forced islamization of Iraq . . . trying to institutionalize women's oppression, and all kinds of discrimination against women."[19] Furthermore, "It is clear to the world that in those countries where shari'ah law is practised—or simply where groups of Islamic militias operate—freedom of expression, speech and association is under threat, if not totally absent. The rights of non-Islamic religious minorities are invariably violated and women suffer disproportionately."[20]

In 2004, Mahmoud and OWFI successfully led an international campaign to defeat the inclusion of shari'ah law in the interim Iraqi constitution. Yet two years later, the issue was back on the agenda. The new Iraqi constitution, according to Mahmoud, "is a mass of confusing contradictions. While it states that men and women are equal under law it also decreed that sharia law—which considers one male witness worth two females—must be observed."[21] Mahmoud also opposes the religious nature of the constitution, which begins with the name of Allah. She argues that a constitution is about law, not religion, so there is no need to include religious practices, aside from a guarantee of freedom of worship. "Religion must be privatized. Religion is a personal matter and should not be brought into everyday life."[22]

Mahmoud has strong views about religion and veiling:

> The veil is not merely a piece of "cloth," but a sign of the oppression of women, control over their sexuality, submissiveness to the will of God or a man. The veil is a banner of political Islam used, to segregate women. . . .
>
> More than ever I hear many women claiming that wearing the veil, burqa or niqab is their own choice. I totally reject this view. Not wearing the veil can create harsh problems for women—if it doesn't cost them their life, as in Iraq, it can cost them long-term isolation from their community.[23]

Mahmoud's campaign against the new constitution again made international headlines, particularly after a fatwa was issued against her in February 2007 by Ansar al-Islam, the notoriously brutal Kurdish jihadist group. However, such threats do not deter Mahmoud: "I will continue doing what I am doing now, going around the world cultivating support for women in Iraq and Kurdistan as well as exposing the violence and gender apartheid that Islamists are imposing on millions of women in the region."[24]

To explain her opposition to the US occupation of Iraq, Mahmoud provides the example of US troops preventing OWFI from staging a demonstration against the rape and abduction of women.

During the insurgency, some control passed "to a bunch of thieves, warlords and tribalists, whose only interest is consolidating and extending their own power."[25]

It was this sentiment that led to the establishment of the Iraqi Freedom Congress, which unites the efforts of OWFI, the Federation of Workers' Councils, and the Student Struggle Union on a more political level. The organization works within Iraq, for example, establishing safety forces in neighborhoods, like "Solidarity" in Kirkuk, and also works internationally, gathering political, moral, and financial support. The last mentioned is important to achieving the congress's plans of establishing its own satellite TV station in Iraq, so it can spread the message to every household and mobilize more support at grassroots level within Iraq. Mahmoud makes a clear distinction between the IFC and other "resistance" movements, which she sees as having the narrow goal of simply ending the US occupation of Iraq.

YANAR MOHAMMED

We used to have a government that was almost secular. It had one dictator. Now we have almost 60 dictators—Islamists who think of women as forces of evil. This is what is called the democratization of Iraq.[26]

Yanar Mohammed, an architect and sculptor, was born and raised in Iraq at a time when women had rights on a par with those in the West. Taking advantage of the opportunities of free tertiary education, she earned both her undergraduate and her master's degrees from Baghdad University. In 1993, she moved to Canada with her husband and son, partly to escape the dim economic prospects in her home country under international sanctions. After the fall of the Saddam regime in 2003, Mohammed heard from a friend about the worsening situation of Iraqi women. She returned to Iraq and cofounded the Organization of Women's Freedom in Iraq (OWFI), whose primary aim is the introduction of a secular constitution for Iraq. Her outspokenness and campaigning on behalf of Iraqi women have won her both acclaim and numerous death threats.

Although the Iraqi women were promised freedom and democracy by both the United States and the various interim Iraqi governments, their situation has deteriorated dramatically since 2003. Many women and girls live in constant fear of being harassed, beaten, abducted, raped, or murdered. Religious mobs sponsored by Iran and Saudi Arabia turned into legitimate political parties under the eyes of American troops. "Nobody listened to us. To the tribals, to the Islamists, but never to women."[27] A vacuum in power has given opportunities to religious forces to politicize Islam, bring back traditional lifestyles, and take away women's voices and rights.

"The first losers in all this were women."[28] This sentiment led to the establishment of OWFI, the only national women's organization advocating a secular society based on democracy and respect for human rights in accordance with international standards. OWFI shelters Iraqi women targeted in honor killings and sectarian violence; monitors women in jail and assists formerly detained women, such as prostitutes; and most visibly, speaks out loudly and insistently for women's legal rights and secular law in opposition to Iraq's growing Islamism. In a 2004 interview, Yanar Mohammed outlined OWFI's goals:

> The first goal is to achieve equality between women and men and the way to that is a secular constitution and a separation of mosque and state. The second is to have equal representation of women and men in all councils, both social and political. Third, we need to end the compulsory veil, to have some laws that protect a woman's right to the dress code of her choice. Last, our goal is to end segregation in the schools.[29]

To this end, OWFI has three interconnected programs and services: women's community centers, media and communications programs, and women's shelters. Through the first two, OWFI is building up a base of women activists who can promote and lead democratization processes toward achieving women's human rights. OWFI's newspaper, *Al Mousawat* (Equality), is the only written media outlet on women's rights in Iraq with a modern egalitarian outlook. The shelters play a vital role in protecting women fleeing from violence, often honor killings, with an "underground railroad" set up to provide initial safe havens and, later, relocation to other cities or even countries. Their work is becoming more difficult:

> the government . . . said you can't open a shelter without the approval of
> five ministries. Some of these ministries are run by the most notorious
> Islamists in Iraqi politics. They spoke openly against us, denounced us as
> promiscuous women. We looked at conditions they set for us and knew we
> could not meet them. We do not admit in Iraq to these shelters. We do it
> in secret from the government. We have a central office in Baghdad. We
> have to change the location of shelters once a year.[30]

The Iraqi government has also prevented OWFI from visiting women's
prisons where victims of trafficking have been jailed for prostitution.

Yanar Mohammed responded to Baghdad's minister for women's affairs,
who claimed sex trafficking was insignificant: "Let me take her to the night-
clubs of Damascus and show her [trafficked] women by the thousands."[31]

Mohammed asserts unequivocally that war and occupation have cost
Iraqi women their legal standing and their everyday freedoms of dress and
movement. Since the beginning of the occupation, the US administration has
recognized Iraqis according to their ethnic and religious identities. She
believes this has allowed the creation of militias from different religious and
ethnic groups with control over specific parts of the country, even over specific suburbs of the major cities. These groups impose harsh restrictions on
women as a way of indicating their control of a particular area. Mohammed
provides the example of Sadr City, a suburb of Baghdad, considered to be its
proletarian heart and the source of social and political change for Iraq's
future. However, Sadr City has been under the authority of Shiite Islamist
militias. The veils the women wear there are usually black:

> I have never before in my life seen young women dressed like that. In 1993,
> when I left Iraq, I had never seen the black gloves.[32]

> We live in a state of continuous fear—if our hair shows on the street, if
> we're not veiled enough at work. It's a new experience for women in Iraq.
> After four years, it's turned into Afghanistan under the Taliban.[33]

An OWFI petition to the Iraqi government highlighted some shocking statistics: although the police acknowledge that fifteen women are killed in the city of
Basra every month, the ambulance drivers indicate that they pick up many
bodies early every morning as they are paid to "clean" the streets.[34] Islamists
maintain that those women who are counted in the official statistics were promis-

cuous or adulterous. However, OWFI points out that the top of the female death toll list is occupied by PhD holders, professionals, activists, regular office workers, and only then prostitutes. The murders are carried out by Islamist militant squads, gangs, and individuals who call themselves Propagation of Virtue and Prevention of Vice (PVPV). According to Mohammed, the PVPV campaign "terrorizes the female population so as to restrain women into the domestic domain and end all female participation from the social and political scene."[35]

Such assertions may seem to ignore the clause in the Iraqi constitution that requires a minimum of 25 percent of members of the government to be women. In the January 2005 elections for the National Assembly, women won 31 percent of the seats. However, nearly half of the elected women parliamentarians ran on the list of the Shiite alliance, and they have had to toe the conservative line of their party.[36]

Furthermore, Mohammed asks, "What's the use of a Governing Council that is even 50% women if their policies are not women-friendly? You have some political groups that have their women's organizations and these . . . are responsible for honor killings or for preparing the lists of women to be killed. So for us, if a woman is taking over, it doesn't always mean that she will bring women-friendly policies."[37]

In 2003 the Iraqi Governing Council passed Resolution 137, which sought to cancel the Iraqi family law practiced since 1959 and impose shar-i'ah law on the interim constitution, a direct threat to the ideal of a secular constitution. Mohammed and OWFI mounted a campaign, both within Iraq and internationally, to defeat this resolution. Mohammed's efforts resulted in a death threat from the Army of Sahaba, which accused her of having "psychologically disturbed ideas about women's freedom."[38] The resolution inferred that girls as young as nine could be married to much older men, that men had the right to make decisions regarding women's education and work, and that the status of a man in marriage was equal to that of four women and, in inheritance, equal to two. In addition, polygamy, "pleasure marriage (mut'ah), compulsory hijab, stoning women to death [due to] adultery, acid-throwing on them, flogging for disobeying Islamic laws, beating women by their husbands, [and] sexual segregation in public places" would be accepted under the law.[39] Mohammed not only opposed Resolution 137 due to its inherent gender discrimination, but also opposed it on the grounds of the image it created of Iraq for the rest of the world:

> It tells the outer world that we are just being identified according to our
> religions—Muslim Sunni, Muslim Shi'ite, Christian, Assyrian. . . . It does
> not tell the world that we are a society of conflicting political tendencies,
> there is the progressive, there is the conservative; among the progressives
> you have all the colors of the spectrum, among the conservatives you have
> the religious . . . the nationalists—that's the Iraqi society![40]

Just a few years later, the Iraqi constitution is, at best, ambiguous, and at worst,
it is contradictory and discriminatory. Article 14 declares citizens "equal before
the law without discrimination based on gender" yet also states that "no law
that contradicts the established provisions of Islam may be established." The
adoption of shari'ah law, while implicit in the introduction to the constitution,
is clearer in other parts. Articles 39 and 41 refer family law to religion. Previously, the "personal status law" gave women favorable treatment on divorce,
custody, inheritance, and so on in Iraqi civil courts, even during the Saddam
era. The new constitution would allow women to "choose" Shiite, Sunni, and
other systems of religious jurisprudence instead of civil law:

> The tribal lifestyle is being reborn. A woman would be forced by all of her
> tribe to follow whatever system they tell her. The constitution has put
> women in a position where no one will protect them from religious cliques.
> [For example,] If a woman is the third or the fourth wife and she has no
> rights inside her home and, on top of that, there is domestic abuse in her
> house, she is doomed. Under Islamic Sharia law a woman must accept beat-
> ings from her husband. Under Islamic Sharia, she must not revolt because
> she is the third or fourth wife.[41]

Iraq is at a turning point in history. If citizens take this historical opportunity, Iraq could indeed become a democratic society with respect for women's
human rights. OWFI is the only group positioned, and determined enough,
to demand women's rights, achieve full equality, and end honor killings.[42]

Despite the threats against her life and the potential for violence that
accompanies her daily life as a woman in Iraq, Yanar Mohammed is determined to continue to speak up for Iraqi women. She also speaks directly *to*
Iraqi women:

> Do you want to be strong? Do you want to be a decision-maker for the
> future of Iraq? Do you think you are a full human being? Or are you

ashamed of your appearance? So why do you cover yourself with these things? You should know this package is the beginning of slavery, the next step is to be denied work, the next one is denied education, and all of [a] sudden your husband is marrying three other wives![43]

Awards

Nominated and shortlisted for 1325 Award in the Netherlands
Recipient of Eleanor Roosevelt Global Women's Rights Award in 2007
2008 Gruber Women's Rights Prize

The figure under the spotlight is labeled "Boy";
the figure in the dark is labeled "Girl."
Source: Abdulrahaman Azaharani *Al-Watan* (Saudi Arabia), August 15, 2007.

The man is saying: "Look, sweetheart, this is what your life and your future will be like. You're the one who wants to get married, not me. . . .
Think about it and get back to me."
Source: *Al-Quds* (Palestinian Authority), August 10, 2007.

11

ISRAEL AND THE PALESTINIAN TERRITORIES

BACKGROUND

Women fill only five of the 88 seats in the National Legislative Council (NLC). One minister in the Palestinian National Authority (PNA) is a woman.[1]

While the Palestinian Authority (PA), the government of the Palestinian Territories (comprising the West Bank and Gaza Strip), has not ratified the Convention on the Elimination of All Forms of Discrimination against Women (CEDAW), "Various surveys tend to show that there is high support for women's political rights and a similar level of support for women's economic rights—but in areas which concern changes in property relations . . . or in the re-distribution of power within the family or marriage there is a radical drop in support."[2] There is also the impact of groups such as Hamas and their endorsement of Islamic law, which influences the resolution of disputes in areas such as divorce and inheritance.

Perpetrators of domestic violence are rarely arrested or charged and if they are, "the maximum sentence that can be imposed is six months."[3] In addition, "neither the Jordanian nor the Egyptian penal codes in force in the West Bank and Gaza respectively recognise sexual violence committed within marriage."[4]

"As a non-state, the [Palestinian] territories cannot be a party to international treaties such as CEDAW, though [they are] still bound by customary human rights norms."[5] The roadblocks, checkpoints, and curfews imposed by the Israeli authorities to protect against suicide bombers present added difficulties. In addition, the Palestinian Authority has been unable to provide stable government in any area, including a guarantee of women's rights.[6]

Despite all the difficulties, however, there are efforts to advance women's rights. For example, the Women's Unit at the Center for Jewish-Arab Economic Development (CJAED) "advances cooperation between Jewish and Arab women in Israel, and between women in Israel and the Palestinian Authority. . . . The center's work has a multi-tiered approach, which incorporates training, mentoring, regional business networks, a loan fund and public policy work"[7] Continued encouragement of such programs is necessary, particularly for Arab women; in 2006, "more than 50% of Israeli women had economic power or were working, compared with about 22% of Arabic women."[8]

Arab female literacy is considerably higher in the West Bank and Gaza than in neighboring countries; particularly in Israel, where Arab citizens make up about 20 percent of the population.[9]

In a historic decision, two female judges were appointed to shari'ah courts in Hebron and Ramallah. The judges believe they can help women gain their rights within Islam. However, Dima Nashashibi of the Palestinian Women's Center for Legal Aid and Counseling was not convinced of any significant improvements for women. "As long as the law is the law, which is difficult to women, I don't think it will change much."[10]

In January 2006, Hamas won a majority of seats in the Palestinian parliamentary elections and began imposing a stricter Islamic criminal code. According to reports in the Arabic press, Hamas enacted severe shari'ah-compliant punishments in the Hamas-controlled Gaza Strip in December 2008, including "amputation of limbs for stealing and the death penalty, including crucifixion, for actions Hamas deems detrimental to 'Palestinian interests.'"[11]

ASWAT

Aswat, meaning "voices" in Arabic, is an association of Palestinian gay women operating out of Haifa, in northern Israel. Founded in 2002, initially as a Web site, it aims to "raise public awareness, and create a safe environment for gay Arab women within our Arab and Palestinian society."[12]

In Muslim countries with their patriarchal social structure, women who dare to identify themselves as outside the traditional gender roles face exclusion or even violence. Traditionally, lesbians have been invisible in Arab society, and until the establishment of Aswat, Palestinian lesbians had never been organized. However, Palestinian lesbians who live in Israel can display their identity in public. For women who do not wish to attend meetings, the Aswat Web site provides a private space for self-expression.

Rauda Morcos, cofounder of Aswat, was "outed" by an Israeli newspaper. She received threatening letters and phone calls from local Arabs, eventually lost her job as a teacher, and moved from her small town to Haifa.

In March 2007, Aswat hosted an inaugural public conference to celebrate five years of existence:

> Two weeks before the conference the Islamic movement issued a statement to the press denouncing the event and claiming that Aswat is a "fatal cancer" that is "corrupting the Palestinian society, that should be forbidden from spreading in Arab society and should be eliminated from the Arab culture."[13]

In the end, over 350 predominantly Arab women attended the conference: "Palestinian women came from cities, towns and villages, including from Gaza, Ramallah and other West Bank towns."[14] There was also a show of support from some Jewish activists. At the conference, which was addressed by many feminist activists and scholars, Aswat launched a book about same-sex love: *Home and Exile in Queer Experience.*

NISSA WA AAFAQ (WOMEN AND HORIZONS)

Nissa WA Aafaq (Women and Horizons) is an Arab Israeli NGO dedicated to women's human rights and the only feminist organization in the local Arab region. In particular, members are committed to the reinterpretation of Koranic scripture through analysis of original texts, rejecting the traditional misogynist, patriarchal viewpoint, which, they claim, has been utilized to marginalize women. This technique of investigation, they believe, will facilitate the egalitarian gender perspectives necessary to reform the lives of the majority of Palestinian Arab women who live in societies dominated by religious belief and practice.[15]

> The traditionally patriarchal interpretation of religion has had a negative impact on women's rights, rights that were granted to them in the religious Islamic holy scripts. These rights include: the right to education, the right to work, the right to manage their financial affairs, the right to self-determination regarding personal life, and the right to participate actively and fully in public and political spheres.[16]

According to Nissa, Koranic texts favor equality of the sexes but in practice, women are severely disadvantaged. For example, male and female adulterers are considered equally guilty in the Koran, but most Islamic communities reserve maximum or sole punishment for women. Similarly, even though four eyewitnesses are required by the Koran to prove adultery, the slightest hint of an illicit relationship may lead to the "honor killing" of a girl by a male member of her family.

In order to promote a "modern" interpretation with relevance to current life, the Nissa WA Aafaq organization is amassing a resource center and library for feminist research and trying to build working relationships with transnational feminist organizations, particularly in the West. Most Palestinian Arab women, subjected to generations of male domination, have been unaware of legitimate feminist interpretations of the holy texts, but many are now showing an interest, following participation in the Nissa lecture programs. Apart from Arab Israeli women, Nissa courses and conferences have also welcomed Jewish Israeli, European, and American audiences.

Through its activism and its educational campaign, Nissa hopes to counter the stereotype of the submissive, repressed Muslim Arab woman:

> In today's Arab and Islamic world, change is under way, and the status of women has become a critical question. A number of Islamic scholars, both male and female, have been working diligently in search of elements within the Islamic texts that empower women, principles which can be applied to modern life.[17]

12
JORDAN

BACKGROUND

Jordan's constitution protects women by explicitly stating that all Jordanians are equal before the law, have the right to assume public office and the right to work. In 1974, women were given the right to vote and the right to run in general elections. In September 1996, a National Committee for Women was formed in order to formulate general policies related to women in all fields.[1]

Despite the concerns of conservative religious groups, the Jordanian government has made a notable effort in terms of legislation on women's rights and women's general advancement. This is partly the result of the current monarch's attitude. King Abdullah II has shown an interest in women's rights and both Queen Rania and Queen Noor (the queen mother) are major advocates of women's rights. Other positive developments for women in Jordan include a drop in the rate of illiteracy and increased female enrollment at university, where half the students at present are female.[2]

A number of organizations have been established to assist with the move toward gender equality, including the Arab Women's Media Center (AWMC), established in December 1999 "to train journalists and study women's issues. AWMC . . . now has 79 members."[3] Another organization, the Jordanian National Commission for Women (JNCW), was started in 1992 with the purpose of developing programs in cooperation with non-government organizations and the private sector, conducting studies, and assessing legislation.[4]

In terms of elections, Jordanian women, in fact, have a higher rate of participation than men. Yet they are underrepresented in terms of the number of female ministers and senators. In 2003, fifty-four women ran for parliament in the June elections but none were elected. After that, however, King

Abdullah instituted a quota system that resulted in the election of six professional women who became members of parliament.

However, there are still difficulties to be overcome. For example, some, like the former minister for information, Leila Sharaf, have questioned the idea of the quota system. "I was against it at first . . . because I thought that a quota may bring women who are not experienced in public life, women who are too conservative to push for women's rights or that it may slacken the women's movement."[5]

One of the major obstacles to the advancement of women has been the issue of political Islam. As in other countries in the region where religion has pervaded legislation, there has been a clear conflict of interest between the maintenance of clerical and social traditions and the desire to meet international standards. These include the Convention on the Elimination of All Forms of Discrimination against Women (CEDAW), which Jordan ratified and implemented in 1992. However, "reports indicate that discrimination persists in many areas of Jordanian women's lives. Gender-based violence remains a major problem throughout the nation."[6]

King Abdullah is encouraging changes, but attitudes will take time to change. "The 42-year old monarch may find himself facing an uphill battle with Jordan's traditional stalwarts to create the kind of society he wants to become an example to the rest of the Middle East."[7]

RANA HUSSEINI

> *Sometimes I get accused of being used by the West, of being a Western agent, but I'm sorry, I don't need anyone in the West to tell me that killing a woman is wrong.*[8]

Although born and raised in Jordan, Rana Husseini was educated in America and gained her BA (1990) and MA (1993) from Oklahoma City University. In September 1993, she returned to Jordan and started work as a reporter for the *Jordan Times*.[9]

After four or five months of covering routine news events, Husseini wrote about an "honor killing," previously a taboo subject in Jordanian society and one that had been overlooked by the media.[10]

"Honor killings" (already mentioned several times in this work) are the murders of girls or women by their husbands or relatives because they have behaved in a way that is said to have damaged the reputation of the family or the tribe. In some cases these killings are based merely on suspicion or rumor; in others, a woman may be killed over an inheritance or for another reason, but the killer will claim that it was an "honor killing" in order to get a lighter sentence.[11]

> The problem of "honor killings" is not a problem of morality or of ensuring that women maintain their own personal virtue; rather, it is a problem of domination, power, and hatred of women who, in these instances, are viewed as nothing more than servants to the family, both physically and symbolically.[12]

The *Jordan Times* reported nineteen such killings in 2001 and twenty-two in 2002. In March 2005, the *Christian Science Monitor* estimated that these crimes account for one-third of all violent deaths in Jordan. Officially, there are twenty to twenty-five "honor killings" every year.[13] Husseini, however, believes that the real numbers may be double the official estimates.[14] Of the murders reported in 2007, ten were committed by brothers, four by fathers, one by a husband, and one by an in-law.[15]

Younger sons are often pressured into committing these crimes by their family and their community, because the courts treat them more leniently than if they have committed murder for a different reason. In fact, a minor who commits an "honor killing" can continue his education while in detention and will leave prison with no criminal record or social stigma.[16]

If a woman survives an attempt to kill her, or fears that she may be murdered by her family and goes to the police, she is put into protective custody in prison, where she will remain indefinitely.[17] Some forty women are in prison in Jordan alongside serious offenders: several have been there for more than ten years.[18]

The case that "compelled Husseini to get more involved" was that of a sixteen-year-old girl whose twenty-one-year-old brother sedated her with sleeping tablets and raped her.[19] Her brother threatened to kill her if she told anyone, but she had to tell the family when she found she was pregnant. Her brother tried to kill her, but she survived. She had an abortion and was married off to a man fifty years her senior. However, he divorced her six months later and, on May 31, 1994, her older brother killed her.[20]

Husseini began to consistently investigate and report "honor killings" in 1994 and started a campaign to raise awareness of the issue and to push for legal reform.[21] Since breaking the silence on the subject in Jordan, Husseini has spoken about these crimes and associated human rights issues in numerous interviews with national and international media and in lectures and conferences across the world.[22]

Husseini was credited by Queen Noor, wife of the late King Hussein of Jordan, with "almost single-handedly bringing the problem to the attention of the public," and Husseini's campaign has been supported at various times by the late King Hussein and his sons.[23] The Jordanian media now report on "honor killings" and other human rights issues such as domestic violence, child abuse, and sexual abuse.[24]

Husseini works as a consultant with local and international organizations, conducting research on human rights violations against women and children in the Middle East, and she has worked for the United Nation's Development Fund for Women (UNIFEM) campaign to eliminate violence against women in five Middle Eastern countries. She has been a special advisor on women's issues and press freedom in Jordan to Freedom House.[25] Husseini has also written a book titled *Murder in the Name of Honor*.[26]

In 1998, Husseini organized the National Jordanian Committee to Eliminate So-Called Crimes of Honor. The committee conducted a grassroots campaign in 1999 and gathered some 15,000 signatures to a petition for the repeal of Article 340 of the Jordanian criminal code.[27]

Article 340 exempts a man from punishment for assault or murder if he finds his wife or any female relative in the act of committing adultery, or in circumstances that lead him to suspect adultery.[28] Article 98 of the penal code provides a reduction in sentence if a crime is committed in "a fit of fury caused by an unlawful or dangerous act on the part of the victim," and these articles are consistently used in the defense of those accused of "honor killings." The average sentence for this type of crime is around seven and a half months and it can be as little as three.[29]

Amendments to Article 340 have been passed several times in the Upper House of the Jordanian parliament since 1999 but they have been rejected each time by the elected representatives of the Lower House, who believe that the amendments violate religious traditions and are a threat to family values.[30] To date the law is unchanged.[31]

The Jordanian government, however, was the first to attempt to address the problem of "honor killings" in a Muslim state, and has introduced several initiatives over the past few years.[32] A Family Protection Department has been established within the Public Security Directorate to investigate allegations of violence against women. In 2007, the Ministry of Social Development set up Dar al-Wifaq (the House of Reconciliation), to which police can refer women and girls who have been assaulted, sexually abused, or neglected, or who have run away from home.[33]

In January 2008, a Protection from Family Violence Law was passed by parliament. The law facilitates the reporting of abuse or domestic violence, provides for victims to receive compensation, and encourages reconciliation and mediation, but it falls short of criminalizing domestic violence, which was a measure called for in 2007 by the UN Committee on the Elimination of Discrimination against Women.[34]

In April 2008, Queen Rania continued the Jordanian royal family's condemnation of these crimes in an Internet video in which she terms them "horrific" and "inexcusable."[35]

Husseini also exposed Norma Khouri's *Forbidden Love* (titled *Honor Lost* in America) as a fraudulent account of an "honor killing." The book told the story of a woman who was murdered by her father for having an affair with a Christian man, and Khouri claimed to have fled Jordan as a consequence.[36] Husseini objected to suggestions in the book that "honor killings" are mandated by Islam and that thousands of them occur in Jordan each year. She made a close analysis of the book with the president of the Jordanian National Committee for Women (JNCW), Amal al-Sabbagh, and they found that it contained numerous other major inaccuracies and no evidence for the event on which it was based. The JNCW reported the results of the analysis to the publishers.[37]

Husseini argues that it is a misconception that Islam justifies "honor killings." These crimes, she asserts, are part of a culture, not a religion, and occur in Arab communities in other countries.[38] However, many commentators argue that "honor killings" cannot be so easily dismissed as an Arab custom unrelated to Islam, because they also occur in non-Arab Muslim communities: in Pakistan, for example, and among the Pashtuns of Afghanistan and the Kurds in Turkey and Iraq.[39]

The UN estimates that more than five thousand "honor killings" occur each year, mainly in the Middle East, North Africa, and South Asia, but also increasingly in Muslim communities in the West, coincident with a rise in fundamentalism.[40] This number does not include women who are beaten, wounded, or disfigured, or who go into hiding or leave the country.[41]

In March 2008, two Jordanian men convicted in separate cases of killing female relatives were sentenced to six months and three months, respectively, under the provisions of Article 98 of the penal code. The court ruled that the offenses should be considered misdemeanors.[42]

Rana Husseini is the recipient of eight local and international awards, including the Human Rights Watch Award, 2000, the Feminist Majority Foundation award, 2000, the Ida B. Wells award, 2003, for Bravery in Journalism, and a medal from HM King Abdullah II in 2007.[43]

Source: Abdellah Derkaoui *Ad-Dustour* (Jordan), May 18, 2007.

13
KUWAIT

BACKGROUND

The Islamic and traditional opposition to suffrage argues that women's exposure to public life by voting will lead to their moral decline.[1]

Throughout its recent history, Kuwait has faced increasing calls for the rights of women and their participation in the political process. Opposition to these rights has been based on social as well as political grounds. Since Kuwait's liberation from Iraq in 1991, the dynastic interests of the royal family have played a part in maintaining limits on women's rights.

Gender is one of the veils behind which the regime conducts its struggles against the parliament.[2]

Kuwait presents an interesting set of contradictions with regard to women's rights. While over 67 percent of the graduates of Kuwait University are female, women still face discrimination in the courts, where their testimony is given only half the value of men's testimony. They are also unable to pass their nationality on to their children. These limitations exist despite the fact that Kuwait is a signatory to the Convention on the Elimination of All Forms of Discrimination against Women (CEDAW), albeit with reservations based on conflicts with Islamic law.

Kuwait ratified CEDAW in 1994, but women were not granted full political rights until 2005. Following the legislation, a number of women were appointed to important political positions: Dr. Maasouma Al-Mubarak as minister of planning and administrative development in June 2005, and Nouriyah Al-Subeeh as minister of education and higher studies in March 2007. In addition, the president of Kuwait University is a woman.

Progress came after a long period of struggle involving a number of organizations, including the Federation of Kuwait Women's Associations and the Women's Cultural and Social Society.

> The Federation is supported and tightly regulated by the Kuwaiti government. It is the only group allowed to represent Kuwait internationally.[3]

The government is very much in control of the freedoms of these groups, yet activists have not been silent through the decades.

Kuwait's women "do not fit the standard Western 'Arab' or 'Muslim' stereotype. . . . Beginning in the early 1970s, middle- and upper-class women began lobbying for political rights and for fundamental changes in Kuwait's family law."[4] The opposition that such activists have had to face was seen clearly on two occasions related to women's suffrage. The first was the conflict and debate aroused in 1999 when the emir's decree granting rights to women was rejected.[5] The second was the debate aroused by the 2005 law that granted suffrage. "'Ninety percent of Kuwaiti women reject political rights because they know it is against religion,' said the lawmaker [Daifallah Buramya] who warned MPs of a 'big shame' if they approved the bill."[6]

Despite the fact that more political rights have been granted to women, there are many conservatives who see such progress as an affront to religious beliefs. However, as attitudes are changing from the top, the likelihood of acceptance of a greater role for women is increasing.

IBTIHAL ABD AL-AZIZ AL-KHATIB

> *Anyone who is secular is accused of being a heretic, which is absolutely untrue. Secularism is the belief in the separation of religion and state. In other words, religion belongs to God, and the state belongs to all. Every person is free to practice his religion and follow his spiritual path, but all are subject to a civil state. That way, we ensure just treatment for all, instead of Sunnis enjoying more rights than Shiites, or vice versa, and Christians having no rights whatsoever in an Islamic state.[7]*

Ibtihal Abd Al-Aziz Al-Khatib has spoken passionately in defense of secular politics. Religion, she declares, must not be allowed to interfere with the state, as divisive loyalties could emerge, weakening the body politic, for example, in the case of a fatwa that runs counter to national interests.

> There is a strong sectarian bias toward the religious authorities rather than the state, and this is catastrophic for our Arab countries. . . .
>
> I want a state that is not based on religion—a civil state. But one of the conditions is to protect people who want to practice their religion.[8]

NOURIYAH AL-SUBEEH

> *When His Excellency the Prime Minister appointed me minister, he obviously consented that I won't wear a veil. . . . How I dress is a matter of principle, and it [is] not fitting for someone to back down from his principles because of his job.*
>
> *A woman who wears a veil does so out of belief, and this belief must be respected—just as the belief of a woman who does not want to wear a veil must be respected. This is [the essence] of democracy, in my opinion, which is, inter alia, to respect and accept the opinion of the other.*[9]

In April 2007, Nouriyah Al-Subeeh, unveiled and wearing a floral printed black skirt, took an oath in parliament as education minister. A week prior to the swearing-in ceremony, Islamist MP Waleed Al-Tabtabae and the Salafist Ummah Principles Alliance had counseled Al-Subeeh to wear the *hijab*.[10]

Their warnings went unheeded, and her refusal to wear the *hijab* created a furor in parliament when several Islamist members remonstrated vehemently. MP Dr. Daifallah Buramya shouted that she was violating the election law and should not be sworn in. He was referring to Article 1 of the 2005 Election Law, which states that women have political rights on condition they adhere to shari'ah religious law, even though the details of this contingency have never been expounded.[11]

MP Dr. 'Ali Al-'Amir declared that Al-Subeeh had sworn to defend the constitution, which was primarily based on shari'ah regulations and added:

> The education minister should wear a veil in order to prevent any argument, constitutional problems, and disputes within the parliament.[12]

Faced with this outburst, Kuwaiti Parliamentary Speaker Jassem Al-Kharafi urged tolerance and stressed there was no compulsion to wear the *hijab* in the chamber. If indeed there was such a religious law, he added, it would apply everywhere, not only in parliament. Another MP said the parliamentary chamber "is not a mosque where, before entering, men take off their shoes and women put on a veil."[13]

The incident sent ripples of consternation through the academic community. Dr. Shamlan Yousuf Al-'Issa, political science lecturer at Kuwait University, lambasted Islamic political groups for interfering in all aspects of everyday life, "in the name of the religion, and sometimes in the name of custom and tradition."[14]

Egyptian writer Naja Abd Al-Halim remarked:

> It is more appropriate to take an interest in what is in Madame Nouriya Al-Subeeh's head than in what she should have on her head.
>
> Madame Nouriya entered the parliamentary chamber with unusual courage, high confidence, and composure that was the envy of all, especially the women, and we hope that every woman who has suffered from the tyranny, domination, arbitrariness, arrogance, and contempt of a man [will have these traits].[15]

Although women did not gain any seats in the parliamentary elections in 2006, two women were appointed to the cabinet.[16]

The other woman minister, Dr. Maasouma Al-Mubarak, originally minister of planning and administrative development, never faced the wrath of Islamist members of parliament as she always wore the *hijab*.

As a successful single-source petroleum economy, Kuwait has not been compelled to modernize, but Al-Subeeh is driven by the vision of a Kuwait with broader academic and economic development. Achieving these goals entails serious reform of the education system and to this end, Al-Subeeh enjoys the support of the emir of Kuwait, Sheikh Sabah IV Al-Ahmad Al-Jaber Al-Sabah. During the National Education Development Conference, in February 2008, she focused on education as a path to development, recognizing that human talents and enterprise are society's most formidable assets. This theme was expanded by her associates, including Dr. Anas Al-Rushaid, who underscored the importance of women's enfranchisement, free speech, free media, and civil society institutions if Kuwait is to become a competitive regional economic center. One of the major obstacles in the educational curriculum is the emphasis on rote learning as opposed to critical thinking, scientific method, and analysis. Without radically changing this approach to learning, Kuwait will not achieve educational parity with the developed world and overcome the country's dependence on a single source of revenue.[17]

The Islamists, however, did not welcome Al-Subeeh's reformist stance. Adversarial at every opportunity, they accused her of responsibility for the deteriorating education standards and demanded she take responsibility for a case in which three Kuwaiti primary schoolboys were allegedly molested by four Asian workers. Al-Subeeh also stood accused of departmental mismanagement and illegal staff appointments and dismissals.

In response, women's rights activist Nabila Al-Anjeri noted, "She is a strong woman with clear plans to reform the educational system. Islamists don't like this."[18]

ROLA DASHTI

There are some people who want to practice intellectual terrorism as they want to take us years back. But we will face this challenge in order to protect our constitutional rights. Not only for women, but for all Kuwait.[19]

Rola Dashti was named as one of the hundred most influential Arabs in 2007. The holder of a PhD in population economics from Johns Hopkins University, she has been a passionate political activist committed to 100 percent female suffrage in the state of Kuwait, for which she has worked tirelessly, and with considerable success, in association with other Kuwaiti suffragettes. In 2005, she was instrumental in successfully lobbying for an amendment to the electoral law that gave women the right to vote and run for office in municipal councils and parliament, and in 2007, she ran for parliament herself.[20]

She is the first woman to be elected chairperson of the Kuwait Economic Society since its inception in 1970, and in this capacity, acts as a powerful driving force in the reform of civil society institutions and the economic modernization of Kuwait. She is founder of the Women Participation Organization, and she is also on the executive committee of the Kuwait Chapter of Young Arab Leaders. During the Emergency and Reconstruction Program (1990–91) associated with Saddam Hussein's invasion, she managed the Kuwaiti government's contracts.

Dashti has been manager of the Economics Department of the Kuwait Institute for Scientific Research, senior economist at the National Bank of Kuwait, and a consultant to the World Bank. She is currently chief executive of a consultancy firm in Kuwait dealing with privatization and small and medium enterprises (SMEs). Outside Kuwait, she has worked with the Red Cross in Southern Lebanon and also promoted women's activism in rural Tunisia and Yemen.

In her forties, Dashti was brought up in a Shiite family. Her father, a member of parliament, had four wives and twenty-four children.

Although Kuwait's 1960s constitution was meant to guarantee equal gender rights, the 1962 election law restricted enfranchisement to men, and the right to run for office was limited to men over twenty-one who were not in the police force or armed services.

Feminist movements first appeared in the 1960s but were resented by Islamists like the Kuwaiti Moslem Brotherhood, who feared the specter of Western influence and started their own rival nonpolitical women's societies. They also allied themselves to tribal factions and managed to take over the Student Union, the Women's Committee of the Social Reform Society, and the Teachers' Society, competing with the Kuwaiti Salafist organization, which was even more vehemently against women's suffrage than the Moslem Brotherhood. The Salafi offshoot composed of members of the younger generation (the Umma Party), formed in the 1990s, was more positive toward women's suffrage, causing the extremists to retreat. To justify this withdrawal, they said their opposition to women's rights was based only on withstanding corrupting Western values.

When one member of parliament thundered that women in political office would introduce "derelicts, deviants and homosexuals," the Women's Socio-Cultural Society, composed of business and educated women, took him to court and won, stimulating changing attitudes toward women's political emancipation.[21]

It was in this environment, which was more conducive to women's suffrage, that Dashti began her vigorous campaign. She believes in the development of a civil society in which political pluralism with credible opposition parties and democratic institutions can flourish. In this context, complete

enfranchisement of women is central. Bringing women into the active political life of the country will also stimulate women's rights and give women the
opportunity to participate in Kuwait's development.

Dashti faced many obstacles along the path to parliamentary reform,
including the tribal mores of Muslim societies. For these strictly segregated
societies, the concept of independent women, let alone of both sexes mingling in parliament, was anathema. However, Dashti and her fellow suffragettes, like Fatima al-Abdali, were set to produce historic changes,
making use of workshops, rallies, and demonstrations, and even suing the
government over the right to vote.

The landmark decision granting women the right to vote on condition
that they conform to Islamic law was made by Kuwait's legislative body, the
Majlis al-Umma, which voted 35 to 23 with one abstention, on May 16, 2005.
On June 12, 2005, Prime Minister Sabah Al-Ahmad appointed the first
woman minister in Kuwait's parliamentary history when Maasouma Al-
Mubarak, a former lecturer in political science at Kuwait University, was given
the portfolio of planning and administrative development.[22] Later she became
health minister but resigned after two patients were killed in a hospital fire.[23]

The hardest part of the struggle . . . has been the insults and rumors.[24]

As soon as women were granted 100 percent suffrage, Dashti announced she
would run for parliament in the 2007 legislative elections. From the start,
she had to endure insults, taunts, threats, and rumors. Women were also
denied participation in traditional *diwaniyyas*, men's evening meetings
dealing with social, economic, and political matters, considered essential for
aspiring politicians. Prior to the elections, Dashti and other women candidates started attending *diwaniyyas* and organizing their own meetings. At
the beginning of Ramadan they were made welcome at the celebrity
diwaniyya held by the emir of Kuwait, who was in favor of their cause.

Dashti was one of thirty women who stood for parliament in the 2006
legislative elections out of a total of 249 candidates. Of all the women candidates who ran, the best performers were Rola Dashti with 1,540 votes and
Nabila al-Anjari with 1,056 votes.[25]

According to Dashti, these modest gains merited reappraisal in light of
parliament's decision to hold the elections one year early, giving the politically inexperienced and relatively unknown women candidates insufficient

time to prepare. There was also inadequate coordination among women candidates to select the most appropriate districts. In addition, Dashti and her colleagues were forced to put up with false rumors, lies, and vote buying by rival candidates.

Another obstacle was "the negative cultural and media attitude towards women in politics."[26]

Women were terrorized in the name of Islam as being anti-religious . . . blasphemous, anti-patriotic agents of the West.[27]

We were accused of being unpatriotic, of being anti-religion, of being anti-family. They said if women are allowed to run for office, this will promote promiscuity and divorce and homosexuality.[28]

According to Dashti, the Islamists kept reiterating that Islam honors women but their real agenda was to promote a male-dominated society.[29]

Even if women are not elected, simply running for parliament may bring about positive changes. For example, one woman stood for a single issue: that Kuwaiti wives married to non-Kuwaiti husbands should be entitled to transmit citizenship rights to their children. As there was considerable popular support for this cause, her rivals were obliged to concur and adapt their policies accordingly.[30]

Of the 100 percent newly enfranchised women registered to vote, 58 percent cast ballots. This represented over 50 percent of the 340,000 eligible voters and provided good evidence for Kuwaiti women's commitment to political involvement, in contrast to commonly held beliefs about their singular lack of interest.

Dashti is undaunted by tribal sectarianism and Islamic extremists bent on controlling women's lives. Many tribal leaders and conservative clergy are hostile to female enfranchisement, voicing fears that women's electoral rights will result in neglect of the house and family as well as children's Islamic education. Dashti is also aware that Islamists, who increased their number of seats from eighteen to twenty-one in the 2006 election, will probably subvert women's rights in the future. But in spite of all the difficulties and the additional danger of empowering autocratic regimes, she maintains that elections open debate and allow the growth of credible opposition parties.[31]

> Women are breaking down barriers. . . . The turnout of women voters was
> very high, comparable to that of men and the number of women who ran
> was unexpectedly high. . . . Women brought to the campaign a gender
> dimension and issues important to them, and forced men to adopt them.[32]

According to Dashti, the main problem faced by activists like herself
throughout the Arab world is the lack of grassroots commitment to political
reform.[33] Furthermore, any political gains must be consolidated if they are
to become long-term gains, and this will require the older political elites to
train younger members and relinquish their own, often abused and privileged, rights.

Now that there are glimmers of democratic progress in this region,
Dashti believes the United States and the outside world in general must form
supportive partnerships with the grassroots movements and individuals dedicated to the development of civil society institutions. Accompanied by cultural exchange, such efforts would encourage modernization, freer trade, and
reduced dependence on tyrannical regimes.

> Two opposing winds are pulling the region in different directions. The first
> is the wind of destruction that is embraced by Islamic extremism:
> extremism as a mode of thinking, terrorism as a mode of conflict resolu-
> tion, and enclosure as a mode of living. The second is the wind of hope that
> is embraced by liberal democrats. Which wind will prevail depends on how
> we as citizens of this region act and take responsibility.[34]

Awards

2005 Winner of the King Hussein Humanitarian Leadership Prize
2006 Vital Voices Global Leadership Awards: Rola Dashti was one of those
 included in the Women of Kuwait Political Participation Award.

(.........)

Source: Abdulrahaman Azaharani *Al-Watan* (Saudi Arabia), May 5, 2007.

14
LEBANON

BACKGROUND

From bikini-clad girls sunbathing on the beaches of Jounieh, to mothers in hijab (head cover) strolling the streets of Baalbeck, the women of Lebanon are as diverse and contradictory as the environment in which they live. This diversity mirrors the clash of cultures that is Lebanon's distinctive characteristic as a haven for 17 different religious sects.[1]

The impact of different religious groups in Lebanon is a significant issue, as this otherwise Westernized nation, liberal in many ways relative to other nations in the region, is held back in terms of women's rights because of the continuing impact of religious courts. While women have become members of parliament and serve in various positions of responsibility, few have reached senior positions in their fields.

Women gained the vote in Lebanon in 1953, and their interests have been represented by various groups over the decades, for example, the Committee for the Political Rights of Women and the Lebanese Women's Council, both founded by Laure Moghayzel, a prominent activist and lawyer. Other organizations have been established to deal with specific issues, for example, the Lebanese Association for Combating Violence against Women, established in 1994. Unfortunately, the government has failed to create facilities for victims of domestic violence, but there are government organizations such as the National Committee for Lebanese Women's Affairs, which is "committed to achieving full equality between men and women. It aims to ensure the human rights of women, to augment women's access to safe and sustainable means of living."[2]

Lebanon ratified the Convention on the Elimination of All Forms of Discrimination against Women (CEDAW) in March 1993. However, the government still faces criticism regarding not only the reservations it made but also the conflicts with various Lebanese laws. The link between the reservations and the conflicts is, as in other countries in the region, the influence of religion. The problem in the case of Lebanon is the number of religions that the constitution recognizes and allows to have influence through religious courts. For example, on the issue of the Personal Status Law: "Women's role is acknowledged. . . . However, in practice women are confined to their biological functions. Personal status laws threaten women with divorce, homelessness and polygamy. Women are also subjected to . . . prevention from compensation, children's custody and from inheritance."[3] On the issue of the Nationality Law: "The Lebanese nationality law restricts consanguinity to the father. Every person born from a Lebanese father no matter where is deemed Lebanese."[4]

The Personal Status Law raises interesting issues, because each religious court interprets the issues according to its own traditions, "making Lebanese women unequal not only to men but also vis-a-vis each other. For instance, since 1959, non-Muslim women are entitled to the same inheritance as male heirs, while to this day, most Muslim women receive only half of that."[5]

The impact of the number of religions allowed to hold religious courts also means that groups lobbying for women's interests are often forced to deal with politicians unwilling to challenge traditional authority. An area of particular difficulty is civil marriage, which is not recognized in Lebanon. Intermarriage is also not recognized, so problems are usually solved by marrying outside the country, or by conversion—in most cases by the woman.[6] There is also the issue of "honor killings," which still exist in some areas and are dealt with leniently by religious courts, and the issue of adultery is also dealt with in a discriminatory manner.[7]

One positive aspect is the fact that there are people willing to lobby for changes, despite the lack of potential for success. There are women now being elected to parliament as well as to municipal councils, although their numbers are still limited and they have yet to serve long terms in parliament.[8]

LINA ABOU-HABIB

It started from a group of women. . . .
We thought that nationality was very critical for a number of rea-

sons. First of all, the issue applies to most of the countries in the Middle East and North Africa region. Second, not much work has been done around it. Third, women were the silent victims of being denied the right to nationality. And fourth, being denied the right to nationality directly meant being denied social, economic and political rights.[9]

In most countries of the Middle East and North Africa, women are second-class citizens with respect to nationality rights. Only men are considered full citizens with the right to confer their nationality on spouses and children with the concomitant political and social entitlements. In some cases, women are even refused the right to apply for citizenship for their children.

Women are not entitled to nationality and citizenship rights without intervention by a male family member. If they marry foreign men, the husbands and children may need to purchase the costly residency permits required by foreigners. In addition, children of foreigners are not eligible for social security, healthcare, and free or subsidized education, and priority in admission to university is given to citizens. Employment opportunities and job security are also limited, and property ownership is restricted.

Lina Abou-Habib coordinates the Campaign for Arab Women's Right to Nationality. She is executive director of the Collective for Research and Training on Development—Action (CRTD-A), an organization that creates opportunities for women to learn and exchange information about women's rights through networks across the Middle East and North Africa.[10]

Most countries in the Middle East determine that only men are citizens and therefore only men can pass on citizenship to their children. Abou-Habib's goals are the introduction of legal reforms that would recognize women as equal citizens in Arab countries, enabling them to confer their nationality unconditionally on their husbands and children.[11]

When she started the campaign in 2001, Abou-Habib focused on statistical research linking nationality, citizenship, and gender. She also interviewed women married to nonnationals, which revealed their insecurity and their undermined status. Her campaign aims to take test cases to court "on the basis that nationality law violates the spirit of the constitution, which is based on equality between women and men, between all citizens."[12] Mobilizing support has also entailed increasing awareness, encouraging academic debate, and network building with women's NGOs.

Abou-Habib's organization, CRTD-A, is working with the Women's

Learning Partnership and associates in Algeria, Bahrain, Egypt, Jordan, Syria, Morocco, and Lebanon.[13]

In comparison, Egypt has enacted partial reforms that permit women to confer their nationality on their children but not on their husbands. In practice, however, the reforms are applied only selectively by the bureaucracy, which tends to exclude Sudanese and Palestinians. In Algeria, the nationality law was reformed in 2005 to include husbands as well as children. King Mohammed VI of Morocco proposed a new nationality law in 2005, and in October 2006, by royal decree, he granted women the ability to confer their citizenship on their children.[14]

The Lebanese government has not reformed the Nationality Law, driven by a fear that Palestinians will take up nationality and destabilize the Lebanese demography. However, Abou-Habib believes this would be an unlikely outcome.

In dealing with the central issue of discrimination, she has encouraged interested parties to petition the governments of all regional countries to lift their reservations on the Convention on the Elimination of All Forms of Discrimination against Women (CEDAW), in particular Article 9, relating to nationality.

> The real issue is patriarchy and a male vision of citizenship, rather than all the silly political arguments that are being made when we demand women's right to nationality.[15]

MALAYSIA

BACKGROUND

Malaysian women are privileged when compared to women in many other countries in the region, and their status is often held up as a model throughout Southeast Asia and the wider Muslim world.

Since the nation achieved independence in 1957, women have had the right to vote and hold political office. In 1976, the government created the National Advisory Council on the Integration of Women in Development, and in 1983, the government created the Women's Affairs Division. In 2001, the prime minister established the Ministry of Women's Affairs and Family Development, and appointed a prominent female politician as its first minister. Women have also been appointed to prominent positions outside political office. In 2000, for example, Dr. Zeti Akhtar Azis took up the role of governor of the Central Bank, the first woman to do so. In 2001, the government took the step of amending the federal constitution to prohibit discrimination on the basis of gender.

Throughout the 1990s, as Malaysia experienced considerable economic growth, statistics relating to women's health also improved. Maternal mortality rates dropped, life expectancy increased, the mean age of marriage increased, the proportion of women with seven children decreased, and the total fertility rate also decreased.[1] In addition, the government provided sixty days of maternity leave on full pay for up to five deliveries, under the Employment Act. Access to educational opportunities also contributed to the economic and social advancement of Malaysian women, with female enrollment at primary and secondary level at about half the total enrollment, and female intake into universities reaching 50 percent in the mid-1990s.

However, there are still inequalities and cultural attitudes to be overcome. Within education, the challenge for the future is to break down the prevalent gender stereotyping. At tertiary level, women tend to enroll in arts and education courses and less in science and technology, which ultimately limits their access to higher-paying jobs.[2]

Legislation does not always treat Muslim and non-Muslim women equally. For example, in October 1999, the Guardianship of Infants Act was amended to provide equal guardianship rights for men and women, but it excluded Muslim women. The following year, the cabinet had to issue an administrative directive to allow *all* mothers to sign documents related to their children, such as passports and school transfers.[3] In 2006, the daughter of former prime minister Mahathir (a prominent campaigner for women's rights) claimed that Muslim Malaysian women were being treated as second-class citizens and were thus subject to a form of apartheid.[4] These statements were a response to changes in Malaysia's Islamic family law, which made it easier for Muslim men to take multiple wives, divorce them, and take a share of their property.[5]

The main areas of discrimination faced by Malaysian women are citizenship, immigration, violence, and women's rights. The first two in particular reinforce patriarchal attitudes and practices. Malaysian women married to non-Malaysian men who have children born outside Malaysia cannot confer Malaysian citizenship on their children. Foreign men married to Malaysian women cannot receive permanent residence status in Malaysia, which has a negative economic effect, leading to a "brain drain" as educated couples leave the country. Finally, Muslim women do not have equality in regard to divorce, polygamy, custody, maintenance, and division of matrimonial property.

Encroaching Islamization, particularly in the north, has led to fines for headscarves that might be considered transparent and has brought about moves to ban lipstick and high heels, and to enforce separate gender supermarket checkouts and fines for couples sitting too close together on park benches.[6] Fatwas on tomboys and the practice of yoga have also been issued.[7]

However, attempts by Malaysia's home ministry to prevent women traveling alone overseas were quashed following protests by women's groups.[8]

MARINA MAHATHIR

Malaysia used to have the best legislation protecting the rights of Muslim women in the world. And now we've gone backwards slowly.

> *The 13 states are all allowed to make their own laws in this area and therefore you get variations. . . . We have this dual system between Muslim and non-Muslim women. For Muslim women, we are living under a different system—what you in the West call Sharia law. So we are living under a kind of apartheid not based on skin colour but religion.*[9]

Datin Paduka Marina Mahathir is the daughter of the former prime minister of Malaysia Dr. Mahathir bin Mohamad. For the past eighteen years she has written a weekly column, "Musings," for the *Star*, Malaysia's largest English-language newspaper. Her articles deal with social and political issues and have been collected in a book titled *In Liberal Doses*. She lives with her husband and three children in Kuala Lumpur.

Mahathir has had a long involvement in AIDS awareness and the prevention of the spread of the disease, and she served for ten years as president of the Malaysian AIDS Council, an umbrella organization for NGOs involved in AIDS-related programs in Asia.

Her exploration of the different social aspects and consequences of the AIDS epidemic drew her attention to the particular plight of Muslim women. She found that Muslim women are especially vulnerable to infection because their religious convictions and the lack of support for them outside marriage makes them unable to refuse sex with their husbands, even when they are at risk. Mahathir has often been criticized for her outspoken views on social and political issues, but the connection that she makes between AIDS, Islam, and gender inequity, which she calls "The Fatal Confluence," has caused great controversy.[10]

> People are so scared of contradicting them, [ulama (religious teachers)] because they feel these people . . . have more knowledge about Islam and therefore, who are we to say anything. . . . It was the same with my critiques. They never actually dealt with what I was saying, more about my credentials.[11]

On the subject of gender inequity in Malaysia, Mahathir observes that the constitution and various statutes in secular law have sought to protect the freedom and enhance the status of women in Malaysia, but in contrast, Muslim women have been subject to "increasingly regressive" amendments to religious laws that have restricted their freedom and denied them social status. Muslims in Malaysia are governed by Islamic family law and shari'ah law.[12] In the areas of child custody, inheritance, property, divorce, and polygamy, Muslim women have fewer rights and protections under these laws than under the secular law.

Mahathir referred to this imbalance as "an insidious and growing form of apartheid among Malaysian women, between Muslims and non-Muslims,"[13] which was seen as a particularly provocative statement because her father, as prime minister of Malaysia, campaigned against the apartheid regime in South Africa.

> We are unique in that we actively and legally discriminate against women who are arguably the majority in this country: Muslim women. Non-Muslim Malaysian women have benefited from more progressive laws over the years while the opposite has happened to their Muslim sisters.[14]

Mahathir also points out that Malaysia signed, and is legally bound to implement, the UN Convention for the Elimination of All Forms of Discrimination against Women (CEDAW). She argues that gender inequity is not an essential aspect of Muslim society; it is the result of a particularly patriarchal and dogmatic interpretation of the Koran: "A lot of patriarchal notions [are] . . . creeping into what is called Sharia law. To me, that's an injustice not only to women but also to Islam, because we're giving Islam a bad name, by making it seem unjust."[15]

Mahathir coproduces a TV program for young women, *3R—Respect, Relax and Respect, Respond*, and produced a film, *Gol dan Gincu*.[16] She is a member of the Women's Aid Organization and the National Women's Advisory Council, and she is a supporter of the Sisters in Islam NGO, advocating equality and justice for Muslim women.[17]

Mahathir started a blog at rantingsbymm.blogspot.com in December 2006, when she became aware of attempts to control online opinion. She also became a trustee of a fund to help defend two Malaysian bloggers who were sued for defamation by the *New Straits Times*.

> If I have faith in my own religion I should never be uneasy and I should welcome questions. . . . I think it's un-Islamic anyway to be anti-pluralism because it says in the Qu'ran that God made us of different people so that we get to learn to know each other. So, to me, that means he intended us to be diverse.[18]

ZAINAH ANWAR AND SISTERS IN ISLAM

> *Then came the additional amendments beginning in 2003 which added insult to injury. A husband could claim a share of his wife's matrimonial property upon his polygamous marriage; a husband could get a court order to prevent his wife from disposing of her property; polygamy was made easier by amending the condition "just and necessary" to "just or necessary"; and further grounds for divorce were extended to men who already enjoyed the unilateral right to divorce [their wives], without rhyme or reason.*
>
> *The public outrage that followed and the revolt led by women Senators in Parliament was a signal to the Government and the religious authorities that Muslim women have had enough.*[19]

Zainah Anwar is one of the best-known advocates of Islamic feminism in Malaysia. She was educated at the MARA Institute of Technology in Malaysia and gained her master's degree in journalism and international affairs at Tufts University in Massachusetts.[20]

Anwar was chief program officer in the Political Affairs Division of the Commonwealth Secretariat in London and a senior analyst at the Institute of Strategic and International Studies in Kuala Lumpur. She is a freelance journalist, a former political and diplomatic writer for the *New Straits Times*, and a government-appointed commissioner of the Malaysian Human Rights Commission. Her book, *Islamic Revivalism in Malaysia: Dakwah*, has become a standard reference work for students in the study of Islam in Malaysia.[21]

In 1988, Anwar helped establish a research and advocacy group, Sisters in Islam (SIS),[22] of which she is executive director. SIS seeks equality for Muslim women within the discourse of Islam and based on the tenets of the Koran. Anwar writes and speaks publicly on Islam and women's rights, both in Malaysia and abroad.[23] Her weekly column on Islamic family issues in Malaysia's major daily newspaper became so popular that a legal office was established to deal with the responses.[24]

Controversially, Anwar contests the right of the mullahs to interpret the Koran for all Muslims, believing that while the Koran is the infallible word of God, its interpretation is human and therefore can, and should, be debated. She observes that "a lot of the problems that we have today with regard to women's rights in Islam has to do more with interpretations of the Koran, a process that has been dominated by men, within the context of patriarchal societies."[25]

Anwar argues that discrimination against women is not an integral part of Islam, and she challenges the particular interpretation of the Koran that emphasizes the superiority of the male and subjugation of the female. "The mullahs say all men are superior to all women and therefore women cannot be regarded as equal to men. They tell me that a Muslim man has the right to divorce his wife at will, the right to take second, third and fourth wives, the right to demand obedience and the right to beat his wife if he thinks she is misbehaving. They say I cannot question these rules as they are God's law."[26]

Anwar's own study of the Koran "was a very liberating experience, really, to find all these verses in the Koran that talk about justice. All these verses that talk about compassion, that talk about mercy, that talk about men and women being each other's garment, that talk about equality, and that men and women will be equally rewarded for doing good."[27]

The mullahs, she claims, interpret the Koran without reference to the sociohistorical context in which certain of its provisions made sense. "It is not Islam that discriminates against women. It is not the verses in the Koran. It is the way these verses have been interpreted by men living in patriarchal societies who wish to maintain their dominance and their superiority and control over women."[28]

The religious bureaucracy in Malaysia has power in the thirteen states and at the federal level on all matters to do with "Personal Law," which can become legally binding even without being subject to the legislative process.[29] The question, therefore, of who interprets the Koran, and how they do so, affects the lives of millions of Malays.

> The decision-making process must be participatory and must reflect the diverse and changing nature of . . . society. Those practices and legal provisions that give the ulama the sole power to decide on matters of religion, and criminalise those with differing opinions, must be abrogated.[30]

Two states in Malaysia, Kelantan and Terengganu, are under the control of the Islamic party, the Parti Islam Se-Malaysia (PAS), and have passed shar-i'ah laws, which regulate offenses by Muslims against the precepts of Islam, providing punishments such as cutting off hands and feet, stoning to death for adultery, and execution for those who leave the faith. At present, these penalties cannot be carried out in these states, because they conflict with the constitution and with federal jurisdiction, but there is segregation between men and women in public places, women are made to cover their faces and hair, they are not allowed to perform in public, and many traditional Malay performing arts are banned.[31]

Most Muslims, male or female, are reluctant to challenge the pronouncements of the mullahs, because they feel they don't have sufficient knowledge and risk being accused of straying from, or betraying, their faith. In fact, in March 2003, the Ulama Association of Malaysia attempted to charge Zainah Anwar and five other writers with "insulting Islam," but Sisters in Islam managed to gain sufficient public support to prevent the action from going ahead.[32]

In January 2006, SIS and Zainah Anwar were also successful in repealing amendments to the family law that would have made polygamy and divorce easier for men. Parliament had passed the amendments, but agreed to review them following a media campaign led by Anwar.

> The Cabinet ordered the Attorney General—and not the religious department—to find solutions. They recognized that the religious department and its obscurantist apparatchiks are the source of the problem.
>
> It was the first time that the forces of progress were sitting in the same room "on equal terms" [with] the mullahs.[33]

In the same month, the prime minister gave assurances that a section of the constitution that invalidated civil law in favor of shari'ah law would be reviewed and the attorney general would consult with a cross-section of society to establish a new policy on family law. His statement followed a public outcry about the burial of Moorthy, the first Malaysian to scale Mount Everest. In this case, a superior court judge had overruled civil law on the grounds that he had no authority over Islamic clerics who claimed Moorthy was a Muslim. A Muslim burial was therefore enforced despite his widow's appeals and the fact he was a practicing Hindu.[34]

> A model progressive Muslim country cannot show the world that it makes laws that discriminate against women and that [it] allows its religious authorities to snatch away the body of a dead man from his grieving Hindu family.[35]

Despite these developments, Zainah's opinions have made her many enemies, and ironically, having just written a piece on the freedom of the press for the *New Straits Times*, she was fired from the paper in late July 2007, with a week's notice. The reason given for her dismissal was a lack of space in the publication. In her last column on July 27, Anwar had appealed to the government to maintain press freedom "in the face of challenges from new media."[36]

Anwar stepped down from Sisters in Islam in March 2008, after twenty years of dedicated work.[37] However, she continued to campaign for women's rights within Islam, and in February 2009, she led an international conference in Malaysia on "Equality and Justice in the Muslim Family."[38] According to Anwar, "Women are not being bad Muslims when they demand equality, demand justice, demand their husbands stop beating them. . . . You can be a feminist . . . and still be a good Muslim. We don't see any contradictions in those demands."[39]

The congress was used to launch Musawah, a Malaysian-based global movement to end discrimination and violence against women in Muslim societies.[40] Opposition to the meeting came from some Malaysian Islamic groups, who said the women had no right to question the opinions and rulings of trained Muslim scholars and spread "propaganda" against Islam.[41]

16
MOROCCO

BACKGROUND

Since his accession to the throne in 1999, King Mohammed VI has shown a commitment to women's rights by proposing a wide variety of legal and social reforms. During the reign of his father, King Hassan II, Morocco ratified the Convention on the Elimination of All Forms of Discrimination against Women (CEDAW) in 1993 and submitted progress reports to the United Nations in 1994, 1997, and 2000. Each report outlined the steps taken toward reforming the legal code and improving the status of women. Since his coronation, King Mohammed VI has appointed three women, including a royal advisor, to senior positions. The king has stated that he believes empowering women is vital to solving poverty and unemployment in Morocco.[1] Following elections in 2002, Morocco became the only Arab nation to have women making up 10 percent of the members of parliament, and the thirty-seven-member cabinet appointed by the king included three female ministers.[2]

One of the most fundamental measures taken by King Mohammed VI to improve women's rights was the introduction of a new family law (*moudawana*) in October 2003. This and other significant changes followed years of intensive lobbying by Moroccan activists using secular and religious arguments.[3]

> The Family Law should not be considered as . . . legislation devised for women only, but rather as a code for the family: father, mother, and children. The proposed legislation is meant to free women from the injustices they endure, in addition to protecting children's rights and safeguarding men's dignity.[4]

The legislation means that women are now allowed to be considered their own guardians, and are therefore not legally bound by the decisions of their male relatives with regard to marriage, education, and employment. The family law raised the legal age for marriage to eighteen, imposed tight restrictions on polygamy, and granted women equal rights in divorce. Perhaps most important, the king made clear in the legislation that men and women were equal before the law, both secular and Islamic:

> [We should] adopt a modern form of wording instead of that which undermines the dignity of women as human beings. Make husband and wife jointly responsible for the family, in keeping with the words of my ancestor the Prophet Sidna Muhammad . . . who said that men and women were equal before the law, and also with the saying: "Only an honorable man will honor them [women]; and only an ignoble man will humble them."[5]

In 2005, King Mohammed VI affirmed his commitment to gender equality, children's rights, and family cohesion by announcing that Moroccan women will be able to transmit their nationality to children born of non-Moroccan fathers.[6]

However, while the king has done much to improve the legal status of Moroccan women, the realities of everyday life, in terms of access to education, healthcare, and employment opportunities, are vastly different for women in urban areas and for women in rural areas. Notably, the Criminal Code contains no specific provision making domestic violence a punishable offense.[7] According to the World Bank, economic status is as much a determinant of who will receive an education in Morocco as gender.[8] Overall female adult illiteracy is 64 percent, but in rural areas it can be as high as 90 percent.[9]

Since the mid-1990s, the government has allocated more funding to women's health, including family planning, prenatal care, and postnatal care. Approximately 42 percent of pregnant women receive prenatal care nationally, but in rural areas the figure drops down to 20 percent. The use of contraceptives also reflects the divide between urban and rural areas, with about half of urban married women using contraceptives, in comparison with 39 percent of their rural counterparts.

Women make up over a third of the workforce in Morocco, predominantly in the agricultural and service sectors. In rural areas, women suffer higher unemployment rates than men, and many thousands move into the cities every year to work as housemaids. According to Amnesty International—Morocco, they work for long hours at low pay and frequently experience physical abuse at the hands of their employers.[10] In urban areas they have more opportunities in professional jobs; one-third of doctors and one-quarter of university professors are women.[11]

For some of the most highly educated, demanding equal rights does not imply freedom from gender-oppressive shari'ah law. On the contrary, according to Islamist and feminist Nadia Yassine, "Our religion is very . . . friendly to women. In theory, in our sacred texts, we have many rights."[12] Yassine advocates the creation of a democratic Islamic republic based on shari'ah law and she campaigned heavily against King Mohammed's reforms.[13]

Although the conservative views of Islamic feminists like Yassine are anachronistic in a modern society, their strategies are powerful. According to Abdou Filali-Ansary, director of the Institute for the Study of Muslim Civilizations at Aga Khan University in London, "Their strength is that they are challenging a despotic regime from within the parameters of the Muslim heritage; they build on the legitimacy of religious discourse to challenge despotism."[14]

FATIMA MERNISSI

The Prophet Muhammad encouraged his believers in seventh century Medina to free their slaves, as he himself had freed his. But that historical legacy did not influence the position of some of the Conservative Arab leaders, who resisted the slavery ban by camouflaging it as an attack on the umma, the Moslem community, which is exactly what they are doing today with women's rights. They know too well that they cannot promote democracy without liberating women. Their resistance to women's rights is in fact, a rejection of democratic principles and human rights.[15]

Fatima Mernissi was professor of sociology at the University of Rabat from 1973 to 1980. Since then she has been a member of a research institute at Muhammad V University, Rabat, Morocco.

The "repulsion" felt toward the concept of women's liberation, Mernissi claims, may be related to fear and aversion of the *jahiliya*, the pre-Islamic sexual norms described in the Koran, in which women were free to dismiss male sexual partners and reject paternal legitimacy.[16] Since Muslim men are not taught how to deal with assertive women, they are repulsed by them.

Women's liberation means more than just that, for Mernissi argues it signals the death of the heterosexual unit. The sexes are socialized to view each other as adversaries, but social equality opens up ideas of friendship and love that threaten the social fabric.

> Muslim ideology, which views men and women as enemies, tries to separate the two, and empowers men with institutionalised means to oppress women.[17]

Mernissi explains that the concept of Umma, or the community of believers, was instituted to enable the family to be used as a buttress to uphold Islamic law.[18] The Prophet created "a patrilineal monotheistic state"[19] dedicated to upholding the Umma. The family was used as an auxiliary to this order, controlled by a patriarch and mirroring the patriarchal order. The premise behind this idea is male domination, recognition of male sexuality, and the belief that men should prioritize Allah as the most important aspect of their lives. It also contains the misogynistic fear of *fitna*, meaning chaos, also associated with beautiful women. Mernissi states that these are the principles that have directed relations between the sexes in Muslim countries for fourteen centuries.[20] Sexuality was confined within an Islamic definition, and the linkage with shari'ah law has been a major influence on relations between the sexes.[21]

Since the structure of the family as an institution is perceived as being divinely ordained, it therefore cannot be subject to change. The family functions as a mini patriarchy, and the Muslim man maintains social order by preventing his wife's ability to cause chaos.[22] Mernissi writes that a man's right to subordinate his wife is enshrined in law, as is men's divine right to maintain authority over women, who are seen as their adversaries. This is not only a right but a duty, as seen by the denigration of men as pimps or cuckolds when they cannot fulfill this role. Men are also granted access to other women for sexual gratification, be they prostitutes or additional wives.[23]

The sexual behavior of women must be contained as it reflects upon the male in charge, and the "honor" of a family is linked to the sexual purity of the females. Mernissi asserts that this necessitates the abuse of women. Since men must control another person in order to enhance their own reputation, instead of proving themselves on their own merit, it is not inconceivable that a man might vent his frustrations on a woman, as she holds the key to his social standing.[24] When women's behavior was confined to the domestic or religious spheres, it could be much more easily patrolled, which possibly explains men's resentment of women's liberation. A woman working in an office, attending school, or driving with a male can ruin the "honor" of her male relatives, and such activities are therefore subject to restrictions.[25] In Morocco, men's access to women is more effectively controlled in rural areas than in urban districts, which are more susceptible to Western influences. Mernissi believes that "sexual segregation, one of the main pillars of . . . social control over sexuality, is breaking down," and this leads to love between men and women.[26]

The gains of the women's rights movement are seen as eroding the traditions of an aspirational golden era. Mernissi argues that this is why many men oppose the Westernization of their countries, for in their perception, it is not only a surrender of their customs but leads to depravity. It might also involve sexual liberation, which removes women's bodies from the possession of a father or husband, and leads to women wishing to choose their own partners and requiring birth control or abortions.[27] Hairdressers and beauty parlors would increase in number, making women more beautiful and therefore more dangerously seductive. Westernization might also lead to demands for literacy and other tools of assertion.[28] In Muslim society, this is behind the idea that only men have the skill to choose which aspects of Westernization they will embrace or discard. Women are not seen as competent enough to make the right decisions.[29]

Mernissi asserts that equality of the sexes contradicts Islam, as "heterosexual love is dangerous to Allah's order."[30] It goes against the view of women's place in the social order, which is subordinate to the men in their family. However, Mernissi notes that in Islamic law, women have the potential to be equal to men. Their inequality, however, is needed as part of the family structure and Umma to maintain the social order.[31] It is the potential danger and power of women that needs to be restrained, and therefore polygamy and sexual segregation must be used as means of control.[32]

> The suppression of a man's right to polygamy would mean that women have their say in the law, that society is not run by and for men's whims alone. Where a Moslem government stands on the question of polygamy is a good way to measure the degree to which it has accepted democratic ideas. And if we do take it as an indication of democracy, we see that very few Moslem countries are up-to-date on human rights. Tunisia and Turkey are the most progressive.[33]

The Muslim social structure in its entirety "can be seen as an attack on, and a defence against, the disruptive power of female sexuality."[34] This is because, Mernissi argues, women are not considered fully human, and it is acted out through cultural institutions such as polygamy, divorce by repudiation, and sexual segregation.[35] Girls are taught to limit their sexuality and are warned against it, whereas boys experience completely different treatment. A cult of the phallus exists, and a common game is to teach boys the connection between the penis and sovereignty, by constantly pointing and linking the words together.[36] With age, and with the knowledge of practices such as repudiation and polygamy, a boy forms the impression that his sexual satisfaction is of paramount importance. However, he cannot afford the mandatory bride-price until at least his midtwenties, which may frustrate him during adolescence. Political activism is not available as an outlet for expression, and he therefore turns on the women in his family, on whom he can vent his dissatisfaction.[37] It is therefore the women who continually suffer for the frustrations of their men.

Published Works: Chronological overview of books in English by Fatima Mernissi

Beyond The Veil: Male-Female Dynamics in Modern Muslim Society (Bloomington: Indiana University Press, 1987).

Doing Daily Battle: Interviews with Moroccan Women (Piscataway, NJ: Rutgers University Press, 1989).

The Veil and the Male Elite: A Feminist Interpretation of Women's Rights in Islam (New York: Basic Books, 1992).

Islam and Democracy: Fear of the Modern World (Cambridge, MA: Perseus Books, 1992).

Women's Rebellion and Islamic Memory (London: Zed Books, 1993). Translated by Emily Agar.

Dreams of Trespass: Tales of a Harem Girlhood (Cambridge, MA: Perseus Books, 1994). UK edition titled *The Harem Within*.

Forgotten Queens of Islam (Minneapolis: University of Minnesota Press, 1997). Translated by Mary Jo Lakeland.

Scheherazade Goes West: Different Cultures, Different Harems (New York: Washington Square Press, 2001).

17
NIGERIA

BACKGROUND

On a daily basis, Nigerian women are beaten, raped, and even murdered by members of their family for supposed transgressions, which can range from not having meals ready on time to visiting family members without their husband's permission. Tragically, husbands, partners and fathers are responsible for most of the violence against these women. . . . Once a woman is married, she is expected to endure whatever she meets in her matrimonial home.[1]

In Nigeria, 50 percent of the population is Muslim. Despite the introduction of a democratic constitution in 1999 that guarantees all basic human rights, including freedom from gender discrimination, a decade later, violations of women's rights in Nigeria are numerous. They fall under the following broad categories: "violence in the home, sexual harassment at school and work, rape . . . punitive widowhood rites, Female Genital Mutilation, forced childhood marriages, sexual violence in conflict situations and during execution of armed robbery, enforcement of gender biased laws, discrimination against the girl child, disinheritance of wives and daughters."[2]

While there are no official studies, research conducted by individuals and NGOs indicates that up to 50 percent of Nigerian women are subject to physical, sexual, or psychological violence,[3] mostly undocumented due to widespread tolerance of violence against women. For example, the criminal justice system provides almost no protection for women from violence in the home or community, according to Itoro Eze-Anaba of the Legal Defense and Assistance Project (LEDAP). He added: "The police and courts often dismiss domestic violence as a family matter and refuse to investigate or press charges."[4] In addition, ten Nigerian states have laws that allow husbands to use physical violence against their wives, and marital rape is not considered a crime.[5]

Cultural and religious beliefs, both traditional and Islamic, perpetuate the idea that once a woman marries, she becomes a possession, with essentially no rights within her husband's family. Indeed, a man's mother or sisters have greater influence over him than his wife. The same beliefs and practices allow polygamy and teach a woman not to expect fidelity from her husband; the resulting promiscuity contributes to a growing HIV/AIDS problem. In 2003, Nigeria accounted for 60 percent of HIV/AIDS sufferers in West Africa, with predictions that the 250,000 new cases in 2000 would rise to 360,000 by 2010.[6] Discussions of sexual relations and sexual health are considered indecent for girls and women, and thus fear of punishment, rejection, and shaming mean that most women suffer all forms of STD, including HIV/AIDS, in silence. Even when a wife is aware of her husband's infidelity, she cannot refuse his sexual demands because of societal expectations that marriage will produce children. Consequently, large numbers of children are born with HIV/AIDS and are orphaned at a young age.

The spread of HIV/AIDS among girls and women is aggravated by the continued practice of female genital mutilation (FGM) using unsterilized instruments. A 1997 World Health Organization study estimated that 60 percent of Nigerian women had been subject to some form of FGM, with the rate jumping to 90 percent in some regional areas.[7]

There is currently no federal law banning FGM,[8] but opponents point to Section 34(1)(a) of the 1999 constitution, which states that "no person shall be subjected to torture or inhuman or degrading treatment."[9] The Women's Center for Peace and Development has concluded that Nigerians continue FGM due to cultural and religious beliefs that "uncircumcised women are promiscuous, unclean, unmarriageable, physically undesirable and/or a potential health risk to themselves and their children, especially during childbirth. One traditional belief is that if a male child's head touches the clitoris during childbirth, the child will die."[10] However, a positive step toward obliterating the practice was taken in February 2008, when the Nigerian government decided to observe the International Day for Zero Tolerance to Female Genital Mutilation.

BAOBAB

The leading Nigerian human rights organization, Baobab for Women's Human Rights, was founded in 1996 by Hajira Usman and Ayesha Imam. Hajira Usman died in 1999.

Baobab grew out of a research project on the status of women's rights in Muslim countries in which several Nigerian women participated. At the completion of the project, Usman and Imam decided to establish Baobab to advance the rights of all Nigerian women (not just Muslim women) in Nigeria's male-dominated society.

Baobab is committed to promote "knowledge, development and exercise of women's rights . . . under religious laws, customary laws and statutory laws."[11] However, Baobab is best known for improving the situation of women in the shari'ah states in northern Nigeria. Baobab is not anti-Islamic; rather, it is nonreligious and apolitical.

Until 1999, contemporary Nigerian Muslim family laws relating to marriage, divorce, child custody, maintenance, and inheritance had been largely uncodified. In 1999, however, some states began to pass a series of new shari'ah acts. Their implementation has been discriminatory against women. Some practices, with no legal basis, have been imposed in areas such as Zamfara State, in the name of "sharianisation." These practices have included the imposition of dress codes on women, attempts to force them to sit at the back of public vehicles, and a midnight curfew in the state capital, Gusau.[12]

Unfortunately, says Ayesha, religious extremists, whom Baobab is careful not to upset or support, claim "that the new Sharia acts of 1999–2002 incorporate perfectly a universal God-given code, and that to raise any issues of possible defects (and therefore of the possibility of removing those defects) is unIslamic, anti-Sharia and tantamount to apostacy [*sic*]—in short a politics of intimidation and threat."[13] According to Ayesha, however, Muslim laws are not unchangeable, to be accepted unquestioningly by all Muslims.[14]

In 2002, Ayesha was the winner of the Canadian John Humphrey Freedom Award for her work in support of women's rights; the award is given annually by the Canadian International Center for Human Rights and Democratic Development.

Ayesha believes that the work of Baobab is not anti-shari'ah, but that it aims to improve shari'ah law:

In my view, it is the duty of Muslims particularly to ensure that laws which claim to be based on Islam do NOT violate women's rights (or any other people's). This is why we have helped to popularise the work of the many Muslim scholars and jurists around the world on the importance and legitimacy of ijtihad (using reasoning to develop legal principles), and, recognising istihasan (equity) and istisahl (the public good) as important principles in drafting laws.[15]

Baobab's activities include monitoring the Nigerian government's compliance with ratified treaties, namely, the Convention on the Elimination of All Forms of Discrimination against Women (CEDAW). Baobab also conducts research on reproductive and sexual rights education and runs programs for women on sexually transmitted diseases such as AIDS.

"Boy" and "Girl."
Source: *Al-Yaum* (Saudi Arabia), July 28, 2007.

The man is saying "[You are] divorced!"
Source: Khaled, *Al-Watan* (Saudi Arabia), August 24, 2007.

18
PAKISTAN

BACKGROUND

*The right to life of women in Pakistan is conditional on their obeying
social norms and traditions.*[1]

Women in Pakistan face significant barriers, beginning at birth. In general, female children are less valued and cared for than male children. Pakistan is one of the few countries where women's life expectancy is lower than that of men and the female infant mortality rate is higher than that for males.[2] According to a UN study, girls receive less nourishment, healthcare, and education.[3]

Over 20 percent of girls between the ages of fifteen and nineteen are married, compared with only 5 percent of males in the same age range.[4] Less than 20 percent of women are economically active. Large numbers of working women face discrimination and sexual harassment, and women are routinely denied equal opportunities for promotion, pay, and benefits.[5]

Discrimination against women is worse in rural areas, where 70 percent of Pakistani women live. In some areas of rural Sindh and Baluchistan, female literacy rates are 2 percent or less.[6] A survey of rural females by the National Institute of Psychology found that 42 percent of parents cited "no financial benefit" as the reason they kept their daughters from attending school and sent their sons instead.[7] In a country where over half of the adult population is illiterate, women make up 60 percent of that group.[8]

It is estimated that domestic violence occurs in 80 percent of Pakistani households. Of the 16,000 cases documented by the Progressive Women's Association (PWA) since 1987, thousands were honor killings and burnings, including over 5,500 *choola*, or "stove deaths," caused by family members who doused a wife with kerosene or gasoline before setting her alight. Deaths were then attributed to burst kitchen stoves. The reasons for burning wives are usually failure to bear a son, hostile relations with mothers-in-law, and husbands who want to marry a second wife but can't afford to keep the first.[9] The Zainab Noor case was the first one investigated by the PWA: "She was burned by her husband who inserted red-hot iron rods in her genitalia and passed electric current through them."[10]

The PWA also deals with the many sulfuric or hydrochloric acid attacks aimed at terrorizing and disfiguring women. Human rights activist and clinical psychologist Shahnaz Bukhari, the director of the PWA, raises funds to pay for victims' surgery and the prosecution of perpetrators. Since 1994, she has recorded 7,800 cases of burning and acid attacks in the Islamabad area alone.[11] The southern Punjab, which has one of the highest incidence of acid attacks, also has strong associations with Islamist terrorist groups Jaish-e-Mohammed and Lashkar-e-Toiba; the latter was implicated in the Mumbai massacres of November 2008.[12]

Human rights monitors and women's groups believe that a narrow interpretation of shari'ah has had a harmful effect on the rights of women and minorities in Pakistan, reinforcing popular attitudes and perceptions such as prejudice against women and non-Muslims:

> Women are considered the property of the males in their family irrespective of class, ethnic or religious group. The owner of the property has the right to decide its fate. The concept of ownership has turned women into a commodity which can be exchanged, bought and sold.[13]

On a daily basis, Pakistani women live in fear of violence at the hands of their family:

> My brother's eyes forever follow me. My father's gaze guards me all the time, stern, angry. . . . [I] stand accused to be declared "kari" [literally, a "black" woman] and murdered.[14]

Girls and women who fear punishment for alleged breaches of honor have few places to hide—there are few women's shelters, women rarely know their way about in the world outside the home, they are unused to public transport, they usually have no money, and a woman traveling on her own is a target for abuse by police, strangers, or male relatives seeking her. Guns, axes, and fire are used against women believed to have brought shame on their family.

Their "crimes" can be illicit relationships, marrying a man of their choice, divorcing abusive husbands, or even rape, but the truth of the allegation is rarely investigated. Police almost invariably take the man's side in "honor killings" and prosecutions are rare. When women are seriously injured by their husbands or families, police discourage them from registering complaints and advise them to seek reconciliation. Even when men are convicted, the judiciary ensures they usually receive a light sentence.

There are several specific pieces of legislation that discriminate against women in Pakistan. The 1990 law of Qisas and Diyat reconceptualized the offenses of assault, manslaughter, and murder, directing them against the victim. This was interpreted to signal "that murders of family members are a family affair and that prosecution and judicial redress are not inevitable."[15]

> In Islam, the individual victim or his heirs retain from the beginning to the end entire control over the matter including the crime and the criminal. They may not report it, they may not prosecute the offender. They may abandon prosecution of their free will. They may pardon the criminal at any stage before the execution of the sentence. They may accept monetary or other compensation to purge the crime and the criminal. They may compromise. They may accept qisas [punishment equal to the offense] from the criminal. The state cannot impede but must do its best to assist them in achieving their object and in appropriately exercising their rights.[16]

The Pakistani penal code provides for provocation as a murder defense,[17] and the courts have allowed that if the provocation (with regard to a man's honor) is grave and sudden, as when someone tells him that his wife has an "illicit" relationship, then he loses all power of self-control and is not fully responsible for his actions.[18] The Hudood Ordinances, introduced in 1979 by General Zia, are religious laws regarding rape and adultery, both falling under the crime of *zina*, illicit sexual relations. If a woman is raped, the Hudood Ordinances require four (male) eyewitnesses to prove her claim. If she cannot provide these eyewitnesses, then she has confessed to adultery and must be punished for this crime instead. In 2006, there were about three thousand women in Pakistani jails because of the Hudood Ordinances.[19]

Prime Minister Benazir Bhutto's promises to repeal the Hudood Ordinances were never realized and it was not until 2006 that the laws were changed under President Pervez Musharraf.

At the age of thirty-five, Bhutto became prime minister of Pakistan and was the first woman to lead a Muslim state.[20] She was assassinated in a suicide attack in Northern Pakistan in December 2007, and her widower, Asif Ali Zardari, became president of Pakistan in September 2008. During her second term in government from 1993 to 1996, Bhutto provided the Taliban with support, without which it could not have come to dominate Afghanistan.

Although a lifelong advocate for women's rights, Bhutto did not reverse discriminatory shari'ah laws or introduce legislation against "honor killings" or domestic violence during her leadership, and most Pakistani women remained illiterate, marginalized, and socially segregated. The gains she did achieve on behalf of women were, however, remarkable for their progress in a strict Islamic and patriarchal milieu.[21] For the first time, women were appointed as High Court judges and the issue of domestic violence was aired in public. A quota of 5 percent for women was approved in the bureaucracy and a women's banking system initiated.[22]

For the most part, however, Pakistani women endure the traditional male control over every aspect of their bodies, speech, and behavior, but exposure to the media and the work of women's groups has led to a tentative but growing awareness of women's human rights. The PWA, for example, runs various workshops that focus on sexual and police violence, bartering of women for land and animals, human trafficking, and violence against children. They have also opposed "marriage" to the Koran, which enforces a life of spinsterhood and Koranic study on girls in order to avoid the transfer of family property to any spouse.[23]

However, as women have begun to assert their independence, the response has been harsh, with the escalation of "honor killings" coinciding with the rise in awareness of their rights. Women's rights activists are also targets. In 2005, Zubeida Begum, who worked for the Aurat Foundation, received death threats and was subsequently murdered together with her seventeen-year-old daughter.[24]

Mysogyny is also demonstrated on the floor of the Pakistani parliament. In August 2008, Sardar Israullah Zehri, a tribal leader and senator from Baluchistan, defended the murder of at least five women in his province who were buried alive in honor killings. In parliament, a month later, he excused the murders as "part of our traditional customs" and, shortly after, was made an advisor to the prime minister's cabinet.[25]

Increasing Taliban control in the Swat region of the North West Frontier Province has curtailed women's rights in the area. According to a local Islamist leader, "Female education is against Islamic teachings and spreads vulgarity in society."[26]

In the same region during 2008, the Taliban destroyed nearly 150 private schools with separate sections for boys and girls[27] and turned others into *madrassas*, or religious seminaries.[28] Over 100 government schools were forcibly closed in 2008, but following a Taliban ultimatum, the rest were ordered shut by January 15, 2009, and several government officials were beheaded.[29] Despite a security pledge by the provincial administration, school owners were too fearful to resist the ban and the Taliban continued its policy of blowing up schools.[30]

A smuggled cell phone video of a public flogging in the Swat region showed a woman being whipped while surrounded by "hundreds of spectators shouting 'Allah-o-Akbar' (God is great)."[31]

It was alleged that the seventeen-year-old victim had committed adultery.[32] Other reports claimed she had left the house without a male kin as chaperone or that a Taliban commander had falsely accused her of flaunting shari'ah law after she spurned his marriage proposal.[33]

In response, Pakistani women's rights activist Asma Jahangir declared: "This is an eye-opener. Terrorism has seeped into every corner of the country. It is time that every patriotic Pakistani should raise a voice against such atrocities."[34]

ASMA JAHANGIR

> *I was born a Muslim and that is still my identity. Islam is no more violent or fanatical than any other religion—it's just that many Muslim countries have politicized religion for the benefit of the rulers. There are Christian fanatics and Hindu fanatics too—put a gun in the hands of any of them and they will terrorize people. Religion should be something personal. It should not be the concern of the state, and no religion has a right to degrade women or erode their human dignity.*[35]

> *I always ask these Islamists, "What kind of justice do you want? Give me specifics." Look how selectively Sharia law is applied here. When*

> *Zia started his Islamization, it was aimed first at women, non-Muslims, and the poor. That served his purpose. It is never invoked against the élite.*[36]

Asma Jahangir was born in Pakistan in 1952, five years after the partition of India and Pakistan and the end of the British Raj. She was the daughter of Malik Jilani, a prominent and outspoken politician who spent years in prison and under house arrest for his opposition to successive military regimes.

An activist from her earliest years, Jahangir was suspended from school when she was seventeen for organizing a student rally to protest against Pakistan's military dictator Ayub Khan. At eighteen, she filed a petition questioning the legality of her father's detention. Eventually, the Supreme Court released Jilani, with an unprecedented ruling against the military's "law of necessity," which they had used for years to legitimize their actions.[37]

Jahangir studied law privately, passed the bar exam in 1978, and received her degree in 1979. In February 1980, with two fellow lawyers and her sister, Hina, she started AGHS Law Associates, the first all-female legal practice in Pakistan. Most of their cases were pro bono; their income was derived from those who could afford to pay. The practice became successful, however, eventually defending more family law cases than any other law firm in Pakistan, and Hina and Asma were made advocates to the High Court in 1981 and 1982, respectively.

In 1980, the sisters and their colleagues were part of a group of women who established the Women's Action Forum. The organization was created to campaign against Pakistan's discriminatory legislation, most notably the evidence law, in which the value of a woman's testimony was specified as half that of a male's testimony, and the Hudood Ordinances.

In 1983, frustrated with endlessly explaining these laws and dealing with their ramifications, Asma staged a public protest with regard to a notorious example of their application. A young blind girl, Safia, was raped but was then herself arrested, imprisoned, and sentenced to death on a charge of *zina* (extramarital sex). When Asma's colleagues and supporters clashed with police, Asma and Hina were arrested and imprisoned for two and a half weeks. "We [their law firm] had been given a lot of cases by the advocate general and the moment this demonstration came to light, the cases were taken away from us," Asma recalled.[38]

In 1986, Asma and Hina set up AGHS Legal Aid, the first free legal aid center in Pakistan. In the same year, realizing that they needed to unify their efforts in order to be effective, Asma, with the Women's Action Forum and other activist groups, formed the Human Rights Commission of Pakistan, of which Asma became secretary-general. Working with the commission brought her into contact with bonded and child laborers, and forsaking most of her other legal work, she visited them in the Bhatta area on a daily basis for more than two and a half years. To make the community more aware of this form of slavery, she wrote a storybook in Urdu about a boy who works as a bonded laborer in order to repay his father's debts. She also filed case after case on behalf of laborers until the High Court ruled in her favor and outlawed forms of bonded labor.

Asma built an outstanding legal career defending the many victims of the Hudood Ordinances and fighting for justice for the powerless and the oppressed. She has defended victims of rape, women seeking divorce from abusive husbands, those accused of blasphemy and facing death by stoning, religious minorities, bonded adults and children, and those who were arrested and then disappeared in the prison system. She has presented a constant challenge to the political and religious leaders of Pakistan on issues of justice and human rights.[39]

As William Dalrymple of the *New Yorker* observed, "Pakistan is a notably patriarchal society, but Jahangir is its most visible and celebrated—as well as most vilified—human-rights lawyer. . . . For Pakistan's liberals, she is a symbol of freedom and defiance, comparable to Aung San Suu Kyi, in Burma."[40]

In 1990, Benazir Bhutto approached Asma about running for office in her government, and in 1994, Bhutto asked her to become the country's first female judge of the High Court. Asma declined both invitations in order to continue her work in defense of human rights. She said she could not work within a system she did not believe in. "It would be hypocrisy to defend laws I don't believe in, like capital punishment, the blasphemy law and laws against women and in favor of child labour."[41]

In 1998, the United Nations Commission on Human Rights appointed Asma Jahangir as special rapporteur on extrajudicial, arbitrary, and summary executions. In that capacity, she has visited Albania, Macedonia, Mexico, East Timor, Nepal, Turkey, and Honduras. "It gives me an opportunity to pick up the issues from the ground and take them right to the top, to the UN level."[42]

Murder and the threat of death have accompanied Jahangir since childhood. When she was thirteen, a man who resembled her father was shot dead as he approached the house, and a second man was badly wounded. In the absence of her parents, Jahangir accompanied the wounded man to hospital. Her family has always believed the assassination was a government-sanctioned attempt on her father's life.

Jahangir received numerous death threats in 1995 for her defense of Salamat Masih, a fourteen-year-old Christian boy sentenced to death for allegedly writing blasphemous words on the wall of a mosque. During the trial, a sniper was discovered taking aim at Jahangir in the courtroom while Islamic fundamentalists chanted, "Death, death, death!" outside. The police released the sniper without charging him.[43] In the weeks after the trial, Asma's family compound was attacked by a group of jihadists searching for Asma and her young son. They took hostage the family of one of Jahangir's sisters. The siege ended when Jahangir called the police and the jihadists escaped.

In 1999, Samia Sawar, a client of Jahangir's, was murdered in the AGHS offices. Sawar's own family had arranged the so-called honor killing when she persisted in seeking a divorce from an abusive husband.[44]

In November 2007, President Musharraf imposed a state of emergency in Pakistan, suspended the constitution, dismissed the chief justice, and arrested more than five hundred lawyers, opposition politicians, and human rights activists. Jahangir was put under house arrest for ninety days, reportedly to prevent her from making "inflammatory speeches." The police also raided the offices of the Human Rights Commission and arrested fifty-five of its members. They were charged with holding "illegal assembly" and remanded to a prison in Lahore. Jahangir pointed out that she was "fortunate" to be under house arrest, because other prominent lawyers were being held in solitary confinement and tortured. She said, regretfully, that Mr. Musharraf had "lost his marbles."[45]

On January 6, 2008, the Pakistan Muslim League (PML-Q), supporters of Musharraf, discovered Asma's two daughters filming torn election posters in Lahore eleven days after the assassination of Benazir Bhutto. The group of armed men beat the girls and their two male colleagues before taking them to the PML-Q's election office. When Jahangir arrived, she was restrained outside at gunpoint. However, she climbed the gate, saw the gunmen taking her youngest daughter to a separate room, and called the local police:

The police took the side of the armed men and pressurized the parents of the friends of her daughters to hand over the video tape which they did. The police then threatened the parents that they should not report this incident otherwise the girls would be kidnapped, raped and killed. The police also pressured the parents to stop Ms. Asma Jahangir from making this incident known and claimed that she would bear the responsibility for whatever might happen in the future.[46]

As of February 6, 2008, Jahangir is head of the Pakistan Human Rights Commission.

Awards

1982 Advocate to the Lahore High Court

1985 Founder of Women's Action Forum

1986 Founding Member of the Human Rights Commission of Pakistan

1992 Advocate, Supreme Court of Pakistan

1995 Martin Ennals Award and Ramon Magsaysay Award

1998 UN Special Rapporteur of the Commission on Human Rights on Extrajudicial, Summary, or Arbitrary Executions

2000 Bernard Simons Memorial Award of the International Bar Association

2009 Litvack Award, Canada

Honorary doctorates in law, Queen's University, Canada, 1998; University of St. Gallen, Switzerland, 1998; Amherst College, Massachusetts, 2003

Published Works

Divine Section: The Hudud Ordinances, 1988

Children of a Lesser God, 1992

Papers on child labor, bonded labor and slavery, women's empowerment, gender and justice, the independence of the judiciary, strategies for human rights, and the electoral process in Pakistan

MUKHTARAN BIBI (MUKHTAR MAI)

I only know one thing and that is how to fight against all odds.
I have no political ambitions. My goal is to fight injustice with
the help of knowledge.[47]

On June 22, 2002, thirty-year-old Mukhtaran Bibi was raped by four men, on the orders of the local *jirga*, or village council, in the Southern Punjab village of Meerwala in Pakistan. The rape was a traditional revenge demanded by the Mastoi tribe because, they said, Mai's brother, Shakur, had brought shame upon them, having been seen with the Mastoi chief's daughter. In fact, the twelve-year-old Shakur had been kidnapped and sodomized by three Mastoi men, and no evidence presented to date indicates that Shakur did more than speak to the woman.

To settle the matter, however, in a hastily gathered tribal meeting, it was proposed that Bibi and Shakur intermarry with the Mastoi, and if Shakur was found guilty of wrongdoing, his family would give the Mastoi some land. The Mastoi agreed, but asked Mukhtaran Bibi to come in person to apologize to them. When she arrived, she was taken into a hut at gunpoint and raped for an hour.

After the gang rape she was thrown out of the hut and left to walk home in her torn shirt, her father covering her with a shawl to shield her from the eyes of the villagers. Within the traditions of tribal honor and the caste system, Bibi would have been expected to kill herself following her humiliation. However, the local imam, Abdul Razzaq, persuaded the family to file charges against the men who were involved, and he brought a journalist to hear Bibi's story. The journalist's report was printed in the local paper and the case became headline news in Pakistan. It was picked up by the international media in the weeks that followed.

On the instructions of the Punjab government, local police arrested fourteen men and charged them with being either actively involved or complicit in the rape. The men who sodomized Shakur were convicted and each sentenced to five years' imprisonment. Of the fourteen arrested for the rape of Bibi, six were sentenced to death in July 2002 in a Southern Punjab court (the four who raped Bibi and the two who ordered that the crime be committed), but eight were acquitted and released. In September, both

Mukhtaran Bibi and the state filed appeals in the High Court in Lahore against the decision to acquit the eight men.

In the same month, Mukhtaran Bibi was given $8,200 compensation by the Pakistani government and began setting up two schools in her village, one for boys and one for girls. In response to an article in the *New York Times*, Bibi received donations amounting to a further $133,000 to help fund the schools. An American aid agency that works in Pakistan, Mercy Corp, was enlisted to manage the funds.[48]

Mukhtaran Bibi became affectionately known in the press as Mukhtar Mai—"respected big sister"—and she came to symbolize the struggle of oppressed women against the patriarchal tribal law that dominates rural Pakistan. The story made national and international news because it was shocking that some authority, however local, had ordered the crime to be committed. It was also unusual in that Mukhtar testified against her attackers and pursued them through the court system.

In Pakistan, under the Islamic laws (the Hudood Ordinances), a rape victim must present four male witnesses to the crime or risk being beaten and imprisoned herself. Obviously, in most cases, this is not possible, so rape generally goes unpunished. Pakistan's Independent Human Rights Commission estimates that a woman is raped or gang-raped every few hours in Pakistan. The number of "honor killings," burnings, and acid attacks, crimes with almost exclusively female victims, is growing each year, in some categories exponentially. Since most incidents are not reported, the real number of attacks on women is likely to be much higher than estimated.[49]

> Gone are those carefree days today.
> I never knew I would be burdened with so much responsibility.[50]

Empowered by local and international concern and given voice by the international media, Mukhtar resolved to devote her life to changing the circumstances in which she had become just one more victim. In so doing, she became an agent for social change against all the odds.

> What mental slavery is this that women in my country do not ask for their rights, fearing that it is against their dignity to do so?[51]

In 2003, she founded the Mukhtar Mai Women's Welfare Organization (MMWWO), which focuses its efforts on three areas of Southern Punjab: Multan (the largest city in the region), Muzaffargarh, and Dera Ghazi Khan.

> Women are facing a lot of problems here, not only at the workplace, but they're also facing domestic violence and abuses. I can only understand one reason for this. They think women are weaker than men. Men have all controls in society. The second reason is illiteracy. Women are uneducated. They don't know their rights.[52]

The purpose of MMWWO is to reduce gender-based violence "through advocacy, sensitisation, awareness raising, media campaigns and networking." MMWWO informs women of their social, political, economic, and legal rights, teaches them to read and write, and assists women to empower themselves economically.

> No doubt, injustice against women in Pakistan essentially emanates from their inability to earn their own money.[53]

The organization helps victims of violence through crisis relief centers that provide legal, medical, psychological, moral, and financial support. From the original school project that Mukhtar started in 2003, there are now three schools providing free education to over seven hundred girls and boys along with school uniforms, books, lunches, and transport services, and a high school is being built. MMWWO also runs a dairy farm and provides an ambulance service.

> We are afraid for our lives, but we will face whatever fate brings for us.[54]

On March 3, 2005, the Lahore High Court reversed the decisions of the local court and acquitted five of the six men who had previously been convicted. The sentence of the sixth was commuted to life imprisonment.[55] Mukhtar, aware of the danger she would be in, faced with the five freed men living in the same village, held a press conference announcing she would appeal to President Musharraf. On March 7, three thousand women rallied with her to demand justice and she traveled to Islamabad to meet with the minister for the interior and, the next day, with the president. The accused men were arrested again, pending an appeal in the Supreme Court.

Mukhtar was invited by Amnesty International to speak in London on June 10, 2005. President Musharraf, however, who later said he feared that Pakistan's image would be unfairly tarnished abroad, placed her name on the exit control list to prevent her from leaving the country. She was also kept under house arrest for fifteen to sixteen days.[56] After national and international protests and the personal intervention of the then US secretary of state, Condoleezza Rice, the prime minister ordered her name to be taken off the list. However, just after Mukhtar received a visa to travel to America to receive an award from *Glamour* magazine, her passport was confiscated again, preventing her from traveling. The passport was returned two weeks later. On another occasion, when she had a speaking engagement in New York on the same day as the prime minister of Pakistan, she was required to cancel her engagement. Since she had to return to Pakistan, the delay meant she could not address the meeting at all.

> I'm so thankful to everyone that they keep a woman like me in mind. . . .
> If some people think I'm a hero, it's only because of all those people who give me support.[57]

Mukhtar has since traveled and spoken in America, Europe, and numerous other overseas locations. She started a weekly blog on the BBC Urdu Web site in November 2006, noting in diary fashion the frequent crimes against women and the social injustices that are a part of her daily life. Mukhtar, who is illiterate, is learning to read and write as a student at her own school, and her words have been written up by local BBC journalist Nadeem Saeed.[58]

In collaboration with Marie-Therese Cuny and Linda Coverdale, Mukhtar has produced a book, *In the Name of Honor: A Memoir*, and a documentary about her, *Dishonored*, has been made by a Norwegian company, Basic Films.

Nicholas Kristof, a *New York Times* journalist who has supported Mukhtar's cause in his column since the beginning, reported that the Pakistani authorities were harassing her and trying to destroy her organization. He quoted Farooq Leghari, a police chief, who said he was transferred away from Meerwala because he tried to protect Mukhtar. Mr. Leghari said that the "harassment and pressure on them is from very high up, from Islamabad" and that Mukhtar and Nadeem could be killed by assassins sent by feudal lords or by the Pakistani government itself. Kristof warned that if anything untoward did happen to Mukhtar Mai, it would come under international scrutiny.[59]

In February 2009, Mukhtar complained that the Federal Minister of State for Defense production had put pressure on her to drop charges against her rapists and accused her of self-seeking publicity.[60]

Mukhtar Mai wed Nasir Abbas Gabol, a police constable, on March 15, 2009. It was an arranged marriage. She demanded unsuccessfully that he divorce his first wife, with whom he has five children.[61]

Awards

August 2, 2005: the Pakistani government awarded Mukhtaran the Fatima Jinnah gold medal for bravery and courage.

November 2, 2005: the US magazine *Glamour* named Mukhtaran as their Woman of the Year.

March 2007: Mukhtaran formally received the 2006 North-South Prize of the Council of Europe for her contributions to human rights.

RAHEEL RAZA (PAKISTAN/CANADA)

> *This struggle for our survival as peace loving, normal Muslims in Canada is no longer about religion. What we are facing is a political ideology gone mad and a battle for power and hegemony in the Muslim world, which has found a niche, and an audience in North America.*[62]

Raheel Raza became aware of the global jihad well before 9/11, after General Zia Islamized the law in her native Pakistan and petrodollars advanced extremist Wahhabi and Salafi ideology. Fearing a sinister Islamist threat to Pakistan and to Canada, to which she immigrated in 1989, Raza took on the challenge of radical Islam. As a result, she became exposed to fatwas and death threats, together with hate mail and accusations of being a "Zionist and Neo-con agent."[63]

Married with two grown sons, she is a writer, public speaker, filmmaker, and interfaith consultant and a recipient of the City of Toronto's Constance Hamilton Award for her promotion of Muslim women's rights.[64]

> For the sake of future generations in the West, we must understand that we are at risk of ghettoizing ourselves and being labeled "the other" if we don't

get with the plan and work towards being the mainstream. If we insist that we can't change, then we're entirely to blame when we remain on the fringes of society.[65]

Her critical and spiritual exploration of Islam in Canada was very different from the rote learning she had experienced while growing up in Pakistan. She became aware of the Islam's similarities to its predecessors, Judaism and Christianity, prompting her subsequent commitment to interfaith dialogue and education.[66] The reform she seeks is to *reclaim* the positive ideals of Islam and reject the jihadist political message.

> To fully understand the political Islamist . . . you have to know that the Wahhabi/Salafi ideology, which blows like a wind from the desert, is the idea that Islam is the only solution and that Muslims must rule the world and force everyone to become Muslim . . . the hard core political message that was born on the death bed of the Prophet and is only good for power and control.
>
> This path dehumanizes women and minorities and doesn't respect Muslims who follow a different path. This has led to theocracies like Iran and Saudi Arabia where the men rule through fear and faith has been made into a terrorizing force rather than the message of reform.[67]

Not all Muslims agree with Raza. Radicalization, they argue, is not so widespread and she is spreading "ludicrous hate and fear mongering," a form of racism that must be resisted.[68]

In her book *Their Jihad . . . Not My Jihad!* Raza contrasts the "true" interpretation of jihad as striving for personal development with the jihad of violence and holy war that she deplores and fears.[69]

> In Canada I feel like I'm fighting not only for the soul of Islam but for the safety of Canada. All around us we are battling against the MSA's (Muslim Student Associations) in educational institutions which are quite radical. . . . When the political leaders want to meet leaders of the community, they go to the same leaders who preach hate and division. Multiculturalism has only fueled ghettoization.[70]

In addition, she believes that appeasement of Islamists has become widespread: "Why do we allow an Imam in Scarborough to openly flout Canadian law by performing polygamous marriages? He's also known to recruit youth to fight a jihad in Afghanistan against our Canadian soldiers."[71]

Raza has warned about the infiltration of pro-shari'ah politicians and Islamist organizations like the Canadian Islamic Congress (CIC) into Canadian political parties that endorsed the New Democratic Party (NDP): "the left-leaning NDP has shown an incredible lack of understanding of the Islamist agenda and how soft jihads are using democratic institutions by manipulating our respect for multiculturalism."[72]

However, when only one Muslim was elected in October 2008, Islamophobia was blamed. According to Raza, Canadians were tired of accommodating "politics disguised as religion."[73]

> In the long-term Islamism seeks to establish an Islamic state in North America, but this is barely mentioned by the suave and polished young Islamists. . . . While a Taliban style overthrow is unlikely, in the short term, Islamists hope to fundamentally change western foreign policy in favor of the foreign governments that fund them and organizations they ideologically adhere to, such as the Muslim Brotherhood.[74]

She cautions that all Muslims will suffer for the acts of a few unless they stop "screaming Islamophobia" and confront the radicals and counter the designs of Iran and Saudi Arabia.[75] "There is no rampant Islamophobia in Canada—only an attempt at gradual Islamization."[76] Islamists, she argues, have found fertile soil in Canada, where they can propagate their ideology with impunity and infiltrate government.

> Canadians are so afraid of being called racist, that they won't stand up to religious extremism. . . . Politicians bend over backwards for the sake of votes totally disregarding the voices of Muslims like me, who are saying be careful of what you agree to and what's under your nose because it will come back to bite you.[77]

> While the jihadist propaganda continues and the Islamists strengthen their hold on the community, working to implement religious schools, religious laws and religious accommodation through the back door, what's happening to the handful of resisting voices?
>
> We're ignored by the politicians, threatened by the Islamists and harshly critiqued by our own community.[78]

19
QATAR

BACKGROUND

The legal system allows leniency for a man found guilty of committing a "crime of honor," or a violent assault against a woman for perceived immodesty or defiant behavior; however, such honor killings are rare.

Women may attend court proceedings but generally are represented by a male relative; however, women may represent themselves if they wish. The testimony of two women equals that of one man, but the courts routinely interpret this on a case-by-case basis.[1]

Qatari women are achieving an increasingly egalitarian role in society, albeit slowly. Sheikh Hamad bin Khalifa al-Thani, ruler of Qatar, has introduced democratic reforms since coming to power in 1995.[2] Considering that Qatar had its first ever elections in March 1999, the reforms represent progress. Female candidates took part in those elections but were not sufficiently supported by the electorate, even though women made up 44 percent of the eligible voters.

Women in Qatar represented about 14 percent of the labor force and their adult literacy rate is over 88 percent.[3] These statistics, combined with the encouragement provided by the nation's ruler, indicate progress for the women of Qatar.

One of the most public advocates of the right of women in Qatar is Her Highness Sheikha Mozah, wife of the emir. "Her Highness has given prominence to the role of Qatari women and created an environment that encourages them to meet their social obligations and participate in public life. [She] endorses women's conferences, which discuss . . . and recommend solutions for the problems and challenges that confront women who work outside the home."[4] Such encouragement is also apparent in the creation of government-affiliated organizations established to deal specifically with women's issues. These include the Women's Affairs Department, which aims to find employment opportunities for women congruent with their nature and social role. A second example is the Women's Affairs Committee, which, as an affiliate of the Supreme Council for Family Affairs, proposes policies and plans to advance the cause of women in various arenas.[5]

"As of April 2007, Qatar had not ratified the Convention on the Elimination of All Forms of Discrimination against Women (CEDAW)."[6] However, Qatar does appear to be working toward some of the obligations listed in the convention. For example, Sheikh Hamad appointed Sheikha bint Ahmed al-Mahmud to the position of minister of education in April 2003.[7] In addition, three sections of the Ministry of Justice are headed by women: the Fatwah and Research, Translation and Official Newsletter, and Legislation sections.[8] While these may be considered token appointments, they are a significant step in a country where women have only recently taken a public role.

There is significant traditional opposition to women's public roles that has not been eradicated:

> The majority of Qatar's citizens, male and female, oppose women taking an active role in public life. The traditional Islamic background of the nation, particularly among the older generation, has fostered a critical attitude towards westernization and women's rights.[9]

SHEIKHA MOZAH BINT NASSER AL-MISSNED

> By encouraging critical thinking and processing of knowledge we are creating full, well-rounded human beings . . . that will enable Qatar to build up its society.[10]

Sheikha Mozah Al-Missned's father was imprisoned by Emir Khalifa bin Hamad al-Thani, reportedly for calling publicly for a fairer distribution of wealth in Qatar, and the Missned clan went into exile in Kuwait. However, in 1977, Mozah Al-Missned married the emir's son, Sheikh Hamad bin Khalifa al-Thani.[11]

In 1995, Sheikh Hamad, having gained the support of the various al-Thani factions, deposed his father in a bloodless coup and became the new emir of Qatar.[12] The sheikh energetically set about transforming the small, traditional nation into one of the most progressive in the region. Qatar has since begun to play an international role as both the home of Al-Jazeera television and a US ally in the Middle East. Qatar also gained a nonpermanent seat on the UN Security Council, its application having received unprecedented support from Israel for an Arab state.[13] Qatar's most outstanding achievement is in the equilibrium it has achieved in adopting a progressive social policy while maintaining its Islamic identity.[14]

The sheikha has played an indispensable role in this achievement by championing the emancipation and empowerment that women have experienced in the region. She is the second wife of the emir of Qatar and the mother of seven of his children. She is also the first and only ruling spouse in Qatar to take a public role in national and international affairs.[15]

Her focus has been on education and social reform, and she has orchestrated numerous national and international development projects.

> Youth can be both the driving force toward economic growth and the badly needed source of innovative thinking required to instigate a genuine Renaissance between the West and Muslim countries. Education lies at the heart of a revival of cooperative relations.[16]

The sheikha is chairperson of the Qatar Foundation for Education, Science, and Community Development, a private nonprofit organization founded in 1995. In 2003, the foundation opened Education City, to provide high-quality degree programs and academic collaboration and to sponsor community projects, with representatives from the best universities in the world.[17] Another project of the Qatar Foundation, the Science and Technology Park, connects academia with industry.

Sheikha Al-Missned is also president of the Supreme Council for Family Affairs, a government institution that promotes the role of the family in society, and vice chair of the Supreme Education Council, which has supervised a comprehensive restructuring of Qatar's K-12 education system.[18]

In addition, she is chairperson of the Sidra Medical and Research Center project, which has created a world-class specialist teaching facility, the Weill Cornell Hospital in Qatar; chairperson of the Silatech initiative, which addresses the challenge of youth employment in the Middle East and North Africa region; and she is chairperson of the Arab Democracy Foundation in Doha.

In 2003, UNESCO appointed the sheikha as a special envoy for basic and higher education, to promote a number of international projects to improve the standard and availability of education worldwide.[19]

> We are trying to make students think and analyze instead of making them memorize descriptive information. . . . The students must know English in addition to the Arabic language. . . . They must know the history of their country and they should know that they are living in a society based on the exploitation and export of oil and gas. They should also know the impact of changes taking place in the Middle East and the Gulf. . . . We are trying to change the University of Qatar from a traditional university to one based on international standards.[20]

In June 2003, the sheikha established the International Fund for Higher Education in Iraq, which is dedicated to the reconstruction of institutions of advanced learning. In 2005, she was invited to become a member of the High Level Group for the UN Alliance of Civilizations, which was established by then UN secretary-general Kofi Annan.[21] In addition to her education reforms, she set up the region's first woman's refuge and upgraded public transport for foreign workers.[22]

In 2007, Sheikha Mozah was given the Chatham House Award in recognition of her commitment to progressive education and community welfare in Qatar and her advocacy of closer relations between Islamic countries and the West. The award is given to the statesperson who is considered to have made the most significant contribution to international relations in the previous year.[23]

Also in 2007, *Forbes* magazine named her one of the hundred most powerful women in the world, and the *Times* (London) named her one of the twenty-five most influential business leaders in the Middle East.[24]

The sheikha has become an icon and role model for the people of Qatar "as someone who has found a balance between modernity, and fidelity to the core values of Islam and Arab culture."[25]

> When asked on the occasion of a speech at Chatham House about the situation of women in Qatar, she answered by pointing out two young women sitting in the front row saying, "These two women are ministers in Qatar. I need not say more."[26]

SAUDI ARABIA

BACKGROUND

The abuse of women's rights in Saudi Arabia is not simply the unfortunate consequence of overzealous security forces and religious police. It is the inevitable result of a state policy which gives women fewer rights than men, which means that women face discrimination in all walks of life, and which allows men with authority to exercise their power without any fear of being held to account for their actions.[1]

Women lead severely restricted lives in this desert kingdom, which has been criticized for practicing "gender apartheid."[2] Segregated where they eat, work, and pray, women need permission for almost everything, including education, employment, or buying an airline ticket. Women cannot vote or run for public office. Unless they are close relatives, men and women do not sit together in the same room. In public dining areas, men eat in the main restaurant but women are relegated to smaller "family areas" away from the public eye.

They must be chaperoned by a husband or male relative, and in a public place, women are compelled to wear the *niqab*, or full face veil, and the *abaya*, a long black robe that absorbs the heat. In contrast, men wear white, reflecting heat.[3] In addition to the *niqab*, an influential Saudi cleric has ordered women to cover one eye to avoid seductive eye makeup.[4]

Citizens are denied generally accepted human rights, including freedom of association, freedom of expression, and diversity of religious practice. According to Amnesty International, fear and secrecy are pervasive:

> The fear is maintained by: the constant risk of arbitrary arrest; harsh punishments for anyone who dares to criticize official policies; the mutawa'een (religious police)[5] who have, in practice, unfettered powers to harass and detain anyone they believe has breached the strict moral codes.[6]

Detainees are denied access to lawyers and may be subjected to mock trials, torture, flogging, amputation, and beheading.[7] The Mutaween threaten, beat, and arrest women who breach the dress code.[8] During a fire at a girls' school in March 2002, they refused to allow eight hundred girls trapped in the locked building to leave, because they were not wearing the headscarves and *abayas* mandatory for the public space. Some girls who tried to escape were beaten back by the religious police. Fifteen girls died in the blaze and fifty were injured.[9]

Secrecy penetrates almost every state institution:

> There are no political parties, no elections, no independent legislature, no trades unions, no Bar Association, no independent judiciary, no independent human rights organizations. The government . . . ignores requests by such organizations for information. . . . There is strict censorship of media within the country and strict control of access to the Internet, satellite television and other forms of communication with the outside world.[10]

The most frequently targeted victims include political dissidents, activists among the Shia minority, migrant workers, and people who break the moral codes.[11]

All legal issues related to women are decided under religious law, and interpreted by the Council of Senior Ulama (religious scholars) with the permission of the king. Muslim clerics, who enforce the social code, preach that "women's rights" are Western ideas that are being imposed on the nation.

In ratifying gender-based religious decisions, the government has given men a considerable legal and social advantage. For example, a man can obtain a divorce easily by request, whereas a woman must appeal for a legal decision. The testimony of a woman is regarded not as fact but as presumption. Male kin must give written consent if a woman requires medical treatment, and when traveling, she must be chaperoned by a male member of the family, a *mahram*, in order to avoid harsh penalties.[12] Women are also forbidden to drive a car or ride a bicycle.[13]

In 2007, a nineteen-year-old woman and her former boyfriend were each sentenced to ninety lashes after they were taken from a car at knifepoint by seven men and both were raped. All involved were penalized, but the woman was charged with the crime of being with an unrelated man. She became known as "the Qatif girl" after the city of Qatif in the Eastern Province, where the rapes took place. After she went to the media denying the charges, a Saudi court increased her penalty to two hundred lashes and suspended her lawyer. Following international outrage, however, the Saudi foreign minister called the ruling a "bad judgment," and the case was sent for review.[14]

Although the government signed the Convention on the Elimination of All Forms of Discrimination against Women (CEDAW), albeit with reservations with regard to any conflict with Islamic law, most of the provisions of the convention have not been implemented. However, a reform was introduced to allow Saudi women who marry foreigners to retain their nationality.[15]

According to the World Bank, 33 percent of women in Saudi Arabia are illiterate compared with 17 percent of men, but their educational opportunities have improved and they now make up 58 percent of university students. Women are excluded, however, from courses such as engineering and architecture, and constitute only 5 percent of the labor force.[16] Enforced segregation of men and women in the workplace limits women's choices of employment, which are usually restricted to healthcare, education, and the civil service.[17] Despite the segregated employment allowed to them, many women adapt and advance. Increasingly, problems may arise when university-educated women are secluded in the home and are unable to find suitable sex-segregated jobs.

Although women are rarely visible in public life, there have been exceptional examples: Princess Al-Jawhara Fahad bin Mohammed bin Abdel Rahman al-Saud was appointed assistant undersecretary for education affairs in 2000, and Princess Dr. Al-Jawhara bint Fahd Al-Saud was appointed as president of Riyadh University for women in April 2007.[18]

The position of Saudi women in society is characterized by idealization and infantilization; their identity is defined by relationships to fathers, husbands, and brothers. The responsibility they bear for the honor of their male kin and tribe is safeguarded by prescribed appearance and behavior, and they are expected to dedicate their lives primarily to husband, family, and domestic duties in a strictly sequestered existence. In some houses there are even rooms that have separate entrances for men and women.[19]

Marriage presents alternatives, all restrictive to women. Apart from polygyny, shari'ah-compliant marriages include *misyar*, in which a man may visit his wife at her family's home without incurring any financial responsibility. *Mesfar* allows temporary marriage to a *mahram* to allow women to travel abroad with a legal escort, and *wanasa* can be utilized by older men to marry young girls. Some religious authorities claim that fathers can arrange the marriage of their female toddlers but consummation must be delayed until the girl turns nine.[20]

According to the Koran, women can inherit half the share of a man, but in practice, it is frequently held in trust. Similarly, a bride's *mahr*, or dowry, is often kept by her family. As men usually manage the financial affairs and Islamic law does not recognize the concept of joint property, husbands commonly use their wives' assets as their own. Women can transact business and have separate bank accounts, but in most cases they leave economic management and control to men.

Attitudes to gender issues can be divided into three main types.[21] Traditionalists, who are in the majority, believe that segregation of women, the veil, and polygyny are basic to political and religious obedience and fear that Islamic traditions are threatened by Western, modernizing influences. Liberal modernists, who promote engagement with the West and relaxation of government-enforced Islam, believe women can have careers, providing they do not sacrifice parental responsibilities. The ultraconservative Salafis, who adhere to the principles of the first three generations of Islam, believe Saudi women should not work and that any reforms must take place within Islam. A small group of radical Salafis believe there is a "war" between the West and Islam, and blame the ruling elite for moral degeneration and lack of protection from a rapacious United States.[22]

Religion has determined social policy in the kingdom since its inception. The Saudi dynasty emerged in the central Arabian area in 1744 when Prince Muhammad ibn Saud, ruler of a city near Riyadh, formed a politico-religious alliance with a Muslim cleric, Muhammad ibn Abd-al-Wahhab, on the understanding that Prince Muhammad would zealously advance the cause of a purified Islam in line with ancient practice. During the period of the first Saudi state, the House of Saud became the dominant tribe, capturing the holy cities of Mecca and Medina from the Ottomans, who responded by driving out the House of Saud.

However, the Al Saud family and Wahhabi ideology survived to form a second Saudi state after the recapture of Riyadh in 1824. Battles with another dynastic tribe, the Al Rashid, also brought about the downfall of Al Saud, but a third and current Saudi state was founded in 1902 by Abdul Aziz ibn Saud with the reconquest of Riyadh and the subjugation of the Nejd and

Hejaz regions. The United Kingdom recognized the sovereignty of Abdul Aziz in the Treaty of Jeddah, and in 1932, these regions were unified to form the Kingdom of Saudi Arabia.

Central to the alliance between the Wahhabi clerics and the House of Saud was a long-term mission to eliminate all other ideologies and enforce Wahhabism in schools and mosques. In return, the Saudi dynasty received a religious imprimatur to oversee Islam's holiest sites in a symbiotic alliance that remains to this day in the interlaced religious and political roles of the clergy and the monarchical government.

The clergy's current power and authority still derive from the puritanical and extremist teachings of ibn Abd-al-Wahhab,[23] with more recent input from radical Egyptian Salafis who were embraced by Saudi Arabia in the 1960s in an effort to undermine the Egyptian pan-Arabism of Nasser. The result was a Wahhabi-Salafi mix containing a violent, jihadist strand.[24] Saudi school books reflect this ideology but the authorities have discussed revision of textbooks to exclude prejudice and incitement against people of other religions and non-Wahhabis.[25]

The vast oil reserves discovered in 1938 and developed after World War II have generated enormous financial rewards and pivotal geopolitical leverage. For example, Saudi investment in the United States represents almost 8 percent of the American economy and if this is withdrawn, the effects could be dire.[26] Massive petrodollar finance has also enabled the export of Wahhabi-Salafism to mosques and educational institutions worldwide.[27]

The perceived corruption of the rulers and unequal distribution of wealth have encouraged Islamist fervor.[28] Another factor has been Khomeini's Iranian Revolution, which challenged Saudi Arabia's Islamic preeminence and forced the leadership to adopt a more pious image.[29] Confrontation with modernity has also triggered increased piety, offering the certainties of Islam and a redefinition of identity.[30]

The first Gulf War served to strengthen resistance to reform by strengthening radical Islamists, who were affronted by the presence of an American base near the holiest shrines in Islam. In addition, the retrograde outlook of Wahhabism has been magnified in response to the challenges of modernization and globalization.[31] These forces have intensified Islamic observance and anti-Western attitudes among Saudi men and women in general.

When it comes to reform, the hands of the ruling elite are tied by their dependence on the religious authority, which confers legitimacy and tends to blame external powers for putting pressure on the government whenever it attempts to modernize. Any reform will be slow, but a "giant step" was taken when the kingdom allowed a mixed gender public audience for a Saudi comedy movie despite pressure from conservative clerics bent on strengthening Wahhabi orthodoxy.[32]

King Abdullah brought in a significant reform in February 2009, when he appointed Norah al-Faiz to the position of deputy education minister (for women's education), the most senior post ever held by a Saudi woman. In the reshuffling of the cabinet, Sheikh Ibrahim al-Ghaith, the hardliner chief of the *mutaween* religious police, was removed and Sheikh Saleh al-Lihedan, head of the Supreme Council of Justice, was dismissed, generating widespread condemnation in the Arab world. Small concessions to women's rights allowed women to study law and register a business without first hiring a male manager.[33] In addition, since January 2008, lone women, Muslim or non-Muslim, have been permitted to stay in Saudi Arabian hotels without a male guardian, providing a local police station is informed.[34]

REVIEW OF REFORMS

A selection of twenty-two women and three men (see chapter 28, "Male Muslim Activists") reformers are mentioned here or profiled below. Most are media activists. Fifteen women are journalists and eight of them write for the English-language Saudi daily, *Arab News*; the others are writers and columnists for Saudi Arabic daily newspapers and Internet dailies. Two also write for a London Arabic daily. Their critiques and analyses have a wide readership.

The types of reform they demand are mainly social, dealing with the right of women to drive, domestic violence, and education, and on the whole, they take the form of critiques, commentary, and analysis. According to columnist Fatima Al-Faqih, Saudi women face prohibitions that are endless. Of all the demands for reform, the most notable has been the determined campaign to permit women to drive cars, led by human rights activist Wajeha Al-Huwaider and by Fouzia Al-Ayouni.[35] This is part of a larger campaign demanding wider-ranging reforms. These efforts have been supported by other writers and media activists such as Suheila Hammad, Dana Al-Ghalib, and by Saudi men, Raid Qusti, Sleiman Al-Sleiman, and Suliman Al-Salman.

Some activists, including Suad Al-Shumari, have observed there is no religious injunction against women driving.[36] The campaign to drive, which took the form of demonstrations and petitions, led to Al-Huwaider's detention by the Mabahith, Saudi Arabia's secret police, and was widely reported in the West. Success was claimed when it was announced that the driving ban would be lifted as part of King Abdullah's program for reform. Warning of the cultural and logistical changes required to overcome what appears to be simply a legislative obstacle, Qusti has drawn attention, for example, to the problem of driving license photographs in a country where uncovering a woman's face is considered a sin.

Reform regarding domestic violence came to the fore when television presenter Rania Al-Baz was almost beaten to death by her husband. The extensive publicity given to her story instigated the first ever study on domestic violence in Saudi Arabia, revealing a widespread and intergenerational culture of silent, abused women. In this context, social scientist Badriyya Al-Bishri has cynically observed Saudi society's tendency to blame the victim and women's compliant acceptance of abuse,[37] whereas outspoken architect Nadia Bakhurji urged the establishment of NGOs to work with victims.

Many activists have stressed the need for educational reforms, ranging from teaching tolerance in schools and sports to self-defense for girls. Extensive reforms are advocated by Samar Fatany, particularly to the law college curriculum, which, she says, should not be confined to Islamic jurisprudence. According to columnist Halima Muzaffar, the spreading culture of fear and death in girls' schools could lead to extremist ideas like martyrdom. Given a national curriculum focused on rote learning even at the tertiary level, and religious distaste for critical thinking and interpretation, Buthayna Nasser laments that Saudi society's progress is hindered.[38] Women, who make up 55 percent of graduates but only 5 percent of the working population, also need to be integrated into the workforce, according to Maha Akeel.

Princess Adelah, daughter of King Abdullah and an advocate and worker for women's empowerment, believes women must be given the opportunity to participate in all areas of development in order to accelerate social progress in the kingdom. She also maintains that her father does not believe women are inferior to men and he would like to see their greater involvement in society. Western media, she says, stereotypes Arab women and overlooks their significant ambition and progress, but she believes that the greater transparency since 9/11 will help remove these distortions.[39]

None of the reformers question the religious basis for law and government or argue for a secular state. Their critique of religion centers rather on the distortion of Islam's teaching about women and their view of a true and peaceful Islam that has been subsumed by an aggressive and violent heretical strain. According to the reformers, women had political and economic rights in the era of the Prophet, and authentic Islam does not require them to cover their faces or live a sequestered life. They generally agree that Islam has been misused to defend social inequalities, resulting, for example, in the imposition of a *mahram*, or male guardian who controls and infantilizes a woman by choosing her spouse and grants her permission to travel, acquire property, apply for a divorce, take a graduate degree, and so forth. Journalist Nourah Al-Kereiji insists that the issuance of women's ID cards should not require a guardian's consent and that such ID cards must be recognized as valid identity documents by banks and government departments.[40] Hatoon Al-Fassi has written of the greater independence enjoyed by women in the pre-Islamic and early Islamic periods and believes that some discriminatory practices, such as that of the male guardian, probably have their roots in Greek and Roman rather than Arab traditions.[41]

Al-Fassi is the only reformer in this group who comments on reforms necessary among Western Muslims, based on her observations as a visiting academic in the UK. While acknowledging that Muslims in Britain are victims of racism and marginalization, Al-Fassi has been critical of university Islamic societies for fostering an environment in which extremism flourishes by inviting provocative speakers who flaunt racism as well as discrimination against women and the exclusion of women in their Friday sermons.[42]

Columnist Hasna Al-Quna'ir challenges extremist clerics directly, accusing them of altering the meaning of the hadith to justify their depiction of women as untrustworthy and subhuman, and she believes a serious cultural reconstruction would be required to overcome the deeply ingrained misogyny.

Television newscaster Buthayna Nasser lambastes men who force women to wear black in the fierce heat while men are allowed to wear white. Even a hint of color can lead to fines or prison sentences for shopkeepers selling such garments.[43] According to Nasser, "They should focus on fighting vices, not women. I do not understand why they force us to wear black in such a hot country while men can wear white."[44]

For Bakhurji and Saudi columnist Maha Al-Hujailan, the *abaya*, or mandatory black cloak is a symbol of segregation, not consistent with early

Islamic history. Al-Hujailan goes further, identifying the garment as a means of limiting vision and speech and as part of a culture of male domination built on oppression and fear.

Saudi scholar Suheila Hammad has been critical of new rules set in place since 2006 to remove women from the Kaaba, the holy, cubed structure inside the Grand Mosque in Mecca and the point to which Muslims turn while praying.[45] Hammad drew attention to this decision as an example of the discrimination the state practices against women.

Author and journalist Zeynab Hifni is scathing about religious authorities who label any hadith favorable to women as unreliable and trust those hadiths that denigrate women.[46] For Qusti, Saudi Arabia is a country dominated by men who exclude women from any public presence and view them as inferior in intelligence. Badriyya Al-Bishri refers to the condescending attitudes of men who denigrate her columns that highlight women's issues,[47] while Dania Al-Ghalib focuses on the guilt that is heaped upon Saudi women. Al-Huwaider makes the point that discrimination starts at birth and is reinforced by a process of fear and submission. According to Al-Hujailan, women have internalized this fear. Men, says Al-Baz, draw strength from their domination, especially the power of unchecked domestic violence.

Shari'ah marriage laws devised to favor men were challenged by women's rights activist Suad Al-Shumari in a television debate, when she confronted a Saudi cleric who averred that according to shari'ah law, girls aged nine can be married. Al-Shumari proclaimed that old men who marry young girls were "sick." She also disputed whether Islamic religious law binds women to accept the guardianship of male kin.[48]

Rajaa Al-Sanea, a twenty-four-year-old Saudi writer who advocates vocational reforms to empower Saudi women financially, caused a sensation with her controversial novel *The Girls of Riyadh*, officially banned in Saudi Arabia but selling on the black market for up to ten times its cover price.[49] Al-Sanea faced intense criticism for her portrayal of Saudi men and her condemnation of Saudi society, including discrimination against divorced women.

One reformer, Nadia Bakhurji, took up the issue of political reform. Starting with her decision to contest the elections to the Board of the Council of Saudi Engineers in 2005, she shocked the country, but won a seat on the ten-member board, the only female among seventy-one candidates. In the same year, she stood for election to a municipal council after identifying a loophole in the legal stipulations, inspiring five other women to stand. In the event, the women were prevented from running because there were no separate polling stations for women. However, Bakhurji plans to run again and is also advocating a quota for women in municipal elections.

In the London Arabic daily *Al-Sharq Al-Awsat*, Thuraya Al-Shihiri castigated Islamist groups for their doublespeak about their supposedly good intentions in implementing shari'ah. In truth, she says, their agenda is to foment revolution in Arab and Muslim states and take control through political Islam, utilizing every means to achieve their ends, including *takiyya* (concealing one's faith), designed to deceive by conveying double messages. If they come to power, she warns, they will segregate and oppress women in the name of religion and justify the persecution of Muslims by *takfir* (accusing other Muslims of heresy).

The past few years have seen an increasing number of activist female Saudi journalists in the Arab press, probably associated with reforms under King Abdullah, a notable development in a country where censorship is routinely practiced. Saudi women, usually excluded from male-dominated courses like engineering, are drawn to a more accessible profession like journalism. Notwithstanding government control of the Internet and blocking of Web sites, the milieu of global media networks must expose Saudi women journalists to women's rights issues in other countries, creating an awareness of the contrasts with their own society. Education abroad and increased travel must also stimulate challenging comparisons.

Even though Saudi Arabia has been a breeding ground for radical Islam and a state sponsor of it, none of the reformers, except for Thuraya Al-Shihiri, have confronted Islamic extremism, perhaps in the fear that sustained criticism would only serve to sideline dissidents and disqualify them from the debate. In any case, demands for reforms might be considered hopeless; even those sanctioned by the House of Saud could be quashed by the clerical authorities on whom the government depends for the conferring of legitimacy. In this context, it is interesting to note that Thuraya Al-Shihiri's article about Islamist doublespeak was published in the London Arabic daily *Al-Sharq Al-Awsat* and not in a Saudi newspaper.

In addition, there is little possibility of support from activist organizations or NGOs in a country without a civil society and in which freedom of assembly and freedom of association are forcibly denied. Even so, Al-Huwaider and Al-Salman managed to form fledgling organizations promoting reform, debate, and research.

Compared with women in surrounding Arab states, Saudi women are less advanced. In Bahrain, Kuwait, Qatar, and Jordan, an unequivocal drive for constitutional reform favoring human rights and women's rights has come from the top, although seriously hindered by internal Islamist forces. In such environments, women's rights discourse has led to the formation of nongovernmental organizations created to network, lobby, and achieve women's political participation and reform.

MAHA AKEEL

> *Doesn't an adult, mature woman have a say in matters concerning her own private life? Why is it only the man's wishes are looked at?*[50]

Maha Akeel is a journalist for the Middle Eastern English-language daily *Arab News*, based in Jeddah, Saudi Arabia. In November 2007, she published an article on the reformist Web site Aafaq in which she condemned Saudi society for infantilizing women and called for traditional beliefs that segregate women from the rest of society to be addressed. She has also spoken out against the conformism inherent in the education system.[51]

Akeel is quick to point out that most legal and societal inequalities are dishonest in their use of Islam as a tool of defense:

> A woman, even a 70-year-old woman, cannot travel abroad without the written, signed and notarized permission of her male guardian, who might be her son or nephew. Is this the respect we give our mothers, and we know how highly respected mothers are in Islam?[52]

The written consent of the male guardian, who is not limited by age or generation, is compulsory in all matters pertaining to women's lives, and whatever her age, her education, or her background, she is not seen as responsible enough to be master of her own affairs or body. Instead, she is forced to live her life according to the dictates of her male guardian. For Akeel this reveals the irony of the question: "At what age and under what circumstances is a woman in Saudi Arabia considered an independent, sane, responsible adult?"[53]

Akeel highlights marriage as one area that showcases the domination of male kin, for the opinion of a woman is not perceived as a necessary consideration when her father chooses her husband.

> Why is it that the system and society do not raise objections to a father marrying his 13-year-old daughter to a 70-year-old man but objects to a 40-year-old woman deciding to marry someone suitable against her father's wishes?[54]

An important issue for Akeel is that of the ulterior motive of the male guardian. His choice of husband for his charge is based on what is most suitable for him; the woman's opinion is not necessarily a point of concern. She may be forced into marriage against her will, kept from a marriage she desires against her will, or forcibly divorced against her will, all because both major and minor decisions about her life are made by somebody else.[55]

The examples given are not irregular, extreme cases, says Akeel. On a daily basis, Saudi women are humiliated in their "struggle to go about their normal life."[56] Everyday tasks become an ordeal; the journey to school or work becomes hazardous simply because women are entrusted to male drivers who may be criminals but still have a right to drive, a right denied to women.

In cases in which a woman wishes to acquire property, she cannot proceed without a male guarantor; to travel abroad she needs male permission; to apply for divorce or child custody she needs male permission and a male representative; and in court cases she must have two men who are willing to identify her, as her own self-identification is insufficient.

Akeel believes the key to reform lies in education, enabling Saudi Arabia to utilize the potential workforce of women, who make up 55 percent of graduates but only 5 percent of the working population.[57]

RANIA AL-BAZ

> *In Saudi Arabia, women do not have much of a place besides the kitchen and the bed. A wife is just a pleasure object for a man. The man can do whatever he wants with her with impunity. But now things are starting to change. Little by little, women are demanding more rights. I am happy to be involved in that noble cause.*[58]

On April 4, 2004, prominent Saudi television presenter Rania Al-Baz was beaten unconscious by her husband, Yunus Al-Fallatta, following an argument.

> I shouted for help from the neighbours but they did not come. A man who beats his wife is not such a rarity in Saudi Arabia. You don't get involved.[59]

Convinced he had killed her, Al-Fallatta dumped his wife outside a hospital.

Barely recognizable after her husband had smashed her head repeatedly against the marble floor of their home, Al-Baz suffered thirteen facial fractures and had to undergo extensive surgery. "I was in a pitiful state. I could hardly breathe. My family, friends and colleagues came to my bedside. They all said the same thing: you must do something. Take advantage of the fact that you are well known to teach this man and others like him a lesson."[60]

For many battered Saudi wives, the story might have ended there, given that they are the silent victims in a country where women cannot vote, drive a car, or leave home without a chaperone.

Al-Baz, however, made international headlines when she permitted newspapers to print the horrific images of the injuries she had sustained. "I was a celebrity. It is not every day that you get a television star being attacked on your beat."[61] The published photos shocked the world, Saudi society, and the Saudi royal family, who offered financial and emotional support. In the following month, the first Saudi research on domestic violence against women was conducted by a Saudi university.

Al-Baz aimed to highlight the plight of battered Saudi women:

> Every violent man will be able to see the suffering that he causes and every woman who is afraid of falling into a similar situation will be able to avoid what happened to me.[62]

A few weeks after the beating, Al-Fallatta came out of hiding and handed himself over to the police. Following a six-week trial, he was found guilty of grievous assault (reduced from attempted murder) and was sentenced to a public flogging and six months in jail. This was a landmark decision. Although Saudi law gives women protection from domestic violence, no woman prior to Al-Baz had pressed charges against her husband.

Al-Fallatta was released after three months, when Al-Baz pardoned him in exchange for his agreement to grant her a divorce and custody of their two boys. Divorce initiated by a woman in Saudi Arabia is very rare, although women have the right to divorce their husbands according to shari'ah law.

In 2005, Al-Baz appeared on *The Oprah Winfrey Show* "Women across the Globe," which featured eleven female victims of violence, each representing a different country and culture. Al-Baz was criticized for neglecting to emphasize the support she had received at home and for portraying Saudi women as victims of a backward, violent society.[63]

For some women, Al-Baz's decision to go public turned her into a heroine; in the eyes of other Saudis she is an outcast:

> Forgiving her husband, her reconstructed new face made up, her hair unveiled and tinted with colour, coming out and talking to Oprah Winfrey, she is now an outcast. She dared to unveil and dared to change. The good she did by bringing to light the long-held taboo of talk of abuse, the opening of women's shelters since, the campaigns against violence that began, all forgotten by a society that took issue with her unveiling. Her husband had the right to it. She invited violence.[64]

Al-Baz has written her memoirs and has devoted herself to counseling women on how to deal with abusive husbands.

> I give practical advice about medical help . . . finding a lawyer. I always tell them they must report their husbands.
> By revealing what happened to me, I have provoked a debate. That's what is new in Saudi Arabia. People are talking.[65]

She now lives in Paris, having left her children with her mother in Saudi Arabia.

MAHA AL-HUJAILAN

> *The abaya makes women appear humiliated, submissive, and blindly obedient to men; and for men, it represents their sexual thoughts and desires for women.*[66]

Maha Al-Hujailan is a Saudi columnist who has written articles criticizing the oppression of women in Saudi society. She has condemned the clothing restrictions for women and the culture of fear that characterizes women's experience of marriage. This fear, she says, is felt by every married woman at the thought of her husband taking another wife and forces her to be compliant and passive in order to avert his displeasure and punishment.

> According to [our] culture, [only] a woman who lives in this sort of fear and anguish properly fulfills her role as wife, while a woman who feels assured that her husband will not take another wife comes to disdain her husband and her family life. . . . [It is assumed that] if it weren't for this overt or covert threat, the woman would not behave herself.
>
> . . . this culture, and [its norms] have become part of their mental and psychological baggage. Perhaps this [upbringing] has caused them to believe that a good man who respects them is nothing but a weak and unstable man. . . . In their opinion, an ideal man is a violent one who humiliates his wife. This is the ideal upheld by the society in which they were raised.[67]

Al-Hujailan explains that the *abaya*, the black robe that envelops the whole body, is relatively new to Saudi women; their grandmothers would not have been familiar with the garment in their youth. However, it has become a symbol of the kingdom.[68] The *abaya*, argues Al-Hujailan, is more than just a garment. It is used to "deny that a normal human being [is] under the black material."[69]

> The abaya indeed covers a typically weak and frightened character . . . who views herself as a sexual entity confined in a well-defined space she can never escape from. This is why the whole culture of the abaya imposes so many restraints upon women.
>
> . . . she must walk slowly, must look down when walking and keep her eyes more or less in front of her—no glancing from side to side in other words. She must not talk to anyone or laugh loudly and must certainly not address any remarks to anyone lest they misunderstand her purpose in doing so.[70]

It symbolizes the concealment of women from the world and transforms them uniformly into meek, silenced women. It would be shocking for society to see a woman wearing an *abaya* talking and laughing freely.[71] Aside from the restrictions that the *abaya* places on a woman's movement, especially that of the feet and hands, it also limits her vision and her ability to speak properly.[72]

How did men succeed in convincing women to transform the free personality that Allah endowed them with into enslaved characters wearing an abaya?[73]

Pointing to the *abaya's* social and religious function is not enough to justify its use, Al-Hujailan argues, because one must understand that it creates and perpetuates certain standards of behavior between the sexes.[74] Created by a patriarchal culture, men have distorted Islam to support the submission of women.[75] By exploiting the good nature of women, asserts Al-Hujailan, men led them to believe that the template for male-female relationships was dominant versus submissive and that men love "the weak and submissive elements of a woman's nature. [Men] then named these elements respect, honor and correct behavior."[76]

Women themselves have internalized this idea, even thinking up new ways to prove their submissiveness and creating "more complicated garments which would confine [women] more than ever before . . . part of a strange phenomenon in which women enjoy being deprived of their free will."[77]

The culture that surrounds this garment is not only evident within the distribution of power but can also be seen in the banning of girls from physical education. Girls playing sports does not conform to the standards set by the *abaya*, for as Al-Hujailan says: "The abaya confines; exercise does the opposite."[78]

WAJEHA AL-HUWAIDER

I wish I knew why the situation of the women in certain Arab states is not condemned by the countries of the world, and does not enrage their citizens. Why do the human rights activists ignore their suffering as though they do not even exist? Why isn't the cry of these millions of women heard, and why isn't it answered by anyone, anywhere [in the world]? Why? Why? Why?[79]

Wajeha Al-Huwaider, the "Arab Rosa Parks,"[80] is a Saudi-born woman who holds an MA from George Washington University and has developed a reputation in the Arab world as a fiery activist in the drive for human rights and women's rights.[81] She has been vocal in her calls for democracy and her criticism of the misogyny and racism endemic in Saudi Arabian society and government.[82]

> Saudi society is based on masters and slaves, or, to be more precise, masters and maids, because the masters are the men, and the slaves are the women.[83]

On International Women's Day, March 8, 2004, she was honored by International PEN, which drew attention to Al-Huwaider and her causes. In November 2004, she was given the 2004 PEN/NOVIB Free Expression Award in The Hague for her work in promoting freedom of expression and the advancement of women's rights. She also writes poetry and short stories.

Wajeha Al-Huwaider was a leading journalist at the Arabic-language daily *Al-Watan* and the English-language daily *Arab News*, but in August 2003, she was prohibited from being published in the Saudi press because of her sardonic portrayal of discrimination against women in Saudi Arabia. Since she was banned from publishing in 2003, she has written for Arab reformist Web sites such as Elaph and Middle East Transparent, often discussing the long-term unsolved problems in the Arab world:

> Our problems [which have continued] for a very long time remain unsolved . . . even though solutions were found decades ago . . . like implementing human rights; struggling against discrimination . . . espousing children's rights; fighting unemployment, illiteracy, and administrative and financial corruption; developing education . . . separating religious authorities from political authorities; and other matters that seem like an unachievable dream to every Arab citizen. . . .
>
> The first reason for the backwardness, ignorance, and atrophy in the Arab countries is that the important minds among the bright elites and the wise pathfinders are still struggling on all levels and in all classes.[84]

Al-Huwaider commutes from her home in Bahrain to Saudi Arabia, where she works at Aramco as a program and evaluation analyst.

On August 4, 2006, a year to the day after King Abdullah bin Abd Al-Aziz acceded to the throne, Al-Huwaider held a demonstration, standing alone with a placard that read "Give Women Their Rights." The Mabahith (secret police) were notified and at first detained her but then released her with a warning. This did not end the matter, however, as on September 20 she was again detained. This time she was threatened with more serious consequences and her career was put in jeopardy. Her release was conditional on her signature of a pledge to relinquish the battle for human rights, including her publication of articles and correspondence with foreign journalists and organizations. Furthermore, she was denied a copy of the document. The secret police restricted her movements and did not permit her to return home to Bahrain until September 28. A protest she had organized for September 23, a Saudi national holiday, was canceled following these events, as the other participants who had been scheduled to appear withdrew for fear of reprisals.[85]

The Right to Drive

Wajeha Al-Huwaider is best known for leading the campaign (together with Fawzia Al-Ayouni) to allow women the right to drive in Saudi Arabia, a right denied to them under the law with the support of Wahhabi Islam. The League of Demanders of Women's Right to Drive Cars was formed to collect signatures for a petition that was presented to King Abdullah in September 2007. Many names were collected via an e-mail appeal and others in public places. The petition noted that women in Islam had always had the right to freedom of movement and had been able to use whatever mode of transport was available at the time without infringing religious doctrine. The campaign received international attention and was covered by global news outlets. The *Wall Street Journal* even recommended a Nobel Peace Prize nomination for Al-Huwaider. The league called on dignitaries like Nelson Mandela, Princess Adelah, and Princess Lolwah Al-Faisal to add their voices to the campaign.[86] Many obstacles confronted the league, including harassment and fear of violence, and the e-mail address set up for signatories was repeatedly encoded and blocked. In January 2008, it was announced that the driving ban would be lifted as part of King Abdullah's program for reform.[87]

This success has not checked Al-Huwaider's desire for change. The League of Demanders of Women's Right to Drive Cars was formed as part of a larger organization started by Al-Huwaider and Al-Ayouni: the Association for the Protection and Defense of Women's Rights in Saudi Arabia, which was intended to function as an umbrella organization demanding wider-ranging reforms and targeting domestic violence, female circumcision, and political rights.

A central tenet of Al-Huwaider's campaign is the recognition of women's human rights as a legal, not a religious, matter. King Abdullah himself accepts that the issue of women driving is not religious but social.[88] Al-Huwaider argues that Arab regimes that deny women their rights should be forced to adhere to the international human rights declarations that they themselves have ratified.

Attitudes of Arab Men to Women

Al-Huwaider provides a cautionary tale for single Arab women who may be worried about spinsterhood:

> Let us look together at the Arab men, beginning with their original land—the Arabian Peninsula. One of the most prominent traits of the men in this region is that they have an inferiority complex. . . . [Saudi men] are the ones who spend the most in the world on aphrodisiacs, so as to achieve a sense of the potency that is in crisis. . . .
>
> They are narcissistic, and [they think that] maintaining guardianship [of women] is manly. . . .
>
> Let us proceed a little further . . . from the land of Syria, which is oppressed to the marrow, through Jordan, where rotten tribalism prevails, to Lebanon . . . all countries with peoples who are eroded economically. The pennies are grabbed by the wealthy . . . but poverty is not the flaw, ladies.
>
> The flaw is . . . the connection that they draw between the nation's honor and the blood of its women [as manifested by "honor killings"]. . . .
>
> Let us move now to "the mother of the world" [Egypt]. . . . Status gnaws at the hearts of its men. . . . All they are interested in are titles such as "Bey," "Pasha," and "Your Honor."
>
> And now to the North African countries . . . chewing on the nonsense of the Green Book [by Al-Qaddhafi]. . . .
>
> Let us look also at the country where the culture of death prevails [Algeria]. [This is] a country of massacres that continued for 10 years, where men enjoy shedding the blood of innocents. . . . Cold weapons are the means sacred to them and to their winding path, which they believe will lead them to Paradise and set them among the black-eyed virgins and men who remain young forever [these are mentioned in the Koran, 56:17, 76:19, and, according to tradition, they serve those who dwell in Paradise]. . . .
>
> What else is there to talk about, ladies? . . . It is a thousand times better to be an old maid than to marry a man in this miserable [Middle] East.[89]

On the anniversary of the murder of a teenage Kurdish girl, Al-Huwaider spoke out against "honor killings." Du'a Al-Aswad was stoned to death on April 7, 2007, in Iraq by a lynch mob whose members filmed themselves on their mobile phones.

> Du'a Al-Aswad is a victim of the wild male madness called "honor." . . . This entire part of the world [is full of] defeated and dejected men, whose only way to gain some sort of victory is by beating their women to death.
>
> But killing her was not enough for them. After she was dead, they mutilated her young body, kicking her and piling more rocks on top of her. Then they broke out in cries of "Allah akbar," and "there is no god but Allah" as though they had just won a strategic battle.
>
> They were like the stones they hurled at her—frozen and devoid of all compassion.
>
> I say to the women . . . : "Good for you for managing to raise beasts who delight in harming you and in shedding your blood and the blood of your daughters. [And] good for the countries and governments that attribute more importance to the lives of animals than to your lives and the lives of your daughters."[90]

Disdainfully, Al-Huwaider compares the treatment of women, especially in the Gulf States, to that of prisoners in Guantánamo Bay.[91] She compares the lives of Arab women, who are unable to venture outdoors without permission from their husbands or fathers, to prison inmates controlled by their jailers.

In some respects, Arab women are even worse off than the prisoners in Guantanamo, especially in regards to the mandatory Arab women's attire, which is severely restrictive in size and color and incompatible with the sweltering heat of the Middle East. In contrast, the prisoners at Guantánamo Bay have access to far more practical and suitable clothing, allowing for some sunlight and fresh air against their cheeks. Worst of all, imprisonment at Guantánamo is only temporary, whereas Arab women have been tethered for hundreds of years and the chains persist throughout their lives. To compound the injustice, thousands of voices around the world have protested against the treatment of prisoners in Guantánamo, but the UN and world at large remain silent about the plight of Arab women, oppressed for centuries and imprisoned "in the dungeons incorrectly referred to as "their homes."[92] Al-Huwaider condemns a world that is not enraged by the suffering of Arab women.

Among the Arabs, the cycle of discrimination against the woman usually begins at home. From a young age, the son receives the lion's share . . . in love, in outlay, in status, and even in education.[93]

In Saudi Arabia, Al-Huwaider maintains, discrimination against women is ingrained in young minds from the moment of birth. Sons receive preferential treatment over their sisters, with better-quality education, care, and material goods lavished upon them. Boys are given more encouragement and expected to have an independent future, while their sisters are sidelined into the roles of wife and mother. "This abhorrent cycle of discrimination in which the Arab woman lives began hundreds of years ago. . . . It is a strangling cycle that wastes the abilities of half of society."[94] Saudi schools are segregated by sex, and while Al-Huwaider notes that schools in general work to achieve submission and conformity, girls are acculturated to their submission and docility in far more potent doses than their brothers.

Nor is old age any protection against discrimination and misogynistic legislation. A Saudi Arabian court sentenced a seventy-five-year-old woman to forty lashes and four months' imprisonment for having two unrelated men at her home.[95] Al-Huwaider deplored the judgment. "It's made everybody angry because this is like a grandmother. Forty lashes—how can she handle that pain? You cannot justify it."[96]

Women inevitably lean toward self-hatred, for they are told they are lewd and sometimes "impure,"[97] but Al-Huwaider is quick to point out the inconsistencies here. If women are "mentally and religiously deficient," how were the wives of the Prophet able to pass on his teachings? Women are described as weak and overemotional, yet they are entrusted with the youth of the nation. If women are innately evil and constitute satanic temptations to men, why do men take up to four wives? How is it possible that women are so incompetent that they cannot be masters of themselves, when the Prophet's wife Aisha managed to lead an entire army into battle?[98]

The fear gnaws away at [women's] sense of being independent entities, and harms their self confidence every day. Thus they always fail at removing the oppression. The real reason for this fear among Saudi women is that there is no law to protect them from violence and discrimination.[99]

Al-Huwaider believes *fear* has been the major tool of submission for Saudi Arabian women and can be categorized as both internal and external. The internal fear derives from the community control exercised by women's families and tribes, and the external fear is related to the wider control wielded by social, political, and religious institutions. These are the enslaving controls that prompted the central mission in Al-Huwaider's life: to champion women and campaign for changes in the law to protect Arab women.

Entrenched Saudi laws do not safeguard women against violence and discrimination:

> The laws grant female citizens only half a voice, diminish women's rights, classify them as having only partial sense, denigrate their importance, doubt their capabilities, permit beating and banishing them, permit their caging within four walls, allow their husbands to treat them as they see fit, and allow them to be bought and sold according to legal agreements. When women fail [in matters forbidden by religious law], the laws welcome their barbarous execution.[100]

Consequently, many Saudi women are afraid to speak about rights for fear of retribution. Al-Huwaider calls on the government to erase this fear by ending oppression and utilizing women's strengths in the interests of the nation. She predicts that repressive policies will cause the downfall of Arab governments when the people become fully aware of their constraints:

> What Arab rulers must understand before they miss the opportunity, and before a flood of enraged people reaches them, is that they are digging their graves with their own hands. The day will come when these graves will swallow them and their thrones, without mercy, if they persist in repressing and eliminating the pathfinders and national elites.[101]

Al-Huwaider does not seek to denigrate Islam; she believes it is the discriminatory legislation of Arab countries that oppresses women:

> The unresolved problems of women are not religious, but purely legal. . . .
> The time has come to annul the chauvinistic interpretations that incite to violence, and . . . removal of their rights.[102]

Al-Huwaider observes the hypocrisy of all the Arab regimes that have ratified the 1948 Declaration of Human Rights, which commits them to justice and equality, yet have failed to promote or enforce the declaration in legislation or spirit. Women are still considered chattels, and men, defending existing laws, insist that Arab societies are respectful of women.

> These laws are clearly no longer suited to an era in which cats and dogs in the developed world have more rights than Arab women, and more even than those of Arab men.[103]

HASNA AL-QUNAIR

> *There was [a preacher] who warned women against shaking a man's hand, saying that, according to one of the sheiks, a woman who shakes the hand of a man that is not her husband is guilty of . . . "adultery of the hand."*[104]

As a columnist at the Saudi Daily newspaper *Al-Riyadh*, Dr. Hasna Al-Qunair has condemned some extremist preachers in Saudi Arabia for their practice of altering the meaning of hadith in order to justify their hatred and dehumanization of women.[105] These distortions are used to "excite the viewers' emotions, entreating them to defend the virtues that the women corrupt."[106] Women are depicted as untrustworthy, subhuman creatures, whose "opinions are not valid"[107] and who must be beaten in order to be controlled.[108]

> [This situation] stems from . . . the historical circumstances and the specific context which formed the background for some of the religious laws and rules that [discriminate] against women.[109]

Also, Al-Qunair argues, more of a distinction must be made between religious rituals and duties and disputed behavioral codes such as the code concerning face-coverings.[110] In order for women to be free from discrimination, Al-Qunair believes that society needs to be restructured.[111]

> The woman is the victim of this insular culture, and her only salvation would be a reorganization of the cultural structure of [our] entire society.[112]

THURAYA AL-SHIHIRI

Our insistence [on reacting] by chopping off heads is a paradigm no less dangerous to humanity than paradigms like Nazism and Fascism.[113]

Thuraya Al-Shihiri is a Saudi journalist who has criticized the reaction of many Muslims to the offensive cartoons published by a Danish newspaper in 2005. The controversy over the cartoons received worldwide publicity when riots broke out in protest. Al-Shihiri argued that this was hypocritical, as other newspapers published positive and factual accounts of Islam, with a Belgian newspaper even distributing free copies of the Koran in Flemish.[114] In the end, the real damage was done not by the cartoons but by the public image of the rioters.

Al-Shihiri is skeptical of Islamist groups, whom she describes as power hungry men who want to impose political Islam, a false brand of Islam, on the rest of society.[115] "These groups . . . are willing to use every means including takiyya [concealing one's faith]. They convey double messages and use doublespeak. . . . Their words do not reflect their actions. They have made hypocrisy a way of life, and for them, the end justifies the means." If Islamist groups were to attain power, she warns, scientific progress and women's freedoms would be seriously curtailed.[116]

Keeping in mind that Islamists believe in "the concept of *takfir* [accusing other Muslims of heresy or apostasy—accusations that could be used to sanction their deaths] . . . how will 'those who continue to [believe] in it' [i.e., the Islamists] further their aims to dominate the Muslim world? What are their full and detailed plans?"[117]

NADIA BAKHURJI

It is not in our culture to tolerate. We are very judgmental. This is wrong. We need to educate people to be tolerant rather than judgmental. Who do we think we are? Very early, we teach children that if this person is Hejazi it means one thing, if Najdi something else. Or that black means this, and white means that. Or for example, she's a woman. Let's judge her. It does not matter what she says; she's just a woman. All these judgments make you guilty instead of innocent. This kind of narrow-mindedness which is programmed . . . socially from an early age needs to be changed. The only way we can move forward is to get rid of this ignorance.[118]

Nadia Bakhurji is a leading Saudi architect who has explored the boundaries of women's roles in her country, especially with regard to their poor visibility in the workforce. Bakhurji has sought to remedy this situation by promoting gender equality and a greater voice for women and children in Saudi Arabia, instead of the "virtual" representation they have at present:

> Women and children are represented virtually in this country. It doesn't mean through the Internet; it means they are represented by a man. A man represents them. We have to get rid of that. Women should represent themselves.[119]

Progress may come only when each generation sets the example for the next, and businesswoman Bakhurji hopes to provide a model for others to follow.[120] She shocked the country with her announcement that she would contest elections to the Board of the Council of Saudi Engineers in 2005. The only female among seventy-one candidates, she came fifth in the elections and was therefore able to take her seat on the ten-member board.[121] As part of her agenda, she pledged to assist woman engineers in a professional capacity, create job opportunities for women, and combat the discrimination against women engineers that holds them back from progressing in their field; she had experienced such discrimination at the beginning of her career.[122]

Earlier in 2005, Bakhurji became the first Saudi woman candidate in the elections to municipal councils. Identifying a loophole in the legal stipulations with regard to candidates, she inspired five other women to stand as well.[123] In a country where women are publicly segregated and still denied voting rights, female candidates for election proved a problem for the government. All women were eventually prevented from running because the government did not have "the logistical systems in place. . . . For example, polling stations for women, and women . . . trained to supervise polling stations."[124] However, buoyed by the supportive reaction to her candidacy, Bakhurji planned to run again in 2009.

An influential member of the Arab International Women's Forum,

Bakhurji has publicized her vision for equality among men and women, noting the stereotyped gender misconceptions that lie at the heart of Saudi male-female relations.

> I believe there is too little communication between the sexes and even between government departments. There is too little official awareness of what women think, what they need, and how they, along with men, could be productive in building society and the economy.[125]

Bakhurji's aim is to empower women and enable them to represent themselves at a governmental level where they are not currently represented.[126] In revealing her strategies, she shows a keen awareness of women's needs, promoting a mechanism for the voices of ordinary women to be heard:

> NGOs provide the means for a normal person—who may have nothing to do with politics— [to] make [his or her] voice heard and most importantly, listened to. NGOs can make sure that changes do in fact occur.[127]

The establishment of NGOs to work with victims of domestic violence would provide an important service and might also act as a deterrent:

> For example, if we in the Kingdom had an NGO that dealt with violence against women, Rania's case [that is, the case of the Saudi TV broadcaster who was severely beaten by her husband] would have gone to that NGO and the NGO would have supported her. It would have made sure she had proper legal representation in court and it would have made sure she received a just settlement. And that her husband would not get away with what he did.[128]

NGOs could also point to discrimination against women in the workplace and school texts.

Bakhurji places a firm emphasis on tolerance and an enlightened education for young people, in order to promote gender equality and cultivate children who are able to perform to the best of their ability. She also advocates dialogue with minority ethnic groups to unify the country.[129] Primarily, she says, an educational overhaul is required to rid society of gender, tribal, and racist stereotypes, as well as to teach the skills of dispassionate debate, tolerance, and compromise:

Let's face it. We do not know how to negotiate. We get heated and emotional and we lose the point. I believe that negotiation should be taught in school; we should learn how to debate. How can we defend our values and beliefs without knowing the basics of negotiating? We must have an educated point of view.[130]

Bakhurji also recommends positive discrimination for women in municipal elections, a national council for women, and counseling centers for families. Basically, what is required is a civil society prepared to facilitate communication between ordinary people, minority groups, and leadership, and to sponsor investment in community projects. To this end, she advocates collaboration with regional states of similar culture such as Bahrain, Egypt, and Jordan.[131]

SAMAR FATANY

Reforming the educational system and raising the standard of our schools and universities remain the biggest challenges Saudi Arabia faces today.[132]

Samar Fatany is a prolific radio and newspaper journalist and one of the most influential media activists advocating reform in a direction that would move Saudi Arabia away from a single-source oil economy toward a knowledge-based economy. Through her columns, she has outlined some of the initiatives and achievements to date.

In a major reform of the education curriculum in Saudi Arabia, King Faisal University's Preparatory Program (UPP) has developed a Western-style program by academics from the United States, Canada, Australia, the United Kingdom, and South Africa to institute critical thinking in preparation for university studies.

The program marks a radical departure from the nation's traditional teaching methods that employ rote memorization. . . . Problem-solving abilities will motivate young Saudis to learn more and foster the curiosity that is at the heart of research and progress.[133]

Oxford University Press has been co-opted to instruct Saudi primary teachers in English-language studies. According to Fatany, "Introducing English in our schools at an early age will allow our students to master the language and learn to better understand the latest technological and scientific developments in our world today."[134]

"Educated and qualified women," she declares, must also "be given the chance to play a role in modernizing our government and society."[135] "When we marginalize women who are qualified and ready to serve, or when we refuse to acknowledge that 54 percent of our college graduates are women who are treated as second-class citizens, we only ensure a bleak future as more competitive nations capitalize on our inability to come to terms with modern reality."[136]

A bold campaign to promote social responsibility, transparency, women's empowerment, and dialogue was launched by the National Dialogue Center. Featured on television, debates focused on previously taboo subjects like regulated discrimination against women in the name of Islam and the unfair and degrading system of male guardians who control women's lives.

Fatany believes these issues "need to be raised, as they constitute a clear violation of human rights by all world standards and any religious belief."[137] Unfortunately, she says, "ignorance about their legal rights and under-appreciation by society are the reasons for the current plight of Saudi women."[138]

> Our educated and progressive women should accept a greater responsibility to lead by example to remove the suspicions of those who are against modernization and progress.[139]

> The media also has a role to play and should expose the self-styled "pious" men who advocate the marginalization of women.[140]

Fatany is aware that the excessively strict and conservative Islam practiced in Saudi Arabia is often unpalatable to Muslims in other countries. "Many Muslims today hold it against us for spreading a rigid interpretation of Islam and influencing innocent and ignorant Muslims who are under the impression that Saudi scholars could never say anything that is wrong. It is time we addressed these issues before we do more harm to Muslims and to our Islamic faith."[141]

Fatany also advocates an overhaul of the Saudi judiciary, so that the law college curriculum is not confined to Islamic jurisprudence and shari'ah law is standardized.[142] "It is essential for our scholars to be globally connected with the needs and concerns of the international Muslim community. The codification of the Shariah law is, therefore, necessary."[143]

LUBNA HUSSAIN

> *The whole concept of girls' education needs to be addressed and revamped with a more enlightened and radical approach. Our current standard of education is untenable internationally. Whereas most countries have joined in a global race toward academic excellence and superiority, we haven't even ventured toward the starting line yet.*[144]

Lubna Hussain is a Saudi journalist who has written about the situation of women in the kingdom with emphasis on the inequalities that the cultural system presents: "Yes we wear the veil and no, we don't drive, but that doesn't mean that we are regressive, backward and uninspired."[145]

Hussain has become exasperated at the stereotypes surrounding the women of her country. Saudi women are almost always described as veiled and banned from driving; to Hussain it is "disconcerting to think that we are defined by only two factors among a myriad of complications that are never alluded to."[146]

Islam, she notes, was in the past progressive in its treatment of women. The Western suffragette movement in the twentieth century demanded some rights that Muslim women already had under Islam, such as owning and inheriting property.[147] The distortion of Islam, she contends, was generated by its interpretation through the lens of male supremacy.[148]

> Educate a man and you liberate an individual, educate a woman and you emancipate a nation.[149]

Speaking on behalf of Saudi women, Hussain claims that what Muslim women really want is the earlier Islam that promoted knowledge and education. They need the tools with which to enter the workforce, and to this end, she advocates more vocational courses for women.[150]

Hussain has been fierce in her criticism of the Saudi judicial system and its ruling in the case of "the Qatif girl," who was sentenced to ninety lashes for being alone with a male nonrelative.[151] The case justifiably caused irreparable damage to the world's image of Saudi Arabia, Hussain lamented.[152] It also sent a message to women all over the country not to expect help from the courts in a crisis, and told lawyers not to involve themselves in such cases, as they would be suspended.[153]

HALIMA MUZAFFAR

> *Teachers are spreading "the culture of death" without any supervision or control. . . . Whether inadvertently or intentionally, the girls' schools are inculcating extremism. . . . Why is the Ministry of Education and Culture ignoring these ideological attempts to transform . . . future mothers who will be easily manipulated by a terrorist father, brother, or husband—because [in their early school years] they were polluted by [ideas] of terror, death, and rejection of this world?*[154]

Halima Muzaffar, a Saudi columnist, wrote an article warning about teachers who frighten schoolgirls with horror stories about death, religion, and immorality, for example, tales about the angels Munkar and Nakir and the Angel of Death who kill nonobservant Muslims.[155] In response to Muzaffar's article, readers sent in many personal stories, including that of a schoolgirl who was in shock after her teacher had forced the class to watch an execution.

She believes "the culture of death" is responsible for the propagation of *takfir*, the malign terrorist ideology with sinister potential that accuses other Muslims of heresy and accordingly sanctions their deaths. "We have had enough generations of closed[-minded people] who know nothing but death and perdition."[156]

21
SOMALIA

BACKGROUND

Women should be treated as women and their share given as such and not as part of clans. If women [are] treated as part of the clan, men will never give the rightful share to women.[1]

The question of women's participation in the workforce is largely secondary to the question of national economic development. The lack of infrastructure, investment, rampant unemployment, and environmental degradation are severe barriers to economic recovery.[2]

When the regime of Siad Barre was overthrown in 1991, Somalia ceased to function as a modern state, descending into a civil war that resulted in a country divided between warlords and their militias. Women and children were frequently victims of the violence between warring clans. The war also had a devastating impact on the economy, from which it has yet to recover. The lack of infrastructure and investment, and the rampant unemployment and environmental degradation presented severe barriers to economic recovery.

In 2000, the various clans met to devise an interim constitution and temporary government. Of the 245 seats in the Transitional National Assembly (TNA), women held twenty-five. Each of the four major clans was represented by five women, with the remaining five from minor clans. The women, however, formed a bloc to represent female interests across clan lines, and the TNA government had two female ministers. The constitution stipulated that the transitional federal parliament (which was to replace the TNA) would have a quota of 12 percent of women. However, women accounted for only 8 percent of the 275 parliamentarians.[3]

Activist Asho Usman Ugas declared, "We are lobbying not only for the women's percentage in parliament, but we are advocating for a package for women's inclusion in every aspect and level of the new government."[4]

The legal status of women in Somalia is currently dictated by the laws of the prewar civil and criminal code, but these laws have not been enforced for a decade. The constitution prohibits discrimination on the basis of gender, but Somalia is still not a signatory to the Convention on the Elimination of All Forms of Discrimination against Women (CEDAW). Furthermore, under the personal status code, women are entitled only to half the inheritance of their brothers.

The health and education standards of Somalia are among the worst in the world. Somali women have a high fertility rate of 7.2 births per woman.[5] The lack of public services and clean drinking water has had a severe impact on child health, and the rates of child morbidity and mortality are among the highest in the world. A survey undertaken in 2006, the Multiple Indicator Cluster Survey (MICS), estimates the infant mortality rate (IMR) at 86 per 1,000 and the under-five child mortality rate (U-5MR) at 135 per 1,000.[6] Somalia's literacy rates are among the lowest in national rankings, with 26 percent female and 50 percent male literacy.[7] The primary school enrollment rate is around 20 percent with about 48 percent of the students being girls, despite the fact that women make up 65 percent of the total population.[8]

Somali women continue to be the victims of violence, particularly rape, which is common in refugee camps. In 2002, the aid agency CARE estimated that approximately forty women were raped every month in four refugee camps.[9]

Despite the numerous obstacles to women's achievement of public positions of power, many women's groups continue to strive for peace and for improvement in the status of Somali women. However, many of these groups are hampered by the lack of a national communications infrastructure and the difficulty of coordinating efforts in a country still crippled by the aftermath of war. Four major networks of women's organizations make up 90 percent of Somali women's groups: the Coalition of Grassroots Women's Organizations (COGWO), the IIDA Women's Development Organization, We Are Women Activists, and the NAGAAD[10] umbrella organization. In March 2004, these four groups launched a nationwide campaign against female genital mutilation (FGM), which is inflicted on almost every girl.[11] Infibulation, the extreme form of FGM, is commonly associated with difficult or prolonged delivery and is one of the main causes of Somalia's maternal mortality, which is one of the highest in the world. In spite of the many difficulties faced by Somali women, they make up nearly half of the workforce.

AYAAN HIRSI ALI (SOMALIA/HOLLAND/USA)

Islam is the new fascism. Just like Nazism started with Hitler's vision, the Islamic vision is a caliphate—society ruled by Sharia law—which women who have sex before marriage are stoned to death, homosexuals are beaten, and apostates like me are killed. Sharia law is as inimical to liberal democracy as Nazism.[12]

Ayaan Hirsi Ali was born in Mogadishu, Somalia, on November 13, 1969. Her father was a graduate in anthropology from Columbia University and a candidate for the Somalian parliament, but he was imprisoned in 1972 after the government was overthrown by the Siad Barre coup.[13]

When she was five, in her father's absence and against his wishes, Ali, her sister, and her brother were subjected to traditional circumcision on the instructions of her grandmother. Her sister tore her wound while urinating and had to be resewn, resulting in a severe illness, from which she never recovered psychologically.[14]

When she was six, Ali's father escaped from prison and the family fled to Saudi Arabia. They lived in Mecca and the children were enrolled in gender-segregated schools. In the girl's school, the teaching featured rote learning from the Koran, focused on what was *haram*, or forbidden. Every Friday, Hirsi Ali relates, capital punishments were carried out, including beheadings, the flogging of men, the stoning of women, and the cutting off of hands and feet. After three years, the Saudis expelled Ali's family because of her father's continuing political activities, and they moved to Ethiopia then eventually settled in Kenya.[15]

In Nairobi, Hirsi Ali attended the English-language Muslim Girls' Secondary School. As a teenager, she was persuaded by a charismatic teacher to adhere to the rigorous Saudi Arabian interpretation of Islam. She read the works of radical Islamists, such as the Egyptians Hasan-al-Banna and Sayyid Qutb, who aimed to counter the effect of Westernization through jihad and active revolution. She wanted to be a part of this jihad, which would create global Islamic rule, defeating "the Jews and the godless West," perceived to be intent on destroying Islam. She wore the *hijab*, supported the Islamist Muslim Brotherhood, and ironically, in view of later events, agreed with the 1989 fatwa against Salman Rushdie.[16]

After secondary school, Hirsi Ali took a one-year course at Valley Secretarial College in Nairobi. In 1992, when she was twenty-three, her father arranged a marriage against her will, to her cousin, a Canadian Somali. The two were traveling to Canada via Frankfurt when Hirsi Ali took the opportunity to escape to Amsterdam, arriving there in July 1992. She requested political asylum in the Netherlands, saying she had come from Somalia. Giving her grandfather's surname, she was granted a resident's permit and later became a citizen.[17]

She took various casual jobs while she learned Dutch, and also took a one-year course in social work. She then enrolled at Leiden University, gaining her master's degree in political science in 2000. While earning her degree, she worked as a Somali-Dutch interpreter and translator for the social services. She also worked with immigrant women in asylum centers and women's refuges, encountering many women who had been beaten or were potential targets of "honor killings."[18]

Hirsi Ali's experiences and her continuing education, particularly her study of *The Atheist Manifesto* by Leiden philosopher Herman Philipse, caused her to question her religious beliefs. The events of 9/11 shocked her, and she was dismayed to realize that she could find their justification in the Koran.

> The little shutter at the back of my mind, where I pushed all my dissonant thoughts, snapped open after the 9/11 attacks, and it refused to close again. I found myself thinking that the Quran is not a holy document. It is a historical record, written by humans. . . . It is a very tribal and Arab version of events. It spreads a culture that is brutal, bigoted, fixated on controlling women, and harsh in war.[19]

In 2002, she renounced her faith and became a vocal critic of Islam, writing articles and speaking on television and in the public arena. She received the first of many death threats in a message from her father, who phoned to relay warnings from Somalis in Europe regarding her safety.[20]

On leaving Leiden University, Hirsi Ali became a fellow at the Wiardi Beckman Foundation and a political researcher for the Dutch Labor Party (PvdA). In 2003, however, she left the Labor Party and was elected to the

Dutch parliament as a member for the People's Party for Freedom and Democracy (VVD).[21]

> I was a one-issue politician, I decided.[22]

> I wanted Holland to wake up and stop tolerating the oppression of Muslim women in its midst. . . . I wanted to spark a debate among Muslims about reforming aspects of Islam. . . . This could only happen in the West, where Muslims may speak out. . . . I wanted Muslim women to become more aware of just how bad, and how unacceptable, their suffering was.[23]

Hirsi Ali also favored more emphasis on cultural and religious rather than simply socioeconomic issues. Specifically, her proposals included the abolition of sectarian religious schools, the reduction of generous unemployment benefits, and the registration of "honor killings."[24]

In January 2003, the same month in which she was elected to parliament, she gave an interview to the Dutch newspaper *Trouw*, in which she made an observation about the Prophet Muhammad:

> All Muslims believe in following his example, but many of the things he did are crimes. When he was in his fifties, he had sex with a nine-year-old girl. By our standards, he was a pervert. He ordered the killing of Jews and homosexuals and apostates, and the beating of women.[25]

The interview was subsequently published under the headline "Hirsi Ali Calls Prophet Muhammad a Pervert." There was an explosive response; hundreds of people demanded she should be punished, and she received death threats on her answering machine. Evaluated as a maximum security risk, she was forced to move house.[26]

In 2003, Hirsi Ali's book *The Caged Virgin: An Emancipation Proclamation for Women and Islam* was published. The book relates her journey from "faith to reason." It outlines her political campaign to call attention to the crimes, particularly against women, being committed in the name of Islam in Europe; and it reveals her impatience with the reluctance of liberals and feminists to condemn these crimes out of what she sees as a misplaced regard for multiculturalism over and above human rights.[27]

> This obsession with subjugating women is one of the things that makes
> Islam so low. And the agents of Islam from Riyadh to Teheran, from Islam-
> abad to Cairo know that any improvement in the lives of women will lead
> to the demise of Islam and a disappearance of their power.[28]

In 2004, Hirsi Ali came to international attention when Theo Van Gogh, the
producer of her film *Submission*, was murdered. *Submission* is a monologue by
a woman wearing a transparent burqa, with verses from the Koran inscribed
on her body. It deals with the prescriptions in the Koran for the treatment
and behavior of women and the potential for abuse that such prescriptions
can create:

> Oh Allah, Most High, you say that men are the protectors and maintainers
> of women because you have given the one more strength than the other; I
> feel at least once a week the strength of my husband's fist on my face.[29]

On November 2, 2004, a member of the jihadist organization known as the
Hofstad Group shot and killed Van Gogh in Amsterdam. A letter was affixed
with a knife to Van Gogh's body, which had been ritually mutilated. The letter
threatened Hirsi Ali with the same fate. After the murder, the Netherlands
government provided her with bodyguards and kept her in secure locations.

In March 2006, along with Salman Rushdie and Irshad Manji, Hirsi Ali
was one of twelve signatories to a letter published as a response to the
Muhammad cartoons controversy. Titled "Manifesto: Together Facing the
New Totalitarianism," the document is a declaration of the need to fight for
secular values, universal human rights, and personal freedom in the face of
Islamic totalitarianism.[30]

After three and a half years in the lower house of the Dutch parliament,
Hirsi Ali resigned on May 16, 2006, after a television program publicized
the fact that she had initially fabricated details about herself in order to be
allowed to remain in the country. In her leaving statement, she pointed out
she had made no secret of the deception in interviews with the media and
with members of her political party. In the statement, she mentioned the
pressures of living under armed guard and said her neighbors had won a
court decision to evict her because they believed her presence was a threat to
their safety. These factors, she said, had contributed to her decision to leave
Dutch politics.[31]

Subsequently, Hirsi Ali took up a position at the American Enterprise Institute (AEI), a think tank with neoconservative associations, based in Washington, DC. In September 2006, Ali's autobiography, *Infidel*, was published and quickly became an international best seller.

> I wrote "Infidel" to answer the question asked of me by my publisher, my colleagues, by associates in Holland—"Ayaan, how did your own process of enlightenment go? How did your own journey from being born and raised in a pre-modern, devout Muslim family to an ultra-modern society like the Netherlands go? And what is it that you value in our moral framework, and what is it that you don't?" "Infidel" is the answer to that.[32]

Pulitzer Prize winner Anne Applebaum wrote in her review of the book:

> "I am Ayaan, the daughter of Hirsi, the son of Magan."
> In the first scene of Infidel, Ayaan Hirsi Ali is a child of 5, sitting on a grass mat. Her grandmother is teaching her to recite the names of her ancestors, as all Somali children must learn to do. "Get it right," her grandmother warns. "They are your bloodline. . . . If you dishonor them you will be forsaken. You will be nothing. You will lead a wretched life and die alone."
> Thus begins the extraordinary story of a woman born into a family of desert nomads, circumcised as a child, educated by radical imams in Kenya and Saudi Arabia, taught to believe that if she uncovered her hair, terrible tragedies would ensue. It's a story that, with a few different twists, really could have led to a wretched life and a lonely death, as her grandmother warned. But instead, Hirsi Ali escaped—and transformed herself into an internationally renowned spokeswoman for the rights of Muslim women.[33]

Her critics, however, argue that she speaks and writes about Muslims as if they were a homogenous group and "grossly misrepresents Islam" as if there were no moderate version,[34] to which she responds:

> Let's make a moral distinction between Islam and Muslims. Muslims are diverse. Some, like Irshad Manji and Tawfiq Hamid, want to reform their faith. Others want to spread their beliefs through persuasion, violence or both. Others are apathetic and do not care much for politics. Others want to leave it and convert to Christianity, like Nonie Darwish, or become atheist, like me.[35]

However, she adds, "Islam unreformed, as a set of beliefs, is hostile to every-thing Western."

> In a free society, if Jews, Protestants, and Catholics have their own schools, then Muslims should have theirs, too. But how long should we ignore that in Muslim schools in the West, kids are taught to believe that Jews are pigs and dogs? Or that they should distance themselves from unbelievers and that jihad is a virtue?[36]

> Anywhere where sharia is implemented, you see incredible inhumanity. People's hands are cut off. Women are confined to their homes and are stoned. . . . Homosexuals are hanged or must hide. That is Iran, Saudi Arabia . . . Afghanistan under the Taliban. Parts of Somalia are now under Sharia rule. Anywhere there is Sharia rule, there is violation of human rights.[37]

In 2005, Hirsi Ali she was named by *Time* magazine as one of the hundred most influential people in the world. She has received several awards for her work, including Norway's Human Rights Service's Bellwether of the Year Award, the Danish Freedom Prize, the Swedish Democracy Prize, and the Moral Courage Award for "commitment to conflict resolution, ethics, and world citizenship."

A proponent of liberal thinkers John Stuart Mill, Frederick Hayek, and Karl Popper, she believes the legacy of the Enlightenment is under threat, not only from fanatical Islamists with absolutist ideas but also from collec-tivists, modern relativists, and complacency in the West. The resultant rise of fanaticism and superstition, she says, must be attacked with active pro-motion of self-knowledge, critical thinking, and debate, principles that gen-erated ideas central to the Enlightenment. She is not opposed to those who worship the Prophet Muhammad, only to the suppression of debate that Islam demands.

> I want to be able to say that Mohammed had some reprehensible qualities without being thrown in jail, without being demonized.[38]

HAWA ADEN MOHAMED

The Somali woman has no say in political decisions. She has no say in family decisions. Recently, for the first time, we elected one female minister to the Somali Puntland State, and one in the federal government, but this is just tokenism. It is not enough.[39]

Hawa Mohamed has led the movement to stop female genital mutilation (FGM) in Somalia, where 98 percent of females fall victim to the procedure. She is the founder and chief executive officer of the Galkayo Education Center for Peace and Development (GECPD) in the Puntland province, northeastern Somalia, an organization that aims to eradicate FGM and also empower women through education.

Hawa's mother died when she was a young child. Her schooling was intermittent as she was burdened with many domestic responsibilities. However, when she was fourteen, Hawa was able to attend school regularly and came to appreciate the importance of catching up on education lost earlier in life. She underwent FGM herself when she was eight years old and barely recovered, due to complications from the wounds. Her older sister died following the procedure when she was seven.

According to Hawa, Islam is often used to legitimize FGM or female circumcision but no relevant instruction is found in the Koran.[40] However, FGM is frequently a prerequisite for marriage, and defenders of the practice claim it ensures virginity and reduces sexual desire, thereby controlling female sexuality.

I don't see FGM stopping in my lifetime. We have to change the mentality of people, and the change has to come from the family.[41]

A long-standing tradition throughout Africa, FGM is commonly practiced in Egypt and other parts of the Middle East. Approximately two million girls a year will undergo the procedure, entailing scraping, burning, or excision of parts of the female genitalia, and ranging from partial or total removal of the clitoris (clitoridectomy) to removal of all external genitalia and the sewing together of the sides of the vulva, leaving a small vaginal opening (infibulation).[42] The operation is usually carried out in unsanitary conditions and without anesthetics by village women who use the same non-sterilized implement on a number of girls, increasing the risk of tetanus, HIV, and other communicable diseases. Basic cutting tools are used, including blunt knives, lids of tin cans, broken glass, and razors.[43] Apart from the severe pain and shock that results, death may follow hemorrhage and infection. Long-term psychological trauma and difficulties with menstruation, sexual intercourse, and childbirth are common, as are recurrent urinary tract infections and excess scar tissue.[44]

Hawa's ordeal, her sister's death following FGM, and the political and domestic marginalization of women eventually inspired her to dedicate herself to women's rights and the abolition of FGM in Somalia.

During the civil war that followed the overthrow of President Mohamed Siad Barre in 1991, Hawa fled to Canada, where she continued to work for women's rights in her home country. Acutely aware of the dire situation for women in Somalia, she returned to start the Juba Women's Development Center in Kismayo, a port town devastated by civil war and teeming with thousands of refugees, mainly women and children. Warlords attacked and plundered the city in 1999, causing many to flee, including Hawa, who escaped to the Puntland region. There, in the town of Galkayo, 700 km north of the Somali capital, Mogadishu, she established the GECPD and a girls' school in 1999. Most girls in Somalia could never afford to go to school, and only boys from wealthy families were sent. There was little interest in literacy, women's rights, or for that matter, any human rights, in a country ruled by brutal, competing warlords. Moreover, Hawa was accused of turning girls away from Islam and trying to "change the girls into boys."[45] A grenade was thrown into her compound, and on another occasion, the surrounding wall was knocked down.[46] Hawa and her colleagues were accused of being "traitors to Somali culture and the Islamic religion" and were vilified by mullahs in their Friday sermons.[47]

Undaunted, she started the school with 120 girls. "In the beginning, we had no facilities and the girls had to sit on the floor."[48] For financial support, she sought the assistance of expatriate Somalis, who funded the first project. Subsequently, the center could point to its performance record and qualify for international aid from NGOs and the United Nations. GECPD was also able to benefit from civil society NGOs in Somalia and internationally.

Although Hawa advanced the women's rights movement in the Puntland area, the ongoing civil war created insurmountable problems, and in 2004, tired of the lack of progress, GECPD organized a demonstration,

"Zero Tolerance For FGM," on International Women's Day. The rally attracted over 20,000 people, including the vice president of Puntland and five cabinet ministers, and provided a focus for discussion of FGM, a subject that is still taboo.[49] "The demonstration created debate, a debate which is still going on today. And dialogue at least brings new questions."[50]

About 750 girls now attend primary school classes in Galkayo, 2,400 adults are enrolled in literacy classes, and Hawa's literacy projects have reached over 7,600 women.[51] Her pet project, "second-chance education," was inspired by her own opportunity to go to school when she was fourteen, and was set up specifically for women between eighteen and twenty-five who missed out on school because of the civil war.[52] Another "second-chance" group of 830 girls attend afternoon classes after they finish domestic duties or work to support their families in the morning.[53]

A hostel was built for the poorest of the refugee schoolgirls in need of basic food and shelter. There is also an outreach program for internally displaced people in Galkayo, and in Harfo village, 70 km north of Galkayo, Hawa established an orphanage and day school.[54] Apart from receiving general education, girls learn about the dangers and mythology of FGM, as well as human rights, women's rights, leadership, and how they can contribute to peace and rebuilding in Somalia.

In 2005, in a ceremony in Austin, Texas, Hawa Aden Mohamed received the eleventh annual Amnesty International Ginetta Sagan Award. The prize recognized her outstanding achievements in defending the rights of women and children, often at considerable personal risk. The $10,000 prize she received went toward the completion of a women's and girls' hospital.[55]

"The Woman in Arab Society."
The fetus is labeled "Female."
Source: *Syria News* (Syria),
June 21, 2007.

22
SUDAN

BACKGROUND

A woman's value in Sudan is based on the number of cows paid for her dowry. To divorce, a woman must pay back those cows—a nearly impossible task.[1]

After gaining independence from Britain in 1956, Sudan developed a tradition of strong civic institutions, including trade unions, women's groups, and student organizations. The successive constitutions granted equal rights and duties to all Sudanese people, irrespective of gender, religion, or ethnic background. Women gained the right to vote in 1953, and in 1964, the right to sit on the judiciary. With access to free education, women achieved senior positions in a number of fields, becoming academics, doctors, police officers, and army officers.

However, few Sudanese can remember a time when their country was at peace. There have been two civil wars between the Muslim North and the Christian and animist South, in 1955–72 and 1983–2005; the latter became Africa's longest-running civil war, with two million killed and four million forced from their homes.[2] Since the Bashir regime came to power in 1989, Sudan has been on a downward spiral, with women targeted for rape and torture by armies and militias. According to Women for Women International, the casualties of the civil war include two million rape victims.[3]

Fatima Ahmed Ibrahim, a former parliamentarian, president of the Sudanese Women's Union, and activist for both women's and human rights, explained, "Women . . . [were] raped routinely because this . . . [was] seen as a way of putting more Islamic babies into the world."[4]

As the conflict between North and South was coming to an end, a rebellion broke out in 2003 in Darfur, the western part of Sudan. Women in Darfur are at great risk: "Government forces and allied armed groups . . . are waging war on women's bodies."[5] Former US secretary of state Colin Powell labeled the conflict in Darfur as genocide.[6]

> Reports by Amnesty International have revealed that some women have been raped in front of their relatives, and other women have been forced into sexual slavery. . . . Rape is being used as a weapon of terror and ethnic cleansing.[7]

Following such assaults, many women are deserted by their families because they are "disgraced." Many women also believe they cannot marry because they are "damaged."[8]

The civil war and the conflict in Darfur have created both hardship and opportunities for women in public life. Those who have been displaced and forced into refugee camps have few economic opportunities and are frequently forced to turn to prostitution and the illegal brewing of alcohol to support their families when men leave to join the fighting. Women composed 42 percent of the labor force in 2003,[9] but since the Darfur conflict erupted, most have struggled to make ends meet. In addition, statistics show that 93 percent of Sudanese women have lost at least one family member, 40 percent report having been beaten, 99.8 percent have no electricity, 87 percent do not have running water, 91 percent have no formal education, and 94 percent are illiterate.[10]

> In Sudan, a girl is more likely to die in childbirth than complete primary school.[11]

The issue of legal status and political representation in Sudan are complex. Women are allocated at least 10 percent of the seats in every state council, and the government has appointed female ambassadors. In 2000, the president appointed an advisor on women's affairs to a cabinet position and announced legislation for two years' paid maternity leave.[12] However, in the same year, the governor of Khartoum issued a decree prohibiting women from working in public places.[13] Furthermore, Sudan is not a signatory to the Convention on the Elimination of All Forms of Discrimination against Women (CEDAW).

In January 2005, a Comprehensive Peace Agreement (CPA) was signed to end the twenty-one-year civil war and establish an interim framework for a national government. Key parties, however, have yet to agree on the various strategies proposed for its implementation. While there is hope that the CPA could have stabilizing effects on the country as a whole, full implementation is considered to be fraught with obstacles due to the country's sociopolitical and economic landscape.

Despite promises in the CPA to help women advance politically, socially, and economically, for example, improving access to maternal and child healthcare, women activists doubt that gender equality will ever become a reality.

AWATIF ELAGEED

> *In the areas where there is plenty of rainfall, part of the land belongs to the community, whereas in the irrigated regions, land was distributed only to the men, not to the women. . . . Just 13 percent of women own any land at all.*[14]

In her feminist curriculum, Awatif Elageed teaches Sudanese girls about projects that provide economic assistance to women in the rural areas. Her doctoral thesis, which was awarded by Humboldt University of Berlin in 2007, dealt with women who worked in the Gezira Scheme in central Sudan.[15] A sociologist and gender specialist, Elageed's research interests are also focused on the displaced women of Darfur and south Sudan.

Elageed is a devout Muslim who actively supports the causes of women's rights and interfaith dialogue in her native country. She is also a lecturer at the Ahfad University for Women, unique in Africa and initiated by Babiker Badri in 1898, although not established until 1907 by his son. Badri held that basic Koranic instruction should be made available to women, not only men.

Like some of her colleagues, Elageed's salary is paid by a Protestant organization, the German Church Development Service (EED), but she sees no inherent conflict in this. "All of us, Christians and Muslims, believe in one God."[16]

Although she believes "some Muslims are not tolerant enough," Elageed is opposed to Western hostility to headscarves. She has forgone the *hijab* for herself, as "simply wearing a headscarf is not enough. Other, more important rules must be observed."[17]

Elageed promotes the university's educational campaign against female genital mutilation (FGM), which affects 80 percent of Sudanese women. As she explains, the more extensive female circumcision called "pharaonic" and allegedly originating in ancient Egypt, was minimized and named Sunnah, meaning "Muhammad's doctrine." Consequently, FGM became more closely associated with Islam and therefore it became "more difficult for us to put an end to this practice."[18]

FATIMA AHMED IBRAHIM

> *These Islamic extremists are nothing but parasites. They claim to govern on behalf of God and yet they do nothing but enrich themselves. I can give you names; some of my own relatives who were very poor are now very rich. They send their children to schools in Britain and put their money into banks in Switzerland.*[19]

Fatima Ahmed Ibrahim was born into an academic family in 1933 in Omdurman on the White Nile opposite Khartoum. Her father was a teacher and her grandfather was an imam and a judge, before becoming headmaster of the first Sudanese boys' school. Ibrahim, her mother, and her sisters were the only females to study at the school.[20]

> I was brought up into a learned family. I have two sisters and four brothers, and we opened our eyes into the big library in our house, from which we got early knowledge of literature, poetry and politics.[21]

Ibrahim became a feminist activist while in secondary school. She published a women's rights community newsletter called *Elra'edda* (Vanguard) and wrote articles on women's issues for the newspapers. Upon graduation, she followed her father and grandfather into the teaching profession.

In 1952, Ibrahim cofounded the Sudanese Women's Union (SWU). The union focused on suffrage, equal opportunity in education and careers, and the promotion of women's literacy. This mission, however, brought the organization into conflict with agencies of the political right such as Jabihat El-Methaiq Elaslami (Islamic Pledge Front).

In 1954, Fatima joined the Sudanese Communist Party (SCP) and soon afterward became a member of its Central Committee.

I was convinced by the party's analysis and views on the causes of the suppression of women and their seclusion and barring from the spheres of work and production. . . . It had merit for the establishment of the first organization for women in the Sudan e.g., Women's League, in 1947.[22]

In 1955, she started and edited a magazine for the Women's Union, *Sawt al Mar'a* (Women's Voice), even though women weren't permitted to become journalists at the time. The journal played a pioneering role in the resistance to the prevailing military dictatorship on issues such as state policy, law, and education:

It was the first [Sudanese] publication to use the caricature and it was banned several times, nevertheless, the voice of women highlighted the women question, the problems of childhood, the women's movement and the real position of Islam toward women.[23]

As chair of the SWU, Ibrahim offered membership to all Sudanese women and opened branches in a number of different provinces. She transformed the union into a broad-based popular organization, despite the suspensions and restrictions imposed on it by three consecutive military regimes in the Sudan.[24]

In 1964, Ibrahim helped to organize the overthrow of the Abbud military regime by the people and in 1965, became the first female MP in the Sudan and, indeed, the whole of Africa and the Middle East. She campaigned against compulsory marriage, underage marriage, and polygamy as well as promoting Sudanese women's right to vote and to equality in work and education.[25]

Ibrahim and her husband, Al-Shafie Ahmed Elsihkh, were decorated by President Nasser of Egypt, who, she relates, "requested us to contribute with our experiences in the field of the trade union's movement and women['s] movement in Egypt."[26]

Most of the women's rights that Ibrahim demanded were granted by parliament in 1968. In 1969, however, Jaafar al-Nimeiri took power by military coup. Initially, the SCP supported him, but after a dispute that led to a short-lived countercoup in July 1971, Nimeiri returned to power. He executed the leaders of the countercoup and the members of the SCP who had supported them. Fatima's husband, who was president of the SCP, was tortured and killed. Fatima was placed under house arrest for two and a half years, and subsequently arrested many times during the period of the Nimeiri regime.[27]

> I swore after the martyrdom of Al-Shafie, not to marry [again], and to raise
> our son Ahmed in an honorable manner and to proceed in the course of the
> struggle for the sake of the poor and the suppressed, even if this course led
> me to the same fate, and I am still honoring this determination.[28]

At one point, because of her continued opposition, Nimeiri threatened to sentence Ibrahim to life imprisonment, but he backed down in the face of Ibrahim's popular support:

> Before the announcement of the judgement the body of the court contacted
> [al-Nimeiri] telling him that any issuance of punishment will lead to a mass
> explosion. He decided to make a round by his helicopter to see by himself the
> assembled masses, and actually he saw the situation and agreed to free me.[29]

Ibrahim and the resistance movement triumphed in 1985 and ended Nimeiri's regime.

In 1989, when an Islamist government took power, the SWU was banned and Ibrahim was again imprisoned. She was released after Amnesty International interceded on her behalf, and she left the Sudan to undergo an operation in London. Fearing for her safety, friends and relatives prevailed upon her not to return to the Sudan.

In the UK, Ibrahim continued to campaign for women's rights in the Sudan and, with other expatriate Sudanese, protested human rights violations such as the flogging of female students at Ahfad University for not wearing the veil and the illegal abduction and conscription of students. She also established a center for the rehabilitation and training of young leaders.[30]

In 1991, Ibrahim was elected president of the Women's International Democratic Federation and, in 1993, was given a UN award for outstanding achievements in the field of human rights.[31]

Ibrahim returned to the Sudan in 2005, after reconciliation between the government and the opposition, and became an MP representing the SCP. Once again, she took up her positions as a member of the Central Committee of the SCP, president of the SWU, and editor of the *Women's Voice*.[32]

In 2006, Ibrahim was awarded the Ibn Rushd Prize for Freedom of Thought, as "a politically engaged woman, who has rendered outstanding services to promoting democracy through her political work."[33]

On March 19, 2007, Ibrahim announced she was retiring from her parliamentary and executive roles although she would remain a member of the Sudanese Women's Union and the Sudanese Communist Party, which she has served for so many years.[34]

Her books and publications include the following: *Our Harvest during Twenty Years*; *Arab Women and Social Changes*; *On the Questions of Personal Matters*; *The Sudanese Working Women's Questions*; *It Is Time for Change* (Arabic); and *A Roaring Outcry to Shake the World Conscience* (English).[35]

TARAJI MUSTAFA (SUDAN/CANADA)

Taraji Mustafa is a Sudanese Canadian human rights activist with views widely divergent from the leadership in her native Sudan. In the fall of 2006, she established the Sudanese-Israeli Friendship Association. She also planned to establish a branch office in Israel. Similar support for Israel was voiced by the leader of the Sudan Liberation Movement, Abd Al-Wahed Al-Nur.[36]

Mustafa's organization was founded in Canada, as the Sudanese government would never have given permission to register any such association.

She said she had been strongly biased against Jews and Israel, an outcome she ascribed to the propaganda instilled in Sudanese children by the resident Arab media. While living in Canada, however, she encountered Jews and became aware of her prejudice.

After announcing the Sudanese-Israeli Friendship Association, Mustafa was overwhelmed by inquiries from Sudanese worldwide, including lawyers who planned to challenge their government for stamping Sudanese passports with a prohibition against travel to Israel.[37] "My phone did not stop ringing for two days. . . . There were students who called me . . . in order to approach student groups in the universities."[38]

She is convinced that a large number of Sudanese, especially those who have traveled abroad, are aware of the unfair, typecast image of Israelis presented by the Arab media and are keen to befriend Israelis.[39]

Moreover, she believes the Sudanese have no reason for automatic loyalty to their Arab co-religionists, as the Arabs "have failed in making us feel we are Arab brothers. There has always been a stereotypical view of the Sudanese people." She believes "the Arab media in its entirety—TV, Web sites, movies, and songs—should be held responsible for this racist behavior. . . .

We are sick and tired of the stereotyping of blacks in the media, in series aired in the Gulf countries."[40]

As for the Palestinians, she is keen to remind them of Sudanese assistance in the past. For example, Jaafar al-Nimeiri rescued Yasser Arafat during the Black September conflict in Jordan.

Some of Mustafa's compatriots were brought up on a "daily diet of Jew and Israel bashing in Sudanese media, school textbooks and government policy,"[41] and her views sparked criticism and insults. The question of revoking her citizenship was discussed in the Sudanese parliament, and in her hometown of Hamilton in Canada, she was vilified by community imams.[42]

When Mustafa, together with other activists in Canada, initiated a pressure group to advocate on behalf of Darfur, the first response came from a Jewish organization. Similarly, the Israeli government granted asylum to dissident Sudanese denied protection in Arab countries. Many of those who fled to Egypt were killed or injured by Egyptian security forces in Mustafa Mahmoud Square in December 2005. Others were killed in Iraq, and those who escaped were refused entry by Jordan.[43]

Mustafa has also defended the rights of Christians in the Middle East. In this context, she has criticized Egyptian Patriarch Shinoda, who banned the Christian pilgrimage to Jerusalem: "Patriarch Shinoda himself is a victim of the Arab media which distorts the consciousness of the Arab individual."[44]

SYRIA

BACKGROUND

The Constitution provides for equality between men and women and equal pay for equal work. Moreover, the Government has sought to overcome traditional discriminatory attitudes towards women and encouraged women's education by ensuring equal access to educational institutions. . . . However, the Government has not changed personal status, retirement, or social security laws that discriminate against women.[1]

The Syrian Arab Republic accepted the Convention on the Elimination of All Forms of Discrimination against Women (CEDAW) in 2003.[2] However, while efforts are being made to advance the cause of women, traditional ideals and practices limit their progress.

Adult literacy for females is over 78 percent and women make up 40 percent of the labor force.[3] Syrian women have taken advantage of opportunities in higher education and females hold 39 percent of seats in universities. However, "The role of women is . . . restricted by constraints on funding, which is more readily allocated to men."[4] The number of women in influential positions, such as public office, is limited by traditional attitudes. Although, in 2006, Dr. Najah Al-Attar was appointed second vice president for cultural affairs, there are only thirty women members of parliament out of a total of 250.[5]

The current Ba'ath regime in Syria, in power since 1963, has promoted the cause of women at various levels, for example, recruiting women into the armed forces and establishing the General Union of Syrian Women in 1967.[6] In a 2003 statement, the president of the union, Soad Bakkur, commented that it was created "with the aim of mobilizing women within a single organization and enhancing their level of education, political awareness, and level of skills to prepare women for a more effective and fuller role in social and economic development."[7]

Despite President Bashar al-Assad's approach to equality for women, however, there are still issues of conflict with traditional practices, which are evident in the application of family law. For example:

> "Under the Syrian Code, a wife's right to maintenance ceases when she works outside the home without her husband's permission."
>
> "A woman who leaves her marital home without legitimate reason is defined as having violated marital law."[8]
>
> "Women over the age of 18 have the legal right to travel without the permission of male relatives; however, a husband or father could file a request with the Ministry of the Interior to prohibit his wife or daughter's departure from the country."
>
> While rape is a felony, punishment can be suspended if a rapist decides to marry his victim.[9] In addition, "there are no laws against spousal rape."[10]

The issue of "honor killings" exists, but there are no reliable statistics on these crimes or on violence against women in general. A study concluded in April 2006 "found that nearly one married woman in four surveyed had been beaten."[11]

GEORGETTE ATIYA

An indomitable fighter for women's rights, Georgette Atiya was born in 1950 and grew up in Qunietra on the Golan Heights, the only girl in a family of six boys. Her father was a member of the Syrian armed forces. During the war with Israel in 1967, her family fled to Damascus. In desperation, she was emboldened to request a meeting with the then defense minister, Hafez al-Assad, on the basis of her membership of the Ba'ath Party.[12] To her surprise, he found her a small house to rent, and she was to keep it for the next thirty years.

In Damascus, she attended university and worked as a schoolteacher during the day and went to Women's Union meetings in the evening. In

1977, she held a controversial, full and frank discussion with her students about the *hijab*. Later, she was condemned by the local sheikh. Together with three hundred other teachers, she was accused of being a communist and dismissed from her job.

At the same time, she became aware of the Muslim Brotherhood's payments to promote Islamism:

> I was very worried. I heard that this group (the Muslim Brotherhood) were paying women to wear the hijab and [jilaabah (long coat)] and were holding private lessons in Koranic discourse, paying people to attend. Then I realised that they had a political intention, not just an Islamic one.[13]

Discouraged by these events, Atiya moved to Paris, where she met many French writers and feminists such as Françoise Sagan, Simone de Beauvoir, and Danielle Mitterand, wife of the former French president. In this rich intellectual environment, she thrived and developed her feminist vocation.

When her mother fell ill in 1996, Atiya returned to a Syria in cultural decline but, determined to make a difference, she set up an artistic salon in her home and decided to establish the feminist Atiya Publishing House in Beirut. She also has political aspirations with the aim of working toward political reform and was a candidate for election to the Syrian parliament in 2003. Her slogan "For Bread and Democracy" reflected her own impoverished background.

> It's not whether I get elected or not, actually, it's the continuation of the process that's the important thing.[14]

Atiya is still outspoken on issues that are seriously controversial in her home country. For example, during an interview on Syrian TV, she said:

> The Palestinian woman's womb is a factory for the conflict; it produces fighting children. After this fighting child is produced, he is taught: "This is your land, this is your country, you will fight for it, stand on it, and die for it."[15]

WAFA SULTAN (SYRIA/USA)

In 1991, when I was relatively new to this country [the United States] and struggling financially, I was offered $1,500 per month by the Saudis to cover my head and attend a mosque. In California, when you tell any American about this, he says, "Who cares?"

You have to care and you have to pay attention! Not caring and not paying attention is why we ended up with the events of September 11—events the likes of which I expected and predicted well before.[16]

Wafa Sultan was born in 1958 into a large Sunni Muslim family in Damascus, Syria, and she grew up a devout Muslim in Banyias, a small town on the Mediterranean coast.[17] She recalled being brought up with a sense of shame because she was female:

> I remember as a little girl trying hard to avoid passing by my father while he was praying because Mohammed once said that if a dog or a woman passes by a man while he was praying he had to rewash himself and pray again, otherwise his prayer wouldn't be accepted.
>
> I remember hearing as an eight-year-old girl that a woman is nothing but shame. Her marriage will cover up one-tenth of her shame and her grave will cover up the rest of it. Can you imagine, at eight, being consumed by shame just because you are female?[18]

Sultan attended medical school and qualified as a psychiatrist at the University of Aleppo in northern Syria. While she was a student, she says, she witnessed the murder of her professor, Dr. Yusef al Yusef, in 1979, by the Muslim Brotherhood, which was seeking to destabilize the Assad regime.

For Sultan, "the sound of the bullets became associated . . . with Allah," and she studied the Koran and the hadith to find out "whether Islam is inherently violent, or whether its adherents misunderstand its teachings." Her study convinced her that "the root was in Islam itself."[19] "Martyrdom is deeply rooted in our teachings. . . . With the help of Saudi money and Wahabbism, what was written in our holy book came to life."[20] Although she lost her faith in Islam at the time, she still considers herself a Muslim.[21]

In 1989, Sultan and her husband went to Southern California on tourist visas before seeking American citizenship. Their two children joined them two years later, and Sultan had a third child in America. She took various jobs as she learned English and studied for her American medical license.[22]

The events of 9/11 were a second seminal event for her:

> At the very first day following this hideous catastrophe, I screamed as loud as I could, "Wake up America! Islam is here," and since then I continue to voice that message.[23]

On June 5, 2005, an essay of Sultan's about the Muslim Brotherhood was published on the Critic Web site (www.annaqed.com), which is run by a Syrian expatriate. The essay, titled "The Muslim Brotherhood: Who Are They Trying to Fool?" warned that the brotherhood, regardless of appearances, was a radical and violent organization. Dr. Sultan was invited to appear the following month on Al-Jazeera Television to debate Dr. Ahmad bin Muhammad, an Islamist Algerian professor of religious politics.[24]

In that debate, she considered the source of the motivation of a suicide bomber:

> In our countries, religion is the sole source of education, and is the only spring from which [a] terrorist drank until his thirst was quenched. He was not born a terrorist, and did not become a terrorist overnight. Islamic teachings played a role in weaving his ideological fabric, thread by thread, and did not allow other sources—I am referring to scientific sources—to play a role. It was these teachings that distorted this terrorist and killed his humanity. It was not [the terrorist] who distorted the religious teachings and misunderstood them, as some ignorant people claim.[25]

On February 21, 2006, Sultan took part in Al-Jazeera's *The Opposite Direction* with Dr. Ibrahim Al-Khouly, an Egyptian professor of religious studies from Al-Azhar University, taking up the debate on Samuel Huntington's "clash of civilizations" theory:

> The clash we are witnessing around the world is not a clash of religions, or a clash of civilizations. It is a clash between two opposites, between two eras. It is a clash between a mentality that belongs to the Middle Ages and another mentality that belongs to the 21st century.
>
> The Muslims are the ones who began the clash of civilizations. The

Prophet of Islam said: "I was ordered to fight the people until they believe in Allah and His Messenger." When the Muslims divided the people into Muslims and non-Muslims, and called to fight the others until they believe in what they themselves believe, they started this clash, and began this war. In order to stop this war, they must re-examine their Islamic books and curricula, which are full of calls for takfir and fighting the infidels.[26]

The *New York Times* estimated that the video clip of the debate was viewed more than a million times.[27]

In 2006, *Time* magazine included Wafa Sultan in a list of a one hundred "Pioneers and Heroes," "whose power, talent or moral example is transforming the world." *Time* said, "Sultan's influence flows from her willingness to express openly critical views on Islamic extremism that are widely shared but rarely aired by other Muslims."[28]

Sultan differs from many critics of extremist or political Islam who condemn what they see as a violent, heretical strain of Islam rather than Islam itself, which she roundly denounces:

I have decided to fight Islam; please pay attention to my statement; to fight Islam, not the political Islam, not the militant Islam, not the radical Islam, not the Wahhabi Islam, but Islam itself. . . . Islam has never been misunderstood, Islam is the problem. . . . [Muslims] have to realize that they have only two choices: to change or to be crushed.[29]

I personally don't believe Islam can be reformed. But my view is very much needed among those who wish to reform it. There are two choices: rejection or reform. My voice forces the reformists to work even harder. The first step is for the West to put pressure on Islamists to respect my right to reject Islam as much as I respect their right to believe in it. Once Muslims are free to choose, the rest will take care of itself. The real solution, in other words, is transformation, not reformation.

Muslim women have everything to gain by a transformed Islam and nothing to lose. They've already lost everything. Muslim men, on the other hand, won't relinquish their powers so easily.[30]

A major issue for Sultan is the "distorted" view that women are honorably treated within Islam, when in reality, they are "subjugated to a level lower than beasts—not to mention the laws of inheritance, testimony in court, the beating of a wife who refuses to go to bed with her husband, and 'honor' crimes." Indeed, she is convinced that "the Islamic faith was created to serve Muhammad, and to legitimize his desires and urges." For example, "When the Prophet Muhammad married the child 'Aisha, this was not an act of honor toward her childhood. . . . When Muhammad married the Jewish woman Safiya, upon his return from a raid in which he killed her father, brother, and husband, this was not an act of honor toward her."[31]

Not only pilloried by Islamists, Sultan has also been reproached by non-Muslims for failing to support and promote a peaceful Islam.[32]

She has received numerous phone and e-mail death threats.[33] In March 2008, a news report stated she had gone into hiding with her family following the announcement of a fatwa in response to an Al-Jazeera appearance in which she endorsed the publication of the Muhammad cartoons as a right of free speech.[34]

> I believe that most people in the West genuinely desire to preserve our true democratic liberal values. My fear is that we confuse liberalism with multiculturalism by allowing a minority Islamic fascistic ideology to assert itself as the dominant cultural force. So, in order to win this battle, we must unite whether we are conservatives or liberals, democrats or republicans, right or left, and defend our way of life; human-rights, freedom of speech, modernity, equality and forward thinking.[35]

> Many Muslims . . . are hostages of their own belief system [but] because of the internet, they are exposed to different cultures. . . . Given the freedom to choose, I believe they are ready to mix Islam with other thoughts, to improve it.[36]

SYRIAN WOMEN OBSERVATORY

> *Those who think that they can impose their conditions are so wrong.*
> *Whatever obstacles we face, we will continue running our activities and doing whatever we think is of benefit to our society and country. We will continue preparing for local, regional and international workshops and symposiums.*[37]

Advocating for women's rights as a nonregistered NGO in Syria requires dedication, courage, and the strength to overcome many obstacles. In October 2006, delegates from the SWO team headed to Sweden for a symposium on "honor killings," initiated by the SWO in collaboration with the Euro-Med Youth Program. The symposium had been approved by the Syrian authorities. However, when the delegates arrived at the Jordanian border, they were stopped by unidentified persons. Then they were told to wait for instructions from "higher authorities."

> We have the right to ask bitterly and with a voice shrinking in pain: Who dares to do that? . . . And what are those hidden "upper authorities" that have such a strong desire not to declare their identity?[38]

Government policy prohibits independent NGOs like the Syrian Women Observatory, and therefore members face the risk of arrest and detention.[39] They are unable to accept grants from abroad or attract other members. In addition, under the Private Association and Institution Act no. 93 of 1958, there is no right of assembly except for religious meetings.[40] Any meeting must be registered in advance, and permission is often refused. The only government-approved women's advocacy group is the General Women's Union (GWU).[41] Formed in 1967, the GWU receives government support and officials are usually selected from within the Ba'ath Party.[42] The Syrian regime, however, is not the major obstacle, as the principal opposition to women's rights groups derives from extremist Islamist groups that maintain a powerful influence in government.

The Syrian Women Observatory Web site[43] monitors discrimination and violence against women and children, building up a database. The site also features discussion papers on sexual health, adolescence, disabilities, and civil rights, and links to other Web sites, including the Arab Organization for Human Rights in Syria, the National Organization for the Advancement of the Role of Women, and the Democratic Youth Organization in Syria.

SWO is committed to the eradication of "honor crimes." Although reliable statistics are not available for Syria, some human rights activists believe Syria has one of the highest numbers per capita. Under Article 548.1 of the Syrian penal code, any man who comes upon a female relative committing adultery or any other illegitimate sexual acts, and inadvertently injures or kills one or other party, may be treated leniently.[44] The interpretation of the legislation can be very broad, encompassing local gossip or a woman just having a conversation with a man. In most cases, the decision to commit homicide is made by the family as a group, and an underage male member is chosen for the task so that a prison sentence may be avoided, as in the case of a fourteen-year-old boy who killed his sister in April 2008 because she "had a relationship with another teenager."[45]

In September 2005, the Syrian Women Observatory launched a major campaign and petition against "honor killings," titled "Stop the Murder of Women, Stop the Honor Crimes!"

> Let us just now say: No! [to] the Article[s] 548, 239, 240, 241, 242 of the Syrian Penal Law! No! [to] acquitting the criminal killers! Yes! [to] . . . just punishment without any mitigation or excuses![46]

The campaign attracted many supportive articles from Muslim and Christian clergy, writers, lawyers, and ordinary citizens in Syria. Posted on the Syrian Women Observatory Web site, the petition demanded the amendment of the above articles of the Syrian penal code, which granted immunity or reduced sentences to men who murder female relatives. The importance of this issue in Syrian society became clear when there was an immediate response, producing thousands of signatories, mainly in Syria. After several months, the Syrian press came on board.

Bassam al-Kadi, a male women's rights activist and team member of SWO, gave a great deal of publicity to the case of Zahra Ezo, a sixteen-year-old girl who died in January 2007. Zahra was kidnapped by a family friend, bringing shame to her family and tribe. The kidnapper went to prison, but Zahra, still at risk from male members of her own family, moved to a refuge in the Damascus girls' care center. During the nine months she spent there, she was visited by her brother, who came to kill her with a butcher's cleaver, and when her uncle came to visit, he approached her holding a knife. Finally, Zahra left the center, got married, and appeared to be reconciled with her family. Her brother, however, eventually found an opportunity to kill her and she died of multiple stab wounds.

> Zahra, the victim of religious institutions that still collude with these murders . . . the victim of bureaucracy and closed minds . . . we all killed Zahra! we all participated in holding the black knife![47]

In other postings, al-Kali mourns more victims:

> Will the appetite of those who defend segments 548 and 192 of the Syrian
> penalty law ever be fulfilled?! . . . Jasmine Kefaya was murdered by her
> brother in Edleb, "Eman Watta" . . . was divorced by her husband because
> he thought she wasn't loyal to him, so he sent her to her parents' house . . .
> her brother slew her. . . . Remember: we will not sleep; we will not shut up
> until this killing stops.[48]

Dr. Kinda Shammat (Faculty of Law, Damascus University) reviewed violence against women on the SWO Web site and held that forcible marriage
was also a "kind of violence" against women.[49]

A posting by Dr. Bassam Al-Mohammad presented the findings of a
study on domestic violence given during a seminar titled "Domestic Violence and Ways to Prevent It." The study was a collaborative effort of the
Forensic Medicine Department at Damascus University and the Forensic
Medicine Institution–Hamburg/Germany in 2004–2005 in Homs. In a
sample of 216 women, 98 percent were found to be exposed to violence by
their husbands, and in 99 percent of these cases, the violence was recurrent.
Furthermore, 47 percent of the women were under twenty years of age.[50]

Increasing awareness of violence against women prompted a field study
that was carried out under the supervision of the GWU and formed part of a
report by the UN Development Fund for Women. The report, released in
2006, included a random sample of about 1,900 Syrian families from all
regions and found that almost one in four married women had been beaten.[51]

In an article posted on the SWO Web site, lawyer Abdullah Ali discussed marital rape:

> Sexual coercion is almost commonplace in some social circles, but the
> secrecy which surrounds it, whether by the husband or the wife, makes the
> coercion cases rare in the courts.
>
> The [Syrian] legislature allows the husband to force his wife to [have]
> sexual intercourse. . . . This is consistent with the view of [a] religious
> fatwa issued by Al-Azhar Mosque.[52]

In a posting titled "The Return of Slaves in the Modern Age: The Maids in
Syria," lawyer Ahmad Manoha expressed concern about female domestic
workers who were denied any legal protection against "a new kind of slavery."[53]

In a posting on July 16, 2008, the Syrian Women Observatory presented its position on the application of the Convention on the Elimination of All Forms of Discrimination against Women (CEDAW) in Syria:

> Even though the Syrian government has ratified CEDAW . . . this is not applied in Syrian courts. In a study prepared by the Federation of Women (2005), the Syrian government has acknowledged, for the first time, that the violence against women is a widespread phenomenon.[54]

"Domestic Violence and the Children." The man says:
"It took you an hour? Bring the coffee."
Source: *Al-Watan* (Oman), June 28, 2007.

24
TUNISIA

BACKGROUND

Tunisia was a French protectorate until independence was granted in 1956. Habib Bourguiba became president and remained in his position until he was deposed in 1987 by Gen. Zine El Abidine Ben Ali. Bourguiba had suppressed Islamic radical plots against the state, but Ben Ali initially attempted to promote Islamic identity by releasing Islamist activists from prison and forging an alliance with the Islamic Tendency Movement. With the rise in Islamic fundamentalism, however, Ben Ali eventually banned Islamist political parties and jailed activists.

In comparison with other countries in the Arab region, Tunisia is the most enlightened with respect to women's rights. The original 1956 Tunisian Code of Personal Status was revolutionary, as there were no explicit references to Islam. In addition, the government's novel use of *ijtihad*, an independent reasoning approach to Islamic legal practice compared with traditional thinking, facilitated reforms for women regarding marriage, divorce, and child custody. Reducing the control of male kin over marriage also increased women's independence significantly. Successive reforms have followed, including those of 1993, which incorporated international human rights principles.

In line with these developments, a number of governmental women's organizations were established, including the Ministry of Women and Family Affairs, the National Women and Development Commission, and the National Council for Women and the Family. Civil Society groups emerged and flourished. These included the National Union of Tunisian Women (UNFT), involved with education; the Tunisia Association of Democratic Women, aimed at raising awareness of women's issues; and the Center for Studies, Research, Documentation, and Information on Women (CREDIF).

In 1985, Tunisia signed the Convention on the Elimination of All Forms of Discrimination against Women with reservations in cases of conflict with

339

Islamic principles. Women's rights in Tunisia are protected by legislation, and the most significant achievements have occurred during the government of President Zine el Abedine Ben Ali. Gender-sensitive legislation has included equal rights for all citizens, a woman's right to give her own family name to her children if she is a single parent, punishment for rape, spousal rape, and sexual harassment, and severe punishment for domestic violence. However, discriminatory shari'ah law still applied to inheritance and family law. For example, daughters could inherit only half the estate left to sons, and family law entitled the husband to hold most of the property acquired during marriage, including that solely acquired by his wife. Muslim women were forbidden to marry non-Muslim men.[1]

In terms of education and employment, adult female literacy rates rose from 55 percent in 1995 to over 64 percent in 2003, and 36 percent of women were in paid employment, making up over 30 percent of the workforce.[2] In 2007, women made up 32 percent of the workforce.[3]

Despite an increasing number of women employed in the health field, textiles, agriculture, and journalism, some social and economic discrimination persists in the private sector. The government has established schemes to assist women setting up small- to medium-sized businesses, and the number headed by women is steadily increasing. More rights, including maternal leave provisions and protection of employment, were introduced in 1996.[4]

In politics, more women are serving in senior government positions, representing over 13 percent of the total, and in line with gender equality, mandatory military service for women was introduced in 2000.[5]

Progressive preindependence initiatives were established by a number of reformists, most important Tahar Al-Haddad, who believed Tunisia could not develop into a modern society without women's emancipation. In his book *Tunisian Women in Sharia and Society*, published in 1930, he argued for women's education, the abolition of polygamy, and greater freedom in marriage and divorce. Al-Haddad's book presented the philosophical basis for the Code of Personal Status, proclaimed on August 13, 1956, under President Habib Bourguiba.

Since 1987, under the direction of President Ben Ali, these successes have been strengthened. For example, a wife's obedience to her husband has been replaced by a commitment for husband and wife "to treat each other with benevolence, live in harmonious relations and avoid any prejudicial action against each other" (Article 23 of the Code of Personal Status).[6] A divorced mother could now be entrusted with full custody of a child (Article 67), and the mother could refuse consent to the marriage of a minor child (Article 6).[7]

On Women's Day in 2006, President Ben Ali announced the preparation of new laws granting divorced mothers custody of their children and the right to live in their own home. There was also a bill to "unify the minimum marrying age, making it 18 for both sexes."[8]

Tunisian first lady Leila Ben Ali has been a significant role model in the campaign for women's and children's rights. In recognition of her achievements, she received the Peace 2005 prize awarded by the foundation Together for Peace.[9]

In her exploration of women's rights in the countries of the Maghreb (Algeria, Tunisia, and Morocco), Mounira Charrad explains the noticeable differences between these countries in terms of women's rights, in spite of similarities in religion, culture, kinship structure, and reformist ideologies at the time of independence. Differences in the evolution of family law, she maintains, reflected the extent to which governments relied on tribal alliances to gain and sustain power.[10]

In Tunisia, a strong central bureaucracy dating from precolonial and colonial days promoted centralized, urban political leadership and loss of tribal power, including the male kinship's control of women in marriage. As the links to the extended patrilineage weakened, the legitimacy of the nuclear family and loyalty to the nation-state were strengthened. The reformist postcolonial government also acted to marginalize and eliminate tribal power.[11]

Tribal allegiances in Morocco were mainly unaffected by the divide and rule policies of the colonial period. In addition, the Code of Personal Status (Mudawwana, 1957–58) left marriage to the extended male kin, who maintained control in order to safeguard tribal property. The monarchy, which took over after independence, exploited tribal coalitions in order to make alliances and act as arbiter in disputes, thereby preventing the emergence of any single powerful contender for power.[12]

In contrast to Tunisia, the colonial period in Algeria had weakened and destroyed some tribes, but a great deal of support for the extended patrilineage remained within the rural population. After independence, the Algerian socialist-nationalist government played the conservative Islamist and democratic reformists off against each other. By adopting the model of the extended patrilineage in the 1984 Algerian family code, the government also sought the support of rural migrants to urban areas, a group that had more sympathy with traditional values.[13]

IQBAL AL-GHARBI

Any misogynist can find what he seeks in a partial reading of Islam's teachings—since [it is written in the Koran that] men are the custodians of women, the husband is entitled to banish his wife and to discipline her with beatings. He is permitted to rape her . . . [and] the testimony of two women is considered equivalent to that of one man.[14]

Dr. Iqbal Al-Gharbi, a lecturer in psychology at Al-Zaytouna University in Tunis, notes that woman is glorified and praised for her devotion and motherhood in prose and poetry, but the reality is a sad contradiction of the ideal:

All the international reports highlight the Muslim world's many failings in gender equality . . . such as the 60% illiteracy among women, and women's [low] representation in decision-making. . . . Moreover, the 2003 U.N. [Arab] Human Development Report attributed the failure of development in our region to three main shortcomings: lack of knowledge, lack of freedoms, and lack of gender equality.

The negative image of women has been integrated into Muslim society by various means. Religious discrimination has its origins in privileges assigned to men and denied to women, such as prophecy, divine mission, jihad, call to prayer, sermons, the caliphate. Although the Koran may favor gender equality, these historical, chauvinistic traditions have persisted. . . . Some customs blame the Muslim nation's misfortunes on women in the tradition of the temptress Eve and the lascivious Zalikha, wife of Potiphar, who attempted to seduce Joseph. Consequently, the shame of treachery and deception have prevailed.[15]

Al-Gharbi also believes Muslim women are infantilized by a marital relationship built on patriarchal authority and fear of divorce and destitution:

The inability of Muslim society to accept women as mature beings is what causes our failure [of] modernity, since modernity is first and foremost the right of the individual—man or woman—to own his or her own body and mind.[16]

Al-Gharbi has written about blind adherence to the Koran and shari'ah religious law. She believes the application of shari'ah would cause harm to Islamic society and must be avoided. For example, many Christian Arabs would feel the need to emigrate, as happened in Syria and Jerusalem. In addition, the Islamic world would become "a world joke for amputating the hand of someone who stole a quarter of a dinar, stoning [adulterous] lovers, publicly giving 1,000 lashes to anyone who imbibes a glass of wine, and breaking the necks of [Muslims] who adopted another religion or of those who do not act according to any religion."[17]

Historically, Islamic regimes have made use of logic and wisdom, rather than tradition, when expedient. For example, the second caliph, Omar bin Al-Khattab, abrogated the Koranic punishment for theft, even though the verse commands hand amputation: "As for the thief, both male and female, cut off their hands. It is the reward for their own deeds (Koran 5:38)."[18] However, Islam was pursuing vast conquests at the time and "such objectives cannot be achieved with a military consisting of one-armed men."[19]

MUNJIYAH AL-SAWAIHI

Munjiyah Al-Sawaihi calls on Arab intellectuals "to address the problem of the woman courageously and with strong resolve" and resist being intimidated by religious authorities.[20] Dr. Al-Sawaihi, a lecturer in Islamic studies at the Higher Institution of Religion at Al-Zaytouna University in Tunis, is passionate about promoting women's rights in the Arab world and thankful she lives in Tunisia where women are not marginalized by law.

Some religious authorities, Al-Sawaihi believes, are to be ridiculed and berated for interpreting religious texts to suit their agenda:

On one of the Islamic satellite TV channels, the Koranic verse about wife-beating was interpreted to mean beating with a toothpick—blows that do not wound or break [bones], avoiding the face. Bravo! What genius in innovative interpretation and reading of a religious text!

She berates Arab and Islamic countries for allowing the persistent subjugation of women. A woman's face, she laments, is "the property of the man, and she must not uncover it. Has he any honor in the world of today?"

For Al-Sawaihi, the Tunisian divorce laws are central to women's emancipation and are unlike the laws in other Muslim countries. For example, a husband does not have arbitrary power to divorce his wife; divorce can only be granted by a court of law. In addition, violence against women is a punishable offense. Custody of children and decisions on their education and rearing may be granted to mothers, and fathers are forbidden to take children abroad without their mother's permission. Alimony and child support must be paid by the father, and failing that, a special fund exists for payments to divorced mothers. Significantly, the child of a Tunisian mother and a non-Tunisian father is granted Tunisian citizenship.

RAJA BIN SALAMA

Dr. Raja bin Salama, a Tunisian writer, is scathing about the mullahs who want women to be veiled and subjugated to men, wearing "black woollen robes that turn women into faceless creatures, lumps of flesh sold at tribal auctions." The hijab, she says, signifies: "No courting. No loving. No looking. No touching."

Arab poetry, Salama claims, is full of romantic love but not for wives: "The songs and poems 'honor the woman.' . . . But love runs counter to the manly ideology based on control."

Most educated, open-minded Muslim Arabs who could defend women against oppression choose to keep the status quo. Even the well educated are prepared to endorse *muta* marriage (temporary pleasure marriage), which is a "type of prostitution," and "keep silent" about an adult's freedom to choose relationships:

> [They] seek to enshrine in law that type of prostitution that Islam recognizes as mut'a marriage—and those amongst them who express solidarity with the problem of women . . . keep silent regarding basic issues such as the adult's freedom to maintain any relationship with anyone he wishes, and to be master of his own body, heart, face, hands, and tongue.

Instead of finding enjoyment in the beauty of the natural body, today's puritanical Muslim Arabs, she laments, are absorbed with head coverings and sin.[21]

SAMIA LABIDI

Ultimately the solution lies in separating religion from politics, particularly in that part of the globe that is still suffering from this amalgam between . . . temporal . . . and spiritual power. I know that our task smacks of the impossible since in Arab-Muslim countries the word "secularism" is hardly pronounced. They do not even dare to think of it, and yet religion and nationalism remain the two greatest dangers that threaten humankind today.[22]

Samia Labidi was born in Tunisia in 1964. She attended Islamic school from the age of three and grew up in a traditional but tolerant family. She was aware then that Islam served the interests of the men around her, describing her experience of religion in her childhood as that of "a hidden Islam, which was present only to confirm and render credible habits deeply etched in the hearts and minds of men of the time."[23]

The family's attitude to Islam changed, however, when she was eleven years old and her sister married one of the founders of the Islamist organization Mouvement à Tendance Islamiste (MTI), known as El Nahda (the Renaissance). Her new brother-in-law was a militant member of the organization, and his presence galvanized the family into a more demanding form of religious practice. "From one day to the next, the entire family got down to work with passion to catch up for lost time and redeem the sins of the past."[24]

Labidi was a willing student of the "true Islam," wearing the veil from the age of eleven, reading the Koran, and learning the hadith:

I followed all the lessons about the legal element in Islam to improve my knowledge of, and better penetrate, the divine mystery. I wished to take an interest only in the basic fundamental elements of Islam independent of all the different interpretations of men who had monopolized this domain in tailoring the texts to their desires. I wanted to develop a personal point of view without having to refer to anyone else; I used the dogma to reach the essential, the quintessence of the so-called divine message.[25]

At the beginning, the adherence of women to Islamism was in the spirit of a movement to liberate women from the chains of tradition and to save them from the devaluation of that Western women experienced as sexual objects. To give back to woman her true place which was hers by rights pleased me.[26]

Labidi's mother could not accept the restrictive situation and asked for a divorce, leaving Tunisia to live with her brother in France. And eventually Labidi herself became disillusioned:

I felt more and more chained up and crushed by the dogma that interfered in the smallest detail of one's daily life. My mind was sterilized gradually, unable to have access to freedom of thought, to myself. The shackling of women had to be pursued without any letup; otherwise men risked losing control of the situation. Women continued to be treated like incapable beings who need to be systematically under the guardianship of a close male relative in order to move, to exist, or even to breathe. I realized gradually that the promises of equal rights and duties they dazzled us with were but bait that lured us into a premeditated trap that closed over us immediately.[27]

After seven years, at the age of eighteen, Labidi decided to reject this form of Islam and, in her turn, left Tunisia, arriving in Paris on July 14, 1983. She enrolled at X University Nanterre, where she earned master's degrees in philosophy and sociology, graduating in 1992. She learned to speak and write French, English, Arabic, and Hebrew.[28]

Two years before she graduated, in 1989, Labidi became interested in Shia Islam, which her younger brother Karim practiced, as opposed to Sunni Islam: "I immersed myself in Shi'a doctrine . . . one can discuss the nature of the divine without falling into blasphemy, which is far from the case in Sunnism, where it is forbidden to ask who God is."[29]

In 1989, however, Karim gave her an account of his activities over the past several years. He had been recruited through the Iranian Cultural Center in Paris and taken to Afghanistan to serve in al Qaeda, but eventually he saw through the ideology and escaped the organization:

I had the choice of believing his version of the facts and his desire to repent, and denouncing him; between giving and refusing help. I opted for the former solution, to give him the benefit of doubt, in agreeing to translate his testimony from Arabic to French, and above all to edit it so that it would act as a warning against this type of spiral.[30]

Her brother's story was confirmed when her brother-in-law was interrogated by the French authorities and later put under house arrest because of his terrorist activities. In 1993, Labidi decided to describe her brother's experience in a book that would serve as a denunciation of Islamic terrorism. She published the book in her own name, "in order not to give in to this fear that these terrorists wish to sow in the hearts of those who criticise them." *Karim, Mon Frère: Ex-intégriste et Terroriste* (Karim, My Brother: Ex-fundamentalist and Terrorist) was released in November 1998.[31]

Labidi argues that the West remains blind to the danger of Islamic terrorism, which, she believes, is sponsoring the establishment of Islamic states in Arabian-Muslim countries and simultaneously undermining the West from within:

> When will the West realize that Islamist danger is planetary, that the Islamists are individuals who work and think on an international level in order to prepare for the coming of the Mahdi (Messiah), who will govern according to their logic the entire earth in the name of Islam? . . . What the Arabian-Muslim countries have been undergoing for decades to combat the rise of Islamist movements does not seem to have any importance for the Western countries. Shouldn't one ring the alarm bells instead of picking on the regimes in power?[32]

Labidi and her brother have since worked together to combat fundamentalism and Islamic terrorism, "whose worst acts," they believe, "are still to come." In August 1997, they created the Association d'Ailleurs Mais Ensemble (AIME),[33] of which Labidi is president. In May 1999, they launched a magazine, *T'AimeICT*, with the aim of encouraging secularism in Arab countries, particularly the Maghreb region in northwest Africa.[34]

In 2001, Labidi published *D. Le Zéro Neutre*,[35] the first in a projected series of seven books that takes on religious fundamentalism through metaphysical argument:

> The characteristic of this book is to show that what one attributes systematically to God is nothing but human abilities whose ins and outs we still have not mastered. It is a book that believes in humankind, in all its divine splen-

dour. Nothing exists outside him, the ensemble of human genius can only come from the interior of ourselves independently of all exterior intervention. God the protector does not exist, he is only the fruit of our imagination.[36]

Her next book, in 2003, was a humanist, secularist novel, *Mazel Azel*,[37] which concerns humanity's search for God and expresses her belief that "what I am seeking and what I will pursue to the end of my life is not God, but humanity."[38]

> Today in the West, we no longer have the right to criticize Islam, from near or far, at the risk of our lives. Even reformist, practicing Muslims are fingered as criminals, simply because they dared to say that Islam should question itself and its values and adapt to the third millennium if it wants to remain on the scene, just as Christianity and Judaism [have] done.[39]

FAWZIA ZOUARI

Feminist Fawzia Zouari is proud of Tunisia's break with the harsh misogyny that exists in most of the Arab world. Zouari was born in Kef, northwest Tunisia. She obtained her doctorate in French and comparative literature at the Sorbonne and has lived in Paris since 1979. A novelist who deals fearlessly with the position of women in the Islamic world, she has worked for the magazines *Qantara* and *Jeune Afrique* and for ten years at the Institute of the Arab World.

On the fiftieth anniversary of Tunisia's Personal Status Code of 1956, Zouari spoke about the centrality of these laws in protecting women's rights. Even though women in some Arab countries have rights, these rights are not sealed in law and are therefore not enforceable. They may be wealthy landlords and yet they remain infantilized, second-class citizens. It would be difficult, Zouari declares, to believe in the rhetoric of freedom when these women are "stripped of all public initiative, from the right to vote up to the right to drive a car."[40]

She applauds the Tunisian Personal Status Code, which gave Tunisian women greater emancipation than anywhere else in the Muslim world. They are free to enter any employment, and many hold down senior positions.

Although larger numbers of women are choosing the veil, Zouari believes Tunisian women will continue to demand control of their lives, and refuse to relinquish their precious liberties or allow a reversal of history. She believes there is no turning back:

> The game is up. Men, my dear friends, it is too late. Tunisian women, who are accustomed to freedom, will not go back to the house. They, who have learned to hitch their own destiny to the future of their country, will not let themselves be intimidated by the sirens of puritanism, even if it triumphs elsewhere in the lands of Islam. Those who showed the way half a century ago no longer have the right to disappoint. At the head of the procession, the guides do not have the right to turn back, nor to have any doubts about their destination, lest they go backwards in history.[41]

Published Works in French

The Caravan of Dreams, éd. Olivier Orban, Paris, 1998
This Country of Which I Die, éd. Ramsay, Paris, 1999
The Islamic Veil, éd. Favre, Paris, 2002
Turned Over, éd. Ramsay, Paris, 2002
To Finish Some with Shahrazad, éd. Edisud, Aix-en-Provence, 2003
This Veil Which Tears France, éd. Ramsay, Paris, 2004
The Second Wife, éd. Ramsay, Paris, 2006

"Domestic Violence: For Every Action, There Is an Equal and Opposite Reaction."
On the large boxing glove: "Pressures."
Source: Ali Alghamdi *Al-Watan* (Saudi Arabia), May 5, 2007.

25

TURKEY

BACKGROUND

Turkey led the Muslim world in introducing reforms in women's rights and was also ahead of many Western countries in granting women suffrage and political representation. Mustafa Kemal Ataturk, credited with most of these achievements, was the creator of the modern Turkish republic. He supported the nationwide liberation campaign by women in the 1920s and 1930s and praised their many contributions to Turkish society.

> In Turkish society, women have not lagged behind men in science, scholarship, and culture. Perhaps they have even gone further forward.[1]

In 1926 a new civil code was adopted, which abolished polygamy and affirmed equal rights for women in education, divorce, custody, and inheritance. By the mid-1930s, all Turkish women had the right to vote[2] and the national assembly had seventeen female representatives, and in 1934, Turkey became the first nation in the world to have a woman elected to its Supreme Court.

Addressing the parliament in 1935, Ataturk stated, "I am persuaded that the exercise of social and political rights by women is essential for mankind's happiness and pride. You can rest assured that Turkish women will contribute jointly with the world's women towards world serenity and safety."[3]

However, since the 1990s, Turkey has witnessed a resurgence in Islamic fundamentalism, and women's lives (and bodies) have become the stage on which the effort to modernize Islam is played out. The Turkish government has sporadically enforced a ban on headscarves for students and teachers in universities since the 1960s but, in 1997, implementation of the ban intensified when the Turkish Army compelled the government to implement the ban without exception. Since that time, women wearing the headscarf have been barred from taking positions in the state bureaucracy, taking up elected posts in parliament, appearing as attorneys in court, working as teachers in private schools and universities, and pursuing tertiary education. The Turkish government lifted this ban with regard to universities in February 2008. For women, the issue has caused a split between secular and Islamist groups that had previously started to develop closer relationships.

Pressure from women's groups helped to force major reforms of Turkey's civil code in 2002. A clause that identified the man as the head of the household and obliged a wife to seek permission to go out to work was removed.[4] Women's groups also collaborated in a campaign for expanded women's rights in a new penal code. Passed by the Turkish parliament in 2004, the code imposed tougher sentences for the murder of women by male family members in "honor killings."[5] The campaign also coincided with an Amnesty International report, which stated that at least a third and possibly up to half of all Turkish women have experienced domestic violence.

"Violence against women by family members spans the spectrum from depriving women of economic necessities through verbal and psychological violence, to beatings, sexual violence and killings."[6] The Amnesty report also highlighted that "Violence against women is widely tolerated and even endorsed by community leaders and at the highest levels of the government and judiciary."[7] The police were criticized for failing to investigate alleged violence and the courts censored for blaming women who had been attacked, raped, or killed.

While some view Turkey as a leader in championing women's rights throughout the Middle East, providing "a cultural bridge between the Middle East and the Western world,"[8] the draft constitution proposed in 2007 would, if implemented, be a significant blow to women's rights. The current constitution obliges the government to ensure equality for all, a clause that women's groups fought hard to include. In contrast, the new draft describes women as a "vulnerable group" in need of "protection." Over eighty women's groups have united to oppose the draft constitution, asserting, "If the government accepts this it will show their ideology and mind-set about women and men. . . . we don't need protection. We need equality and ask for that, not protection."[9] The women's groups, both secular and Islamist, believe the draft constitution provides an opportunity to push for more rights, not fewer, including a clause insisting on a temporary quota for women in order to eliminate discrimination. They argue it is the only way to improve Turkey's very poor rating on gender equality compared with most European countries.

A 2008 Turkish study, in which almost 12,800 women were interviewed, revealed that four out of ten women in Turkey were victims of domestic violence or sexual abuse, including 25 percent or more from the higher socioeconomic groups. Most cases were never officially reported.[10]

NEBAHAT AKKOÇ AND KA-MER

> *The system . . . structured on a basis of violence, has defined the roles of men and women, has regarded women as someone's daughter or wife or mother, has given men the right and responsibility to monitor women. This is the root of the violation of equality and freedom.*[11]

From 1984 to 1999, thirty thousand to forty thousand people were killed in the conflict between the Turkish military and the Kurdistan Workers Party (PKK). In those years, Nebahat Akkoç and her husband, Zubeyr, were Kurdish primary schoolteachers who were active in Kurdish politics and in the human rights movement. Nebahat's husband, who was murdered in 1993, was thought to have been killed by agents of the state, but the Turkish government denied any involvement. After her husband's death, Nebahat became more involved in the local human rights associations and was herself arrested and tortured.

In coming to terms with her experience of torture at the hands of the Turkish police, Nebahat began to develop a new philosophy, which focused on the concept of state violence extending from the family home:

> After this torture and during the torture, I realized that this is a cycle of violence, that perhaps the policemen doing the torture saw violence in their own family and because of that are committing this torture. I realized then that I need to do something against violence.[12]

Nebahat was well aware of the violence and discrimination suffered by local women and now had direct experience of discrimination as a widow, and of torture as a detainee. She began to study feminist literature and from that point on her activism centered on gender politics.

Ka-Mer Women's Organization

Nebahat Akkoç, together with a group of local women, founded the Ka-Mer Women's Organization in 1997. Traditional cultural mores in the region dictate the exclusion of women from social, economic, political, and cultural life and despite the introduction of new legislation to protect and support women, for the most part, they lack the knowledge and confidence to take advantage of their rights.

The Ka-Mer organization seeks to meet the needs of local women in practical ways and to educate them about their legal rights and their economic potential. To this end, the organization has created a network of centers that provide services for local women. The first center, which became the model for the subsequent ones, was established in 1997, in Diyarbakir, the largest city in the region. There are now twenty-three centers and the network continues to expand.

The centers provide home-cooked Kurdish meals and childcare facilities for women who take part in the organization's activities, such as counseling and educational courses. Intensive ten-week courses are run for groups of twenty women at a time and serve to develop each participant's ability to challenge misogyny and abuse in the family, with a clear understanding of participants' legal and economic rights. The flagship Ka-Mer course explores gender roles, sexual discrimination, sexuality (formerly a taboo subject), and the economic rights of women. More than 2,000 women have taken the course in Diyarbakir, and more than 15,000 have been reached by the organization.

> We want the right to think and act freely: We want a world where people
> are not polarized and everyone is enriched by various senses of belonging
> and can live on the basis of their own decisions.[13]

Ka-Mer also helps women to become independent of male family members by fostering economic self-sufficiency. Participants are invited to develop ideas for their own commercial projects, for example, restaurants, gift shops, and clothing shops, and they are offered low-interest loans of $200 to $7,000. Participants are encouraged to spread the ideas and ideals of female empowerment in their local communities, and successful entrepreneurs are invited to return a proportion of their profits to Ka-Mer. The organization is run on a nonprofit basis, with one-fifth of its income derived from small fees charged for childcare services and restaurant meals, and most of the remainder from donations by other organizations.

Ka-Mer has a hotline for women and girls who are at risk of being killed by male family members for perceived immorality, and in these cases, the organization provides accommodation, medical services, and legal aid. Negotiators from Ka-Mer meet with relatives of potential victims to persuade them that the practice of "honor killing" should be abandoned. This service saved the lives of about a hundred women between 2003 and 2006.

Initially Ka-Mer struggled to survive because it was viewed with hostility by both the Turkish state and the Kurdish independence movement and even by the existing feminist organizations in Turkey. Nebahat's focus on violence within was seen as undermining the Kurdish nationalist movement. Ka-Mer was labeled a traitor's organization and accused of being in league with the Turkish authorities. However, they were no more in favor of Ka-Mer ideals and activities than were the Kurds, and they put pressure on Nebahat to stop.

> People said that we were feminists, and that feminists equalled prostitution. But right now, people understand that feminism equals defending women's human rights. We've taught them.[14]

Nebahat and her co-workers received threats from both sides, which only began to lessen as more women went to the centers and joined the organization.

In the past decade, Ka-Mer has become the leading force in the women's movement in Turkey, operating in every region in South and South Eastern Anatolia. The organization influences and informs policy on the prevention of violence against women, and Nebahat is consulted by the European Parliament, the Turkish government, and local elected officials, both Turkish and Kurdish.

Awards Given to Nebahat Akkoç

> One of thirty-six people honored by *Time* magazine with the Middle Eastern and European Heroes Award in 2003
>
> Presented with Amnesty International's Ginetta Sagan Award in 2004 in honor of Ka-Mer's work in the field of women's human rights

KA-DER

[Men] have said "yes" to human rights, women's rights, education, health, economy and even gender equality in the civil rights code and the penal code. But they hope that politics stays theirs. . . . It's the final rampart that affirms their force and their vision of the hierarchy that remains men's.[15]

To elect is not enough, we want to be elected and to govern![16]

The Association for the Support and Preparation of Women in Politics) (KA-DER) was founded in 1997 as the first nonpartisan Turkish political women's movement. The organization is dedicated to gender equality assisted by positive discrimination at all levels of government. Like-minded men are also welcome as members, but no members are permitted to foist their political views on others, and the chairperson is excluded from membership of any political party. With seventeen branches in major cities and over three thousand members in eleven provinces, KA-DER incorporates all women, affiliated or nonaffiliated, to political parties.[17]

Although a third of Turkish women are illiterate,[18] the majority of university students are women. Women are also successful in the legal profession, and in spite of underrepresentation in politics, Tansu Çiller from the DYP party became the first female prime minister in 1993. Women feature strongly in business and finance but generally, successful businesswomen have not been interested in feminist issues.

In global ratings of women in politics, Turkey is ranked number 162, with 4.4 percent of women in parliament and less than 1 percent of mayors. In contrast, women represent 31 percent and 12 percent of parliamentarians in Germany and France respectively.[19]

KA-DER's basic platform is a protest against underrepresentation and it has aimed for 33 percent of women in parliament. The organization is also committed to secular government and civil society with the full participation of women, including practical training for women in public life. Women are encouraged to stand for office, with strong ideals of service to women and society at large and firm views about opposing intolerance and fanaticism. To assist women candidates, KA-DER runs educational courses on government process and operates a hotline. It is cautious, however, of political parties that accept a quota of women simply to bolster their own image.[20]

The zany symbol of KA-DER is a fake mustache, flaunted by women activists to spotlight men's control of the Turkish parliament and gain the attention of political parties. By focusing on the mustache, an icon of Turkish men's virility, the organization has achieved immense publicity. This creative strategy and the slogan "Is it necessary to be a man to enter Parliament?" turned a $100,000 advertising campaign into the equivalent of a $10 million operation.[21] As an added bonus, the advertising company, Adrena, did not charge for the campaign, which was designed for the run-up to the elections in 2007. KA-DER also won the support of more than a hundred NGOs and persuaded many of Turkey's high-profile women in the arts and business world to sport mustaches. The media then took up the story and featured women celebrities sporting mustaches in newspapers, in popular magazines, and on television.[22]

In order to train women for civic and political life, KA-DER organizes intensive education courses on aspects of politics as well as techniques of communication, presentation, organization, and leadership. Women interested in candidature are taught to understand the system of election, including familiarity with the vast electoral constituency boundaries and the method of nomination from a list. Serious candidates are encouraged to develop sophisticated strategies to rise to the top of these lists.

Seyhan Eksioglu, former president of KA-DER, resigned from the organization when she stood for the Justice and Development Party (AKP) in Turkey's sixteenth general election in July 2007. She is aware of the challenges faced by a sophisticated organization like KA-DER, which defies the traditional image of women as wives and mothers and promotes the view of women as serious politicians. Reform, she asserts, is required to overcome centuries of discrimination against women who were thought to be over-emotional and inadequate to the task of successfully combining household and politics.

Apart from policies to overcome illiteracy and end violence against women, Eksioglu believes KA-DER must demand full implementation of the UN Convention on the Elimination of All Forms of Discrimination against Women, which was ratified by Turkey.

Eksioglu would like political parties to endorse a gender quota, enabling

30 percent of parliamentarians to be women.[23] Positive discrimination was indeed exercised by the Motherland Party (ANAVATAN) and the Grand Unity Party (BBP), which did not take fees from women candidates in the general election of July 2007. In addition, the Democratic Society Party (DTP) declared that 40 percent of the people on its candidate list would be female.[24] At the final count, forty-eight women were elected to parliament, representing 8.7 percent of the assembly.[25]

> We worked very hard, and the result of the campaign is that the percentage of women in Parliament has been doubled. But we cannot rest on this success, we must continue.[26]

KA-DER Campaigns

1997–2002 Campaign to Change the Civil Code

1997–2005 Campaign for Gender/Women's Quota

2003–2005 Amendments to the Turkish penal code in Favor of Women (with Women's Platform)

2003–2008 For Tomorrow from Today, a campaign for women's participation and representation in local politics

8.brabea@alriyadh.com
www.alriyadh.com

Source: *Al-Riyadh*
(Saudi Arabia),
May 31, 2007.

UNITED STATES OF AMERICA

MONA ELTAHAWY

> *Muslims are killing Muslims in Darfur. . . . The sad fact is that more Muslims today are dying at the hands of Muslims than by acts of Israelis, Americans, or any other perceived enemies.*[1]

E gyptian-born journalist and media activist Mona Eltahawy was born in Port Said, Egypt, in 1967. A "proud liberal Muslim," she has lived in Cairo and Jerusalem and was the first Egyptian journalist to live and work in Israel. Eltahawy was a news correspondent for Reuters, sending reports and opinion pieces to various newspapers including the *Guardian* (UK) and *US News* and moved to the United States in 2000. In 2006, she was a Distinguished Visiting Professor at the American University in Cairo (AUC).[2]

At the age of fifteen, Eltahawy was sexually harassed in Mecca during the Hajj pilgrimage, even though her body, apart from her face and hands, was completely covered. Subsequently, she learned that 98 percent of foreign women tourists and 83 percent of Egyptian women had similar experiences in Egypt. Moreover, the perpetrators blamed the victims "because of the way they dressed," and the harassment was usually unreported because Egyptian women feared for their reputations.

> This shame is fuelled by religious and political messages that bombard Egyptian public life, turning women into sexual objects and giving men free rein to their bodies.
>
> The state itself taught Egyptians a most spectacular lesson in institutionalized patriarchy when security forces and government-hired thugs sexually assaulted demonstrators, especially women, during an anti-regime protest in 2005, giving a green light to harassers.[3]

While living in Saudi Arabia with her family, Eltahawy became a feminist at the age of nineteen, a response that "was both a survival mechanism and a rebellion" against the oppression of females in the country. During her exploration of Islam, however, she discovered that the misogynistic interpretations were out of keeping with the earliest form of the faith that gave Muslim women rights as yet unknown to European females.[4] Muslim women in the West, she says, are subject to a hypocrisy exemplified by two cases in France. In one instance, a secular French court sided with a Muslim husband who wanted annulment of the marriage because he claimed his wife was not a virgin, and in another case, French citizenship was denied to a Muslim woman because she was committed to wearing the full veil, or *niqab*. "So basically one woman wasn't submissive enough and the other was too submissive."[5]

Her critics have labeled Eltahawy a "neocon" who was prepared to excuse the "inciteful and hateful" way the Prophet was depicted in the Danish *Jyllands-Posten* Muhammad cartoons controversy. In addition, they assert that she has insulted Muslims by accusing them of exaggerated outrage.[6]

Eltahawy is not deterred. She has drawn attention to women suicide bombers in Iraq and the motivations of al Qaeda in Iraq, which enlisted the women. Apart from their greater ease in getting through checkpoints, she believes that the use of women "taunts men into recruitment." For al Qaeda, schooled in Wahhabi Islam, "women are nothing more than the virgins waiting by the dozen to service the male bombers in the next life."[7]

In the interests of freedom of speech, Eltahawy has strongly defended Middle East bloggers like Saudi Arabian activist Wajeha al-Huwaider, who used the Internet to collect petitions demanding women's right to drive. The petitions were then delivered to King Abdullah:

> A desire to express themselves and a determination to use blogs and social networking sites like Facebook and Myspace to circumvent censorship has created a thrilling equation in the Arab world: one man/woman + internet = very angry dictator.[8]

ASRA NOMANI

We are standing up for our rights as women in Islam. We will no longer accept the back door or the shadows, at the end of the day, we'll be leaders in the Muslim world. We are ushering Islam into the 21st century, reclaiming the voice that the Prophet gave us 1400 years ago.[9]

Nomani's mantra: It's time to take the slam *out of Islam.*[10]

Since the kidnapping and murder of her close friend Daniel Pearl in 2002, Asra Nomani has campaigned against segregationist practices and attitudes within mosques in the United States. Her message has reached a broad audience, with her work featured in many publications, including the *Washington Post*, the *New York Times*, *Time* magazine, *American Prospect*, *Slate*, *Sojourners Magazine*, *People*, and others. Although her courageous actions have been likened to those of Rosa Parks and Martin Luther King Jr., she has received death threats, and online jihadist message boards have called for a fatwa to be issued against her.

Asra Nomani was born in Bombay, India, in 1965. At the age of four, she migrated to the United States with her family, living in New Jersey for six years before relocating to Morgantown, West Virginia, where she still lives today. She graduated from West Virginia University in 1986 with a BA in liberal studies and continued her studies in international communications at American University, receiving an MA in 1990.

Nomani started work at the *Wall Street Journal*, and throughout her fifteen years with this publication, she wrote about issues that had little to do with her Islamic upbringing, covering the commodities market, the airline industry, and international trade and travel.

The first significant turning point in her life was the attack on the World Trade Center on September 11, 2001, which compelled her to take leave from the *Wall Street Journal* and travel to Pakistan. Her dispatches for *Salon* magazine earned her an Online Journalists Award. During the time she spent in Pakistan, she befriended Daniel Pearl. His kidnapping and subsequent murder affected her deeply, as Pearl and his wife had been staying with Nomani in Karachi. She was actively involved in the investigation into Pearl's disappearance until she discovered she was pregnant; her Pakistani boyfriend told her to get an abortion and left her when she declined. Nomani's "crime" of continuing an illegitimate pregnancy carries a penalty of death by stoning under shari'ah law.

She then returned to her family in the United States and began writing *Standing Alone in Mecca: An American Woman's Struggle for the Soul of Islam*. The birth of her son inspired her to undertake a pilgrimage to Mecca, another turning point in her life. Nomani was stunned to learn that in the Masjid al-Haram, the Sacred Mosque, men and women prayed together side by side, an act that was unheard of in mosques in the United States. (Since 2006, new rules have removed women from the often crowded space.)[11]

Upon her return to Morgantown, Nomani felt like a second-class citizen, entering her mosque through a back door and praying on an upstairs balcony, segregated from the men, including her father, who had helped to establish the original mosque in 1981 and to rebuild the Islamic Center of Morgan-town (ICM) in 2003.

Her father, Zafar Nomani, supports her activism. He told her: "Muhammad was one of the greatest feminists. Islam first gave rights to women 1,400 years ago. . . . When I see Islam today and the way people behave towards women, I am very sad. I am for women's rights, respect, women's equality. Islam teaches that."[12]

Nomani recalls feeling sick and depressed every time she climbed the stairs to the separate women's area in the ICM. She also felt confused as to why she, who had "interviewed the Taliban, corporate titans, and political leaders . . . didn't dare peek over the edge of the balcony in my own mosque."[13] Searching for inspiration, Nomani found "courage, clarity and vision"[14] in three historical figures: the "mother of the Civil Rights Movement," Rosa Parks, feminist suffragette Alice Paul, and the Prophet Muhammad.

Reactions to Nomani's attempt to pray alongside the men in her mosque were, and continue to be, irreconcilable. Fellow members of her congregation petitioned the mosque to have her banished for "disrupting worship and spreading misinformation about Islam."[15] Representatives of the mosque justified the segregationist practice, not with teachings from the Koran but with tradition, pragmatism, and modesty, arguing that separating the sexes was more conducive to focusing on the prayer itself and prevented men and women from gazing upon one another when prostrating.

In contrast, religious scholar and historian Reza Aslan supported Nomani's protest. According to Aslan, "This conception of the separation of men and women is something that never occurred during the prophet's life-time. What she has done is perfectly in line with Islamic values, traditions and the prophet's own desire to have men and women working side by side, praying side by side and even fighting side by side."[16]

In 2005, Nomani took her protest a step further, when, on March 1, she posted her "99 Precepts for Opening Hearts, Minds and Doors in the Muslim World" to the doors of her Morgantown mosque. Nomani does not reject the obvious comparisons to Martin Luther and even draws inspiration from the feminist pioneers within other faiths. "We are at a crossroads similar to the one Christians and Jews found themselves in before women were accepted as rabbis, ministers and pastors."[17]

Weeks later, Nomani organized the first public woman-led prayer by a mixed-gender congregation in the United States, held in New York City on March 18, 2005. She began her "Muslim Women's Freedom Tour" shortly thereafter. The tour encouraged Muslim women to assert themselves in their mosques by holding mixed-gender prayer services led by women in halls usually reserved for men. As with her 2003 protest, reactions have revealed both criticism and praise. Her critics allege that both events were staged simply to promote her book, *Standing Alone in Mecca*, which was published in February 2005. The prayer event in New York City, they point out, was not even held at a mosque (three had refused and an art gallery withdrew its offer after a death threat), but in the Episcopal Cathedral of St. John the Divine, and only six individuals attended the second, at Brandeis University. However, others laud her efforts and admire Nomani for "fighting the good fight," for example, Asma Gull Hasan, Pakistani American lawyer and author of *Why I Am a Muslim: An American's Odyssey*:

> A lot of women our age, first-generation Americans, young Muslims who don't like the conservative attitudes of the mosque, either keep attending blindly and ignore the rhetoric or just stop attending altogether. I don't go to a mosque because I get so irritated with how women are treated.[18]

Nomani has countered the criticisms of self-promotion with an argument of sheer practicality. Her publisher was sending her around the country; therefore it made sense to combine it with the Freedom Tour, which she regards as "doing my heart's work." "I think it's incumbent on Muslims with intellect, hope and love in our hearts . . . to go into the houses of worship and really try to transform the Muslim house from within."[19]

She saw two years of campaigning against segregationist practices in mosques come to fruition in July 2005, when the country's major Muslim organizations issued a report titled "Women Friendly Mosques and Community Centers: Working Together to Reclaim Our Heritage," recommending various reforms, including an affirmative action program to have women sit on mosque boards. At Nomani's own mosque in Morgantown, the rules banning women from the front door and the main hall have been reversed, and a woman has been elected to office for the first time.

Nomani also draws strength from the actions of Muslim women internationally. In November 2005, she participated in a conference of twelve Muslim women scholars on Islamic feminism in Barcelona, Spain. Initially, she had reservations, when one Barcelona city official questioned whether Islamic feminism was merely an oxymoron and a young Muslim man attending the conference stated that "In Islam, there is no place for feminism."[20] However, shortly after Nomani had outlined her efforts to integrate mosques in the United States, she was stunned and inspired by the willingness of the audience to back women in their struggles against what she terms the "gender jihad."

> We Muslim feminists view it as a struggle that taps Islamic theology, thinking and history to reclaim rights granted to women by Islam at its birth but erased by manmade rules and tribal traditions masquerading as divine law.[21]

The participants, including Muslim women from Malaysia, Mali, Nigeria, France, Canada, the United Kingdom, the United States, and refugee camps in Western Sahara, shared their stories of regional reform. Using various methods, the women began challenging the customs that deny Muslim women basic human rights from the mosque to the bedroom, including gender segregation, mandatory veiling, forced early marriages, death for sex outside marriage, domestic violence, and strict domestic roles. All of the participants rejected their image as the "bad girls" of Islam, explaining that they are not anti-shari'ah or anti-Islam. Rather, by using the Koran and the Sunnah, the traditions and sayings of the Prophet Muhammad, they see their efforts as part of a wider peace movement. Nomani herself, in a move reminiscent of Martin Luther King Jr., proposed a plan she called "The Islamic Dream," an attempt to coordinate the efforts of people around the world and develop a new approach for Islam in the twenty-first century.

To this end, in September 2006, Nomani cofounded Muslims for Peace with other Muslim women. The following month, she was awarded a reporting fellowship from the South Asian Journalists Association to report on a Muslim woman activist building a women's mosque in her native India. Since August 2007, Nomani has been a visiting professor at Georgetown University's School of Continuing Studies, leading the Pearl Project, a faculty-student project examining the murder of Daniel Pearl.

Award

Online Journalists Award, 2001

Selected Published Works

Tantrika: Traveling the Road of Divine Love (San Francisco: Harper, 2003).
Standing Alone in Mecca: An American Woman's Struggle for the Soul of Islam (San Francisco: Harper, 2005).

AMINA WADUD

> *In the period immediately following the death of the Prophet, women were active participants at all levels of community affairs—religious, political, social, educational, intellectual. They played key roles in preserving traditions, disseminating knowledge and challenging authority when it went against their understanding of the Qur'an or the prophetic legacy.*
>
> *Today more women are active in the discussion and reformation of identity than at any other time in human history. By going back to primary sources and interpreting them afresh, women scholars are endeavoring to remove the fetters imposed by centuries of patriarchal interpretation and practice.[22]*

Wadud received widespread publicity on March 18, 2005, when she led an unsegregated congregation of about sixty men and forty women in Friday prayers at Synod House, part of the Episcopal Cathedral of St. John the Divine, on Manhattan's Upper West Side. The event was sponsored by the Muslim Women's Freedom Tour, Muslim Wakeup! and the Progressive Muslim Union of North America, and was filmed by international media organizations including the two major Arab satellite networks, Al-Jazeera and Al-Arabiya. As mentioned (Asra Nomani), three mosques had refused to host the event and a fourth venue, an art gallery, was dropped after a bomb threat.[23]

Amina Wadud was born on September 25, 1952, in Bethesda, Maryland. Her father was a Methodist minister and her mother was descended from Muslim slaves of Arab, Berber, and African ancestry dating back to the eighth century. In 1972, without knowing her maternal ancestry at the time, Wadud became a Muslim.

In 1975, she received a bachelor of science degree from the University of Pennsylvania; later she gained an MA in Near Eastern studies and a PhD in Arabic and Islamic studies from the University of Michigan. She also studied advanced Arabic in Egypt at the American University in Cairo, Koranic studies at Cairo University, and philosophy at Al-Azhar University. Between 1989 and 1993, Wadud was an assistant professor at the International Islamic University in Malaysia. She became a professor of Islamic studies at Virginia Commonwealth University, Richmond, Virginia, in 2007 and is currently a visiting scholar at the Starr King School of the Ministry in California.

The mother of five children, Wadud has become internationally known as an expert lecturer, speaker, and consultant on the subject of women in Islam and on the practice of Islam in the United States. After six years of research, her book *Qu'ran and Woman: Re-reading the Sacred Text from a Woman's Perspective* was published in March 1999.[24] Her book contests the traditional patriarchal reading of the text and argues that the essential language of the Koran is free from gender bias and prejudice.[25]

In August 1994, she delivered a Friday sermon on "Islam as Engaged Surrender" in the Claremont Main Road Mosque in Cape Town, South Africa. This was an unprecedented break with the tradition that the sermon is always given by a male and led to calls for Wadud to be removed from her position at Virginia Commonwealth University.

The mixed congregation Friday prayers that she led in March 2005 generated intense controversy. As the Assembly of Muslim Jurists stated in response to the event, the traditional view held by the majority of Islamic scholars is that women cannot lead the Friday prayer or deliver the sermon. Sheikh Yusuf Al-Qaradawi, a leading figure in the Muslim Brotherhood, said that a woman could lead the service for other women and her family, "instead of coming up with the heresy of women leading men in prayers."[26]

However, other respected Islamic scholars, including Javed Ghamidi, the founding president of the Al-Mawrid Institute of Islamic Sciences in Lahore, Pakistan, said there is nothing in the Koran or the prophetic tradition to prohibit women from leading congregations in prayer, and Egypt's Grand Mufti, Sheikh Ali Guma, supports women leading prayer with the approval of the community.[27]

There have also been less tolerant responses. Saudi Arabia's Grand Mufti, Abdul Aziz al-Sheikh, declared Wadud to be an "enemy of Islam" who has "violated the law of God,"[28] and the media in Egypt and Saudi Arabia called Wadud a "deranged woman" who "collaborates with Western infidels to corrupt Islam." Wadud has received fatwas and death threats and at times has needed the protection of armed guards.[29]

There is no consensus opinion, and what became known as the "Wadud Prayer" forced even conservative Muslim organizations to publicly address the issue. The question of whether women can become imams and lead prayer meetings is a focal point for a deeper ongoing discontent with the gender inequality that exists within the practice of Islam worldwide, and an articulation of the desire for reform. Khaled Abou El-Fadl, professor of Islamic studies at UCLA, said that the Wadud Prayer expressed the frustration of many learned Muslim women and that fundamentalists fear a "ripple effect, not just in the U.S. but all over the Muslim world."[30]

The Progressive Muslim Union followed the Wadud Prayer with a Woman-Led Prayer Initiative to encourage further debate between conservative and progressive Muslims and to facilitate and document similar events. Amina Wadud continues to lead mixed prayer services.

In 2006, Wadud's book *Inside the Gender Jihad: Women's Reform in Islam*, dealing with gender injustices and oppression, was published.[31]

> Sharia is thoroughly patriarchal. . . . You cannot legislate with regard to the well-being of women without women as agents of their own definition, and Sharia was not concerned with that construction. Sharia was happy to legislate for women, even to define . . . the proper role of women, and to do so without women as participants. So obviously that is a major flaw and the only way for that aspect of Sharia to be corrected would be a radical reform in the way in which it is thought.[32]

Source: Khaled, *Al-Watan* (Saudi Arabia), July 11, 2007.

ELHAM MANE'A

> *I call on you, my Muslim sister, to take off the veil. This is an honest call. . . . Its intention is not to defile you, nor to encourage you to [moral] lassitude. I call on you to exercise [free] thought and to use your own mind.*
>
> *I am not calling on you to stop praying, fasting, or believing in Allah. I call on you to take off the veil. . . . Be yourself—a woman, and not [a collection of] private parts.*[1]

Reformist Yemeni columnist Dr. Elham Mane'a urges Muslim women to be aware of the religious and political propaganda associated with Islamic dress before embracing the veil. She claims that the veil (*hijab*) emerged from admiration of the Iranian Islamic Revolution and the imposition of mandatory Islamic dress for women. This revolution, which she believes betrayed the middle classes and left-wing groups who helped the clerics oust the shah, served as the focus for Islamic arousal and the model for Islamic expression in the region:

> Since this revolution was the first true awakening in the region, it was considered by many to be an example worthy of imitation—both [the revolution itself] and the garb that the women began to wear.

Mane'a stresses that the propagation of the *hijab* as mandatory Islamic dress was made possible through colossal petrodollar funding for relentless Wahhabi propaganda. A natural ideological merger with the Muslim Brotherhood created further dissemination of ideology, new Islamist groups, and ultimately changes in Muslim attitudes. She emphasizes that the veil is a political issue: Iran, Saudi Arabia, and the Muslim Brotherhood are committed to political power and depend on religion for their authority. The arguments used to convince women to wear the veil have taken several forms:

> The first argument is based on the assumption that the Arab man is a lecherous animal that cannot control its urges, and therefore, one must be on guard against it. . . .
>
> This premise is unfair to the Arab man, whom we know as a brother, as a father, as a husband, and as a human being. . . .
>
> He is capable of controlling his urges. . . .
>
> This first argument also includes a humiliating premise about women, since it portrays the woman as nothing more than a sex tool—not as a human being but as [a collection of] private parts.
>
> The second argument is based [on] the premise that there is a connection between wearing the veil and the establishment of a good society.
>
> On the contrary, the forced segregation [of the sexes] has led to homosexual relations . . . [and] has not prevented some of the girls from having [sexual] relations out of wedlock. After that, they usually have surgery to reconstruct the hymen.
>
> The third argument rests on the premise that [Islam] has a firm position on the issue of the veil, while the fact is that there are many [different] religious texts on the subject.
>
> [When you read them] you will see that not only is there an abundance of texts, but that they also have numerous interpretations. . . .
>
> As a matter of fact, the third argument, which claims that it is religion that imposes wearing the veil on women, is the weakest argument, since we never heard it before the late 1970s, and we didn't see it implemented until the orthodox interpretation of Islam became the most prevalent interpretation in the Arab and Muslim world.

28
MALE MUSLIM ACTIVISTS

SULIMAN AL-SALMAN (SAUDI ARABIA)

Helping women to get their rights, which are ignored or suppressed by law or customs doesn't conflict with Islam, which does not prevent women from utilizing their own money, driving or choosing their own husbands.[1]

Al-Salman believes women are severely hampered by regulations that restrict their movements outside the home and force overwhelming social dependency on men. He stood for municipal elections in 2005 with a campaign in support of women's rights. Although he failed to win a seat, he continued his activism on behalf of women, and after two years of negotiations with the Ministry of Social Affairs, he obtained approval to form Ansar Al-Marah, the first civil society for women's rights in Saudi Arabia.

Other existing women's societies were mainly set up for the purpose of humanitarian relief. Ansar Al-Marah, which was established in January 2008, has twenty-one members, mainly activists and academics, who will aim for increased awareness, research, and institutional changes beneficial to women. The organization, however, has been criticized for having a Westernizing agenda incompatible with Islam.[2]

SLEIMAN AL-SLEIMAN (SAUDI ARABIA)

Beforehand, there was no justification for women driving cars, but women have begun going to work, to their jobs, their shops, to the market. We are living in modern cities. Our demand to allow women to drive is a pressing and natural demand. It is a woman's natural right to drive a car.[3]

Sleiman Al-Sleiman is a Saudi man who has consistently campaigned for Saudi women to be allowed to drive. He appeared in a television debate in May 2007 and argued that women needed to drive because they were now going to work, and a modern country should allow modern practices.[4]

He assured the panel that women would still "respect the Islamic moral values when they drive,"[5] in contrast to Dr. Sleiman Al-'Eid, head of the Islamic Culture Department at King Saud University, who warned that women driving would erode the system of modesty. The panel included a woman, Intisar Falamban, who said she did not need to drive because she had a chauffeur. Al-Sleiman insisted that not all women were fortunate enough to afford a chauffeur, and even if they were, they would not always feel safe with him. It is not feasible, he argued, that women should rely on a husband or male guardian to drive them everywhere, for such people are not always available.[6]

Al-Sleiman characterized his ideological rivals as "the same people who are against the education of women, and are against television and cellular phones with cameras. They are against anything new."[7]

BASHIR GOTH (SOMALIA)

> The warlords used brute force to coerce people and the Islamists use brute religion to dehumanize people.
>
> They hide women not because Islam orders their mummification but because Islamists suffer from a masculinity problem. They think he who is not a master of his wife cannot be a master of others. Power and tyranny is their ultimate goal.
>
> Anyone who wants to see where the Islamists would like to lead Somalia should only see how they treat women, music and ideas.[8]

Somali journalist Bashir Goth blames Saudi Arabian Wahhabi Islamist influence for the increasing discrimination against and oppression of Somali women. He maintains this ideology is heretical and opposed to authentic Islam. The Islamist rulers of Mogadishu, he says, promised peace and tolerance after they drove out the warlords. They vowed not to enforce shari'ah law or Islamic dress for women but then persecuted women who didn't comply. In addition, they promoted Islamic courts, terrorized areas that showed any resistance, and set out to Arabize and Islamize all Somali regions in the Horn of Africa.

In Goth's opinion, groups of Somali clerics like the self-styled Authority for Promotion of Virtue and Prevention of Vice are the agents of Wahhabism, the puritanical form of Islam practiced in Saudi Arabia:

> [They] hide under the cloak of religion and scare people with their indiscriminate use of terms such as blasphemous, infidels, apostates, sacrilegious, atheists, westernized minds and many others. They use the available democratic atmosphere to herd us towards the abyss.[9]

Goth warns that the Wahhabi form of Islam is poised to replace Somali Islamic practice and establish an Islamic emirate unless Somalis resist religious fanaticism and interference and Somali intellectuals find the courage to speak up.

He believes Wahhabi Islamists will impose the submission of women (and men) by a religious police force like the Mutaween in Saudi Arabia. It was this moral police corps that forced girls to return to their blazing school building and face incineration because, in their haste to escape, they had left their headscarves behind.[10]

> These fanatics are on a mission to eliminate co-education schools, shroud young girls and deprive them of their healthy childhood social interaction with boys. They want to bury them alive and teach them from an early age that the female body is an eyesore to public decency. . . .
>
> It is this obsession with sex, this concept of viewing women only as an object of sex, created for man's libido relief that turned women's body into a thing of shame. . . . If we let them have their way, these prophets of "purity" would soon be on a mission to destroy what has remained of our culture. . . . They want to edit, re-write and censor the treasures of Somali oral literature.[11]

The attitudes and methods of the Islamists are already evident in floggings for petty crimes and threats of the death penalty for those who don't perform the five-time daily prayers. Moreover, Goth believes women will bear the burden of repression, entailing segregation and religious enslavement:

> It is time . . . to speak out. If we don't do it today, we won't be able to do it tomorrow. Because there will be no tomorrow as our country descends into 7th century Arabia.[12]

ABUL KASEM (BANGLADESH/AUSTRALIA)

What I found was shocking. Sometimes, I just could not believe what I was reading. Thus, I completely discarded the explanations, apologies, and tafsirs [interpretations] from the erudite Islamic scholars and started to use my own brain, common sense, and judgment to find the truth.

After I found the "real Islam," I could not look straight into the eyes of my mother. I could not sit comfortably with my sisters. I could not be at ease with my wife. I was forced to pick up the pen (read keyboard) to tell all the mothers, sisters, and wives of Islamic faith what Sharia/Islam means for them.[13]

Kasem selected over eighty verses out of hundreds related to women and women's rights. His sources include the Koran, the hadith, and Imam Ghazali, whose book *Ihya Uloom Ed-Din* is said to be second only to the Holy Koran.[14]

Men are superior to women.

The Koran

Men are protectors and maintainers of women; women must be devoutly obedient, if not then beat them. (4:34)

The Koran

Wives are tilths: sow in them in whatever manner you like. (2:223)

Sunaan Abu Dawud (Hadith)

A man will not be asked as to why he beat his wife. (11.2142)

A woman who complains about the beatings she receives from her husband is not the best woman. (11.2141)

Men have a right to four wives and any number of sex slaves.

The Koran

For men four free women wives (some say nine) at a time and any number of slave girls is permitted. (4:3)

Women annul prayers.

Sahih Bukhari (Hadith)

A prayer is annulled by a passing woman, a dog and a monkey.

Mishkat-ul-Masabih (Hadith)

An ass, a pig, a Jew, a Magian and a woman annuls a prayer. (Vol. 2, p. 114, Hadis no. 789)

Most women are deficient in intelligence.

Sahih Bukhari

Majority of women are in hell because they are deficient in intelligence. (1.6.301)

Ghazali

They (women, servants) are evil and possess little intelligence. (Vol. 2, p. 34)

Women are forbidden to travel alone.

Sahih Bukhari

A woman cannot travel without her husband or Dhi-Mahram, no man can visit her. (3.29.85)

Women are slaves and men are their owners.

Ghazali

Women are prisoners in a man's hand. Men have taken them as trusts from God and God has made their sexual parts lawful for men. (Vol. 2, p. 33)

Hedaya (manual of Sunni law)

A woman is a servant and the husband is the person served. (P. 47)

Islamic marriage is about sex for money.

Sunaan Abu Dawud

A woman becomes lawful if you give her a dower of two handfuls of flour or dates; a contract or temporary marriage can be done for a handful of grains. (11.2105)

Teaching twenty verses of The Koran is enough as a dower to marry a woman. (2.11.2106)

Sunaan Abu Dawud

If you marry a pregnant woman then her vagina is lawful if you pay the dowry, after she gives birth, flog her; the child becomes your slave. (11.2126)

Hedaya

Maintenance of a wife is the custody for the purpose of enjoyment. (P. 141)

A woman should never be elected as a ruler.

Sahih Bukhari

People ruled by a woman will never be successful. (5.59.709)

If a woman wishes to get rid of her tyrannical husband she must refund the "sex money" (*mahr*) she received from him during marriage.

Sahih Muslim (Hadith)

A woman must return the Mahr if she wants a divorce from her husband. (7.63.197, 198, 199)

A husband has the right to have sex with his wife by force (the right to rape).

Hedaya

You can enjoy a wife by force. (P. 141)

Women are easily expendable—a divorced woman gets no maintenance or alimony from her ex-husband.

Sahih Muslim

No lodging and maintenance for an irrevocably divorced woman; Muhammad asked one such woman to be lodged with a blind man, Ibn Umm Maktum. (9.3519, 3522, 3530)

Women bring bad luck.

Malik's Muwatta (Hadith)

A woman, a horse and a house bring bad luck. (54.8.21, 22)

Men should always oppose women.

Ghazali

Hazrat Umar said, "Act opposite to women as there is reward in opposing them." (Vol. 2, p. 34)

Women may undergo female circumcision.

Sunaan Abu Dawud

Female circumcision—do not cut severely as that is better for a woman and more desirable for a husband. (41.5251)

In contrast, there are four often-quoted verses in the Koran where women are considered equal to men (compiled by Azam Kamguian, "Islam and Women's Rights," Center for Inquiry).

Their Lord responded to them: "I never fail to reward any worker among you for any work you do, be you male or female, you are equal to one another." (3:195)

As for those who lead a righteous life, male or female. While believing, they enter paradise; without the slightest injustice. (4:124)

Anyone who works righteousness, male or female, while believing, we will surely grant them a happy life in this world, and we will surely pay them their full recompense for their righteous works. (16:97)

Whoever commits a sin is required for just that, and whoever works righteousness—male or female—while believing, these will enter paradise wherein they receive provision without any limits. (40:40)

Abul Kasem was born in Bangladesh, where he attended a secular school. As a child, his father taught him to recite from the Koran and he was instructed in the Islamic rituals and texts by a mullah, who taught that "Muslims are the only inheritors of the earth, that we must never mix with the non-Muslims, we must hate them, humiliate them verbally, and if possible, physically."[15]

When the riots broke out between India and East Pakistan (now Bangladesh), Kasem was in high school. Witnessing the brutality of the Islamists and seeing the mutilated bodies of his Hindu friends proved to be a life-changing experience, especially after he discussed the events with ordinary Muslims who believed Hindus had no right to be in their Muslim country and deserved to be killed. In any case, they said, killing non-Muslims brings rewards.

The genocide perpetrated by the Islamic Army of Pakistan, assisted by local Islamists, in 1971, killed about 3 million Bengalis and included the rape of about 250,000 women. Islamists vindicated their actions by referring to the Koran, the hadith, and shari'ah law. Kasem sought the opinion of a local imam, who explained that the Bengalis, having deviated from authentic Islam, deserved the wrath of Allah as dispatched by the Pakistani army. At that point, Kasem decided to research the Islamic texts for himself.

After reading numerous works by Islamic scholars who extolled the virtues of Islam for women, Kasem came to believe that the Prophet did improve the status of women in comparison to their situation in pre-Islamic times, but he was struck by the unfairness and barbarity experienced in reality by vast numbers of women in many Muslim societies. These disparities led him to dissect the texts more closely.

> Sura an-Nisa' 4:34 . . . As to those women On whose part ye fear Disloyalty and ill-conduct Admonish them (first), (Next), refuse to share their beds, (And last) beat them (lightly); But if they return to obedience, seek not against them Means (of annoyance): For God is Most High, Great (above you all).[16]

The word "lightly" was not part of the original verse but was added later by the translator, Yusuf Ali.[17] Kasem makes the point that Yusuf Ali added the word to avoid embarrassment and "make the verse more civilized."[18]

For Kasem, this verse defines women as objects under the control of men who are entitled to dispense corporal punishment according to their whims. Trapped by men's belief in their rightful ownership of wives, women would have no recourse at the hands of a tyrannical husband.

Kasem contrasts these traditions with secular law. For example, in Australia, where he lives, physical or mental abuse of a spouse is a serious punishable offense, and government authorities have the power to remove victims to a secret location until the court hearing. This secular law is incongruous with the Koranic verse and would be considered un-Islamic.

In the Islamic republic of Iran, violence against wives is taken further by religious leaders such as Hojatoleslam Imani: "A married woman should endure any violence or torture imposed on her by her husband for she is fully at his disposal. Without his permission she may not leave her house even for a good action (such as charitable work). Otherwise her prayers and devotions will not be accepted by God and curses of heaven and earth will fall upon her." Moreover, just the charge of adultery by a husband can result in the wife's being punished by stoning to death.[19]

Many Islamist apologists assert that Islam does not advocate polygamy. In response to this claim, Kasem quotes the following hadith:

The best Muslims had the largest number of wives (Shahih Bukhari 7.62.7).

The best Muslim men should have incredible sex power (Shahih Bukhari 7.62.142).[20]

According to Kasem, the priority in Islamic marriage is procreation rather than love and companionship. Furthermore, he believes the Islamists have a hidden agenda to advance the cause of Islam through women's potential to change the demographics. Not only are women essential merchandise and pleasure machines, but they are also breeding factories.[21]

Islamists affirm the religious and moral responsibilities to honor and respect women and punish any violation. However, for Kasem, any Muslim woman who believes Islam grants her justice, freedom, and gender equality is simply gullible and vulnerable to those mullahs who support the views expressed by misogynist verses and feel no need to protect women from being victimized by men.[22]

The West is also an easy target of Islamist misrepresentations. According to Kasem, Islamists adopt the sophisticated and well-tried historical techniques such as *taqiyya* (telling lies) and *kitman* (adopting deception) that were used in the past when advancing into enemy territory. In this way, Islamists are able to confound a credulous West and acquire trust.[23]

We cannot bury our head like an ostrich and pretend that everything is fine and dandy with Islam because some uneducated Mullahs have said so. It is necessarily not so. The truth must be told no matter what price one has to pay.[24]

LAFIF LAKHDAR (TUNISIA)

We Muslims need to stop considering the proliferation of children as a religious obligation. We need to stop depriving non-Muslim women married to Muslim men of their rights to guardianship over their children and of inheriting from their Muslim spouses and children. We need to stop the sexual disfigurement of girls through circumcision. We need to stop insisting on women's inequality to men in civil rights, and on polygamy, which is a catastrophe for Muslims in their countries and in the diaspora.[25]

Tunisian reformist Lafif Lakhdar worked closely with Ahmed Ben Bella, Algeria's first president. He also followed the PLO from Jordan to Beirut, where he became a prominent left-wing intellectual. Disillusioned by the events of the Lebanese civil war and leftist ideology, he went to live in Paris.

Lakhdar was a columnist for the London-based Saudi Arabian daily *Al-Hayat*, but his liberal views were unacceptable and he was suspended for two months. In October 2002, during an interview on Al-Jazeera TV, he expressed strong views about the stoning of women and also about modernization in the Muslim world, including secularization, more freedom of movement for women outside the home, and gender equality with respect to legal testimony and inheritance. Following this interview, he was immediately fired by *Al-Hayat*.[26]

He was also boycotted by Al-Jazeera after appearing on their popular program *The Opposite Direction*, when he refuted the claims of Holocaust deniers.[27]

Lakhdar demands the elimination of the verse that commands wife beating:

[The] Koran 4:34 commands: "Beat them." I have demanded the abrogation of this verse, i.e., that it not be put into practice, because it is no longer in conformity with the universal values of the age. . . . The Islamic Tunisian historian Mohammed Talbi also demanded its abrogation.[28]

He also speaks about the *hijab* with derision:

> [Forbidding the *hijab*] restores esteem to a woman's body. How so? A man's body is partly shameful—from the navel to the knee. A woman's body is shameful in its entirety, apart from the face and the hands. Muslim women aren't equal to Muslim men even in the value of their bodies!
>
> One French psychoanalyst thinks that French Islamists demand [that women wear] the hijab because a woman's hair makes them think of hair she has elsewhere, and this inflames their passions. This reduces women to sex.
>
> The subconscious meaning of this is that every woman with her hair uncovered is a whore whom any Muslim is entitled to violate. This is why the Islamic jurisprudents forbade Muslim slave girls to wear the hijab, and likewise non-Muslim women—i.e., Muslims have the right to violate them whenever they want.[29]

According to Lakhdar, international bodies should legislate against the stoning of women and the UN Security Council should pass a resolution calling for military intervention in the case of Islamist stoning of women.[30] The adoption of secularist principles, separation of religion and state, full citizenship for women, and freedom of religion, he believes, are essential preconditions for the emancipation of Muslim women and do not preclude the retention of culture and national characteristics.[31] Furthermore, says Lakhdar, Muslim women, like the national and religious minorities "who are denied full citizen's rights by theocracy," could conceivably be the most powerful advocates of secular government as they have the most to gain.[32]

> A great number of Muslim women have internalized the Islamic jurisprudence, which was written by men and for men. This is what one French sociologist called "symbolic violence," meaning that the victim—in this case the Muslim woman—accepts the view of her executioner.[33]

SALMAN MASALHA (ISRAEL)

Islam is in my view a prescription for going back in time, to the pre-Islamic period of benightedness. The solution is to build a liberal and democratic society that places the individual in the center, and more than anything the woman at the heart of this center.

. . . The Islamic motto of "Islam is the solution" must be replaced by "the woman is the solution." Women must be educated, encouraged, and enlightened. In a home with an educated and productive wife, the children will grow up to be educated and productive. A large part of the backwardness and tragedy of the Arab world lies in its abhorrent treatment of women.[34]

Poet Salman Masalha, a Druze citizen of Israel, was born in 1953 in Al-Maghar, a Druze Arab town in the Galilee, northern Israel. He spent time in an Israeli military jail in the mid-1970s for refusing to join the Israeli army on the grounds of conscientious objection.

Masalha has a PhD in classical Arabic literature from the Hebrew University, Jerusalem, where he taught Arabic language and literature and was the coeditor of the concordance of early Arabic poetry.[35] He is also a member of the editorial board of *Masharef*, an Arabic quarterly journal.[36] His published work includes many volumes of poetry in Arabic and Hebrew, and a large number of his poems have been translated into English, French, and other languages. Apart from questions of identity, his poems deal with universal issues.

Salman Masalha is adamant about the Arab world's imperative need to confront its backwardness, due in large part, he claims, to the oppression of women by the nomadic Arab culture, which is characterized by a perverse sense of male honor. In this mind-set, a man's honor does not depend primarily on himself but on the behavior of the females in his family, who must be controlled and punished for transgressions.

The situation of the individual in Arab countries is like the situation of the individual in the deeply-rooted nomadic tribal Arab mentality. . . . Everything concerning the individual honor of the Arab is nonexistent. For this reason, the Arab man goes far outside himself in search of his repressed selfhood—[he turns] to the weakest link in his environment, namely, the woman—his wife, sister, daughter, etc.[37]

Masalha believes the Arab male's need to control women's bodies is simply an effort to secure his "honor," which he lacks "socially and politically."

The developed world, Masalha believes, owes much of its progress to the emancipation and high value given to women in Western society. Masalha believes that prolonged oppression of women deprived Arab society of the potential contribution of half of its members:

> The deeply-rooted male tribal mentality that later cloaked itself in religious Islamic ideology is the very heart of the problem. After this outlook (stated in Koran 4:34)—that "men have authority over women"—took root . . . what then remained for the repressed half of Arab society [i.e., women] to do for the benefit of this society?[38]

In order for the Arabs to advance, says Masalha, urgent changes need to take place. Separation of religion and state is of primary importance. Illiteracy, rated at 50 percent in the Arab world and actually much higher, according to Masalha, must be corrected. However, the most important mission for Arab society, he believes, is the liberation of women and the acknowledgment that men's self-respect and self-worth are dependent on their own conduct and not the behavior of female family members. Instead of subjugating women, their needs must be given immediate priority, with rights to education, political enfranchisement, and control over their own fertility.

> The Arab feminist movements must take the initiative and demand legislation to mandate family planning—so that the woman will no longer be seen as a baby factory.[39]

RAID QUSTI (SAUDI ARABIA)

> *From the first second you set foot in King Abd Al-Aziz International Airport in Jeddah or King Khaled International Airport in Riyadh you see only men. I would not blame a first-time visitor for thinking that creatures from outer space had zapped all the women. But sadly, the fact is that women have no public presence whatsoever in Saudi Arabia. They exist only behind closed doors.*[40]

Raid Qusti is a columnist for the English-language Saudi daily *Arab News*. Throughout his career, he has made a point of highlighting the imbalance in power between men and women in the Saudi state. His columns have been critical of many aspects of society that discriminate against women, such as the vagueness of Saudi law in relation to social conduct and the Mutaween, or religious police, who impose their own version of puritanical laws on the population.[41]

Qusti is committed to the reforming of women's position in society. The sexual segregation of Saudi society, he writes, "almost amounts to a phobia when men and women are together,"[42] and this is one reason why he finds the idea of foreign tourism to Saudi Arabia laughable, reflecting "our intolerance and rigidity."[43]

> Families going to recreation centers will be shocked to find that there is a day for men and one for women. In other words, families will be split, with the sons going with the father on one day and the daughters with their mother on another.[44]

On the issue of women driving, Qusti is fully in favor of it, but laments the difficulties in store once driving becomes legal. Many Saudis believe that

> if women were allowed to drive, soon some would . . . discard the Hijab and Abaya as well. . . . In 1991 a group of Saudi women protested against the law banning them from driving and took to the streets in their cars and threw away their Abayas and Hijabs . . . if women were allowed to drive it would merely encourage them to leave the house unsupervised for no good reason.
>
> There are in my opinion two main obstacles that hinder women from driving here . . . the mentality of men, many of whom continue to see women as lesser creatures in terms of intelligence and capability [and] the fact that the uncovering of a woman's face in public is not only a social taboo but is believed . . . to be a sin.[45]

Changing the law cannot change a culture that is not suited to the idea of women driving. The need for female traffic police would have to be overcome, and the practical problems regarding photo licenses and uncovered faces would discourage many women.[46] The only solution, Qusti argues, would be to change the structure of power that views women as inferior and to distinguish carefully between traditions and religious law. However, these societal reforms could take years.[47]

Qusti notes that Saudi segregation is not supported by the Prophet's hadith. Women in early Islamic history traded in markets, healed the wounded, publicly mixed and debated with men, and fought in battle.[48] Segregation of the sexes in modern-day Saudi society, he says, "is utterly misplaced and wrong in the 21st century."[49]

He makes a point of applauding positive steps undertaken toward the public visibility of women. For example, he devoted an entire article to the appointment of Buthayna Nasser as the first female newsreader for the newly launched Al-Ikhbariya news channel in 2004.[50]

He also draws attention to the way segregation affects women's quality of life and livelihood in the Saudi state. For instance, women doctors attending a medical symposium in 2006 were asked to leave, even though hospitals are mixed places.[51] Another example was the treatment of "Yara," a woman, and her male colleague who were arrested and imprisoned for the crime of having coffee together. Yara was accused of *khulwa* (seclusion with an unrelated man).[52]

Qusti has also written about how the laws controlling women can affect men, for example, in the case of a Nigerian convert who was accused of being alone with an unrelated woman and imprisoned after helping his elderly female neighbor get to the hospital.[53]

In Qusti's view, "women have no public presence whatsoever in Saudi Arabia."[54] They are literally faceless in the domestic space too. Some Saudi men and women have never even seen their own mother's face, or the faces of other female family members.[55]

Al-Kharj native Muhammad Abdullah has never seen his wife's face. "We've been married for ten years and I've never seen it, not once," he said. The *burqa* "is stuck to her face 24 hours a day":

One day I tried to remove the Burqa while she was asleep. She was furious. She left and went to her parents' house and returned only after I had signed an undertaking that I would never attempt to do such a thing again.

Saud Al-Otaibi also found his wife fiercely loyal to the custom. "I tried to blackmail my wife by saying I'd marry another woman if she didn't show me her face, he said. But he was in for a surprise. "Instead of giving in she said, all right, marry someone else. And she set me up with a friend of hers who wasn't so strict in her adherence to the custom, and I married her."[56]

Qusti has called his country "a handicapped society . . . which [relies] on only half the country's human resources—the male half."[57] In answer to critics who rebuke him as "un-Saudi," he declares that he is a good patriot: "A person who truly loves his country does not pretend that it is a society of angels and free of all problems."[58]

His articles also take care to praise the authorities and NGOs when they take positive steps, such as producing the first human rights report in Saudi Arabia, published by the nongovernmental National Society for Human Rights (NSHR) in 2007. The report reviewed discrimination against Saudi women, among many human rights violations.[59]

"[Bride and Groom] of Compatible Age."
Source: *Al-Riyadh* (Saudi Arabia), April 19, 2007.

TRANSNATIONAL ORGANIZATIONS THAT SUPPORT MUSLIM WOMEN'S RIGHTS

WOMEN LIVING UNDER MUSLIM LAWS (WLUML)

Of continuing concern is how some otherwise more progressive forces, the mass media, donors, etc. have accepted the appropriation of human rights discourse, the language of democracy, and arguments of "cultural specificity" by fundamentalists who claim to be "moderates."[1]

In 2002, Women Living under Muslim Laws convened a major international meeting on the "Warning Signs of Fundamentalisms." Following this meeting, a collaborative Web resource was built by WLUML, the Association for Women's Rights in Development (AWID), and Rights and Democracy in order to pool and store information, increase awareness of dangers, and develop strategies for response in vulnerable countries and communities.[2]

Special attention was paid to the mechanisms used by various fundamentalist movements to gain adherents and maximize their sphere of influence and control. The methods identified included provision of education and welfare, especially if these services were not made available by the state, and effective use of inexpensive communication technology like audiocassettes and the Internet to preach Islamist, anti-Western hatred and incitement to violence and murder. Attention was also focused on the hoards amassed by these movements through arms and drug smuggling and also their special efforts to recruit Muslim women to the Islamist cause.

Another observation has been the utilization of human rights and women's rights concepts and terminology by Islamist groups to advance their cause with Western human rights organizations and well-intentioned liberals.

The Global Campaign to Stop Stoning and Killing Women was launched by WLUML in 2007 in response to the continuing practice of stoning in countries like Pakistan, Indonesia, Iran, and Nigeria. WLUML unequivocally condemned this form of punishment, which it views as a distortion of religion and a justification for the abuse of women:

> Women constitute nearly all those condemned to death by stoning. Why? Because discriminatory laws and customs almost always assign more guilt to women than to men in any manner of action that is seen as violating "norms" of sexual behaviour, especially any instance of alleged sexual relations outside marriage (zina). Men are entitled to marry more than one woman and can use this justification for sex outside marriage. They are also more mobile and can more easily escape punishment.[3]

WLUML (see its Web site at www.wluml.org) is an international solidarity group that provides support and information for women living under Muslim laws. It operates in over seventy countries, wherever women's lives are dictated by Islamic laws or customs, and aims to support women in gaining more control over their lives. The organization was formed in 1984 by nine women from Algeria, Morocco, Sudan, Iran, Mauritius, Tanzania, Bangladesh, and Pakistan, in response to several high-profile cases of abused women in Muslim countries.

According to WLUML, Islamic authorities perpetuate the myth of one homogenous Muslim rule of law and way of life. On the other hand:

> WLUML focuses on laws and customs and the concrete realities of women's lives. This includes the often diverse practices and laws classified as "Muslim" (resulting from different interpretations of religious texts and/or the political use of religion) and the effects these have on women, rather than on the religion of Islam itself.[4]

Apart from its support of Muslim women living in countries where Islam is the state religion, WLUML also extends its support to secular Muslim women, those living in non-Muslim countries, and non-Muslim women and children subject to Muslim laws.

The aim of the organization is to empower seemingly helpless and marginalized women by ending their isolation, mobilizing active support, and promoting dialogue and tolerance:

WLUML actively endorses plurality and autonomy, and consciously reflects, recognizes and values a diversity of opinions. Individuals and groups linked through the network define their own particular priorities and strategies according to their context.[5]

The primary concerns are, however, the effects of Islamic fundamentalism, militarization, and widespread violence on women's lives.

There is no formal membership of WLUML; it is rather a network of people sharing resources and coordinating actions like petitions and letter writing. Recognizing that women's rights are universal, the organization reaches out internationally to other feminist and progressive groups, exchanging resource materials and publishing informative and analytical articles in English, French, and Arabic. WLUML publishes regular news updates and provides legal advice and assistance for asylum applications. Of most importance are the international alerts and campaigns initiated and circulated by the organization.

Alerts and campaigns for action have included the following:

The case of Mokarrameh Ebrahimi, who spent ten years in an Iranian prison awaiting execution by stoning for adultery. A campaign by WLUML with international collaboration resulted in her release in March 2008, together with her son Ibrahimi, aged four and born in custody.

Nineteen-year-old Saudi Arabian gang-rape victim, "the Qatif girl," was sentenced to 200 lashes for being alone with an unrelated man. She was granted a pardon by the king of Saudi Arabia, as a result of pressure from organizations coordinated by WLUML.

When the reformist Iranian feminist magazine *Zanan* was shut down by government authorities in February 2008, WLUML campaigned against the action with an online petition.

In February 2008, an appeal went out to activists and other concerned people to phone and fax Iranian officials in order to stop the regime from carrying out the death sentence by stoning of Zohreh and Azar Kabiri.

The many publications of WLUML include an occasional journal in the dossier series, occasional papers, and the quarterly newssheet, which projects the voices of activists and various articles on women's issues.

In addition to the collective energy generated by linking through WLUML, networkers see a deep value in knowing through WLUML that others elsewhere share one's values and may be experiencing similar difficulties, and that prompt support in situations of both personal and national political crisis is available.[6]

Assisting Women's Participation in the Economy: Haifa Al Kaylani and AIWF

> *Arab women can play a greater role building bridges of understanding to connect with other cultures. They need to network within the region and beyond to the international community and both contribute to and benefit from that cross-cultural enrichment.*[7]

Haifa Al Kaylani is driven by a personal mission to break down stereotypes of Arab women and assist them in business, the world she knows best. She believes women are the key to peace and prosperity and no real progress is possible without their contribution:

> There is no development in any society without women playing their rightful role. This is very important for the future development of the region as optimizing and fully utilizing all the human resources and is an essential factor in this growth.[8]

She takes these concepts further, adding:

> when women prosper, families and communities prosper. Educational attainment is the key to empowerment, and women can be the engines of change and development.
>
>   . . . We live in a world without borders, and the Arab world is at the heart of the globalized economy. Arabs are expected to work hard and strive to negotiate with partners across borders to establish their role in the global village.
>
>   For women to take part in this transformation, they need to master business and information technology to speak to the world.[9]

Women could also play a vital role in fostering much-needed cultural ties between Arab and international communities.

Al-Kaylani likes to remind her audiences that UN Resolution 1325, which says that women should be "involved in peace processes and participate in peace negotiations next to men. Women should no longer be viewed as victims but as promoters of peace instead":

> Women so empowered can take an active role in ending hostilities, first and foremost by raising the next generation. If educated and enlightened they will be able to teach their children the importance of dialogue, opening channels to present their positions—but not in a combative manner.[10]

Haifa Al-Kaylani was born in Palestine and raised in Lebanon. A highly educated woman, fluent in five languages, she attended the American University of Beirut and Oxford University and received a master's in economics before working as a junior economist for the United Nations. She is married to a diplomat, Wajih Al-Kaylani, with whom she has one son, Sirri, a lawyer. The family moved to London in 1976.

Heavily involved in public life, Al-Kaylani sits on the board of many charities, cultural institutions, and NGOs. She is international vice president of the Women's Leadership Board at Harvard University; an advisory board member of the Suzanne Mubarak Women's International Peace Movement; a member of the advisory board of the Middle East Institute, School of Oriental and African Studies, University of London; a member of the advisory board of Tanaka Business School, Imperial College, London; and a member of the board of trustees of the British Edutrust Foundation.[11]

These roles have given her wide experience and influence in government and international circles, which she has put to use in developing projects to assist Arab and other Muslim women. Of particular concern is the future of Muslim women and children in Europe. Improving access to education and jobs may be the key to integration, she believes. In her speech at a Conference titled "Muslims and the West: Living Together—But How?" Al-Kaylani stressed that

> Improving education and job opportunities for immigrant Muslim women will better the chances for their children and increase the prosperity for their families and local communities, and foster their closer integration within the wider community.
>
> There are Muslims in Europe who see their identity as resting on the concept of Umma, but there is also a growing group of young Muslims

born in Europe who wholeheartedly identify themselves in their values, behavior, and appearance as Europeans.[12]

Al-Kaylani's major achievement has been the foundation and leadership of the London-based Arab International Women's Forum (AIWF; www.aiwfonline.co.uk),[13] which she established in 2001 as a voice for Arab women in business, the civil service, and public life; it was the first nonprofit, nongovernmental, nonpolitical, and nonreligious organization of its kind. Bolstered by her determination and the slogan "Building Bridges, Building Business," the high-profile organization evolved rapidly.

Eventually, AIWF encompassed a network of about 1,500 associations, corporations, and individuals in forty-five countries, aimed at promoting Arab businesswomen and community leaders in the world of international markets and politics.[14] Women who use the services of AIWF also benefit from role models and mentoring, and they are given opportunities to attend workshops on entrepreneurship, management, decision making, and working with major international corporations.

Following "Women as Engines of Economic Growth in the Arab World," a program initiated by the forum in 2005, AIWF produced a report focused on the need for governments and business corporations to end all forms of discrimination and improve access to education, vocational training, and information technology. The forum's board of trustees includes successful Arab women, whose areas of expertise range from public service to large business corporations.

> We are there to effect positive growth and development, and with it peace and prosperity by focusing on women's roles in the Arab world and the international community.[15]

Awards

2006 Haifa Al-Kaylani was named as one of twenty-one Leaders for the Twenty-first Century by *Women's eNews* in New York.

2007 She was named as one of the Muslim Power 100 Leaders in the United Kingdom and received the Education Excellence Award.

2008 She was the recipient of the World of Difference Lifetime Achievement Award presented by the International Alliance of Women.

AGAINST HONOR KILLINGS

International Campaign against Honor Killings (ICAHK)

> *It is unbelievable, but it is a dark reality; tens of thousands of women are killed in the name of the most barbaric and backward phenomenon—so-called honor which has been practiced in tough male dominated traditions, religious, nationalist and patriarchal communities, in their home land and diasporas, in peace or during war.*[16]

Rand Abdel-Qader, aged seventeen, was a student of English at Basra University when she met Paul, a British soldier. In 2008 they had a few brief, innocent conversations, but when Rand's father found out, he accused her of bringing shame on his honor. Enraged, he suffocated his daughter in order to restore the family honor. In spite of freely admitting to the murder, he received no punishment.[17]

Even very young girls are not immune. In the case of a four-year-old Palestinian girl who was raped by a man in his midtwenties, the child was left by her family to bleed to death because they believed her misfortune would sully their honor.[18]

> Some Palestinian women, facing a loss of honor and certain death, have been offered a chance "to die with dignity" by strapping on explosives and killing Israelis.[19]

The International Campaign against Honor Killings (ICAHK) has brought attention to individual cases and to the large number of victims throughout the world:

> According to the United Nations reports, every year, 5000 women are murdered under the pretext of honor killing worldwide. This is just the tip of the iceberg and reality is far darker. The victims of "honor killings" are far more [numerous] than the innocent victims of international terrorism.[20]

Many believe the figure of 5,000 to be a gross underestimate, as it does not include women in remote rural areas whose births and deaths are never recorded and those who are pressured by their families to commit suicide.

The provocation could be talking to a male who is not a relative, or even networking on the Facebook Web site, as in the case of a young Saudi Arabian woman.[21] Victims of rape are particularly vulnerable to the serious charge of *zina* (extramarital sex) and consequent accusations of destroying the family honor.

> Often the murder is planned by the family who come together to decide her fate and select her executioner. In European countries this is often a younger brother, to take advantage of more lenient sentencing for juveniles. In many other countries, murderers receive token punishment or none at all; in some they are even applauded. The lack of appropriate punishment is justified by questionable interpretations of Islam, or by remnants of colonial French and British law which allow for reduced sentencing for crimes of passion, even though honor crimes are far older than either the religion or the law.[22]

These summary executions, common in the Middle East, are also on the rise in immigrant communities in Europe and the rest of the West.

Although "honor killings" are not confined to Islamic communities, there is a preponderance of them in those Muslim communities where a man's honor is bound to the women he "owns," and the practice is tied to the Islam of the Middle Ages:

> Al-Ghazali is a theologian who died back in 1111 but is still a very lively and actual authority today. . . . Since then the woman [has been] regarded as an instrument for the unlimited usage of man in order to secure his individual power and pleasure as well as the biological survival and expansion of Allah's collective community.
>
> When a Muslim male beats, rapes or even kills a woman, we are faced with a deeply rooted behaviour pattern. . . . It is called "honor" because it is supposed to secure male power and prevent the society from falling into "Fitna," . . . namely, disturbance or even upheaval in the community. In other words, keeping women under control saves the "peace of Islam."[23]

STOP! Honor Killings is a Web site dedicated to mourning yesterday's victims and preventing new cases. It includes a database of stories about victims and testaments from those who have suffered attempts on their lives. The Web site also offers a confidential advisory service that can be accessed immediately by women at risk.

The International Campaign against Honor Killings (ICAHK), which was launched from the STOP! Honor Killings Web site, is committed to eradicating honor crimes. Its board members include Nadia Mahmoud, cofounder of the Organization for Women's Freedom in Iraq and cocoordinator of the Middle East Center for Women's Rights (MECWR); Azam Kamguian, founder of the Committee to Defend Women's Rights in the Middle East; and Houzan Mahmoud, head of the Iraq Freedom Congress—Abroad.

These activists believe that women's rights must be considered universal, with no defense of killers using the pretext of cultural practice. "Honor killings" should therefore be recognized as punishable acts of murder and any laws that defend the murderers or mitigate the crimes must be repealed. In addition, every effort should be made to reeducate societies and assist potential victims to seek asylum.

According to ICAHK, the success of the campaign depends on a persistent struggle against misogynist ideas in education and the media. However, the positions of ICAHK and similar NGOs, in particular, the Committee on the Elimination of Discrimination against Women (CEDAW), are closely identified with international human rights law. This stance presents an obstacle for women's rights as the universalism versus relativism debate is still not resolved.

For Houzan Mahmoud the position is clear: "I condemn these brutalities against women and have dedicated my life to fight for their liberation. I feel a great bitterness that many of those young women who wanted to rebel and protest against tribal, religious and patriarchal barriers are now dead."[24]

LAHA (For Her)

> *I'm doing an MA on feminism. . . . In the conservative place where I live I've seen enough that made me a hard-core feminist. . . . Activism is my whole life and the only thing that reminds me I'm still useful.*[25]

These words were written by Ahmad Ghashmary, founder of LAHA.[26] LAHA, "For Her," is also an acronym for Living Ahead Her Ambition. A Middle Eastern women's rights initiative, it was created by a young Jordanian male feminist, Ahmad Ghashmary, so concerned about the oppression of women in his society that he was driven to initiate change. Founder members of LAHA come from Jordan, Syria, and Egypt.

Ghashmary took up the issue of gender equality when he heard about his neighbor, a young woman whose father prevented her from attending university. His "Women in a Maze" essay on "honor killings" won a prize in the Hands across the Mideast Support Alliance (HAMSA) contest, launching Ghashmary into the activism circuit, and he capitalized on this success by creating the LAHA blog. Written mainly in Arabic, his articles are ardent protests against repression in his society.

Ghashmary is especially passionate about wiping out "honor crimes," and he calls for changes in legislation: "The problem is not simply social attitudes in some families. Courts in countries like Jordan and Syria routinely give light punishments to men who kill their female relatives. Murderers are often given only brief jail terms because judges claim to understand the motivation behind the killing." However, he believes "people in Arab societies are beginning to be more aware of the danger and barbarity of these rituals."[27]

In another essay, Ghashmary refers to Shakespeare's insights into the tragedy and foolishness of "honor killing" when Othello expresses remorse after killing his wife, Desdemona:

> Othello: then must you speak of one that loved not wisely, of one not easily jealous, but being wrought, perplexed in the extreme; of one whose hand like the base Indian threw a pearl away richer than all his tribe.[28]

Ghashmary ponders about the many misguided "Othellos" in the Middle East:

> The last Othello I heard about [was] from Syria, and what a hair-raising story that was! This person had unjustified suspicions that his wife was cheating on him and one night he heard noises coming from the roof of his house in a late hour; brave Othello [took] his gun and went up to find out who was there. He didn't find [anyone], but his sick mind told him that [it] was his wife's lover trying to get in. . . . He shot HIS WIFE . . . and she died. . . . It was found out later that the noises were [those] of a CAT![29]

In the context of violence against women, LAHA also includes articles on female genital mutilation. In December 2007, Ghashmary included an article about an Islamic cleric in Egypt who filed a lawsuit against the minister of health for banning the practice, even though many religious authorities disagreed with him:

Sheikh Youssif al-Badri claimed the ministerial decree violated the Egyptian constitution as well as Islamic principles. He argued "the practice is necessary in curbing women's sexual inclinations."[30]

Ghashmary hopes the LAHA initiative will form a regional network for like-minded male and female activists who want to see grassroots reform. And he is convinced of the urgency:

We cannot lose half of our society.[31]

The future is in our hands. We need to act now.[32]

Gay and Lesbian Rights: Al Fatiha and the Safra Project

Nine countries have laws in place that prescribe the death penalty for same-sex activities: Afghanistan, Arab Emirates, Chechnya, Iran, Mauritania, Pakistan, Saudi Arabia, Sudan, and Yemen.[33]

Many Muslim gay men and lesbians [struggle] to reconcile their sexual orientation with their religion and culture. They often feel that they are forced to make a difficult or impossible choice: either to abandon Islam or to [suppress] their sexual orientation. For most people, particularly those living in Muslim countries, there usually is no choice but the latter. Those who are forced to flee often continue to struggle with this question.[34]

In many authoritarian Muslim countries, harsh sodomy laws are enforced and same-sex acts are punishable by fines, prison sentences, public whipping, or death. Even in the West, where Muslims live in a liberal or secular culture, LGBTIQQ (lesbian, gay, bisexual, transgender, intersex, "queer," and questioning sexual orientation) Muslims are treated as outcasts. In particular, the conservative, homophobic outlook in many Muslim societies has created a hostile environment for homosexuals, who invariably encounter rejection by their families and friends.

The Al Fatiha[35] organization based in Washington was established by Faisal Alam as a place for LGBTIQQ Muslims to find a supportive network in the face of the discrimination, repression, and isolation they invariably face within mainstream Muslim communities. In 1997, Alam began by reaching out across the United States through an Internet chat room and the next year, a group of forty convened for a conference, which culminated in the creation of Al Fatiha ("The Opening"; "Sura Al-Fatiha" is the first chapter of the Koran). Incorporated in 1999, the organization provides a safe environment for those looking for support among likeminded Muslims and a religious life, reconciled within Islam. Al Fatiha, with chapters across the United States, Canada, Britain and growing, has become a powerful advocate for the rights of LGBTIQQ Muslims.

The organization offers an active forum for debate and acceptance but the battle is still in its infancy. An early and important initiative was the organization of regional and international meetings and conferences, where many LGBTIQ Muslims had their first opportunity to meet with others who shared the same difficulties. As well as regional conferences in the United States, annual international conferences have been held since 2000, including seminars and workshops spanning personal, cultural, human rights, and media issues.

Most LBTQQ Muslim women in the West are expected to be under the supervision of their father, brother, uncle, or husband throughout their whole lives and any public knowledge of a sexual transgression like lesbianism would invite harsh penalties.

Like most Muslim women, they are forced to marry young; their husbands can divorce them easily, throw them out, take another wife, and gain custody of the children. Those who don't marry are still trapped, as they are not permitted to live alone, a status that brings "dishonor" to the family. Due to the high incidence of domestic violence, they are reluctant to provoke attacks by "coming out," and there is virtually no Muslim community support or information about legal rights.[36]

The mental health system cannot deal adequately with their psychological problems as counselors lack resources on Islam and homosexuality and refrain from discussing sexuality due to concerns about cultural insensitivity. Many LBTQQ Muslim women believe their sexual orientation is sinful according to Islam, and their inability to reconcile their religious beliefs with sexual identity often results in psychological crises and depression.[37]

Add to this mix a culture that is culturally at odds with the more risqué mainstream homosexual community, and these women have nowhere to turn:

I didn't understand who or what I was. There was no support out there for me and it was frightening to think that there was nowhere to go.[38]

The Safra Project (www.safraproject.org) brings together religious and secular LGBTIQQ Muslim women of all ages and backgrounds in the UK, where there are an estimated 140,000 South Asian Muslim LBT and gay people.[39] *Safra* means "journey" or "discovery" in Arabic, Farsi, and Urdu. The organization was started in October 2001 by women faced with a combination of prejudices in relation to gender identity, religion, race, and culture and with no accessible or appropriate social and legal services to assist them.

A preliminary investigation conducted in 2001–2003, using data from some eighty LGBTIQQ women and fifteen service providers, produced a report on its initial findings in 2002.[40] The report identified the need for support groups and workshops not compromised by fears of cultural insensitivity and for more hostels and safe houses for victims of domestic violence and those forced to leave the family home.

In 2003, the Safra Web site was launched to further build and organize a support community, publicize research findings, and share her-stories.

In the words of Tamsila Tawqir, Safra Project coordinator, "My focus on 'diversity as strength' comes from the Safra Project's view that we need to understand and accept, not just tolerate, the multiple identities of people and the diversity in religion. . . . That is the challenge for all of us."[41]

Often consulted by government policy makers, the organization assists in the drafting of antidiscrimination, domestic violence, and partnership rights legislation, and has partnered with organizations like the Birmingham Council, the Refugee Council, and Student Action for Refugees. In addition, it runs workshops and holds conferences that provide opportunities for LGB-TIQQ Muslim women and also others to improve their knowledge and develop solidarity and support. Some policies formulated by the organization have been implemented in the Middle East, as in the case of ASWAT, the Palestinian-based women's association.

Although not a faith group, Safra has addressed relevant Islamic feminist issues in articles posted on its Web site. Leaving the issue of gender preference aside, the articles point to the many progressive Muslim reformists who claim that the Koran affirms gender equality. In contrast, shari'ah law, they maintain, was formulated by men on the basis of the hadith (the compilation of sayings and practices of the Prophet Muhammad), in order to advance the patriarchal prejudices and practices of a bygone era that have little relevance to the modern world. They emphasize that the hadith was originally open to interpretation (*ijtihad*) but this option was closed between the tenth and fourteenth centuries, largely preventing future challenges.

With respect to homosexuality, shari'ah law allows sex only within a heterosexual marriage, thereby excluding same-sex relationships. Most traditional Muslim scholars refer to Koranic verses like the story of Lut (similar to Lot in the Bible) for the view that homosexuality is a sin, but the Koran does not specify punishments, so they apply shari'ah penalties similar to those pertaining to heterosexual acts like adultery.[42]

ARAB HUMAN DEVELOPMENT REPORT

The Plight of
Arab Women
for Equality

The *Arab Human Development Report 2005 (AHDR): Towards the Rise of Women in the Arab World* was the fourth in a series prepared by the United Nations Development Programme (UNDP).

The president of the Arab Gulf Program for United Nations Development Organizations, Prince Talal Bin Abdul Aziz of Saudi Arabia, stated:

> Religion has no connection with any of the mistaken practices that are carried out against women. Our societies, however, give precedence to custom over true worship and provide foundations for assumptions that have no grounding either in the Holy Qur'an or in the authenticated practices and sayings of the Prophet (the Hadith). Most of the sufferings of Arab women are attributable to the accumulation of such customs and traditions.[1]

There have been attempts at reform, with movements such as Egypt's Kefaya! (Enough!), the Syrian Damascus Declaration, Irhalu! (Get Out!) in Yemen, and Khalas! (It's Over!) in Libya.

> While Arab governments announced a spate of reforms . . . violations continued to increase.[2]

OBSTACLES TO THE ADVANCEMENT OF WOMEN

Health

Arab women must face the risks associated with high morbidity and high mortality rates, particularly in non–oil producing countries. Qatar has a mortality rate of 7 per 100,000 births, whereas poor Arab countries face a mortality rate of 1,000 per 100,000 births.[3] The average fertility rate is also higher than in the rest of the developing world: 3.8 live births in the Arab countries compared to 2.9 in the rest of the developing world.[4] If this birth rate continues, the populations of Arab countries will double every twenty years, and this will add to problems related to social services and infrastructure.

Education

In general, female access to education is less than that of males. However, Lebanon, the Palestinian territories, Tunisia, and some oil-producing countries have a higher rate of enrollment by women than men. Another problem is discrimination against women when setting entrance criteria for professional schools. For example, in Kuwait a female candidate for engineering and petroleum studies must achieve a grade point average of 83.5, whereas a male needs only 67.9.[5]

At the beginning of the twenty-first century there were sixty million illiterate adults in the Arab world, that is, 40 percent, most of whom are impoverished and rural women. This rate is higher than both the global average and that of developing countries.[6]

Economic Activity

The low rate of participation by women in the economic activities of Arab countries is associated with limited economic growth, high unemployment, and the traditional perception of men as the breadwinners. As a result, women are the last to be recruited and the first to be fired.[7]

Political Life

Despite the fact that women have the right to vote in the vast majority of Arab countries, the Arab region is at the bottom of the list in terms of the number of women in parliament.[8] Females in cabinet positions have been rare. Egypt appointed its first female minister in 1956, Iraq in 1959, and Algeria in 1962, but the positions have generally been second tier. Also, women's positions in political parties have been mostly symbolic.[9]

Poverty

Although according to the UNDP report there is no "feminization of poverty," indices show that conditions are less favorable for women.[10]

In rural areas, there is a practice of sending girls to serve "in a form of neo-slavery" in urban homes.[11] These girls are commonly illiterate and do not earn enough to better their conditions through savings and education. Their situation is similar to that of women migrant workers, who in Qatar, Oman, and Kuwait make up more than 70 percent of the female labor force.

> The harsh and degrading treatment meted out to foreign female domestic workers is a mark of shame on the brow of societies that ignore it.[12]

Culture

Although Islam introduced the concept of the Islamic community or umma, to replace identification with tribes, the Arabs maintained their rigid, patriarchal structures, which acted to progressively exclude women from positions of authority and influence.[13]

> Men have always been given priority and preference in jurisprudential studies relating to women. This is a predisposition that entrenched itself as a result of reading the Qur'an with a bias in men's favor.[14]

> Hundreds of popular proverbs imply that women should be segregated. They project an attitude akin to that which led to the burying of girls alive. In order to justify their retrograde spirit, these proverbs use moral and other arguments expressed in the language of tales and myths.[15]

Relations within the family have continued to be governed by the father's authority over his children and the husband's over his wife, under the sway of the patriarchal order.[16]

The battle for the liberation of women in Arab thought and everyday life needs to be redoubled. In varying degrees, hostility towards women remains a scarring feature of ideas, attitudes and feelings among individuals and communities in most Arab countries.[17]

A Strategic Vision

The UNDP report notes:

an Arab renaissance cannot be accomplished without the rise of women in Arab countries. . . . Directly and indirectly, it concerns the well-being of the entire Arab world.[18]

Arab States should review the reservations that they have registered with regard to CEDAW [see the Convention on the Elimination of All Forms of Discrimination against Women, below] in order to:

- Remove all reservations against Article 2 of the Convention, which prescribes the principle of equality . . .
- Remove reservations that use the pretext that the provision in the Convention is contrary to national law.[19]

A system of quotas for women should be instituted in the legislative and representative assemblies.[20]

A review of criminal legislation and criminal procedures should be undertaken to eliminate all legal texts that contain discrimination against women. This should cover texts that discriminate in punishment for the crime of adultery; those that discriminate in reducing the punishment for crimes of honor committed by a husband rather than a wife; and those that absolve the perpetrator of a crime of rape from punishment if he marries the victim of the rape.[21]

Arab legislators must act to adopt the most enlightened efforts in shari'a and other religious laws for achieving conformity with the principle of equal treatment for men and women, one that accords with the overall intentions of Islamic and non-Muslim religious law.[22]

In conclusion, however, the report concedes that what it has offered is "no more than intellectual grist for forces of renewal in the Arab countries."[23]

Convention on the Elimination of All Forms of Discrimination against Women (CEDAW)

Adopted by the United Nations General Assembly on December 18, 1979.

Article 2

States Parties condemn discrimination against women in all its forms, agree to pursue by all appropriate means and without delay a policy of eliminating discrimination against women and, to this end, undertake:

(a) To embody the principle of the equality of men and women in their national constitutions or other appropriate legislation if not yet incorporated therein and to ensure, through law and other appropriate means, the practical realization of this principle;

(b) To adopt appropriate legislative and other measures, including sanctions where appropriate, prohibiting all discrimination against women;

(c) To establish legal protection of the rights of women on an equal basis with men and to ensure through competent national tribunals and other public institutions the effective protection of women against any act of discrimination;

(d) To refrain from engaging in any act or practice of discrimination against women and to ensure that public authorities and institutions shall act in conformity with this obligation;

(e) To take all appropriate measures to eliminate discrimination against women by any person, organization or enterprise;

(f) To take all appropriate measures, including legislation, to modify or abolish existing laws, regulations, customs and practices which constitute discrimination against women;

(g) To repeal all national penal provisions which constitute discrimination against women.

The full text of CEDAW can be found at http://www.un.org/womenwatch/daw/cedaw/cedaw.htm.

NOTES

INTRODUCTION

1. Jill Carroll, "Inside Islam, a Women's Roar," *Christian Science Monitor*, March 5, 2008, http://www.csmonitor.com/2008/0305/p13s03-lign.html (accessed August 24, 2008).

2. For example, Islamists have declared their aim to occupy the White House, as cited in Islamist forum Al-Hesbah, November 7, 2008, Middle East Media Research Institute (Memri) Dispatch Series, no. 2106, http://www.memri.org/bin/latestnews.cgi?ID=SD210608 (accessed March 3, 2009).

3. Rafia Zakaria, "Veil and a Warning," *Frontline* 23, no. 2, January 28–February 10, 2006.

4. Bruce Bawer, "Norway's Very Own Ayaan Hirsi Ali," *Pajamas Media*, November 2, 2007, http://pajamasmedia.com/blog/meet_norways_answer_to_ayaan_h/ (accessed March 3, 2009).

5. "The Arab Media: How Governments Handle the News," *Economist*, February 7, 2008, http://www.economist.com/world/africa/displaystory.cfm?story_id=10666436 (accessed March 18, 2009).

CHAPTER 1: AFGHANISTAN

1. Appeal court judge, Kandahar, September 2004, Amnesty International interview, Afghanistan: "Women Still under Attack—A Systematic Failure to Protect," *Amnesty International 2005*, http://www.amnesty.org/en/library/info/ASA11/007/2005 (accessed February 4, 2009).

2. "The Rights of Women and Minorities in Islam and Muslim Societies," CSID's 8th Annual Conference, April 27, 2007, Washington, DC, p. 4.

3. *The Universal Declaration of Human Rights* (UDHR), December 10, 1948, http://www.un.org/Overview/rights.html (accessed March 17, 2009); *The International Covenant on Civil and Political Rights* (ICCPR), March 23, 1976, http://www1.umn.edu/humanrts/instree/b3ccpr.htm (accessed March 17, 2009); *The UN Convention against Torture* (CAT), December 9, 1975, http://www.hrweb.org/legal/cat.html (accessed March 17, 2009); *The UN Convention on the Elimination of All Forms*

of Discrimination against Women (CEDAW), 1979, http://www.un.org/womenwatch/daw/cedaw (accessed March 17, 2009); *The UN Convention on the Rights of the Child*, September 2, 1990, http://www.un.org/womenwatch/daw/beijing/platform (accessed March 17, 2009); *The Beijing Declaration and Platform for Action, Fourth World Conference on Women, 1995*, September 4–15, 1995, http://www.un.org/womenwatch/daw/beijing/platform (accessed March 17, 2009); *The Rome Statute of the International Criminal Court*, July 17, 1998, http://www.un.org/law/icc/index.html (accessed March 17, 2009).

4. Afghanistan: "Women Still under Attack."

5. "More Young Girls Face Rape in Afghanistan," March 6, 2009, *CNN*, http://www.cnn.com/2009/WORLD/asiapcf/03/06/afghan.women/index.html (accessed March 11, 2009).

6. Ibid.

7. Ibid.

8. Ibid.

9. United Nations World Food Programme (WFP), July 1, Afghanistan, http://beta.wfp.org/countries/afghanistan (accessed February 4, 2009).

10. Library of Parliament Research Publications, Parliament of Canada, January 10, 2008, http://www.parl.gc.ca/information/library/PRBpubs/prb0734-e.htm (accessed March 24, 2009).

11. Salima Ghafari, "Women's Voices Missing from Media," *IWPR*, March 28, 2006, http://www.womenandislam.net/afg/content/news_view.php?id=waitaf_afg.20060402005326 (accessed February 4, 2009).

12. Afghanistan: "Women Still under Attack."

13. Friederike Boge, Friedrich-Ebert-Stiftung, "Women and Politics in Afghanistan: How to Use the Chance of the 25% Quota for Women," Kabul, September 2005, http://library.fes.de/pdf-files/iez/02536.pdf (accessed February 4, 2009).

14. Ibid.

15. Zahid Hussain, "Taleban Threaten to Blow Up Girls' Schools If They Refuse to Close," *Times* (London), December 26, 2008.

16. Nicholas D. Kristof, "Terrorism That's Personal," *New York Times*, November 30, 2008.

17. "The Rights of Women and Minorities in Islam and Muslim Societies."

18. "President Karzai Congratulates Women on International Women's Day—Excerpts from President's Speech," press release from the office of the spokesman to the president, March 8, 2005, Amnesty International, May 30, 2005, http://www.amnesty.org/en/library/info/ASA11/007/2005 (accessed February 4, 2009).

19. Tom Coghlan in Kabul, Catherine Philp, and Suzy Jagger, "President Karzai's Taleban-Style Laws for Women Put Troop Surge at Risk," *Times* (London), April 3, 2009.

20. "Karzai Orders Urgent Law Review," *BBC News*, April 4, 2009, http://news.bbc.co.uk/2/hi/south_asia/7983081.stm (accessed April 4, 2009).

21. Deborah Copaken Kogan, excerpt from *0, The Oprah Magazine*, Afghanistan Women Council, March 2002, http://www.afghanistanwomencouncil .org/in_the_media.html (accessed February 4, 2009).

22. "Murder of a Heroic Woman, Great Threat to the Taliban," *Globe and Mail* (Toronto), September 30, 2008.

23. "Top Afghan Policewoman Shot Dead," *BBC News*, September 28, 2008.

24. "Suhaila Seddiqi," http://www.afghanet.com/biographies/bio.php ?subaction=showfull&id=1126371773 (accessed February 4, 2009).

25. "More Young Girls Face Rape in Afghanistan," March 6, 2009, *CNN*, http://www.cnn.com/2009/WORLD/asiapcf/03/06/afghan.women/index (accessed March 11, 2009).

26. Salima Ghafari, "Women's Voices Missing from Media," *IWPR*, March 28, 2006, http://www.womenandislam.net/afg/content/news_view.php?id=waitaf _afg.20060402005326 (accessed February 4, 2009).

27. Ron Synovitz, "Afghanistan: Author Awaits Happy Ending to 'Sewing Circles of Heart,'" *Payvand's Iran News*, April 4, 2004, http://www.payvand.com/ news/04/apr/1003.html (accessed February 4, 2009).

28. Abdul Waheed Wafa, Carlotta Gall, and Adam B. Ellick, "Empowering Women in Afghanistan," *New York Times*, October 2008, http://video.on.nytimes .com/?fr_story=961ff7a9192db5ee206fa770b6154d586f (accessed February 4, 2009).

29. "American Afghan," *Washington Post*, February 8, 2002, http://discuss .washingtonpost.com/zforum/02/news_sultan020802.htm (accessed February 4, 2009).

30. "Gunmen Kill Director of Women's Affairs for Southern Afghanistan," *International Herald Tribune*, September 25, 2006, http://www.iht.com/articles/ap/ 2006/09/25/asia/AS_GEN_Afghanistan.php (accessed February 4, 2009).

31. Robert Kluyver, "Safia Amajan Obituary," *Guardian* (UK), October 16, 2006, http://www.guardian.co.uk/news/2006/oct/16/guardianobituaries.afghanistan (accessed February 4, 2009).

32. "Afghan Women's Right Advocate Safia Amajan Assassinated in Kandahar," http://www.propagandapress.org/2006/09/26/afgahn-womens-right -advocate-safia-ama-jan-assassinated-in-kandahar (accessed February 4, 2009).

33. Ibid.

34. "Afghanistan: The Woman Who Defied the Taliban, and Paid with Her Life," September 26, 2006, http://www.wluml.org/english/newsfulltxt.shtml?cmd%5B157%5D=x-157-543692 (accessed February 4, 2009).

35. Paul Anderson, "Four Years from 9/11—The Ballot and the Bombs," *Sunday Herald* (Scotland), September 18, 2005.

36. Jon Hemming, interview, "Afghan Women Seek to Outlaw Domestic Violence," Reuters, December 13, 2006.

37. "Their Future at Stake as Afghanistan Votes," *Sydney Morning Herald*, October 6, 2004.

38. "International Editor of the Year," http://www.un.org/Pubs/chronicle/2005/issue3/0305p57.html# (accessed January 1, 2009).

39. Aunohita Mojumdar, "New Face of Afghan Politics," October 9, 2005, http://www.boloji.com/wfs4/wfs464.htm (accessed January 1, 2009).

40. "The Power of One: An Interview with Shukria Barakzai," *Worldpress*, March 16, 2005, http://www.worldpress.org/Asia/2047.cfm (accessed January 1, 2009).

41. Ibid.

42. Ibid.

43. "Journalism in Afghanistan," Media Report, ABC Radio National, June 22, 2006.

44. Library of Parliament Research Publications, Parliament of Canada, January 10, 2008, http://www.parl.gc.ca/information/library/PRBpubs/prb0734-e.htm (accessed March 24, 2009).

45. "International Editor of the Year," acceptance speech.

46. Tom Coghlan, "Women Defy Odds in Afghan Polls," *Telegraph* (UK), November 15, 2005.

47. "The Power of One: An Interview with Shukria Barakzai."

48. "Women and Power in Central Asia (Part 4): Roundtable on the Tajik, Afghan, and Iranian Experiences," Radio Free Europe, December 29, 2005.

49. Hemming, "Afghan Women Seek to Outlaw Domestic Violence."

50. "The Power of One: An Interview with Shukria Barakzai."

51. "Women under Siege in Afghanistan," *BBC News*, Kabul, June 20, 2007.

52. Jill Carroll, "Inside Islam, a Woman's Roar," *Christian Science Monitor*, March 5, 2008, http://www.csmonitor.com/2008/0305/p13s03-lign.htm (accessed January 1, 2009).

53. Ibid.

54. Ibid.

55. Wazhma Frogh, "Ignorantism," November 5, 2004, http://www.iranian.com/Women/2004/November/Afghanistan/index.html (accessed January 1, 2009).

56. Wazhma Frogh, "Politics of Religion," October 26, 2007, http://www.devactivism.org (accessed January 1, 2009).

57. Wazhma Frogh, "Gender Violence to Drugs," http://www.persianmirror.com/community/writers/wazhmafrogh/2004/genderviolence.cfm (accessed January 1, 2009).

58. Ibid.

59. Wazhma Frogh, "Human Rights Violations in the Name of Religion," http://www.persianmirror.com/community/writers/wazhmafrogh/2004/humanrights.cfm (accessed January 1, 2009).

60. Ibid.

61. "On the Eve of the Global Campaign for the Elimination of Violence against Women," November 27, 2007, http://www.devactivism.org (accessed January 1, 2009).

62. Ibid.

63. Ibid.

64. "More Young Girls Face Rape in Afghanistan."

65. Carroll, "Inside Islam, a Woman's Roar."

66. "'An Alternative to the Warlords!' Masooda Jalal's Campaign for President of Afghanistan," *Awakened Woman*, September 23, 2004, http://www.awakenedwoman.com/hamilton_jalal.htm (accessed January 1, 2009).

67. Transcript of the speech delivered by Minister Massouda Jalal on September 8, 2005, in New York, for the Citigroup Series on Asian Women Leaders, on Women's Leadership in Afghanistan's Reconstruction, http://www.asiasource.org/asip/jalal.cfm (accessed January 1, 2009).

68. Ibid.

69. Ibid.

70. "Woman Takes on Afghan Politics: Determined Doctor Pushing Agenda in First Democratic Elections," *NBC News*, September 7, 2004.

71. "Running for President," *News24*, August 12, 2004, http://www.news24.com/News24/World/News/0,,2-10-1462_1571915,00.html (accessed March 24, 2009).

72. "Massouda Jalal Sets Precedent for Afghan Women," AFP, Kabul, January 26, 2004.

73. "Dr. Massouda Jalal: An 'Un-Islamic' Candidacy," *Voices Unabridged*, E-Magazine on Women and Human Rights Worldwide, September 28, 2004, http://www.voices-unabridged.org/format/creat_format.php?id_article=67 (accessed March 24, 2009).

74. "Massouda Jalal," http://www.beautifulatrocities.com/archives/2005/01/masooda_jalal.html (accessed August 8, 2008).

75. Nick Meo, "Afghanistan: The Woman Who Wants to Be President," *Independent* (UK), August 4, 2004.

76. "Woman Takes on Afghan Politics."

77. "Massouda Jalal."

78. "Malalai Joya," Omega Web site, http://www.eomega.org/omega/faculty/ viewProfile/bfeab94d1fd77e79b1823a2266705c84 (accessed February 4, 2009).

79. VDay, "Help Afghanistan's Leading Champion of Women's Rights," http://www.malalaijoya.com/index1024.htm (accessed February 4, 2009).

80. "In the Line of Fire: The *Satya* Interview with Malalai Joya," *Satya Online Magazine*, June/July 2007, http://www.satyamag.com/jun07/joya.html (accessed February 4, 2009).

81. "Profile: Malalai Joya," *BBC News*, November 12, 2005, http://news.bbc .co.uk/2/hi/south_asia/4420832.stm (accessed February 4, 2009).

82. "In the Line of Fire: The *Satya* Interview with Malalai Joya."

83. Sonali Kolhatkar, "If I Arise, Talking with Malalai Joya, Afghanistan's Youngest Revolutionary," *Clamor Magazine* 37, Summer 2006, http://clamor magazine.org/issues/37/people.php (accessed February 4, 2009).

84. Ibid.

85. Ibid.

86. European Parliament, Committee on Foreign Affairs, Candidates for Sakharov Prize for Freedom of Thought 2007, pp. 6–7, http://www.europarl.europa.eu/meetdocs/ 2004_2009/documents/cm/683/683416/683416en.pdf (accessed February 4, 2009).

87. "A Salute to Malalai Joya—Afghanistan's Tom Paine," http://www.nolan chart.com/article4449.html (accessed February 4, 2009).

88. Hamida Ghafour, "One Woman's Words Defy Might of Afghan War-lords," *Telegraph* (UK), August 13, 2004, http://www.telegraph.co.uk/news/world news/asia/afghanistan/1467010/One-womans-words-defy-might-of-Afghan -warlords.html (accessed February 4, 2009).

89. "Kabul: Rally Demands Amnesty for War Criminals; Demonstrators Cried Out 'Death to Malalai Joya,'" *Paz Ahora*, http://www.pazahora.org/Malalai JoyaEnglish.htm (accessed February 4, 2009).

90. "Afghan Parliament Suspends Outspoken Female Lawmaker after Critical TV Interview," *International Herald Tribune*, May 21, 2007.

91. "Censure of Malalai Joya Sets Back Democracy and Rights," Human Rights Watch, May 23, 2007, http://www.afghanwomensmission.org/news/index .php?articleID=67 (accessed February 4, 2009).

92. "Afghan Parliament Suspends Outspoken Female Lawmaker."

93. "Protest Rallies in Support of Malalai Joya around the World," Arian Television, June 23, 2007, http://video.google.com/videoplay?docid=-3057882769 988169074 (accessed February 4, 2009).

94. "Afghanistan: Reinstate Malalai Joya in Parliament; Suspension of Female

MP One Year Ago Is Setback for Democracy," Human Rights Watch, May 21, 2008, http://hrw.org/english/docs/2008/05/21/afghan18897_txt.htm (accessed February 4, 2009).

95. Hamid Ghafour, "A Populist Hero Emerges from under the Rule of the Gun," *Globe and Mail* (Toronto), July 27, 2004.

96. "Profile Malalai Joya," *BBC News Online South East Asia*, November 12, 2005, http://news.bbc.co.uk/2/hi/south_asia/4420832.stm (accessed February 4, 2009).

97. RAWA Web site, http://www.rawa.org (accessed February 5, 2009).

98. Ibid.

99. Ibid.

100. "Avenging Meena's Blood Is Meaningful Only in the Context of Struggle against Fundamentalism and for Democracy," http://www.rawa.org/meenakillers-en .htm (accessed March 24, 2009).

101. Aryn Baker, "60 Asian Heroes," *Time*, November 13, 2006.

102. RAWA Web site.

103. Ibid.

104. Manizha Naderi, "Women for Afghan Women," Women and Postwar Reconstruction Conference, luncheon address, March 13, 2004, www.womenfor afghanwomen.org/about/LanaEOmid.html (accessed February 5, 2009).

105. "The Non-profit Spotlight: Manizha Naderi," *Mideast Connect*, June 12, 2006, http://www.womenforafghanwomen.org/press/MidEast6-12-06.html (accessed March 24, 2009).

106. "Mission Statement, Women for Afghan Women (WAW)," http:// www.womenforafghanwomen.org (accessed February 5, 2009).

107. WAW concept paper, http://www.womenforafghanwomen.org/about/ ConceptPaper.html (accessed February 5, 2009).

108. Naderi, "Women for Afghan Women."

109. "Women and the Constitution: Kandahar 2003," Conference Report, www.womenforafghanwomen.org/events/ConferenceKandahar (accessed February 5, 2009).

110. Naderi, "Women for Afghan Women."

111. Ibid.

112. "Women and the Constitution: Kandahar 2003."

113. Ibid.

114. Ibid.

115. Suhaila Muhsini, "Profile: Suraya Parlika—Champion of Women's Rights," Institute for War and Peace Reporting, Afghan Recovery Report #129, August 13, 2004, http://www.peacewomen.org/news/Afghanistan/Aug04/profile .html (accessed February 5, 2009).

116. Ibid.

117. Ibid.

118. Ibid.

119. David Montero, "Afghan Women Start Businesses, Help Reconstruct a Torn Nation," *Christian Science Monitor*, May 8, 2006, http://www.csmonitor.com/2006/0508/p04s01-wosc.htm (accessed February 5, 2009).

120. Ibid.

121. Stephanie Hiller, "Afghanistan: Women Still in Terror," *People and the Planet*, April 21, 2005, http://www.peopleandplanet.net/doc.php?id=2464 (accessed February 5, 2009).

122. Ibid.

123. "World People's Blog, March 30, 2007," http://word.world-citizenship.org/wp-archive/1176 (accessed February 5, 2009).

124. Feminist Majority (FM) quoted in "Stephanie Hiller, Afghanistan: Women Still in Terror," People and the Planet, http://www.peopleandplanet.net/doc.php?id=2464 (accessed February 5, 2009).

125. Muhsini, "Profile: Suraya Parlika."

126. Christina Troup, "Nobel Peace Prize Hopeful Speaks in S.F.," *Oakland Tribune*, http://findarticles.com/p/articles/mi_qn4176/is_20050401/ai_n14615624/pg_1 (accessed February 5, 2009).

127. Nilofar Sakhi, abstract, "Domestic and External Challenges to Democracy in the Muslim World: Case Studies: Turkey and Afghanistan," Center for the Study of Islam and Democracy, CSID's 7th Annual Conference, "The Challenge of Democracy in the Muslim World, Washington, 5–6 May 2006," http://www.csidonline.org/index.php?option=com_content&task=view&id=269&Itemid=95 (accessed March 24, 2009).

128. "Fulbright Scholar Recalls Her Struggle to Empower Afghan Women," August 25, 2006, http://www.america.gov/st/washfile-english/2006/August/20060825164339ndyblehs0.4105493.html (accessed January 5, 2009).

129. Ibid.

130. Sakhi, abstract.

131. Ibid.

132. "Feminists Yanar Mohammed of Iraq and Dr. Sima Samar of Afghanistan on the Dire Situation for Women under US Occupation and Rising Fundamentalism," Democracy Now! May 14, 2007, http://www.democracynow.org/2007/5/14/feminists_yanar_mohammed_of_iraq_and (accessed February 5, 2009).

133. Sima Samar, "Despite the Odds—Providing Reproductive Health Care to Afghan Women," *New England Journal of Medicine* 351, no. 11 (September 9, 2004):1047–49.

134. Sima Samar, chair, Afghan Independent Human Rights Commission, http://web.bu.edu/ghi/documents/Samar%20Biograph.pdf (accessed March 24, 2009).

135. Waheed Warasta, "Freedom of Expression in Afghanistan," *Dominion*, January 29, 2008, http://www.dominionpaper.ca/articles/1634 (accessed February 5, 2009).

136. "Gunmen Kill Director of Women's Affairs for Southern Afghanistan."

137. Pat Irish, "Dr. Sima Samar Discusses Current State in Afghanistan," April 12, 2007, http://media.www.bcheights.com/media/storage/paper144/news/2007/04/12/News/Dr.Sima.Samar.Discusses.Current.State.In.Afghanistan-2837138.shtml (accessed March 24, 2009).

138. Ibid.

139. Ibid.

140. "Feminists Yanar Mohammed of Iraq and Dr. Sima Samar of Afghanistan on the Dire Situation for Women under US Occupation and Rising Fundamentalism."

141. Shuhada Organization, http://www.shuhada.org.

142. "Afghanistan's Reform Agenda: Four Perspectives," March 2002, Asia Society, http://www.asiasociety.org/publications/update_afghanreform.html (accessed February 5, 2009).

CHAPTER 2: ALGERIA

1. Zahia Smail Salhi, "Algerian Women, Citizenship, and the 'Family Code,'" *Gender and Development* 11, no. 3 (November 2003): 27–35, http://www.learningpartnership.org/citizenship/wp-content/uploads/algerian-women-family-code.pdf (accessed February 5, 2009).

2. Khalida Messaoudi, *Unbowed: An Algerian Woman Confronts Islamic Fundamentalism*, interviewed by Elisabeth Schemla, trans. Anne C. Vila (Philadelphia: University of Pennsylvania Press, 1998).

3. Salhi, "Algerian Women, Citizenship, and the 'Family Code.'"

4. Louisa Ait-Hamou, *Women's Struggle against Muslim Fundamentalism in Algeria: Strategies or a Lesson for Survival?* WLUML publication, December 2004, http://www.wluml.org/english/pubs/pdf/wsf/14.pdf (accessed March 24, 2009).

5. Salhi, "Algerian Women, Citizenship, and the 'Family Code.'"

6. Ibid.

7. Michael Slackman, "Algeria's Quiet Revolution: Gains by Women," *International Herald Tribune*, May 26, 2007, http://www.iht.com/articles/2007/05/26/africa/algeria.1-62108.php (accessed February 5, 2009).

8. Ibid.

9. Nathalie Szerman, "Profile of Reformist Algerian Cartoonist Ali Dilem," Memri Inquiry and Analysis Series, no. 282, June 27, 2006, http://www .memri.org/bin/articles.cgi?Page=countries&Area=northafrica&ID=IA28206 (accessed April 4, 2009). Cartoon translations by Memri.

10. Speech at the Simone de Beauvoir Convention in 1999, Cologne, http:// www.dadalos.org/int/Menschenrechte/Grundkurs_MR3/frauenrechte/woher/ dokumente/dokument_5.htm (accessed February 5, 2009).

11. Ibid.

12. Richard Swift, "Interview with Khalida Messaoudi, Women's Rights Activist—Algeria," *New Internationalist*, March 1995, http://www.thirdworld traveler.com/Heroes/Khalida_Messaoudi.html (accessed February 5, 2009).

13. Ibid.

14. Ibid.

15. Messaoudi, *Unbowed*, p. 56.

16. Excerpt from the fatwa against Khalida Messaoudi, UNESCO education server D@dalos, http://www.dadalos.org/int/menschenrechte/Grundkurs_MR3/ frauenrechte/woher/portraets/messaoudi.htm (accessed February 5, 2009).

17. Swift, "Interview with Khalida Messaoudi, Women's Rights Activist— Algeria."

18. Speech at the Simone de Beauvoir Convention in 1999, Cologne.

19. Messaoudi, *Unbowed*, pp. 64–65.

CHAPTER 3: BAHRAIN

1. United Nations Development Programme, Programme on Governance in the Arab Region (UNDP–POGAR), "Gender and Citizenship: Arab Countries," http://gender.pogar.org/countries/country.asp?cid=2 (accessed July 8, 2008).

2. World Bank Group GenderStats, http://devdata.worldbank.org/gender stats/genderRpt.asp?rpt=profile&cty=BHR,Bahrain (accessed February 5, 2009).

3. Ann Workman, "Interview with Wajeeha Al Baharna," Women's Learning Partnership, March 7, 2006, http://www.learningpartnership.org/advocacy/campaign/ wabinterview (accessed January 9, 2009).

4. Ibid.

5. "Claiming Equal Citizenship: The Campaign for Arab Women's Right to Nationality," http://old.crtda.org/crtd.org/www.wrn/index.htm (accessed February 5, 2009).

6. Ibid.

7. Ibid.

8. Al-Arabiya TV, December 21, 2005, in "Bahraini Women's Rights Activist Ghada Jamshir Attacks Islamic Clerics for Fatwas Authorizing Sexual Abuse of Children," Memri TV Clip no. 978, December 21, 2005, http:// memri.org/bin/latestnews.cgi?ID=SD106005 (accessed January 10, 2009).

9. Ibid.

10. Ibid.

11. Ibid.

12. Committee of Women's Petition President to British House of Lords: "The Struggle for Women's Rights in Bahrain Has Become More Difficult," Memri Dispatch no. 1401, December 20, 2006, http://www.memri.org/bin/articles.cgi ?Page=archives&Area=sd&ID=SP140106 (accessed February 5, 2009).

13. Ibid.

14. Scott Macleod, "Ghada Jamsheer: Activist," *Time*, May 14, 2006.

15. "Bahrain: A Women's Rights Activist Faces Trial and Imprisonment," Bahrain Center for Human Rights, http://www.bahrainrights.org/ref05060301 (accessed February 5, 2009).

16. "Bahraini Women's Rights Activist Ghada Jamshir Attacks Islamic Clerics."

17. "The Struggle for Women's Rights in Bahrain Has Become More Difficult."

18. Ibid.

19. Ghada Jamsheer, "Activist Ghada Jamsheer: Why Aren't Women of the Ruling Family in Bahrain Subject to the Shariah Courts Like Other Women?" AAFAQ, March 14, 2008, http://www.aafaq.org/english/aafaq_today.aspx?id_ news =145# (accessed January 10, 2009).

20. "Worrying Allegations over Government Attempts to Spy on Prominent Women's Rights Activist," Bahrain Center for Human Rights, March 17, 2007, http://www.bahrainrights.org/en/month/2007/03 (accessed January 10, 2009).

CHAPTER 4: BANGLADESH

1. "Bangladeshi TV Takes Aim at Violence against Women," Department for International Development, August 16, 2007, http://www.dfid.gov.uk/case studies/files/asia/bangladesh-women.asp (accessed February 6, 2009).

2. Qurratul Ain Tahmina, "Bangladesh: Women's Policy Sneakily Changed by Government," Women's International League for Peace and Women, July 27, 2005 (accessed July 17, 2008), http://www.peacewomen.org/news/International/ July05/Bangladesh.html (accessed February 6, 2009).

3. Ibid.

4. Dina M. Siddiqi, "In the Name of Islam? Gender, Politics and Women's Rights in Bangladesh," *Harvard Asia Quarterly*, July 27, 2005, http://www.asia quarterly.com/content/view/165/43 (accessed February 6, 2009).

5. Ain Tahmina, "Bangladesh: Women's Policy Sneakily Changed by Government."

6. "Bangladesh," Online Women in Politics, http://www.onlinewomenin politics.org/bangla/bangmain.htm#banglatop (accessed February 6, 2009).

7. Ibid.

8. Ain Tahmina, "Bangladesh: Women's Policy Sneakily Changed by Government."

9. "Bangladesh: Gender, Poverty and the Millennium Development Goals. Country Gender Strategy," Asia Development Bank, 2004, http://www.adb.org/ Documents/Reports/Country-Gender-Assessments/ban.asp (accessed February 6, 2009).

10. "Bangladesh: 21, 000 Women Die Annually in Childbirth," *IRIN News*, June 13, 2008, http://www.irinnews.org/Report.aspx?ReportId=78721 (accessed February 6, 2009).

11. Ibid.

12. Acid Survivors Foundation (ASF), http://www.acidsurvivors.org/index .html (accessed March 28, 2009).

13. Ibid.

14. Ibid.

15. "Taslima Nasrin: 'They Wanted to Kill Me,'" *Middle East Quarterly*, September 2000, http://www.meforum.org/article/73 (accessed November 27, 2008).

16. Ibid.

17. Ibid.

18. Ibid.

19. Taslima Nasreen, "No Woman No Cry," livemint.com, *Wall Street Journal*, May 4, 2007, http://www.livemint.com/2007/05/04000500/No-woman-no-cry -Taslima-Nas.html (accessed February 20, 2009).

20. Speech delivered to the women's forum, Deauville, France, October 15, 2005, Taslima Nasrin Official Web site, http://taslimanasrin.com/index2.html (accessed February 20, 2009).

21. "Taslima Nasrin: 'They Wanted to Kill Me.'"

22. Adrian Morgan, "Taslima Nasreen—A Woman of Moral Substance," August 24, 2007, http://www.islam-watch.org/adrianmorgan/Taslima-Nasreen -Woman-of-Substance.htm (accessed August 22, 2008).

23. "Taslima Nasrin: 'They Wanted to Kill Me.'"

24. Ibid.

25. Speech delivered to the women's forum, Deauville, France.

26. "Let's Think about the Burqa," http://taslimanasrin.com/OPINION.pdf, (accessed August 22, 2008).

27. "Taslima Nasrin: 'They Wanted to Kill Me.'"

28. Morgan, "Taslima Nasreen—A Woman of Moral Substance."

29. Ibid.

30. Taslima Nasreen, "It Feels, Speaks, Smells Like Home," *Outlook India*, May 14, 2007, http://www.outlookindia.com/dossiersind.asp?id=812 (accessed February 20, 2009).

31. Morgan, "Taslima Nasreen—A Woman of Moral Substance."

32. Nasreen, "It Feels, Speaks, Smells Like Home."

33. "Taslima Nasrin: 'They Wanted to Kill Me.'"

CHAPTER 5: CANADA

1. Irshad Manji, "Is Islam to Blame?" *Los Angeles Times*, July 22, 2005, http://articles.latimes.com/2005/jul/22/opinion/oe-manji22 (accessed January 27, 2009).

2. Clifford Krauss, "An Unlikely Promoter of an Islamic Reformation," *New York Times*, October 4, 2003, http://query.nytimes.com/gst/fullpage.html?res=9C0DE3DE153CF937A35753C1A9659C8B63 (accessed January 27, 2009).

3. Andrew Sullivan, "Decent Exposure," *New York Times*, January 25, 2004, http://query.nytimes.com/gst/fullpage.html?res=9C01E5D61E30F936A15752C0A9629C8B63 (accessed January 27, 2009).

4. "Irshad Manji: Encyclopedia II—Irshad Manji—Biography," http://www.experiencefestival.com/a/Irshad_Manji_-_Biography/id/5168464 (accessed January 27, 2009).

5. Ibid.

6. "About Irshad," http://www.irshadmanji.com/about-irshad (accessed January 27, 2009).

7. Sullivan, "Decent Exposure."

8. Irshad Manji, "Islam Needs an Age of Reason," *Washington Post*, Guest Voices, August 16, 2007, http://newsweek.washingtonpost.com/onfaith/guestvoices/2007/08/a_muslim_defense_for_interfait.html (accessed January 27, 2009).

9. Bina Shah, "The Trouble with Irshad Manji," October 3, 2004, www.chowk.com/articles/8145 (accessed January 27, 2009).

10. Irshad Manji, "From Books to Virgins," *Los Angeles Times*, July 22, 2005, http://articles.latimes.com/2005/nov/06/opinion/op-islameducation6 (accessed January 27, 2009).

11. Irshad Manji, "It's Time for All of Us to Embrace Ijtihad," *Globe and Mail* (Toronto), March 24, 2009.

12. Manji, "From Books to Virgins."

13. "The Making of a Kafir," http://www.irshadmanji.com (accessed January 27, 2009).

14. Stephen Brown, "Canada's Salman Rushdie," *Front Page Magazine*, October 2, 2003, www.frontpagemagazine.com/Articles (accessed January 27, 2009).

15. Asla Aydintasbas, "A 'Refusenik' Looks at Her Religion," *Wall Street Journal*, January 27, 2004.

16. Shah, "The Trouble with Irshad Manji."

17. Barry Gewen, "Muslim Rebel Sisters: At Odds with Islam and Each Other," *New York Times*, April 27, 2008, www.nytimes.com/2008/04/27/weekin review/27gewen.html (accessed January 27, 2009).

18. See http://asmasociety.typepad.com/mlt (accessed January 27, 2009).

19. Mujibr Rehman, "Calling All Believers to a Conversation on Islam," *Times of India*, December 11, 2005.

20. Manji official Web site, http://www.irshadmanji.com/sources-and-notes ?itemid=57 (accessed January 5, 2009).

21. Ibid.

22. National Film Board of Canada, 2007, http://www.nfb.ca/collection/ films/resultat.php?type=credit&pid=115165&nom=Irshad+Manji (accessed January 27, 2009).

23. See http://www.irshadmanji.com/moral-courage-project (accessed March 24, 2009).

24. See http://www.irshadmanji.com/about-irshad (accessed March 24, 2009).

25. Ibid.

CHAPTER 6: EGYPT

1. Nadje Al-Ali, "Secular Women's Activism in Contemporary Egypt," http://www.wluml.org/english/pubs/pdf/wsf/18.pdf (accessed July 17, 2008).

2. UNDP, "Arab Human Development Report: Empowerment of Arab Women," 2005.

3. Margot Badran, "Feminism in a Nationalist Century," *Al-Ahram Weekly*, December 30, 1999–January 5, 2000, issue no. 462, http://weekly.ahram.org.eg/ 1999/462/women.htm (accessed December 4, 2008).

4. Ibid.

5. Ibid.

6. United Nations Development Programme (UNDP–POGAR), "Gender and Citizenship: Arab Countries," http://gender.pogar.org/countries/country.asp ?cid=5 (accessed December 4, 2008).

7. Ibid.

8. Gamal Essam El-Din, "Children Accorded Greater Rights," *Al-Ahram Weekly*, June 12–18, 2008, issue no. 901.

9. Michael Slackman, "Voices Rise in Egypt to Shield Girls from an Old Tradition," *New York Times*, September 20, 2007, http://www.nytimes.com/2007/09/20/world/africa/20girls.html (accessed December 4, 2008).

10. Charles Levinson, "Egypt's Growing Blogger Community Pushes Limit of Dissent," *Christian Science Monitor*, August 24, 2005.

11. "Egyptian Blogger Nora Younis Wins Human Rights First Award," *Global Voices Online*, http://globalvoicesonline.org/2008/10/23/egyptian-female-blogger-nora-younis-receives-human-rights-first-award (accessed December 8, 2008).

12. "Egypt: A Modern Myth," www.faits-et-projets.com/decouvrir_egypte_GB.htm (accessed November 29, 2008).

13. Ekbal Baraka, http://www.ekbalbaraka.net/ekbal_baraka.htm (accessed November 29, 2008).

14. Ibid.

15. Ibid.

16. Ibid.

17. Ibid.

18. Hossam Mansour, "Feminists in Egypt," CSS Zen Gardens, http://www.ahl-alquran.com/English/show_article.php?main_id=626 (accessed March 24, 2009).

19. Ibid.

20. Ekbal Baraka, *The Veil* (Cairo: Rosel Yousef, 2002).

21. Abstract, *The Veil*, http://www.ekbalbaraka.net/books_abstract.htm (accessed March 24, 2009).

22. "Censorship, Religion and Sex," http://sidesteppingreal.blogspot.com/2006/12/censorship-religion-sex-update.html (accessed March 24, 2009).

23. Ekbal Baraka, http://www.ekbalbaraka.net/ekbal_baraka.htm (accessed March 24, 2009).

24. "Don't Be Deceived, a Conversation with Nonie Darwish," *Reform Judaism*, http://reformjudaismmag.org/Articles/index.cfm?id=1239 (accessed December 4, 2008).

25. "Egyptian-American Writer Nonie Darwish, Founder of 'Arabs for Israel': 'We Must Begin to View the Jews in a Forgiving Light,'" Memri Special Dispatch Series, no. 1533, April 3, 2007, http://memri.org/bin/articles.cgi?Page=archives&Area=sd&ID=SP153307 (accessed December 4, 2008).

26. Nonie Darwish, *Now They Call Me Infidel: Why I Renounced Jihad for America, Israel, and the War on Terror* (New York: Sentinel, 2006).

27. Ibid., p. 9.

28. "Don't Be Deceived, a Conversation with Nonie Darwish."

29. Darwish, *Now They Call Me Infidel*, p. 13.

30. Nonie Darwish, "Impossible Family Dynamics of Islam," *Front Page Magazine*, January 29, 2003, http://frontpagemag.com/articles/Read.aspx?GUID=E8D B610A-9044-4A03-8E61-DCEDD0EFCEAE (accessed December 4, 2008).

31. Jamie Glazov, "Interview with Nonie Darwish, *Now They Call Me Infidel*," *Front Page Magazine*, December 20, 2006, http://www.frontpagemag.com/ Articles/Read.aspx?GUID=A53FE649-F1F9-4CF0-B80A-9C4ECA46DC10 (accessed December 4, 2008).

32. Ibid.

33. "Don't Be Deceived, a Conversation with Nonie Darwish."

34. Nonie Darwish, "What I Learned from Jews," http://arabsforisrael.com (accessed December 1, 2008).

35. "Don't Be Deceived, a Conversation with Nonie Darwish."

36. Transcript of a speech delivered by Dr. Aida Seif El Dawla at the American University, Beirut, "Public Health as a Human Rights Issue," February 12, 2004, http://fhs-lb.aub.edu.lb/anniversary/seif_al_dawla.html (accessed December 4, 2008).

37. "Fearless Speech," *Al Ahram Weekly*, November 13–19, 2003, issue no. 664, http://weekly.ahram.org.eg/2003/664/eg9.htm (accessed December 4, 2008).

38. "Human Rights Watch Honors Egyptian Anti-Torture Activist," Human Rights Watch, 2003, http://hrw.org/english/docs/2004/10/06/uk9456.htm (accessed March 24, 2009).

39. Transcript of speech delivered by Dr. Aida Seif El Dawla at the American University, Beirut, "Public Health as a Human Rights Issue."

40. Khaleb Diab, "The Virginity Dialogues," *Guardian* (UK), January 2008, http://commentisfree.guardian.co.uk/khaled_diab/2008/01/the_virginity_dialogues .html (accessed March 24, 2009). Reprinted with permission of Guardian News & Media Ltd.

41. "Fearless Speech."

42. Amany Radwani/Cairo, "Fighting for Their Rights" *Time Europe*, October 11, 2004, http://www.time.com/time/europe/hero2004/dawla.html (accessed December 4, 2008).

43. Diab, "The Virginity Dialogues."

44. Ibid.

45. American University Cairo Faculty, http://www.aucegypt.edu/facstaff/ Pages/default.aspx (accessed March 24, 2009).

46. Christine Spolar, "Mubarak's Foes Brave Beating for a Cause," *Chicago Tribune*, May 18, 2005, http://harakamasria.org/node/6215 (accessed March 24, 2009).

47. Charles Levinson, "Egypt's Growing Blogger Community Pushes Limit of Dissent," *Christian Science Monitor*, August 24, 2005.

48. "Egypt: A Test Case for Democracy," *CNN*, http://edition.cnn.com/TRANSCRIPTS/0511/20/cp.01.html (accessed March 24, 2009).

49. Diab, "The Virginity Dialogues."

50. Colleen Ross, "Failing Grade for Academic Freedom in Egypt," December 29, 2005, CBC Toronto, http://www.cbc.ca/news/viewpoint/vp_ross/20051229.html (accessed March 24, 2009).

51. Ibid.

52. Rabab el-Mahdi and Philip Marfleet, eds., *Egypt: The Moment of Change* (London: Zed Books, 2009).

53. Diab, "The Virginity Dialogues."

54. Ibid.

55. Jennifer McBride, "Nawal El-Saadawi," www.webster.edu/~woolflm/saadawi.html (accessed December 6, 2008).

56. Nation Master, http://www.nationmaster.com/encyclopedia/Nawal-el_Saadawi (accessed December 6, 2008).

57. Brian Belton and Clare Dowding, "Nawal El-Saadawi—A Creative and Dissident Life," http://www.infed.org/thinkers/et-saadawi.htm (accessed December 6, 2008).

58. McBride, "Nawal El-Saadawi."

59. Ibid.

60. AWSA Web site, www.awsa.net/profile/index.html (accessed December 6, 2008).

61. Fiona Lloyd-Davies, "No Compromise," *BBC News*, October 26, 2001, http://www.bbc.co.uk/worldservice (accessed August 14, 2008).

62. Zvi Bar'el, "Vilified for Voicing Dissent," *Haaretz*, March 5, 2007.

63. Ibid.

64. Ibid.

65. Ramadan Al Sherbini, "Feminist's Book Is Recalled by Its Publisher for 'Offending Religion,'" *Gulfnews*, February 7, 2007, http://archive.gulfnews.com/articles/07/02/07/10102478.html (accessed December 6, 2008).

66. Bar'el, "Vilified for Voicing Dissent."

67. Keynote Speech of H. E. Mrs. Suzanne Mubarak, World Food Day Ceremony, FAO, Rome, October 16, 2008.

68. Suzanne Mubarak Women's International Peace Movement, http://www.womenforpeaceinternational.org (accessed January 26, 2009).

69. Regional Workshop, Summary Report, "The Road to UNSC 1325, Women, Peace and Security Future Perspectives," May 29–30, 2004.

70. Arab Women Organization (AWO), http://www.sis.gov.eg/En/Women/institutions/Arab/AWO/100402030000000001.htm (accessed January 26, 2009).

71. Marie Vlachová and Lea Biason, eds., *Women in an Insecure World: Violence against Women—Facts, Figures and Analysis* (2005). Geneva Centre for the Democratic Control of Armed Forces (DCAF), http://www.dcaf.ch/women/_publications.cfm?navsub1=11&navsub2=4&nav1=3 (accessed April 3, 2009).

72. "ALECSO Thanks Mrs. Mubarak for Supporting Arab Reading for All Project," *Arabic News*, June 14, 2003, http://www.arabicnews.com/ansub/Daily/Day/030614/2003061433.html (accessed January 26, 2009).

73. International Museum No. 208, UNESCO, http://portal.unesco.org/culture/en/ev.php-URL_ID=4884&URL_DO=DO_TOPIC&URL_SECTION=201.html (accessed January 26, 2009).

74. Address by H. E. Mrs. Suzanne Mubarak, Peace Matters Lecture Series, "New Zealand and Peaceful Conflict Resolution," November 28, 2007.

75. Suzanne Mubarak Women's International Peace Movement, http://www.womenforpeaceinternational.org/EN/Events/EventDetails.aspx?ID=102&Path=National%20Level (accessed March 28, 2009).

76. Ibid.

77. "Speech of Mrs. Suzanne Mubarak after Receiving the Pioneering Women Prize," Egypt State Information Service, June 13, 2006.

78. Dalia Ziada and Jesse Sage, "Jailed for Blogging," *International Herald Tribune*, December 27, 2006.

79. "Egypt Blogger Jailed for 'Insult,'" *BBC News*, February 22, 2007.

80. Free Kareem! http://www.freekareem.org/kareem-faq (accessed March 28, 2009).

81. Tom G. Palmer, "Getting Kareem Freed," *National Review*, March 29, 2007.

82. Free Kareem! http://www.freekareem.org/2006/11/06/muslims-standing-with-kareem (accessed December 8, 2008).

83. "Egypt: Women at the Forefront for Change," *BBC News*, March 19, 2008.

84. Free Kareem! http://www.freekareem.org/category/egyptian-blogosphere (accessed December 8, 2008).

85. Ibid.

86. See http://www.youtube.com/watch?v=uUoJa8QlRFw (accessed December 8, 2008).

87. Dalia Ziada, http://daliaziada.blogspot.com (accessed March 28, 2009).

88. The Initiative for an Open Arab Internet, http://www.openarab.net/en/node/346 (accessed March 28, 2009).

89. Ibid.

90. Hands across the Mideast Support Alliance, http://www.hamsaweb.org/honorme.html#dal (accessed March 28, 2009).

91. "Egypt: Women at the Forefront for Change."

92. Ibid.

93. See http://www.youtube.com/watch?v=uUoJa8QlRFw (accessed December 8, 2008).

CHAPTER 7: FRANCE

1. Emma-Kate Symons, "France Closes Ranks against Burka," *Australian*, July 18, 2008, http://www.theaustralian.news.com.au/story/0,25197,24036168-2703,00.html (accessed March 25, 2009).

2. Eloi Laurent, "Fadela Amara," August 3, 2007, French Politics, http://artgoldhammer.blogspot.com/2007/08/fadela-amara-guest-post-eloi-laurent.html (accessed March 25, 2009).

3. Bruce Crumley, "Acting on the Outrage," *Time*, September 30, 2004.

4. Adar Primor, "Sarkozy's Leftist," *Haaretz*, April 5, 2008, http://www.haaretz.com/hasen/spages/971505.html (accessed January 6, 2009).

5. Fadela Amara and Sylvia Zappi, *Breaking the Silence: French Women's Voices from the Ghetto* (Berkeley: University of California Press, 2006), p. 53. The work was originally published by Editions La Découverte, Paris, France, in 2003, and was translated into English by Helen Chenut.

6. Ibid.

7. Rose George, "Ghetto Warrior," *Guardian* (UK), July 17, 2006, www.guardian.co.uk/world/2006/jul/17/france.politicsphilosophyandsociety (accessed December 8, 2008).

8. Ibid.

9. Amara and Zappi, *Breaking the Silence*.

10. Catherine Raissiguier, "Muslim Women in France, Impossible Subjects?" May 2, 2008, http://www.darkmatter101.org/site/2008/05/02/muslim-women-in-france-impossible-subjects (accessed January 6, 2009).

11. Ibid.

12. Primor, "Sarkozy's Leftist."

13. George, "Ghetto Warrior."

14. Crumley, "Acting on the Outrage."

15. Ibid.

16. "Pan-European Arab Muslim Gang Rape Epidemic," Iris Blog, May 19,

2006, www.iris.org.il/blog/archives/757-Pan-European-Arab-Muslim-Gang-Rape -Epidemic.htm (accessed January 6, 2009).

17. Primor, "Sarkozy's Leftist."

18. George, "Ghetto Warrior."

19. Ibid.

20. Ibid.

21. Ibid.

22. Laurent, "Fadela Amara."

23. George, "Ghetto Warrior."

24. Primor, "Sarkozy's Leftist."

25. George, "Ghetto Warrior."

26. Pierre Mabut and Antoine Lerougetel, "France: Socialist Party Feminist Joins Sarkozy's Cabinet," World Socialist Web Site, July 5, 2007, http://www .wsws.org/articles/2007/jul2007/amar-j05.shtml (accessed January 6, 2009).

27. Raissiguier, "Muslim Women in France, Impossible Subjects?"

28. Primor, "Sarkozy's Leftist."

29. Amara and Zappi, *Breaking the Silence.*

30. Samira Bellil, cited in Nicholas Bamforth, ed., *Sex Rights: The Oxford Amnesty Lectures 2002* (Oxford: Oxford University Press, 2005), p. 172.

31. Rose George, "Obituary: Samira Bellil," *Guardian* (UK), September 13, 2004, http://www.guardian.co.uk/news/2004/sep/13/guardianobituaries.france (accessed August 19, 2008).

32. Ibid.

33. Bruce Crumley and Adam Smith, "Sisters in Hell," *Time*, November 24, 2002, http://www.time.com/time/magazine/article/0,9171,393601,00.html (accessed August 19, 2008).

34. Rose George, "Revolt against the Rapists: France's Women Fight Back," 2003, http://rosegeorge.com/site/revolt-against-the-rapists-frances-women-fight -back (accessed December 6, 2009).

35. Jon Henley, "Gang Rape on Rise among French youth," *Guardian* (UK), May 3, 2001, http://www.guardian.co.uk/world/2001/may/03/jonhenley (accessed January 6, 2009).

36. Crumley and Smith, "Sisters in Hell."

37. Christiane Amanpour, "The New French Revolution," *60 Minutes*, May 16, 2004, http://www.cbsnews.com/stories/2004/05/13/60minutes/main617270 .shtml (accessed January 6, 2009).

38. George, "Obituary: Samira Bellil."

39. Amanpour, "The New French Revolution."

40. George, cited in Bamforth, *Sex Rights: The Oxford Amnesty Lectures 2002.*

41. Slang for gang rapes, literally "your turn" or "pass arounds."

42. George, "Obituary: Samira Bellil."

43. Crumley and Smith, "Sisters in Hell."

44. "Samira Bellil, French Author and Rights Activist, Dies," *Washington Post*, September 9, 2004, http://www.washingtonpost.com/wp-dyn/articles/A7061-2004 Sep8.html (accessed January 6, 2009).

45. George, "Revolt against the Rapists."

46. Amanpour, "The New French Revolution."

47. George, "Obituary: Samira Bellil."

48. Ibid.

49. Ibid.

50. Ibid.

51. Amanpour, "The New French Revolution."

CHAPTER 8: INDONESIA

1. Indonesian feminist Valentina Sagala, in Novia D. Rulistia, "Women's Rights Recognized but Not Completely Fulfilled," *Jakarta Post*, Review 2007, http://old.thejakartapost.com:80/review2007/nat06.asp (accessed November 16, 2008).

2. See http://www.kowani.or.id/html/aim.htm (accessed November 16, 2008).

3. CIA, *The World Factbook*, http://www.cia.gov/library/publications/the -world-factbook/fields/2122.html (accessed March 25, 2009).

4. Sharon Bessell, "Women in Parliament in Indonesia: Denied a Share of Power," Asia Pacific School of Economics and Government, ANU, Discussion Papers, Policy and Governance, 2004.

5. Anne Pohlman, "A Fragment of a Story," *Intersections: Gender, History and Culture in the Asian Context*, no. 10 (August 2004).

6. Rulistia, "Women's Rights Recognized but Not Completely Fulfilled."

7. Bessell, "Women in Parliament in Indonesia."

8. "Indonesia: Exploitation and Abuse: The Plight of Women Domestic Workers" (data taken from 2002 study by the International Labour Organization), Amnesty International, ASA 21/001/2007, February 14, 2007, http://www .amnesty.org/en/library/info/ASA21/001/2007 (accessed April 3, 2009).

9. *Amnesty International Report 2008: State of the World's Human Rights*, http://archive.amnesty.org/air2008/eng/Homepage.html (accessed May 6, 2009).

10. Ibid.

11. *World Health Organization Report*, http://www.searo.who.int/en/Section13/Section390_14241.htm (accessed July 4, 2008).

12. Ibid.

13. "Divorce Rate Up 10 Fold since Reform Era: Ministry," *Jakarta Post*, February 4, 2009.

14. Rulistia, "Women's Rights Recognized but Not Completely Fulfilled."

15. Bessell, "Women in Parliament in Indonesia."

16. "Indonesia: Paramilitary Groups Hijack Islam," *Jakarta Post*, June 9, 2008.

17. Ibid.

18. "Incorporating Sharia into Legal Systems," *BBC News*, February 8, 2008, http://news.bbc.co.uk/2/hi/7235357.stm (accessed March 25, 2009).

19. "In Padang, Islamic Law Is Now Imposed on All," *Asia News*, April 24, 2008, http://www.asianews.it/index.php?l=en&art=12098&size=A (accessed March 25, 2009).

20. "Interview with Aditiana Dewi Erdani, 2007," http://www .quantara.de/webcom/show_article.php/_c-478/_nr-590/i.html?PHPSESSID=133 099 (accessed January 11, 2009).

21. Ibid.

22. Ibid.

CHAPTER 9: IRAN

1. Massoume Price, "Historically Significant Women in Iran and the Neighbouring Areas," *Payvand's Iran News*, March 3, 2008. http://www.payvand.com/news/08/mar/1093.html (accessed February 6, 2009).

2. Elham Gheytanchi, "Chronology of Events regarding Women in Iran Since the Revolution of 1979," June 22, 2000, http://www.encyclopedia.com/doc/1G1-63787338.html (accessed February 6, 2009).

3. Deepa Kumar, "Hands Off Iran—Why Iranian Women Don't Need Rescuing by the US," *Shahrgon*, April 25, 2008, http://www.shahrgon.com/en/index .php?news=34 (accessed July 30, 2008).

4. Fereshteh Nouraie-Simone, ed., *On Shifting Ground—Muslim Women in the Global Era* (New York: Feminist Press, 2005), p. 218.

5. Massoume Price, "Women's Movement," *Iranian*, March 7, 2000, http://www.iranian.com/History/2000/March/Women/index3.html (accessed July 30, 2008).

6. Ibid.

7. Ibid.

8. Ibid.

9. Ibid.

10. "The Society and Its Environment," *Pars Times*, December 1987, http://www.parstimes.com/history/society _environment.html (accessed February 6, 2009).

11. Gheytanchi, "Chronology of Events regarding Women in Iran Since the Revolution of 1979."

12. Ibid.

13. Article 92 of the *qisas* laws, cited in Haleh Afshar, "Islam and Feminism: An Analysis of Political Strategies," in *Feminism and Islam*, ed. Mai Yamani (Berkshire, UK: Ithaca Press, 1996), p. 201.

14. Article 16, cited in Afshar, "Islam and Feminism," p. 202.

15. Ibid.

16. Article 92, cited in Afshar, "Islam and Feminism," p. 201.

17. Article 6, cited in Afshar, "Islam and Feminism," p. 201.

18. Afshar, "Islam and Feminism," p. 202.

19. Article 60, cited in Afshar, "Islam and Feminism," p. 201.

20. Ibid., p. 203.

21. Ibid., p. 20.

22. "Iran's Hardliners Trying to Curb Women's Rights," *New York Times*, October 26, 2007.

23. "WLUML: What Is Happening to Women in Iran," Feminist Peace Network, April 16, 2008, http://www.feministpeacenetwork.org/2008/04/16/wluml-what-is-happening-to-women-in-iran (accessed February 7, 2009).

24. Ibid.

25. Elaheh Farahani, in Y. Mansharof, "Human Rights in Iran," Memri, September 29, 2006, http://memri.org/bin/articles.cgi?Page=archives&Area=ia&ID=IA29606 (accessed February 7, 2009).

26. Ibid.

27. Nouraie-Simone, ed., *On Shifting Ground*, p. 64.

28. Ibid., p. 65.

29. "Iran Cracks Down on Women's Rights Websites," *Feministing*, May 28, 2008, http://www.feministing.com/archives/009274.html (accessed February 7, 2009).

30. "New Law in Iran: Death Penalty for Online Crimes," *Jerusalem Post*, July 8, 2008, http://www.jpost.com/servlet/Satellite?cid=1215330897449&pagename=JPost/JPArticle/ShowFull (accessed February 7, 2009).

31. "Zanan: A Voice of Women, Silenced," *Los Angeles Times*, January 29, 2008, http://latimesblogs.latimes.com/babylonbeyond/2008/01/zanan-a-voice-o.html (accessed February 7, 2009).

32. Mansharof, "Human Rights in Iran."

33. Ibid.

34. "Iran's Hardliners Try to Curb Women's Rights."

35. Lilli Pourzand, in Mansharof, "Human Rights in Iran."

36. Kumar, "Hands Off Iran."

37. "Iranian Women Activists Get Suspended Lashing Sentences," Reuters, April 22, 2008, http://www.reuters.com/article/worldNews/idUSDAH2258752008 0422?pageNumber=1&virtualBrandChannel=0 (accessed February 7, 2009).

38. "Eight Women Rights Activists Arrested in Today's Gathering in Tehran," Iran Human Rights, June 12, 2008, http://www.iranhr.net/spip.php ?article412 (accessed February 7, 2009).

39. Kumar, "Hands Off Iran."

40. Majid Mohammadi, "Iranian Women Activists: In It to Win It," *Washington Post*, March 15, 2007, http://newsweek.washingtonpost.com/postglobal/need toknow/2007/03/iranian_women_activists_in_it.html (accessed February 7, 2009).

41. Ibid.

42. "Stop Stoning Forever," http://www.meydaan.org/english/aboutcamp .aspx?cid=46 (accessed February 7, 2009).

43. Equality Now, July 2008, http://equalitynow.org/english/actions/action _2902_en.html (accessed February 7, 2009).

44. Ibid.

45. Shabnam Rahmati, "Khatami's Performance in Supporting Women's Rights," *Fekr-e Rooz, Weekly Magazine*, May 25, 2003, pp. 7–8, http://www.parstimes .com/women/ebadi _on_khatami.html (accessed February 7, 2009).

46. "The Systematic Repression of the Women's Rights Movement in Iran," *International Campaign for Human Rights in Iran*, May 5, 2008.

47. Dana Shahsavari, "The High Price of Confronting Women," *Rooz online*, February 18, 2007, http://www.roozonline.com/english/archives/2007/02/the_high _price_of_confronting.html (accessed March 5, 2009).

48. Omid Memarian, "Women's Rights Activists Arrested on the Eve of the International Women's Day," *Rooz online*, March 8, 2007, http://roozonline.com/ english/archives/2007/03/womens_rights_activists_arrest.html (accessed February 7, 2009).

49. Maryam Kashani, "Heavy Convictions for Women Activists," *Rooz online*, April 22, 2007, http://www.roozonline.com/english/archives/2007/04/heavy _convictions_for_women_ac.html (accessed February 7, 2009).

50. Arash Motamed, "Women Activists on Their Way to Prison," *Rooz online*, April 29, 2007, http://www.roozonline.com/english/archives/2007/04/women _activists_on_their_way_t.html (accessed February 7, 2009).

51. "Iran: Human Rights in the Spotlight on the 30th Anniversary of the

Islamic Revolution," Amnesty International USA, February 5, 2009, http://www
.amnestyusa.org/document.php?id=ENGMDE130102009&lang=e (accessed March
19, 2009).

52. "The Systematic Repression of the Women's Rights Movement in Iran."

53. Ibid.

54. Ibid.

55. "Mahboubeh Karami (f), Aged 40, Journalist and Women's Rights
Defender," Shiro Khorshid Forever blogspot, June 27, 2008, http://shiro-khorshid
-forever.blogspot.com/2008/07/mahboubeh-karami-f-aged-40-journalist.html
(accessed March 19, 2009).

56. "Mahboubeh Karami Released on Bail," August 26, 2008, Change for
Equality, http://www.4equality.info/english/spip.php?article331 (accessed March
19, 2009).

57. "Nafiseh Azad, Member of One Million Signatures Campaign Released
after 6 Days Detention," Change for Equality, February 5, 2009, http://www
.4equality.info/english/spip.php?article463 (accessed March 19, 2009).

58. "Do Signature Campaign Activists Belong on Trial?" *Women News Network*, July 21, 2008, http://womennewsnetwork.net/2008/07/21/iran-globalreport
802/ (accessed March 5, 2009).

59. "Parvin Ardalan," *Feminist School*, July 31, 2008, http://femschool
.info/english/spip.php?page=print&id–article=49 (accessed February 7, 2009).

60. "Change for Equality Website Blocked for 18th Time," December 8,
2008, Women's Learning Partnership, http://learningpartnership.org/en/advocacy/
alerts/iranwomenarrests0307 (accessed February 7, 2009).

61. Nader Irani, "Pressures Increase by the Day," *Rooz online*, May 2, 2008,
http://www.roozonline.com/english/archives/2008/05/pressures_increase_by_the
_day.html (accessed February 7, 2009).

62. Najafi's blog, in Farsi, can be found at http://noghtehsarekhat.blogsky
.com. At the top is Voltaire's famous statement: "I do not agree with a word you say,
but I will defend to death your right to say it."

63. Her 2002 film *Zendan-e zanan* (Women's Prison) has received the following commendations: nominated for the Grand Prix at the Bratislava International Film Festival in 2002; nominated for the Grand Prix Asturias for Best Feature
at the Gijón International Film Festival in 2002; nominated for Best Feature Film
at the Hawaii International Film Festival in 2002; recipient of the Ecumenical Jury
Award—Special Mention—at the Fribourg International Film Festival in 2003; and
recipient of the Amnesty International DOEN Award at the Rotterdam International Film Festival in 2003.

64. Her awards include those for Best Screenplay at Iran's Fajr International

Film Festival in 1999; the Grand Prix "Cinéma Tout Ecran" at the Geneva Cinéma Tout Ecran in 2003; and Best Director and Best Film at the 51st Asia–Pacific Film Festival in 2006. See "Tamineh Milani," *Mideast and N. Africa Encyclopedia*, http://www.answers.com/topic/tahmineh-milani (accessed August 10, 2008).

65. "Iranian Film Maker Faces Execution," November 6, 2001, http://www.abc.net.au/rn/arts/atoday/stories/s408223.htm (accessed February 7, 2009).

66. Rick Zand, "Iran Not So Far Away: Women's Rights Activists Won't Be Silenced," *Vermont Woman*, July 2008.

67. Michael Theodoulou, "Victory for Women's Rights as Polygamy Law Is Scrapped," *National* (Abu Dhabi), September 10, 2008.

68. "Iran: Human Rights in the Spotlight."

69. Luke Slattery, "Iranians Aroused to Action," *Australian*, November 22, 2008.

70. Aired on *IRIN News*, August 30 and September 1, 2008, as cited in "Iranian TV Campaign against Western Fashion in Iran," Memri Special Dispatch, no. 2122, November 20, 2008, http://www.memri.org/bin/latestnews.cgi?ID=SD 212208 (accessed March 8, 2009).

71. "Iran: Human Rights in the Spotlight."

72. N. MacFarquhar, "Iranian Blogosphere Tests Government's Limits," *New York Times*, April 6, 2008.

73. Ibid.

74. Fereshteh Nouraie-Simone, ed., *On Shifting Ground—Muslim Women in the Global Era* (New York: Feminist Press at the City University of New York, 2005), p. 77.

75. Blog Herald Blog Count, October 2005: over 100 million blogs created. See http://www.blogherald.com/2005/10/10/the-blog-herald-blog-count-october-2005 (accessed December 4, 2008).

76. "Iran Launches Fresh Crackdown on Websites: Report," AFP, May 20, 2008, http://afp.google.com/article/ALeqM5jgPmlgFydl8ifBE-OLsLXcyQYUgg (accessed March 29, 2009).

77. Ibid.

78. Nick Farrell, "Iran Cracks Down on Websites," *Inquirer*, May 21, 2008, http://www.theinquirer.net/gb/inquirer/news/2008/05/21/iran-crackdown-websites (accessed March 19, 2009).

79. "False Freedom," Human Rights Watch, November 14, 2005, http://www.hrw.org/en/reports/2005/11/14/false-freedom?print (accessed March 19, 2009).

80. Ibid.

81. Ibid.

82. Ibid.

83. Ibid.

84. Mona Shahabi, "Passdaran's Journal Warn[s] and Courts Continue Trials of Web Bloggers," *Rooz online*, July 23, 2007, http://www.roozonline.com/english/archives/2007/07/passdarans_journal_warn_and_co.html (accessed March 19, 2009).

85. Shahram Rafizadeh, "Passdaran Warns about a Velvet Internet Revolution," *Rooz online*, November 23, 2008, http://www.roozonline.com/english/archives/2008/11/passdaran_warns_about_a_velvet.html (accessed December 4, 2008).

86. Shahram Rafizadeh, "The Internet Is a Rabid Dog," *Rooz online*, November 2, 2008, http://www.roozonline.com/english/archives/2008/11/the_internet_is_a_rabid_dog.html (accessed December 4, 2008).

87. "I Am Worried about My Mother," *Rooz online*, March 18, 2007, http://www.roozonline.com/english/archives/2007/03/i_am_worried_about_my_mother.html (accessed January 12, 2009).

88. Vicki Chan, "Iran's Bid to Blot Out Bloggers," http://www.bard.edu/bgia/bardpolitik/vol6/09iran_bloggers.pdf (accessed January 12, 2009).

89. Nazila Fathi, "Iran Jails More Journalists and Blocks Web Sites," *New York Times*, November 8, 2004, http://www.nytimes.com/2004/11/08/international/middleeast/08iran.html?_r=1&page&oref=slogin (accessed January 12, 2009).

90. Human Rights Watch, "Iran: Journalists Receive Death Threats after Testifying Presidential Commission Heard Their Testimony of Torture during Detention," http://www.wsisasia.org/ml/communication/200501.month/1246.html (accessed January 12, 2009).

91. "I Am Worried about My Mother."

92. "Regime Trying to Create Iran-only Internet System," December 2004, http://www.pezhvak.com/Pezhvakm/162/pezh162b_42.pdf (accessed January 12, 2009).

93. Chan, "Iran's Bid to Blot Out Bloggers."

94. "Iran: Civil Society Activists and Human Rights Defenders under Attack," Amnesty International Press Release, November 10, 2004, http://web.amnesty.org/library/Index/ENGMDE130392004?open&of=ENG-IRN (accessed January 12, 2009).

95. "Hana Abdi Sentenced to Serve 5 Years Prison Term in Another Province," June 19, 2008, http://www.change4equality.net/english/spip.php?article294 (accessed January 12, 2009).

96. "Flogging and Imprisonment for Nasrin Afzali," *Rooz online*, April 20, 2008, http://www.roozonline.com/english/archives/2008/04/flogging_and_imprisonment_for.html (accessed January 12, 2009).

97. Ironically, *azadi* translates as "freedom" in English.

98. "Woman's Share Is Half of the FREEDOM in Iranian Soccer Stadiums," Inside Iran, June 5, 2006, http://jadi.civiblog.org/blog/_archives/2006/6/5/2006 540.html (accessed March 19, 2009). The blogger, a young Iranian man, apologizes for his inadequate English, but as his Web log is filtered within Iran, he cannot write in his native Farsi about freedom of expression, censorship, and Internet filtering.

99. Laura-Julie Perreault, "Iran: For Feminists in Iran, Freedom Is a Soccer Game," Women Living under Muslim Laws, March 4, 2008, http://translate.google .com/translate?hl=en&sl=fr&u=http://www.wluml.org/french/newsfulltxt .shtml%3Fcmd%255B157%255D%3Dx-157-561212&sa=X&oi=translate &resnum=1&ct=result&prev=/search%3Fq%3DWLUML%2Bafzali%2Bsoccer %26hl%3Den%26rlz%3D1T4GGLG_en___AU273 (accessed March 19, 2009). Web page originally written in French.

100. "Iran: Human Rights Groups Protest Imminent Imprisonment of Delaram Ali," Women Living under Muslim Laws, November 10, 2007, http://www.wluml .org/english/actionsfulltxt.shtml?cmd%5B156%5D=i-156-558421 (accessed January 13, 2009).

101. Maryam Kashani, "You Oppose Women's Rights, Admit It," *Rooz online*, November 14, 2007, http://www.roozonline.com/english/archives/2007/11/you _oppose_womens_rights.html (accessed January 13, 2009).

102. "Iran 'Must Free' Woman Activist," *BBC News*, November 10, 2007, http://news.bbc.co.uk/2/hi/middle_east/7088310.stm (accessed January 13, 2009).

103. "Women Will Not Be Silenced. Delaram Ali in Interview with Rooz," *Rooz online*, November 14, 2007, http://www.roozonline.com/english/archives/ 2007/11/women_will_not_be_silenced.html (accessed January 13, 2009).

104. Fariba Amini, "Interview with Noushabeh Amiri: The Horizon Looks Bright," October 17, 2007, http://www.concernedjournalists.org/horizon-looks -bright-iranian-journalist-looks-future (accessed July 22, 2008).

105. Ibid.

106. Noushabeh Amiri, "Mr. President: Learn from This 'Young Man'!" *Rooz online*, January 15, 2008, http://www.roozonline.com/english/archives/2008/01/mr _president_learn_from_this_y.html.

107. "Iran: Text of Parvin Ardalan's Speech," WLUML, March 26, 2008, http://www.wluml.org/english/newsfulltxt.shtml?cmd[157]=x-157-561112 (accessed March 19, 2009).

108. "Slamming Its Doors on the World," *Time*, January 15, 2006, http:// www.time.com/time/magazine/article/0,9171,1149388,00 .html (accessed January 17, 2009).

109. Shirin Karimi, "Parvin Ardalan Wins Prestigious Olof Palme Prize," *Rooz*

online, February 17, 2008, http://www.roozonline.com/english/archives/2008/02/parvin_ardalan_wins_prestigiou.html (accessed March 19, 2009).

110. Mahsa Shekarloo, "Iranian Women Take On the Constitution," *Middle East Report Online*, July 21, 2005, http://www.merip.org/mero/mero072105.html (accessed January 17, 2009).

111. See Change for Equality, http://www.change4equality.com/english/ (accessed March 19, 2009).

112. Farangis Najibullah, "Iran: Women's Activist Wins Human Rights Award," Radio Free Europe, February 14, 2008, http://archive.rferl.org/reports/Full Report.aspx?report=571&id=2008/02/571-11-04 (accessed January 17, 2009).

113. "Iran Women Arrested over Protest," *BBC News*, March 4, 2007, http://news.bbc.co.uk/1/hi/world/middle_east/6416789.stm (accessed March 19, 2009).

114. Ibid.

115. "Iran: Text of Parvin Ardalan's Speech."

116. Ibid.

117. Ibid.

118. Ibid.

119. Ibid.

120. Homa Arjomand, "A Meeting to Discuss Shari'a Court in Ontario," http://www.butterfliesandwheels.com/articleprint.php?num=66 (accessed March 28, 2009).

121. Homa Arjomand, speech at METRAC (Metropolitan Action Committee on Violence against Women and Children), "Emerging Issues in Women's Equality—A Look at Shari'ah Law," October 28, 2004, http://www.nosharia.com/sp-homa-metrac-28-10-2004.htm (accessed March 28, 2009).

122. International Campaign against Shari'a Court in Canada, http://www.nosharia.com (accessed March 28, 2009).

123. Arjomand, speech at METRAC, "Emerging Issues in Women's Equality."

124. Jamie Glazov, "Protecting Women and Children from Shari'ah," *FrontPageMagazine.com*, January 2, 2008, http://www.frontpagemag.com/Articles/Read.aspx?GUID=355fb5f0-65ca-4bfc-9a4f-59cfc3031e09 (accessed January 19, 2009).

125. Lynda Hurst, "Ontario Shari'ah Tribunals Assailed," *Toronto Star*, May 22, 2004.

126. Review of Ontario's Arbitration Process and Arbitration Act, Canadian Council on American-Islamic Relations (CAIR-CAN), August 10, 2004, http://www.caircan.ca/downloads/sst-10082004.pdf (accessed January 20, 2009).

127. Arjomand, speech at METRAC, "Emerging Issues in Women's Equality."

128. "Indepth: Islam, Shariah Law: FAQs," *CBC News Online*, May 26, 2005, http://www.cbc.ca/news/background/islam/shariah-law.html (accessed March 28, 2009).

129. Glazov, "Protecting Women and Children from Shari'ah."

130. "Indepth: Islam, Shariah Law: FAQs."

131. Arjomand, "A Meeting to Discuss Shari'a Court in Ontario."

132. "Implementation of the Shari'ah Law in Canada," adapted from a speech given by Homa Arjomand at the Humanist Association of Ottawa on April 16, 2004, Ottawa, Canada, http://www.nosharia.com (accessed January 21, 2009).

133. Ibid.

134. Ibid.

135. Arjomand, "A Meeting to Discuss Shari'a Court in Ontario."

136. Glazov, "Protecting Women and Children From Shari'ah."

137. Ibid.

138. Arjomand, speech at METRAC, "Emerging Issues in Women's Equality."

139. Keith Leslie, "McGuinty Rejects Ontario's Use of Shari'ah Law and All Religious Arbitrations," *Canadian Press*, September 11, 2005.

140. "Never Forget Hatun! Campaign against Honour Killing," speech by Homa Arjomand on International Women's Day, March 8, 2006, http://www.islam -watch.org/HomaArjomand/HomaIWD06.htm (accessed March 28, 2009).

141. Homa Arjomand, "8 March Centennial against Political Islam for Secularism in Solidarity with Imprisoned Iranian Activists," speech given in Sweden, March 8, 2008, http://www.nosharia.com/Homa%20Arjomand.htm (accessed March 28, 2009).

142. Glazov, "Protecting Women and Children from Shari'ah."

143. "Journalist Facing Prison," *International Herald Tribune*, March 6, 2008, http://www.wifp.org/fundamentalism.html#anchor5337829 (accessed March 19, 2009).

144. Jeffrey Gedmin, "Voice That Tehran Fears," *Washington Post*, September 19, 2007, http://www.washingtonpost.com/wp-dyn/content/article/2007/09/18/ AR2007091801570.html (accessed March 19, 2009).

145. "Journalist Facing Prison."

146. Ibid.

147. Gedmin, "Voice That Tehran Fears."

148. Ibid.

149. Hashemi Rafsanjani, chairman of the Assembly of Experts and the Expediency Council of Iran, president of the Islamic Republic of Iran from 1989 to 1997, quoted in Parvin Darabi, "Iran's International Human Rights Obligations," July 11, 2008, http://www.homa.org/index.php?option=com_content&view=article&id =100&Itemid=57 (accessed January 17, 2009).

150. See http://www.homa.org (accessed January 17, 2009).

151. Parvin Darabi, "Establishment of the Islamic Republic in Iran and the

Present Situation for Women," http://www.homa.org/index.php?option=com_content&view=article&id=103&Itemid=57 (accessed January 17, 2009).

152. Parvin Darabi, "I Am a Moslem Woman," July 11, 2008, http://www.homa.org/index.php?option=com_content&view=article&id=64&Itemid=55 (accessed March 19, 2009).

153. Ibid.

154. Parvin Darabi, "Women and Islam," July 11, 2008, http://www.homa.org/index.php?option=com_content&view=article&id=63&Itemid=55 (accessed January 17, 2009).

155. The Iranian government not only enforces compulsory veiling but tells women and girls what color they can wear, only dark colors being acceptable. Dr. Homa Darabi's refusal to wear the chador, and the harassment she faced as a result, contributed to her suicide. Before her death, she would argue that the "Hejab Is Not a Woman's Dignity, It Is Woman's Slavery." Parvin Darabi, "Iran's International Human Rights Obligations," July 11, 2008, http://www.homa.org/index.php?option=com_content&view=article&id=100&Itemid=57 (accessed January 17, 2009).

156. Darabi, "I Am a Moslem Woman."

157. Ibid.

158. Ibid.

159. Ibid.

160. Parvin Darabi, "An Open Letter to Christiane Amanpour, 'Iranian Women Better Off Today? Are They?" January 29, 2009, http://www.rozanehmagazine.com/allarticles/AmanpourChristine.htm (accessed January 30, 2009).

161. Interview by *Al-Ahram Weekly*, cited in "Iranian Nobel Peace Laureate Shirin Ebadi Criticizes Iran's Regime," Memri Special Dispatch Series, no. 942, July 26, 2005, http://memri.org/bin/articles.cgi?Page=archives&Area=sd&ID=SP94205 (accessed February 20, 2009).

162. "Iran Nobel Peace Prize Winner," www.answers.com/topic/shirin-ebadi (accessed February 20, 2009).

163. Amir Taheri interview, *Al-Sharq Al-Awsat* (London), October 19, 2003, in "Shirin Ebadi—Iranian Nobel Peace Prize Laureate," Memri Special Dispatch Series, no. 596, October 24, 2003, http://memri.org/bin/articles.cgi?Page=archives&Area=sd&ID=SP59603 (accessed February 20, 2009).

164. Ibid.

165. "Women and Power in Central Asia (Part 4): Roundtable on the Tajik, Afghan, and Iranian Experiences," Radio Free Europe, December 29, 2005, http://www.rferl.org/featuresarticle/2005/12/73d843ae-2271-44d3-a907-cbdb6b252ecd.html (accessed February 20, 2009).

166. Nouraie-Simone, ed., *On Shifting Ground*, p. 267.

167. Mustafa El-Labbad interview, "Ask the People," *Al-Ahram Weekly*, June 30–July 6, 2005, issue no. 749.

168. Nouraie-Simone, ed., *On Shifting Ground*, p. 267.

169. Shahram Rafizadeh, "Hardliner Media Attack Nobel Laureate," *Rooz online*, January 6, 2008, http://www.roozonline.com/english/archives/2008/01/hard liner_media_attack_nobel_l.html (accessed March 19, 2009). After the Islamic Revolution, *Kayhan* became a tool of the theocratic government.

170. "Shirin Ebadi—Iranian Nobel Peace Prize Laureate."

171. "Shirin Ebadi to Take On Authorities over Sivand Dam," *Rooz online*, April 18, 2007, http://www.roozonline.com/english/archives/2007/04/shirin_ebadi _to_take_on_author.html (accessed March 19, 2009).

172. "Shirin Ebadi—Iranian Nobel Peace Prize Laureate."

173. Ibid.

174. Nouraie-Simone, ed., *On Shifting Ground*, p. 269.

175. Mustafa El-Labbad interview, "Ask the People."

176. Nouraie-Simone, ed., *On Shifting Ground*, p. 278.

177. Mustafa El-Labbad interview, "Ask the People."

178. "Shirin Ebadi—Iranian Nobel Peace Prize Laureate."

179. "Dual Legitimacy," *Rooz online*, http://www.roozonline.com/english/ archives/2007/12/dual_legitimacy.html (accessed February 20, 2009).

180. Ibid.

181. "Shirin Ebadi—Iranian Nobel Peace Prize Laureate."

182. Nouraie-Simone, ed., *On Shifting Ground*, p. 269.

183. Mustafa El-Labbad interview, "Ask the People."

184. Nouraie-Simone, ed., *On Shifting Ground*, p. 271.

185. Ibid.

186. Mustafa El-Labbad interview, "Ask the People."

187. Roozbeh Mirebrahimi, "Our Children Have Been Tortured," *Rooz online*, August 22, 2007, http://www.roozonline.com/english/archives/2007/08/our _children _have_been_torture.html (accessed February 20, 2009).

188. Arash Bahmani, "Shirin Ebadi: Freedom of Speech Is Our Right as Well," *Rooz online*, February 26, 2006, http://www.roozonline.com/english/archives/2007/ 02/shirin_ebadi_freedom_of_speech.html (accessed February 20, 2009).

189. Ibid.

190. Maryam Kashani, "You Oppose Women's Rights," *Rooz online*, November 4, 2007, http://www.roozonline.com/english/archives/2007/11/you_oppose _womens_rights.html (accessed March 19, 2009).

191. Shirin Ebadi, "Bravo for This Logic!" *Rooz online*, December 6, 2007, http://www.roozonline.com/english/archives/2007/12/bravo_for_this_logic.html (accessed March 19, 2009).

192. Ibid.

193. Mustafa El-Labbad interview, "Ask the People."

194. Rafizadeh, "Hardliner Media Attack Nobel Laureate."

195. Mustafa El-Labbad interview, "Ask the People."

196. Mehrangiz Kar, "Shirin Ebadi Is in Danger, "September 12, 2008, *Rooz online*, http://www.roozonline.com/english/archives/2008/09/shirin_ebadi_is_in _danger.html (accessed February 20, 2009).

197. Ali Akbar Dareini, "Iran Shuts Office of Nobel Winner's Rights Group," December 22, 2008, http://www.iranpresswatch.org/2008/12/iran-shuts-office-of -nobel-winners-rights-group/?referer=sphere_search (accessed February 20, 2009).

198. Haleh Esfandiari, "Held in My Homeland," *Washington Post*, September 16, 2007.

199. Ibid.

200. Haleh Esfandiari, "Iranian Women Please Stand Up," *Foreign Policy*, November/December 2005, http://www.foreignpolicy.com/users/login.php?story _id=3298&URL=http://www.foreignpolicy.com/story/cms.php?story_id=3298 (accessed March 2009).

201. Woodrow Wilson International Center for Scholars, May 21, 2007, http:// www.wilsoncenter.org/index.cfm?fuseaction=news.item&news_id=236704 (accessed August 13, 2008).

202. Esfandiari, "Held in My Homeland."

203. Memarian, "Imprisoned Haleh Esfandiari Not Well," *Rooz online*, August 22, 2007, http://www.roozonline.com/english/archives/2007/08/imprisoned_haleh _esfandiari_no.hml (accessed January 28, 2009).

204. Esfandiari, "Held in My Homeland."

205. Haleh Esfandiari and Robert S. Litwak, "When Promoting Democracy Is Counterproductive," *Chronicle of Higher Education*, October 19, 2007, http:// chronicle.com/free/v54/i08/08b00701.htm (accessed March 20, 2009).

206. Azam Kamguian, "The Silent Holocaust: Why Humanity Must Achieve Victory over Islam," http://www.islam-watch.org/Azam_Kamguian/Silent -Holocaust-Islam.htm (accessed March 21, 2009).

207. Azam Kamguian, Medusa Conference, 2003, http://www.rowzane .com/000_etelayeha/2310/231030Medusa_English.pdf (accessed March 21, 2009).

208. Azam Kamguian, "We Need to Fight the Battle for Enlightenment," http://www.butterfliesandwheels.com/articleprint.php?num=124 (accessed March 21, 2009).

209. Kamguian, Medusa Conference, 2003.

210. Kamguian, "The Silent Holocaust."

211. Kamguian, Medusa Conference, 2003.

212. Ibid.

213. Ibid.

214. Ibid.

215. Azam Kamguian, "Iran Lies on an Anti-Islamic Bomb: The Rise of a Massive Secularist Movement," International Humanist and Ethical Union, http://www.iheu.org/node/1692 (accessed January 20, 2009).

216. Ibid.

217. Ibid.

218. Kamguian, "The Silent Holocaust."

219. Azam Kamguian, "Islam and the Liberation of Women in the Middle East," http://www.islam-watch.org/Azam_Kamguian/Islam-Liberation-Women-in-Middle-East.htm (accessed March 21, 2009).

220. Kamguian, "The Silent Holocaust."

221. Ibid.

222. Kamguian, "Islam and the Liberation of Women in the Middle East."

223. Kamguian, "Iran Lies on an Anti-Islamic Bomb."

224. CDWRME, ISIS, Center for Inquiry, http://www.centerforinquiry.net/isis/islamic_viewpoints/cdwrme_bulletin_5.

225. Mehrangiz Kar, interview with IranDokht, www.irandokht.com/TV/TVmore.php?PID=22 (accessed January 29, 2009).

226. "Mehrangiz Kar," www.mehrangizkar.net (accessed March 21, 2009).

227. Ibid.

228. "Mehrangiz Kar Speaks on Nobel Laureate Shirin Ebadi," UCLA International Institute, http://www.international.ucla.edu/article.asp?parentid=5537 (accessed January 29, 2009).

229. Ibid.

230. Sam Fayyaz, "Kar: The Mother of Democracy Is Freedom of Expression," National Iranian American Council, November 21, 2007, http://www.niacouncil.org/index.php?option=com_content&task=view&id=956&Itemid=2 (accessed January 29, 2009).

231. "Mehrangiz Kar Speaks on Nobel Laureate Shirin Ebadi."

232. Mehrangiz Kar, interview with IranDokht.

233. "Mehrangiz Kar," www.mehrangizkar.net.

234. Mehrangiz Kar, interview with IranDokht.

235. "Mehrangiz Kar," www.mehrangizkar.net.

236. "Attempts to Persecute Human Rights Defender Mehrangiz Kar by Silencing Her Husband," Women's Learning Partnership, May 10, 2002, www.learningpartnership.org/en/advocacy/alerts/iran0502 (accessed January 29, 2009).

237. "Siamak Pourzand: A Case Study of Flagrant Human Rights Violations,"

May 14, 2004, www.payvand.com/news/04/may/1090.html (accessed January 29, 2009).

238. "Mehrangiz Kar," www.mehrangizkar.net.

239. "Attempts to Persecute Human Rights Defender Mehrangiz Kar by Silencing Her Husband."

240. Ibid.

241. "Siamak Pourzand: A Case Study of Flagrant Human Rights Violations."

242. "Attempts to Persecute Human Rights Defender Mehrangiz Kar by Silencing Her Husband."

243. "Reporters without Borders Outraged at Siamak Pourzand's Treatment in Hospital," Reporters without Borders, April 20, 2004, http://www.rsf.org/print .php3?id_article=9821 (accessed January 29, 2009).

244. "Attempts to Persecute Human Rights Defender Mehrangiz Kar by Silencing Her Husband."

245. "Mehrangiz Kar," http://www.mehrangizkar.net.

246. Ken Gewertz, "Mehrangiz Kar Speaks Truth to Power," *Harvard University Gazette*, http://www.hno.harvard.edu/gazette/2005/04.07/09-kar.html (accessed January 29, 2009).

247. "Iranian Women's Rights Defenders, Mahboubeh Hossein Zadeh and Nahid Keshavarz Remain in Prison," *Payvand News of Iran*, April 16, 2007, http:// www.payvand.com/news/07/apr/1165.html (accessed January 29, 2009).

248. "Arbitrary Arrest of WHRDs in Iran (Ms Nahid Keshavarz and Ms Mahboubeh Hosseinzadeh)," April 5, 2007, http://www.defendingwomen-defending rights.org/iran_arbitraty_arrest.php (accessed January 29, 2009).

249. Ibid.

250. Azar Majedi, "Sexual Apartheid Is the Product of Political Islam: Let's Rise against It!" *Medusa Journal of the Center for Women and Socialism*, http://www .medusa2000.com/englishindex.htm (accessed January 20, 2009).

251. Organization for Women's Liberation—Iran, http://www.womens liberation.net/english (accessed January 20, 2009).

252. Soheila Sharifi, "Portrait of a Leader, Mansoor Hikmat," *Medusa, Journal of the Center for Women and Socialism*, http://www.medusa2000.com/englishindex.htm (accessed January 20, 2009).

253. Azar Majedi, "Biography," http://www.azarmajedi.com (accessed January 20, 2009).

254. Azar Majedi, "What Is Apartheid," www.azarmajedi.com/articles/what %20is%20aparthied.html (accessed January 20, 2009).

255. Azar Majedi, in an interview with Safa Haeri of the Iranian Press Service (IPS), http://www.azarmajedi.com/articles/safa%20haeri.html (accessed January 20, 2009).

256. Ibid.

257. Ibid.

258. Azar Majedi, "Women's Liberation in Iran Today: Preconditions and Obstacles," http://www.azarmajedi.com/articles/Women%27s%20liberation%20in %20Iran.html (accessed March 21, 2009).

259. Azar Majedi, interview with Safa Haeri of the Iranian Press Service (IPS).

260. Azar Majedi, interview with Jamie Glazov, *Front Page Magazine*, January 10, 2008, http://frontpagemag.com/Articles/Read.aspx?GUID=1598104E-1586 -4CEF-9A11-4E12FEE429AD (accessed January 20, 2009).

261. *Medusa, Journal of the Center for Women and Socialism*, http://www.medusa 2000.com/englishindex.htm (accessed January 20, 2009).

262. "Report of Conference on Secularism," *Iran Tribune*, March 20, 2009, http://www.iran-tribune.com/200903202136/Report-of-Conference-on -Secularism.shtml (accessed March 21, 2009).

263. Organization for Women's Liberation—Iran.

264. Ziba Mir-Hosseini, "Iran: Nationalism, Liberation and the Alliance between 'Fundamentalists' and Government Opposition," http://www.awid.org/eng/ (accessed January 28, 2009).

265. Ziba Mir-Hosseini, "The Voice of Feminism, Iranian Style," http://www .culturebase.net/artist.php?3792 (accessed January 28, 2009).

266. Mir-Hosseini, "Iran: Nationalism, Liberation."

267. Mir-Hosseini, "The Voice of Feminism, Iranian Style."

268. Ziba Mir-Hosseini, *Marriage on Trial: A Study of Family Law in Iran and Morocco* (London: I. B. Tauris, 1993, 2002), http://www.uib.no/hff/smi/seminars/ ZIBA%20MIR.pdf (accessed January 28, 2009).

269. "Women Make Movies," http://www.wmm.com/filmCatalog/makers/ fm406.shtml (accessed January 28, 2009).

270. Ibid.

271. Hasan Yousefi Eshkevari, Ziba Mir-Hosseini, and Richard Tapper, *Islam and Democracy in Iran: Eshkevari and the Quest for Reform* (London: I. B. Tauris, 2006).

272. "Women Make Movies: Ziba Mir-Hosseini," http://www.wmm.com/ filmCatalog/makers/fm406.shtml (accessed January 28, 2009).

273. Ziba Mir-Hosseini, "Religious Modernists and the 'Woman Question': Challenges and Complicities," in Eric Hooglund, ed., *Twenty Years of Islamic Revolution: Political and Social Transition in Iran since 1979* (Syracuse, NY: Syracuse University Press, 2002), pp. 74–95.

274. Joy Smith, "Ziba Mir-Hosseini," http://www.debalie.nl/dossierartikel.jsp ?dossierid=32516&articleid=39256 (accessed January 28, 2009).

275. Mir-Hosseini, "Religious Modernists and the 'Woman Question,'" pp. 74–95.

276. Mir-Hosseini, "The Voice of Feminism, Iranian Style."

277. Sabrina Tavernise, "In Quest for Equal Rights, Muslim Women's Meeting Turns to Islam's Tenets," *New York Times*, February 16, 2009.

278. Ibid.

279. "David Brancaccio Interviews Azar Nafisi," PBS transcript, June 20, 2003, http://www.pbs.org/now/transcript/transcript_nafisi.html (accessed January 29, 2009).

280. "VG: Artist Biography: Nafisi, Azar," http://voices.cla.umn.edu/vg/Bios/entries/nafisi_azar.html (accessed January 29, 2009).

281. Julie Salamon, "Professor's Rebellion: Teaching Western Books in Iran, and in U.S., Too," *New York Times*, March 24, 2003, http://query.nytimes.com/gst/fullpage.html?res=9E0CE5D61730F937A15750C0A9659C8B63 (accessed January 29, 2009).

282. Ibid.

283. "David Brancaccio Interviews Azar Nafisi."

284. "VG: Artist Biography: Nafisi, Azar."

285. "David Brancaccio Interviews Azar Nafisi."

286. Ibid.

287. Azar Nafisi, *Reading* Lolita *in Tehran: A Memoir in Books* (New York: Random House, 2003).

288. Ibid., p. 26.

289. "Azar Nafisi," Stephen Barclay Agency, http://www.barclayagency.com/nafisi.html (accessed January 29, 2009).

290. Richard Byrne, "A Collision of Prose and Politics," *Chronicle of Higher Education*, October 13, 2006, http://www.campus-watch.org/article/id/2796 (accessed July 13, 2008).

291. Hamid Dabashi, "Native Informers and the Making of the American Empire," *Al-Ahram Weekly*, June 1, 2006, http://weekly.ahram.org.eg/2006/797/special.htm (accessed March 21, 2009).

292. Ibid.

293. Byrne, "Collision of Prose and Politics."

294. "Azar Nafisi," SourceWatch, http://www.sourcewatch.org/index.php?title=Azar_Nafisi (accessed March 21, 2009).

295. "NSS Supports the Launch of the Ex-Muslim Council of Britain," http://www.secularism.org.uk/83138.html (accessed January 30, 2009).

296. Maryam Namazie, "Islam Must Be Criticized," February 7, 2006, http://maryamnamazie.blogspot.com/2006_02_01_archive.html (accessed January 30, 2009).

297. Juliet Rix, "It's Time to Take a Stand against Islam and Sharia," March

12, 2008, *Times* (London), http://women.timesonline.co.uk/tol/life_and_style/women/the_way_we_live/article3530256.ece?print=yes&randnum=1214875007 991 (accessed January 30, 2009).

298. Ibid.

299. Nick Cohen, "One Woman's War," *Observer* (London), October 16, 2005, http://www.guardian.co.uk/world/2005/oct/16/gender.observercolumnists (accessed January 30, 2009).

300. Hambastegi International Federation of Iranian Refugees, http://www.hambastegi.org/english/index_new.htm (accessed January 30, 2009).

301. Keith Porteus Wood, "Maryam Namazie Secularist of the Year Award," http://www.butterfliesandwheels.com/articleprint.php?num=152 (accessed January 30, 2009).

302. "NSS Supports the Launch of the Ex-Muslim Council of Britain."

303. See http://maryamnamazie.blogspot.com/2006/03/manifesto-together-facing-new_01.html (accessed January 30, 2009).

304. Jonathan Petre, "New Group for Those Who Renounce Islam," *Telegraph* (London), June 21, 2007, http://www.telegraph.co.uk/news/worldnews/1555263/New-group-for-those-who-renounce-Islam.html (accessed January 30, 2009). Reprinted with permission from *Daily Telegraph/Sunday Telegraph*.

305 Namazie, "Islam Must Be Criticized."

306. Rix, "It's Time to Take a Stand against Islam and Sharia."

307. Worker-Communist Party of Iran (WPI), http://www.wpiran.org/English/english.htm (accessed January 30, 2009).

308. See http://www.thirdcamp.com/php/amanifest.php (accessed January 30, 2009).

309. *Rooz online*, June 14, 2006, cited in Y. Mansharof, "Human Rights in Iran (1): Women's Struggle against Discrimination by the Regime," Memri Inquiry and Analysis Series, no. 296, September 29, 2006, http://www.memri.org/bin/articles.cgi?Page=archives&Area=ia&ID=IA29606 (accessed March 7, 2009).

310. Ibid.

311. Ibid.

312. Ibid.

313. "Women's Rights and Women's Lives in Iran," *VOA News*, September 5, 2004, http://www.parstimes.com/news/archive/2004/voa/women_rights.html (accessed January, 2009).

314. Ibid.

315. "Biography, a Glimpse at the Life of Maryam Rajavi," http://www.maryam-rajavi.com (accessed March 7, 2009).

316. Ibid.

317. "Plan for Freedoms and Rights of Iranian Women," National Council of

Resistance of Iran (NCRI), http://ncr-iran.org/content/view/29 (accessed March 7, 2009).

318. The PMOI, also known as Mujahedin-e Khalq (MEK) or Mujahedin Khalq Organization (MKO), is the largest of the groups that make up the NCRI coalition. See http://www.scribd.com/doc/2314510/Peoples-Mojahedin-of-Iran -PMOI-Mission-Report (accessed January 30, 2009).

319. Achrene Sicakyuz and Borzou Daragahi, "EU Removes Iranian Group from Terrorism List," *Los Angeles Times*, January 27, 2009.

320. Ibid.

321. Ibid.

322. Daniel Pipes, "Will Washington Betray Anti-Regime Iranians?" *Catholic Exchange*, July 18, 2008.

323. Sicakyuz and Daragahi, "EU Removes Iranian Group from Terrorism List."

324. "Speech by Mrs. Maryam Rajavi, President-Elect of the Iranian Resistance," April 24, 2008, http://www.iran.mojahedin.org/pagesen/detailsNews.aspx ?newsid=2214 (accessed January 30, 2009).

325. Ibid.

326. "A Brief Biography of Maryam Rajavi," http://www.iran-e-azad.org/ english/maryam/biography.html.

327. Margaret Coker, "Life for Women in Iran Beset by Fate, Culture," May 16, 2007, *Washington Times*, http://www.iranfocus.com/en/index.php?option=com _content&task=view&id=11268 (accessed March 21, 2009).

328. "Women Newsmakers, Rita Henley Jensen and Shadi Sadr Interview," *Women's eNews*, May 19, 2004, http://www.washingtonpost.com/wp-dyn/articles/ A18283-2004May11.html (accessed January 30, 2009).

329. Carline Bennett, "Seven Who Create New Pathways for Success," *Women's eNews*, December 23, 2003, http://womensenews.org/article.cfm/dyn/aid/1639 (accessed January 30, 2009).

330. Meydaan (Women's Field) Web site, http://www.meydaan.org/english/ default.aspx (access blocked August 18, 2008; accessed January 30 and March 21, 2009).

331. "Iran Launches Fresh Crackdown on Websites: Report," *Age* (Melbourne), May 20, 2008, http://news.theage.com.au/technology/iran-launches-fresh -crackdown-on-websites-report-20080520-2giq.html (accessed January 30, 2009).

332. "Two NGO Offices Have Been Closed," Iran Watch Canada, March 16, 2007, http://moriab.blogspot.com/2007/03/news-in-brief-march-16-07-two-ngo .html (accessed January 30, 2009).

333. Coker, "Life for Women in Iran Beset by Fate, Culture."

334. Deborah Campbell, "Iran's Feminists," March 29, 2007, http://thetyee .ca/News/2007/03/29/IransFeminists (accessed January 30, 2009).

335. "Shadi Sadr Describes Iranian Women's Movement," *Women's eNews*, May 24, 2004, http://www.womensenews.org/article.cfm/dyn/aid/1433 (accessed January 30, 2009).

336. Ibid.

337. Soheila Vahdati, "Stop Stonings in Iran, but Don't Confuse the Issue," *Women's eNews*, January 4, 2007, http://www.womensenews.org/article.cfm/dyn/ aid/3021 (accessed March 21, 2009).

338. Ibid.

339. "A Growing Number of Iranian Women Are Being Prepared to Be Executed by Public Stoning," trans. Lily Mazahery, July 26, 2006, http://www.gather .com/viewArticle.jsp?articleId=281474976769970 (accessed January 30, 2009).

340. Ibid.

341. "International Pressure Saves Mother from Death by Stoning," http:// www.amnesty.org.au/adp/comments/19272 (accessed January 30, 2009).

342. "The Systematic Repression of the Women's Rights Movement in Iran," http://www.iranhumanrights.org/themes/womens-rights.html (accessed January 30, 2009).

343. "Stoning Execution Halted," *Rooz online*, June 25, 2007, http://www .roozonline.com/english/archives/2007/06/stoning_execution_halted.html (accessed January 30, 2009).

344. "We Are Not Ashamed of Stoning," September 30, 2007, ISNA/ Women's Field, http://www.isna.ir/Main/NewsView.aspx?ID=News-1004107 &Lang=P (accessed August 18, 2008, but blocked January 30 and March 21, 2009), http://www.meydaan.com/English/showarticle.aspx?arid=373.

345. Ibid.

346. "Authorities Free Two Feminist Journalists but Close Their NGO's," Reporters without Borders, March 23, 2007, http://www.rsf.org/article.php3?id _article=212369 (accessed January 30, 2009).

347. Campbell, "Iran's Feminists."

348. Hossein Derakhshan, "Iran Awakening," *Guardian* (UK), March 16, 2007, http://www.guardian.co.uk/commentisfree/2007/mar/16/iranawakening (accessed January 30, 2009).

349. "Iran: Flogging and Prison Sentences for Women's Rights Activists," WLUML, April 22, 2008, http://www.wluml.org/english/newsfulltxt.shtml ?cmd[157]=x-157-561451 (accessed January 30, 2009).

350. Arian Fariborz, "Interview with Mahsa Shekarloo—Iranian Feminism Online," June 5, 2003, http://www.qantara.de/webcom/show_article.php/_c-307/ _nr-13/_p-1/i.html (accessed January 31, 2009).

351. Ibid.

352. Mahsa Shekarloo, "Of Numbers Greater Than Nineteen," *Bad Jens*, May 22, 2002, http://www.badjens.com/fifthedition/ofnumbers.htm (accessed January 31, 2009).

353. Ibid.

354. Ibid.

355. Mahsa Shekarloo, "Iranian Women Take on the Constitution," *Middle East Report Online*, July 21, 2005, http://www.merip.org/mero/mero072105.html (accessed January 31, 2009).

356. Ibid.

357. Ibid.

358. Maura Casey, "Editor of Feisty Iranian Magazine Faces Prison," *Women's eNews*, February 27, 2001, http://www.womensenews.org/article.cfm?aid=462 (accessed January 31, 2009).

359. "A Feminist among Iran's Fundamentalists," International Women's Media Foundation, http://www.iwmf.org/article.aspx?id=383&c=carticles (accessed January 31, 2009).

360. Ibid.

361. Amal Hamada, *"Zanan*: An Iranian Reformist Women's Magazine," http://www.islamonline.net (accessed January 31, 2009).

362. Casey, "Editor of Feisty Iranian Magazine Faces Prison."

363. "A Feminist among Iran's Fundamentalists."

364. Grace Davies, "Iranian Feminist Magazine under Threat," May 2, 2008, http://www.opendemocracy.net/blog/grace_davies/iranian_feminist_magazine _under_threat (accessed January 31, 2009).

365. Ibid.

366. Farangis Najibullah, "Iran: Women's Magazine Felled by Latest Government Closure," *Payvand's Iran News*, February 14, 2008, http://www.payvand .com/news/08/feb/1131.html (accessed March 19, 2009).

367. M. Nissimov, Y. Mansharof, and A. Savyon, "Iranian Women's Magazine Shut Down for Publishing Investigative Article on Martyrdom Movement," Memri Inquiry and Analysis Series, no. 439, May 22, 2008, http://www.memri.org/bin/ articles.cgi?Page=archives&Area=ia&ID=IA43908 (accessed January 31, 2009).

368. "Letter on Behalf of Shahla Sherkat," press release, February 2008, http://www.iwmf.org/subcatdetail.aspx?sc=pastletter (accessed January 31, 2009).

369. "Iran: Closure of Women's Rights Publication Zanan," *FrontLine*, February 5, 2008, http://www.frontlinedefenders.org/node/1353 (accessed January 31, 2009).

370. Casey, "Editor of Feisty Iranian Magazine Faces Prison."

371. "A Feminist among Iran's Fundamentalists."

372. Ibid.

373. Ibid.

374. Mahmud Sarabi, "Zanan Monthly Is Banned," *Rooz online*, February 4, 2008, http://www.roozonline.com/english/archives/2008/02/zanan_monthly_is _banned.html (accessed January 31, 2009).

375. Heather Harvey, "Trying to Read Grazia in Iran," *Guardian* (UK), January 31, 2009, http://www.guardian.co.uk/commentisfree/2009/jan/31/iran-censorship (accessed February 1, 2009).

376. "Answers to Your Most Frequently Asked Questions about the Campaign," Women's Learning Partnership, February 28, 2008, http://www.learning partnership.org/advocacy/alerts/iranwomenarrests0307 (accessed March 19, 2009).

377. Ibid.

378. "Iran: Women's Rights Defenders Defy Repression: Sussan Tahmasebi," http://www.amnesty.org/en/library/info/MDE13/022/2008/en (accessed March 19, 2009).

379. "Women Look with Hope to New Govt," Reuters, March 14, 2008, http://www.thepeninsulaqatar.com/Display_news.asp?section=World_News &subsection=Gulf%2C+Middle+East+%26+Africa&month=March2008&file =World_News200803147360.xml (accessed March 19, 2009).

380. Ibid.

CHAPTER 10: IRAQ

1. Statement by Azam Kamguian, "Human Rights of Women in Iraq," April 6, 2004, http://www.iheu.org/node/1306 (accessed January 31, 2009).

2. Joseph, "Elite Strategies for State-Building," p. 184, quoted in Human Rights Watch briefing paper, "Background on Women's Status in Iraq Prior to the Fall of the Saddam Hussein Government," November 2003, http://www.hrw.org/ backgrounder/wrd/iraq-women.htm (accessed March 25, 2009).

3. Ibid.

4. Ibid.

5. Ibid.

6. Ibid. Clarification is provided in note 21 of the briefing paper.

7. Ibid.

8. Ibid., note 27.

9. Esra Naama, in discussion, "Human Rights and Women in Iraq: Voices of Iraqi Women," DOSINTLWMN Archives, March 10, 2003, http://statelists.state.gov/ scripts/wa.exe?A2=ind0303b&L=dosintlwmn&P=182 (accessed January 31, 2009).

10. Houzan Mahmoud, "Human Chattel," *Guardian* (UK), May 2, 2007, http://www.guardian.co.uk/commentisfree/2007/may/02/humanchattel?comment page=1 (accessed February 1, 2009).

11. Houzan Mahmoud, "An Empty Sort of Freedom," *Guardian* (UK), March 8, 2004, http://www.guardian.co.uk/world/2004/mar/08/iraq.gender (accessed February 1, 2009).

12. Terri Judd, "Barbaric 'Honor Killings' Become the Weapon to Subjugate Women in Iraq," *Independent* (UK), April 28, 2008, http://www.commondreams .org/archive/2008/04/28/8573 (accessed February 1, 2009).

13. Katha Pollitt, "Democracy Is Hell," May 19, 2005, http://www.rezgar .com/eng/show.art.asp?aid=338 (accessed February 1, 2009).

14. Mahmoud, "An Empty Sort of Freedom."

15. Houzan Mahmoud, "We Say No to Medieval Kurdistan," *Guardian* (UK), April 13, 2007, http://www.guardian.co.uk/commentisfree/2007/apr/13/thefightfor secularisminku1 (accessed February 1, 2009).

16. Mahmoud, "An Empty Sort of Freedom."

17. Houzan Mahmoud, "Human Chattel," *Guardian* (UK), May 2, 2007, http://www.guardian.co.uk/commentisfree/2007/may/02/humanchattel?comment page=1 (accessed February 1, 2009).

18. Mahmoud, "An Empty Sort of Freedom."

19. Houzan Mahmoud, interview with Bill Weinberg, WW4 Report, WBAI Radio, April 1, 2006, http://ww4report.com/node/1798 (accessed March 25, 2009).

20. Mahmoud, "We Say No to Medieval Kurdistan."

21. Judd, "Barbaric 'Honor Killings.'"

22. Houzan Mahmoud, "It's Not a Matter of Choice," *Guardian* (UK), October 7, 2006, OWFI, May 5, 2008, http://www.equalityiniraq.com (accessed February 1, 2009).

23. Ibid.

24. "Death Threats against Women's Rights Defender," WHRD, March 5, 2007, http://www.defendingwomen-defendingrights.org/iraq_deaththreats.php (accessed February 1, 2009).

25. Houzan Mahmoud, "The Price of Freedom," *Guardian* (UK), October 17, 2006, http://www.byliner.com/writer/?id=11424 (accessed March 25, 2009).

26. Bay Fang, "The Talibanization of Iraq," *Ms. Magazine*, Spring 2007.

27. "Fighting for Women's Rights in Iraq," *CNN*, 2007, http://edition.cnn .com/2007/WORLD/meast/06/26/pysk.mohammed/index.htm 1 (accessed February 1, 2009).

28. Amy DePaul, "First Victims of Freedom," *Guernica Magazine*, May 2007, http://www.guernicamag.com/interviews/326/the_black_glove/print.php (accessed March 25, 2009).

29. Lucinda Marshall, "Our Lives Are Worse Now," interview with Yanar Mohammed, Dissident Voice, June 21, 2004, http://www.dissidentvoice.org/June04/Marshall0621.htm (accessed March 25, 2009).

30. DePaul, "First Victims of Freedom."

31. Rania Abouzeid, "Iraq's Unspeakable Crime: Mothers Pimping Daughters," Time, March 7, 2009.

32. DePaul, "First Victims of Freedom."

33. Fang, "The Talibanization of Iraq."

34. "Condemn the Killings of Women in Basra and Umara. End the Genocide on Women of Iraq," OWFI, January 5, 2008, http://www.ahewar.org/eng/show.art.asp?aid=518 (accessed March 25, 2009).

35. Ibid.

36. Fang, "The Talibanization of Iraq."

37. Marshall, "Our Lives Are Worse Now."

38. "Iraqi Women's Rights Activist Receives Death Threat from Islamist Group: MADRE Launches Campaign to Protect Yanar Mohammed," February 6, 2004, http://www.commondreams.org/news2004/0206-01.htm (accessed March 25, 2009).

39. "International Campaign to Reverse the Governing Council's Resolution 137, Which Changes the Iraqi Family Law to Islamic Shari'a," http://www.petitiononline.com/OWFI/petition.html (accessed March 25, 2009).

40. "The Civil Opposition in Iraq," interview with Yanar Mohammed of OWFI by Bill Weinberg, June 28, 2004, http://ww4report.com/static/iraq3.html (accessed March 25, 2009).

41. DePaul, "First Victims of Freedom."

42. "Background of the Organization of Women's Freedom in Iraq," VDAY, 2005, http://www.vday.org/contents/vcampaigns/spotlight/iraq (accessed March 25, 2009).

43. "The Civil Opposition in Iraq."

CHAPTER 11: ISRAEL AND THE PALESTINIAN TERRITORIES

1. United Nations Development Programme (UNDP–POGAR), "Gender and Citizenship: Arab Countries," http://gender.pogar.org/countries/country.asp?cid=14 (accessed February 1, 2009).

2. Ibid.

3. Masshoor Basisy, general director of planning at the Palestinian Authority (PA) Ministry for Women's Affairs, cited in "Few Legal Options for Abused Palestinian Women, Say Activists," IRIN, October 3, 2007, http://www.stopvaw.org/

PALESTINE_Few_Legal_Options_for_Abused_Palestinian_Women_Say_Activists .html (accessed March 11, 2009).

4. Human Rights Watch, cited in ibid.

5. Bojana Stoparic, "Palestinian Women's Rights Lost in Power Shift," *Women's eNews*, May 4, 2005, http://womensenews.org/article.cfm/dyn/aid/2246/ context/archive (accessed March 25, 2009).

6. Ibid.

7. Sharon Wrobel, "Jewish and Arab Women Unite in Spirit of Entrepreneurship," *Jerusalem Post*, November 23, 2006.

8. Ibid.

9. World Bank Group GenderStats, http://go.worldbank.org/AETRQ5 QAC0 (accessed February 8, 2009).

10. Nasser Shiyoukhi and Diaa Hadid, "2 Palestinian Women Become Judges in Islamic Court," Associated Press, February 24, 2009, http://www.google.com/ hostednews/ap/article/ALeqM5jOQd1uzqc-Ee9_Y-qeCO7oL7VN-AD96I3AH80 (accessed March 11, 2009).

11. Nicole Jansezian, "Hamas Reinstates Crucifixions of Christians," *Newsmax*, January 9, 2009, http://www.newsmax.com/newsfront/Hamas_bombs _Gaza_Israel/2009/01/09/169756.html (accessed March 11, 2009).

12. Aswat Group, Mission Statement, http://www.aswatgroup.org/english/ about.php?category=120 (accessed February 1, 2009).

13. "Aswat Gives Voice to Palestinian Lesbians," June 1, 2007, http:// without-a-roadmap.blogspot.com/2007/06/aswat-gives-voice-to-palestinian.html (accessed February 1, 2009).

14. Leslie Feinberg, "Palestinian Gay Women Hold Historic Conference," Workers World, April 12, 2007, http://www.workers.org/2007/world/aswat-0419 (accessed February 1, 2009).

15. See http://www.womenandhorizons.org (accessed February 1, 2009).

16. Ibid.

17. Ibid.

CHAPTER 12: JORDAN

1. "Human Resources," http://www.kinghussein.gov.jo/resources5.html (accessed February 1, 2009).

2. United Nations Development Programme (UNDP–POGAR), "Gender and Citizenship: Arab Countries," http://gender.pogar.org/countries/country.asp ?cid=7 (accessed February 1, 2009).

3. Ibid.

4. Jordanian National Commission for Women, http://www.jncw.jo (accessed February 1, 2009).

5. Leila Sharaf, quoted in Dale Gavlak, "Bringing Jordan's Women into the Fold," February 9, 2004, *BBC News*, http://news.bbc.co.uk/2/hi/middle_east/3462385.stm (accessed February 1, 2009).

6. United Nations Development Programme, "Gender and Citizenship: Arab Countries."

7. Sharaf, quoted in Gavlak, "Bringing Jordan's Women into the Fold."

8. Alasdair Soussi, "Rana's War," *Worldpress*, March 25, 2005, http://www.worldpress.org/Mideast/2053.cfm#down (accessed February 1, 2009).

9. Ibid.

10. Rana Husseini, "Honor Killings," http://www.pbs.org/speaktruthtopower/rana.html (accessed February 1, 2009).

11. Ibid.

12. Adam Jones, "Honor Killings and Blood Feuds," http://www.gendercide.org/case_honour.html (accessed February 1, 2009).

13. "Jordan: 'Honour' Killings Pose a Serious Challenge to the Rule of Law," WLUML, October 31, 2007, http://www.wluml.org/english/newsfulltxt.shtml?cmd[157]=x-157-557614 (accessed March 25, 2009).

14. Husseini, "Honor Killings."

15. Rana Husseini, "Legal Experts Call for Amending Penal Code Articles Invoked in So-called Honor Crimes," *Jordan Times*, May 16, 2008, http://www.jordantimes.com/index.php?news=4745&searchFor=rana%20husseini (accessed February 1, 2009).

16. Husseini, "Honor Killings."

17. Ibid.

18. "Jordan Special Report on Honor Killings," UN Office for the Coordination of Humanitarian Affairs, http://www.irinnews.org/report.aspx?reportid=25021 (accessed February 1, 2009).

19. Husseini, "Honor Killings."

20. Amy Henderson, "JT Reporter Awarded for Her Coverage on Crimes of Honor," *Jordan Times*, March 30, 1998, http://www.jordanembassyus.org/033098004.htm (accessed February 1, 2009).

21. Soussi, "Rana's War."

22. See www.ranahusseini.com (accessed February 1, 2009).

23. Soussi, "Rana's War."

24. "Gendercide: Honor Killings in Jordan," July 30, 2007, http://newmoonnews.blogspot.com/2007/07/gendercide-honor-killings-in-jordan.html (accessed February 1, 2009).

25. See http://www.ranahusseini.com/Biography2.html.

26. Rana Husseini, "Murder in the Name of Honor," OneWorld Publications, March 27, 2008.

27. See www.ranahusseini.com (accessed February 1, 2009).

28. "Jordan Special Report on Honor Killings."

29. "Gendercide: Honor Killings in Jordan."

30. Ibid.

31. "Jordan Special Report on Honor Killings."

32. "Gendercide: Honor Killings in Jordan."

33. "Jordan Still Wrestles with 'Honor' Crimes," Reuters, January 28, 2008, http://www.abc.net.au/news/stories/2008/01/28/2148087.htm (accessed February 1, 2009).

34. "Lenient Sentences for Perpetrators of 'Honor Killings' a Step Backwards for Protection of Women in Jordan," Amnesty International Public Statement, April 23, 2008, http://www.amnestyusa.org/document.php?id=ENGMDE160012008&lang=e (accessed February 1, 2009).

35. Ibid.

36. Ali Abunimah, "A Hoax and Honor Lost for Norma Khouri," *Lebanese Daily Star*, August 29, 2004, http://www.zmag.org/znet/viewArticle/7966 (accessed February 1, 2009).

37. Ibid.

38. Husseini, "Honor Killings."

39. Adrian Morgan, "Mutilation and Killing for Muslim 'Honor' Religious or Tribal Custom?" Family Security Matters, June 26, 2007, http://www.fsmarchives.org/article.php?id=1095290 (accessed February 1, 2009).

40. Mandy Clark, "Honor Killings on Rise World Wide," February 5, 2008, Voice of America, http://www.voanews.com/english/archive/2008-02/2008-02-05-voa19.cfm (accessed February 1, 2009).

41. "Jordan Still Wrestles with 'Honor' Crimes."

42. "Lenient Sentences for Perpetrators of 'Honor Killings.'"

43. See http://www.ranahusseini.com/Awards.htm (accessed March 25, 2009).

CHAPTER 13: KUWAIT

1. United Nations Development Programme (UNDP–POGAR), "Gender and Citizenship: Arab Countries," http://gender.pogar.org/countries/country.asp?cid=8 (accessed February 1, 2009).

2. Mary Ann Tétreault, "Kuwait's Parliament Considers Women's Political

Rights, Again," *Middle East Report Online*, September 2, 2004, http://www.merip
.org/mero/mero090204.html (accessed February 1, 2009).

3. United Nations Development Programme, "Gender and Citizenship:
Arab Countries."

4. Tétreault, "Kuwait's Parliament Considers Women's Political Rights, Again."

5. Ibid.

6. Omar Hasan, "Kuwait's Islamists Vow to Thwart Women's Rights,"
March 2, 2005, *Middle East Report*, http://www.middle-east-online.com/english
/?id=12868 (accessed February 1, 2009).

7. Interview with Dr. Al-Khatib, Al-Arabiya TV, March 14, 2008, "Kuwaiti
Columnist Ibtihal Al-Khatib Criticizes Hizbullah, Declares That a Secular State Is
the Only Way to Protect Religious Rights in the Arab World," Memri Special Dispatch Series, no. 1878, March 24, 2008, http://www.memri.org/bin/latestnews
.cgi?ID=SD187808 (accessed February 1, 2009).

8. Ibid.

9. *Roz Al-Yousuf* (Egypt), April 7, 2007, cited in I. Rapoport, "Kuwaiti Education Minister Would Not Wear the Veil," Memri Inquiry and Analysis, no. 352,
April 7, 2007, http://memri.org/bin/latestnews.cgi?ID=IA35207 (accessed March
25, 2009).

10. "Hijab-less Subeeh Can Be Cause of Next Crisis," *Kuwait Times*, April 1,
2007, http://www.kuwaittimes.net/read_news.php?newsid=MTM0MDk4MDgw
Mg (accessed March 25, 2009).

11. Ibid.

12. *Al-Siyassa* (Kuwait), April 1, 2007, cited in Rapoport, "Kuwaiti Education Minister Would Not Wear the Veil."

13. Ibid.

14. Ibid.

15. Ibid.

16. "US First Lady Briefed about Challenges Facing Kuwaiti Women,"
KUNA, October 24, 2007, http://www.kuna.net.kw/NewsAgenciesPublicSite/
ArticleDetails.aspx?id=1851515&Language=en (accessed February 2, 2009).

17. "Education Key to National Development: Al-Subeeh," *Kuwait Times*,
February 18, 2008, http://www.kuwaittimes.net/read_news.php?newsid=NjY5MD
Q2MDQ1 (accessed February 2, 2009).

18. "Lady MP under Fire in Headscarf Row," *Gulf Daily News*, December 25,
2007, http://gulf-daily-news.com/1yr_arc_articles.asp?Article=203812&Sn=WORL
&IssueID=30280&date=12-25-2007 (accessed February 2, 2009).

19. Nawara Fattahova, "Al-Mubarak Hailed for Honest Work," September
22, 2007, *Kuwait Times*, http://www.kuwaittimes.net/read_news.php?newsid=MTI
zMTYwNTAx (accessed February 1, 2009).

20. Dr. Rola Dashti, March 12, 2006, http://www.zu.ac.ae/leadership 2006/roladashti.aspx (accessed February 1, 2009).

21. Haila Al-Mekaimi, "Kuwaiti Women's Tepid Political Awakening," http://www.arabinsight.org/aishowarticle.cfm?id=183 (accessed February 1, 2009).

22. "House Approves Crowley Resolution Commending Kuwait for Granting Women Voting Rights," July 13, 2005, http://www.planetwire.org/details/5379 (accessed February 1, 2009).

23. "Kuwait Health Minister Resigns after Hospital Fire," Reuters, August 25, 2007, http://www.alertnet.org/thenews/newsdesk/L25686840.htm (accessed August 13, 2009).

24. Faiza Saleh Ambah, "For Women in Kuwait, a Landmark Election," special to *Washington Post*, June 29, 2006, p. A20.

25. "Kuwait: Kuwaiti Women Optimistic Despite Setbacks," July 4, 2006, *WLUML News and Views*, http://www.wluml.org/english/newsfulltxt.shtml?cmd %5B157%5D=x-157-539175 (accessed March 25, 2009).

26. "In Kuwait, Women Are Breaking Down Barriers," *World of Parliaments Quarterly Review*, Web version, issue no. 23, October 2006, http://www.ipu.org/news-e/23-4.ht (accessed February 1, 2009).

27. Ibid.

28. Ambah, "For Women in Kuwait, a Landmark Election."

29. Rola Dashti, "Can There Be Democracy with Marginalization?" Media Monitors Network, July 30, 2005, http://usa.mediamonitors.net/content/view/full/17244 (accessed February 1, 2009).

30. "Elections in the Arab World: Progress or Peril?" Middle East, Brookings Institution, February 12, 2007, http://www.brookings.edu/papers/2007/0212 middleeast_wittes.aspx?p=1 (accessed February 1, 2009).

31. Ibid.

32. "In Kuwait, Women Are Breaking Down Barriers."

33. "Elections in the Arab World: Progress or Peril?"

34. Dashti, "Can There Be Democracy with Marginalization?"

CHAPTER 14: LEBANON

1. Ghada Khouri, "Caught in the Middle: Women in Lebanon," http://www.geocities.com/Wellesley/3321/win13b.htm (accessed February 1, 2009).

2. United Nations Development Programme (UNDP–POGAR), "Gender and Citizenship: Arab Countries," http://gender.pogar.org/countries/country.asp ?cid=9 (accessed February 1, 2009).

3. "A Brief Review of the Current State of Violations of Women's Rights in Lebanon," http://www.lnf.org.lb/windex/brief1.html#a1 (accessed March 25, 2009).

4. Ibid.

5. Khouri, "Caught in the Middle: Women in Lebanon."

6. Ibid.

7. Ibid.

8. United Nations Development Programme, "Gender and Citizenship: Arab Countries."

9. Anna Workman, "Interview with Lina Abou-Habib, Director of Collective for Research and Training on Development-Action (CRTD-A)," March 4, 2006, http://www.learningpartnership.org/advocacy/campaign/labhinterview (accessed February 1, 2009).

10. Collective for Research and Training on Development—Action, http://old.crtda.org/crtd.org/www/why.htm (accessed February 1, 2009).

11. Workman, "Interview with Lina Abou-Habib."

12. Ibid.

13. "Claiming Equal Citizenship: The Campaign for Arab Women's Right to Nationality," http://www.learningpartnership.org/en/node/407 (accessed February 1, 2009).

14. "Kid of Alien Dad May Get Moroccan Nationality," http://theseoultimes.com/ST/?url=/ST/db/read.php?idx=2290 (accessed February 1, 2009).

15. Workman, "Interview with Lina Abou-Habib."

CHAPTER 15: MALAYSIA

1. "Women in Malaysia. Country Briefing Papers," Asia Development Bank, December 1998, http://www.adb.org/Documents/Books/Country_Briefing_Papers/Women_in_Malaysia/default.asp?p=gender (accessed February 2, 2009).

2. Ibid.

3. Ivy Josiah, "There Are No Human Rights without Women's Rights," Women's Aid Organization, September 6, 2001, http://www.asiasource.org/asip/wao.cfm (accessed February 2, 2009).

4. Marina Mahathir's comments, due to appear in her regular newspaper column, were censored and did not appear. The story made international headlines, as her father had been very outspoken against the policy of apartheid in South Africa.

5. Jonathan Kent, "Malaysia Women 'Suffer Apartheid,'" *BBC News, Kuala Lumpur*, March 8, 2006, http://news.bbc.co.uk/go/pr/fr/-/2/hi/asia-pacific/4784784.stm (accessed February 2, 2009).

6. "Malaysia: Women Told to Avoid Lipstick and High-Heeled Shoes to 'Preserve Dignity,'" *Guardian* (UK), June 25, 2008.

7. Carolyn Hong, "Muslim Women Fight for Equal Rights," *Straits Times*, February 18, 2009.

8. "Malaysia Drops Proposed Travel Restriction for Women," Reuters, *ABC News*, May 5, 2008, http://www.abc.net.au/news/stories/2008/05/05/2236062.htm (accessed February 2, 2009).

9. "Deutsche Welle Radio's Nicola Fell Reports on Changing Times for Malaysian Women," *ABC NewsRadio*, November 15, 2008.

10. Ibid.

11. Interview with Yuli Ismartono, July 15, 2006, http://www.the-leaders.org/library/07.html (accessed February 2, 2009).

12. "Islamization and Its Impact on Laws and the Law-Making Process in Malaysia," December 2003, AWID, http://www.awid.org/eng/Issues-and-Analysis/Library/Islamization-and-its-Impact-on-Laws-and-the-Law-Making-Process-in-Malaysia (accessed February 2, 2009).

13. Marina Mahathir, "Our Own Apartheid," March 7, 2006, http://bakrimusa.blogspot.com/2006/03/our-own-apartheid-marina-mahathir.html (accessed February 2, 2009).

14. Ibid.

15. Interview with Yuli Ismartono.

16. See http://www.redfilms.com.my/golgincu/produksi.html (accessed February 2, 2009).

17. MM, "About Me, Rantings," http://rantingsbymm.blogspot.com (accessed February 2, 2009).

18. Interview with Yuli Ismartono.

19. Zainah Anwar, "Unjust and Unnecessary," *Star* (Malaysia), July 6, 2008, http://zfikri.wordpress.com/2008/07/09/zainah-anwar-unjust-and-unnecessary (accessed February 2, 2009).

20. "Zainah Anwar, Founder, Sisters in Islam," http://www.islamproject.org/muslims/muslims_tl5.htm (accessed February 2, 2009).

21. Ibid.

22. Sisters in Islam, http://www.sistersinislam.org.my (accessed February 2, 2009).

23. Ibid.

24. Fereshteh Nouraie-Simone, ed., *On Shifting Ground: Muslim Women in the Global Era* (New York: Feminist Press, 2005), p. xi.

25. Radio National Australia, "Feminist Islam," January 4, 2004, http://www.abc.net.au/rn/talks/natint/stories/s1012873.htm (accessed March 25, 2009).

26. Zainah Anwar, "Ending the Patriarchy," *Time*, March 10, 2003, in

WLUML, http://www.wluml.org/english/newsfulltxt.shtml?cmd%5B157%5D =x-157-528479 (accessed February 2, 2009).

27. "A Faith Unmasked," *Age* (Melbourne), August 12, 2003, http://www .theage.com.au/articles/2003/08/11/1060454122799.html (accessed February 2, 2009).

28. "Sister In Islam," *Tufts University E-News*, December 10, 2002, http:// enews.tufts.edu/stories/983/2002/12/10/SisterInIslam (accessed March 25, 2009).

29. Jane Perlez, "Letter from Malaysia: Malaysia's Big Sister Shakes Up Islam Rule," *International Herald Tribune*, February 16, 2006, http://www.iht.com/ articles/2006/02/16/news/letter.php (accessed February 2, 2009).

30. Zainah Anwar, "Modern, and Moderate, Islam," *AsiaWeek*, September 16, 1997, http://www.hartford-hwp.com/archives/54/091.html (accessed February 2, 2009).

31. Radio National, "Feminist Islam."

32. Helie Anissa, "Muslim Women and Feminist Strategies in Times of Religious Fundamentalisms," Europe Solidaire Sans Frontières, August 2006, http:// www.europe-solidaire.org/spip.php?article3235 (accessed March 25, 2009).

33. Radio National Australia, "Feminist Islam."

34. "Malaysia, Abdullah Freezes Islamic Bill," *AsiaNews*, January 13, 2006, http://www.asianews.it/index.php?l=en&art=5115 (accessed February 2, 2009).

35. Perlez, "Letter from Malaysia."

36. Reporters without Borders, August 21, 2007, http://www.rsf.org/article .php3?id_article=23344 (accessed March 25, 2009).

37. Suhaini Aznam, "A Sister Steps Out," *Star*, March 30, 2008, http:// thestar.com.my/news/story.asp?file=/2008/3/30/lifefocus/20762710&sec=lifefocus (accessed February 2, 2009).

38. "Muslim Women 'Face Crisis over Violence,'" *Australian*, February 15, 2009.

39. Ibid.

40. Musawah: For Equality in the Family, http://www.musawah.org (accessed March 28, 2009).

41. "Muslim Women 'Face Crisis over Violence.'"

CHAPTER 16: MOROCCO

1. United Nations Development Programme (UNDP–POGAR) "Gender and Citizenship, Arab Countries," http://gender.pogar.org/countries/country.asp ?cid=12 (accessed March 25, 2009).

2. Ibid.

3. Sabrina Tavernise, "In Quest for Equal Rights, Muslim Women's Meeting Turns to Islam's Tenets," *New York Times*, February 15, 2009.

4. "King of Morocco Calls for Fundamental Reform in Family Law," Memri Special Dispatch Series, no. 604, November 7, 2003, http://www.memri.org/bin/latestnews.cgi?ID=SD60403 (accessed February 2, 2009).

5. Ibid.

6. United Nations Development Programme, "Gender and Citizenship: Arab Countries."

7. *Amnesty International Report*, 2007, http://www.amnesty.org/en/region/middle-east-and-north-africa/north-africa/moroccowestern-sahara (accessed February 2, 2009).

8. United Nations Development Programme, "Gender and Citizenship: Arab Countries."

9. Ibid.

10. Ibid.

11. Ibid.

12. Daniel Steinvorth, "Our Religion Is Friendly to Women," interview with Moroccan Islamist Nadia Yassine, *Spiegel Online*, July 3, 2007, http://www.spiegel.de/international/world/0,1518,492040,00.html (accessed February 2, 2009).

13. Magdi Abdelhadi, "Accused Morocco Islamist Speaks Out," *BBC News*, September 30, 2005, http://news.bbc.co.uk/2/hi/africa/429386.stm (accessed April 5, 2009).

14. "Back to the Islamic Future," Carter Center (updated August 2007), http://www.cartercenter.org/peace/human_rights/defenders/defenders/morocco_nadia_yassine.html (accessed February 2, 2009).

15. Fatima Mernissi, *The Harem Within* (Doubleday, 1994), p. 175, footnote 1. Partial footnote by Fatima Mernissi from her book, *Dreams of Trespass: Tales of a Harem Girlhood*, © 1994 by Fatima Mernissi. By permission of Edite Kroll Literary Agency Inc. UK edition, *The Harem Within* (Doubleday, 1994).

16. Fatima Mernissi, *Beyond the Veil* (London: Al Saqi Books, 1985), p. 166.

17. Ibid., p. 19.

18. Ibid., p. 17.

19. Ibid., p. 82.

20. Ibid.

21. Ibid., p. 17.

22. Ibid., p. 167.

23. Ibid.

24. Ibid., p. 61.

25. Ibid., p. 161.

26. Ibid., p. 107.

27. Ibid., p. 168.

28. Ibid.

29. Ibid.

30. Ibid., p. 18.

31. Ibid.

32. Ibid., p. 19.

33. Mernissi, *The Harem Within*, p. 38, footnote 4. Partial footnote by Fatima Mernissi from her book, *Dreams of Trespass: Tales of a Harem Girlhood*, © 1994 by Fatima Mernissi. By permission of Edite Kroll Literary Agency Inc. UK edition, *The Harem Within* (Doubleday, 1994).

34. Ibid., p. 45.

35. Ibid.

36. Ibid., p. 162.

37. Ibid.

CHAPTER 17: NIGERIA

1. Stephane Mikala of Amnesty International, in "Half of Nigeria's Women Experience Domestic Violence," May 31, 2008, *Afrol News*, http://www.afrol.com/articles/16471 (accessed March 25, 2009).

2. Nogi Imoukhuede, "Female Genital Mutilation—A Crime in Edo State," July 19, 2004, http://www.rufarm.kabissa.org/articles/fgm.htm (accessed February 2, 2009).

3. Itoro Eze-Anaba, quoted in "Half of Nigeria's Women Experience Domestic Violence."

4. Ibid.

5. "The Women of Nigeria Are Rebuilding Their Beautiful Nation," Women for Women International, http://www.womenforwomen.org/nigeria.htm (accessed February 2, 2009).

6. Celestina Omoso Isiramen, "Women in Nigeria: Religion, Culture and AIDS," International Humanist and Ethical Union, November 1, 2003 (accessed February 2, 2009).

7. US Department of State, "Nigeria: Report on Female Genital Mutilation or Female Genital Cutting," June 1, 2001, http://www.state.gov/g/wi/rls/rep/crfgm/10106.htm (accessed February 2, 2009).

8. Although Edo State has banned FGM, the minimal punishment (a $10 fine and six months' imprisonment) and lack of enforcement have been criticized.

9. US Department of State, "Nigeria: Report on Female Genital Mutilation or Female Genital Cutting."

10. Ibid.

11. Baobab for Women's Human Rights Web site, http://www.baobab women.org/history.htm (accessed February 2, 2009).

12. "Nigerian State Introduces Full Islamic Law," http://www.hrwf.net/ religiousfreedom/news/2000PDF/nigeria_2000.pdf (accessed February 2, 2009).

13. Ayesha Imam, "An Acceptance Speech on Islam and Women's Rights," Urhobo Historical Society, December 10, 2002, http://www.waado.org/NigerDelta/ HumanRights/WomenRights/AyeshaIman.html (accessed February 2, 2009).

14. Ibid.

15. "Nigeria: Ayesha Imam Wins the John Humphrey Freedom Award," Women Living under Muslim laws, July 9, 2002, http://www.wluml.org/english/ newsfulltxt.shtml?cmd%5B157%5D=x-157-3227 (accessed March 25, 2009).

CHAPTER 18: PAKISTAN

1. Hina Jilani, lawyer and human rights activist, cited in "Honor Killings of Girls and Women," Amnesty International, http://www.amnesty.org/en/library/ info/ASA33/018/1999 (accessed February 2, 2009).

2. "Women in Pakistan. Country Briefing Papers," Asian Development Bank, July 2000, http://www.adb.org/Documents/Books/Country_Briefing_Papers/ Women_in_Pakistan/default.asp?p=gender (accessed February 2, 2009).

3. "Women in Pakistan," http://www.onlinewomeninpolitics.org/pakistan/ pakmain.htm (accessed February 2, 2009).

4. "Women in Pakistan. Country Briefing Papers."

5. "Women in Pakistan," http://www.onlinewomeninpolitics.org/pakistan pakmain.htm.

6. Ibid.

7. Ibid.

8. "Women in Pakistan. Country Briefing Papers."

9. Juliette Terzieff, "Pakistan's Fiery Shame: Women Die in Stove Death," *Women's eNews*, October 27, 2002, http://www.womensenews.org/article.cfm/dyn/ aid/1085/context/cover (accessed December 1, 2008).

10. Progressive Women's Association—Pakistan, http://www.pwaisbd.org/ index (accessed December 2, 2008).

11. Nicholas D. Kristof, "Terrorism That's Personal," *New York Times*, November 30, 2008.

12. David Aaronovitch, "Killing Defies Pathetic Explanations," *Australian*, December 3, 2008.

13. Tahira Shahid Khan, "Chained to Custom," March 4–10, 1999, p. 4, cited by Amnesty International, http://www.amnesty.org/en/library/info/ASA33/018/1999 (accessed February 2, 2009).

14. This quotation is from a pubescent girl in a small Sindhi village, cited by Amnesty International, http://www.amnesty.org/en/library/info/ASA33/018/1999 (accessed February 2, 2009).

15. "Honor Killings of Girls and Women."

16. Ibid.

17. Section 300(1) states: "Culpable murder is not murder if the offender, whilst deprived of the power of self-control by grave and sudden provocation, causes the death of the person who gave the provocation." Cited by Amnesty International, http://www.amnesty.org/en/library/info/ASA33/018/1999 (accessed February 2, 2009).

18. "Honor Killings of Girls and Women."

19. "Pakistan, Land, Gold, Women," *CBC News*, February 28 and March 1, 2006, http://www.cbc.ca/news/background/pakistan/mckenna_pakistan.html (accessed February 2, 2009).

20. "Obituary: Benazir Bhutto," *Times Online*, December 27, 2007, www.timesonline.co.uk/tol/comment/obituaries/article3101102.ece (accessed February 2, 2009).

21. Shujauddin Qureshi, "No Better Than a Man? Benazir Bhutto under Fire," http://www.geocities.com/Wellesley/3321/win12b.htm (accessed February 2, 2009).

22. Ibid.

23. See http://www.islamawareness.net/Marriage/Quran/married.html (accessed December 2, 2008).

24. "Zubeida's Family Seeks Musharraf's Attention," *Daily Times* (Pakistan), August 2, 2005.

25. Fatima Bhutto, "Does Pakistan Have No Shame?" *Daily Beast*, February 11, 2009, http://www.thedailybeast.com/blogs-and-stories/2009-02-11/does-pakistan-have-no-shame/p/ (accessed March 18, 2009).

26. Zahid Hussain, "Taleban Threaten to Blow Up Girls' Schools If They Refuse to Close," *Times* (London), December 26, 2008.

27. Ilyas Khan, "Threatened Pakistan Schools Close," *BBC News*, January 16, 2009, http://news.bbc.co.uk/2/hi/south_asia/7832715.stm (accessed January 16, 2009).

28. Hussain, "Taleban Threaten to Blow Up Girls' Schools If They Refuse to Close."

29. Salman Masood, "Video of Taliban Flogging Rattles Pakistan," *New York Times*, April 4, 2009.

30. "Fresh Attacks on Pakistan Schools," *BBC News*, January 19, 2009, http://news.bbc.co.uk/2/hi/south_asia/7836875.stm (accessed January 19, 2009).

31. Farhan Bokhari, "Taliban Flogging Incident Imperils Peace Deal," *Financial Times* (London), April 4, 2009.

32. Ibid.

33. Masood, "Video of Taliban Flogging Rattles Pakistan."

34. Ibid.

35. William Dalrymple, "Letter from Pakistan, Days of Rage," *New Yorker*, July 23, 2007, http://www.newyorker.com/reporting/2007/07/23/070723fa_fact _dalrymple?currentPage=all (accessed February 2, 2009).

36. Ibid.

37. The 1995 Ramon Magsaysay Award for Public Service, "Biography of Asma Jahangir," http://www.rmaf.org.ph/Awardees/Biography/BiographyJahangir Asm.htm (accessed March 26, 2009).

38. Laila Kazmi, "Women of Pakistan, Asma Jahangir," *Jazbah Magazine*, http://www.jazbah.org/asmaj.php (accessed March 26, 2009).

39. Ibid.

40. Dalrymple, "Letter from Pakistan, Days of Rage."

41. "Asma Jahangir," Sawnet Who's Who, http://www.sawnet.org/whoswho/ ?Jahangir+Asma (accessed February 2, 2009).

42. Vikram Sura, "Asma Jahangir, in Her Own Words," *UN Chronicle*, online edition, http://www.un.org/Pubs/chronicle/2002/webArticles/111102_interview _asma.html (accessed February 2, 2009).

43. The 1995 Ramon Magsaysay Award for Public Service, "Biography of Asma Jahangir."

44. Kazmi, "Women of Pakistan, Asma Jahangir."

45. "Arbitrary House Arrest of Ms. Asma Jahangi," November 7, 2007, www.fidh.org/Asia/Pakistan (accessed March 26, 2009).

46. "Daughters of UN Special Rapporteur Asma Jahangir Allegedly Detained, Assaulted and Threatened," WLUML, January 6, 2008, http://www .wluml.org/english/newsfulltxt.shtml?cmd[157]=x-157-559667 (accessed February 2, 2009).

47. Mukhtar Mai, "Against All Odds," *BBC News*, September 28, 2006, http://news.bbc.co.uk/2/hi/south_asia/5371904.stm (accessed February 2, 2009).

48. Nicholas D. Kristof, "A Free Woman," *New York Times*, June 19, 2005.

49. "Trend Analysis of Human Rights Violations," March 1, 2007, http:// www.hrcp-web.org/hrcpDetail_2.cfm?catId=166&catName=Reports (accessed February 2, 2009).

50. Mukhtar Mai, "So Much Responsibility," *BBC News*, November 16, 2006, http://news.bbc.co.uk/2/hi/south_asia/6124926.stm (accessed February 2, 2009).

51. Ibid.

52. Amy Goodman interview, "I Will Go On Until I Have Even the Slightest Hope of Justice," *Democracy Now!*, June 21, 2005, http://www.democracynow.org/2005/6/21 (accessed February 2, 2009).

53. Mukhtar Mai, "So Much Responsibility."

54. Nicholas D. Kristof, "When Rapists Walk Free," *New York Times*, March 5, 2005, http://www.nytimes.com/2005/03/05/opinion/05kristof.html (accessed March 28, 2009).

55. Ibid.

56. "SHAME," SBS Television, Australia, March 5, 2008.

57. Kristof, "A Free Woman."

58. Mukhtar Mai, "So Much Responsibility."

59. Nicholas D. Kristof, "A Woman's Work Earns Her Enemies," *New York Times*, April 8, 2007, http://select.nytimes.com/2007/04/08/opinion/08kristof.html?_r=1 (accessed March 28, 2009).

60. Bhutto, "Does Pakistan Have No Shame?"

61. "Pakistan's Gang Rape Victim Mukhtar Mai Marries Constable," *ChennaiOnline News*, March 16, 2009, http://news.chennaionline.com/newsitem.aspx?NEWSID=1767ec81-b12e-4118-bc28-2334da5ea48e&CATEGORYNAME=INTER (accessed March 28, 2009).

62. Raheel Raza, "Moderate Muslims Struggle to Make Their Voices Heard," *Vancouver Sun*, August 28, 2008.

63. Jamie Glazov, "Reclaiming Islam," *Front Page Magazine*, November 11, 2008, http://www.frontpagemag.com/Articles/Read.aspx?GUID=90F3E95C-FBA9-4FD5-B9B4-8CA14DC09477 (accessed March 28, 2009).

64. "Raheel Raza—Pakistan and Canada," *World People's Blog*, October 28, 2008, http://word.world-citizenship.org/wp-archive/2507 (accessed November 12, 2008).

65. "Raheel Raza: Let's Pull the Veil off Our Minds," October 14, 2006, http://noburka.blogspot.com/2006/10/rahee-raza-says-lets-pull-veil-off-our.html (accessed November 12, 2008).

66. Glazov, "Reclaiming Islam."

67. Ibid.

68. "Truth or Scare: Raheel Raza's Fear Mongering," November 11, 2008, http://muslimahmediawatch.org/2008/11/11/truth-or-scare-raheel-razas-fear-mongering/ (accessed November 12, 2008).

69. Raheel Raza, *Their Jihad . . . Not My Jihad! A Muslim Canadian Woman Speaks Out* (Basel, Switzerland: Basileia Books, 2005).

70. Glazov, "Reclaiming Islam."

71. Kathy Shaidle, "Appeasing Canada's Islamists," *Front Page Magazine*, September 8, 2008, http://frontpagemagazine.com/Articles/Read.aspx?GUID=2EC745 DE-DFD3-4BA2-ABAB-E688A306EAE0 (accessed November 12, 2008).

72. Raheel Raza, "The Islamist Role in the 2008 Canadian Elections," *American Thinker*, November 8, 2008, http://www.americanthinker.com/2008/11/the _islamist_role_in_the_2008.html (accessed November 13, 2008).

73. Ibid.

74. Ibid.

75. Ibid.

76. Raza, "The Islamist Role in the 2008 Canadian Elections."

77. Glazov, "Reclaiming Islam."

78. Raza, "Moderate Muslims Struggle to Make Their Voices Heard."

CHAPTER 19: QATAR

1. US Department of State, "Qatar," http://www.state.gov/g/drl/rls/hrrpt/ 2004/41730.htm (accessed February 2, 2009).

2. United Nations Development Programme (UNDP–POGAR), "Gender and Citizenship: Arab Countries," http://gender.pogar.org/countries/country.asp?cid =15 (accessed February 2, 2009).

3. World Bank Group GenderStats, http://devdata.worldbank.org/gender stats/genderRpt.asp?rpt=profile&cty=QAT,Qatar (accessed March 26, 2009).

4. Embassy of Qatar, Washington, DC, http://www.qatarembassy.net/ women.asp (accessed March 26, 2009).

5. Ibid.

6. United Nations Development Programme, "Gender and Citizenship: Arab Countries."

7. Ibid.

8. Embassy of Qatar, Washington, DC, http://www.qatarembassy.net/ women.asp (accessed February 2, 2009).

9. United Nations Development Programme, "Gender and Citizenship: Arab Countries."

10. Danna Harman, "Backstory: Qatar Reformed by a Modern Marriage," *Christian Science Monitor*, March 6, 2007, http://www.csmonitor.com/2007/ 0306/p20s01-wome.html (accessed February 22, 2009).

11. Danna Harman, "The Royal Couple That Put Qatar on the Map," *Christian Science Monitor*, March 5, 2007, http://www.csmonitor.com/2007/0305/p20s01 -wome.html (accessed February 2, 2009).

12. Basma Al-Mutlaq, "Women in Islamic Countries Call for Greater Reform," *Arab News*, March 14, 2007.

13. "Israel Responds to Qatar's Request: Supporting Its Nomination to the UN Security Council," May 19, 2005, *Arabic News*, http://www.arabicnews.com/ansub/Daily/Day/050519/2005051924.html (accessed February 2, 2009).

14. Harman, "The Royal Couple That Put Qatar on the Map."

15. Al-Mutlaq, "Women in Islamic Countries Call for Greater Reform."

16. Sheikha Mozah Al-Missned, "From Illusions of Clashes to an Awakening of Alliances: Constructing Understanding between 'Islam' and the 'West,'" speech given at Chatham House, London, February 14, 2007, http://www.mozahbintnasser.qa/output/page29.asp (accessed February 2, 2009).

17. Official Web site of Her Highness Sheikha Mozah bint Nasser Al-Missned, http://www.mozahbintnasser.qa/output/page1.asp (accessed February 2, 2009).

18. Ibid.

19. Official Web site of Her Highness Sheikha Mozah bint Nasser Al-Missned.

20. Louay Bahry, "Reform at the University of Qatar: A Profile of Female Leadership," *Middle East Institute*, February 4, 2008.

21. Ibid.

22. Harman, "Backstory: Qatar Reformed by a Modern Marriage."

23. Ibid.

24. Ibid.

25. Al-Mutlaq, "Women in Islamic Countries Call for Greater Reform."

26. Ibid.

CHAPTER 20: SAUDI ARABIA

1. "Saudi Arabia—End Secrecy, End Suffering," Amnesty International Index, MDE 23/09/00, http://web.archive.org/web/20070202030903/www.amnesty.org/ailib/intcam/saudi/briefing/4.html (accessed February 3, 2009).

2. Rita Henley Jensen, "Gender Apartheid Tour in Saudi Arabia," *Women's eNews*, March 7, 2005, http://www.womensenews.org/article.cfm/dyn/aid/2212/context/ourdailylives (accessed March 20, 2009).

3. Ibid.

4. "Saudi Cleric Favors One-Eye Veil," *BBC News*, October 3, 2008, http://news.bbc.co.uk/2/hi/middle_east/7651231.stm (accessed March 20, 2009).

5. The Mutaween, officially known as the Commission for the Promotion of

Virtue and the Prevention of Vice, patrol the streets to enforce laws that ban the fraternizing of unrelated men and women, homosexuality, prostitution, alcohol, Western music considered to be un-Islamic, and the practice or proselytizing of non-Muslim religions.

6. "Saudi Arabia—End Secrecy, End Suffering," Amnesty International Index, MDE 23/09/00.

7. Ibid.

8. Jensen, "Gender Apartheid Tour in Saudi Arabia."

9. "Saudi Police 'Stopped' Fire Rescue,'" *BBC News*, March 15, 2002, http://news.bbc.co.uk/1/hi/world/middle_east/1874471.stm (accessed March 20, 2009).

10. "Saudi Arabia: A Secret State of Suffering," Amnesty International, http://web.archive.org/web/20070202022213/www.amnesty.org/ailib/intcam/saudi/report.html (accessed February 3, 2009).

11. "Saudi Arabia—End Secrecy, End Suffering," Amnesty International Index, MDE 23/09/00.

12. United Nations Development Programme (UNDP–POGAR), "Gender and Citizenship, Saudi Arabia, Women in Public Life," http://gender.pogar.org/countries/country.asp?cid=16 (accessed February 3, 2009).

13. Hazel Heyer, "Saudi Women Traveling Solo Can Now Stay in Hotels," *eTurboNews*, January 22, 2008, http://www.eturbonews.com/958/saudi-women-traveling-solo-can-now-stay-hotels (accessed February 20, 2009).

14. Rasheed Abou-Alsamh, "Ruling Jolts Even Saudis: 200 Lashes for Rape Victim," *New York Times*, November 16, 2007.

15. United Nations Development Programme, "Gender and Citizenship, Saudi Arabia, Women in Public Life."

16. "Al-Sharq Al-Awsat," London, July 23, 2006, translated as "Public Debate in Saudi Arabia on Employment Opportunities for Women," Memri Inquiry and Analysis Series, no. 300, November 17, 2006, http://memri.org/bin/latest news.cgi?ID=IA30006#_edn1 (accessed March 20, 2009).

17. Ibid.

18. United Nations Development Program, "Gender and Citizenship, Saudi Arabia, Women in Public Life."

19. "Women Speak Out in Saudi Arabia," *CBS News*, March 24, 2005.

20. Abeer Mishkhas, "To Each, a Marriage of His Choice," *Arab News*, July 17, 2008.

21. Mai Yamani, *Changed Identities—The Challenge of the New Generation in Saudi Arabia* (London: Royal Institute of International Affairs, 2000), p. 117.

22. Ibid., p. 130.

23. Faiza Saleh Ambah, "Saudi Writer Recasts Kingdom's History," *Washington Post*, Foreign Service, February 4, 2007.

24. Trevor Stanley, "Understanding the Origins of Wahhabism and Salafism," Jamestown Foundation, http://www.jamestown.org/single/?no_cache=1&tx_ttnews [tt_news]=528 (accessed February 3, 2009).

25. "2008 Update: Saudi Arabia's Curriculum of Intolerance," Center for Religious Freedom of Hudson Institute with the Institute for Gulf Affairs, http://www.hudson.org/files/pdf_upload/saudi_textbooks_final.pdf (accessed February 3, 2009).

26. Heyer, "Saudi Women Traveling Solo Can Now Stay in Hotels."

27. "Saudi Publications on Hate Ideology Invade American Mosques," Freedom House, 2005, http://www.freedomhouse.org/uploads/special_report/45.pdf (accessed February 3, 2009).

28. Yamani, *Changed Identities—The Challenge of the New Generation in Saudi Arabia*, p. 116.

29. Mai Yamani, ed., *Feminism and Islam* (London: Ithaca Press, 1996), p. 266.

30. Yamani, *Changed Identities—The Challenge of the New Generation in Saudi Arabia*, p. 116.

31. Hayat Alvi, "The Human Rights of Women and Social Transformation in the Arab Middle East," *Review of International Affairs* 9, no. 2 (June 2005).

32. Souhail Karam, "Saudi Cinema Move Tests Commitment to Reform," Reuters, December 29, 2008.

33. "Saudi King Appoints Woman, Fires Hardline Cleric," *Canberra Times* (Canberra, Australia), February 15, 2009.

34. Heyer, "Saudi Women Traveling Solo Can Now Stay in Hotels."

35. Faiza Saleh Ambah, "Saudi Women Seek Right to Sit in Driver's Seat," *Washington Post*, September 24, 2007.

36. Debate on types of marriage in the Arab world, aired on Abu Dhabi TV, October 27, 2008, cited in "Saudi Cleric and Women's Rights Activist Clash over Types of Common-Law Marriage in the Arab World," Memri TV, http:// www .memritv.org/clip/en/1932.htm (accessed March 5, 2009).

37. "Imagine You're a Woman," *Al-Sharq Al-Awsat* (London), October 9, 2005, Memri Special Dispatch Series, no. 1012, http://memri.org/bin/articles.cgi ?Page=archives&Area=sd&ID=SP101205 (accessed February 3, 2009).

38. Excerpts from a TV debate on women appearing on Saudi TV aired on LBC TV, March 25, 2007; in Memri TV Clip no. 1420, March 25, 2007, http:// www.memritv.org/clip_transcript/en/1420.htm (accessed February 3, 2009).

39. Mai Badr, "Princess Adelah bint Abdullah Talks of Women's Issues," *Arab News*, December 21, 2006.

40. "ID Cards for Women: Why Insist on Guardian's Consent?" *Arab News*, November 22, 2002, Memri Special Dispatch Series, no. 458, January 12, 2003,

http://www.memri.org/bin/articles.cgi?Page=archives&Area=sd&ID=SP45803 (accessed February 3, 2009).

41. Andrew Hammond, "Saudi Scholar Finds Ancient Women's Rights: Hatoon Al—Fassi Argues Women Enjoyed More Rights in Nabataean State than in Saudi Arabia Today," http://www.middle-east-online.com/english/?id=25650 (accessed February 3, 2009).

42. "The Extremism of the Muslims in the West and Our Responsibility," *Al-Iqtisadiyya*, August 21, 2006, cited in Memri Special Dispatch series, no. 1274, http://memri.org/bin/articles.cgi?Page=archives&Area=sd&ID=SP127406 (accessed February 3, 2009).

43. Ibid.

44. Abeer Allam, "Saudi Religious Police Get Tough on Fashion," *Financial Times*, September 27, 2008.

45. "Women Face Curbs in Makka Mosque," Al-Jazeera, August 28, 2006, reproduced at Sweetness and Light blog, http://sweetness-light.com/archive/muslim-women-faces-restrictions-in-mecca (accessed February 3, 2009).

46. Excerpts from an interview with Saudi author Zaynab Hifni, aired on Al-Arabiya TV, May 19, 2006, in Memri Special Dispatch Series, no. 1179, June 1, 2006, http://www.memri.org/bin/articles.cgi?Page=archives&Area=sd&ID=SP 11790 (accessed February 3, 2009).

47. "Imagine You're a Woman."

48. Debate on types of marriage in the Arab world, aired on Abu Dhabi TV.

49. Harry de Quetteville, "Taboo 'Behind the Veil' Novel Tops the Saudi Bestseller Lists," *Telegraph* (London), February 4, 2006, http://www.telegraph.co.uk/news/main.jhtml?xml=/news/2006/02/05/wnovel05.xml&sSheet=/news/2006/02/05/ixworld.html (accessed February 3, 2009).

50. Maha Akeel, "When Is a Saudi Woman Considered an Adult?" Aafaq, November 4, 2007, http://www.aafaq.org/english/inbox.aspx?id_alri=24# (accessed February 3, 2009).

51. Roger Hardy, "Unemployment, the New Saudi Challenge," *BBC News*, October 4, 2006, http://news.bbc.co.uk/1/hi/business/5406328.stm (accessed February 3, 2009).

52. Akeel, "When Is a Saudi Woman Considered an Adult?"

53. Ibid.

54. Ibid.

55. Ibid.

56. Ibid.

57. Hardy, "Unemployment, the New Saudi Challenge."

58. Matthew Campbell, "Testimony of a Broken Face—Interview with Rania

Al-Baz," *Times* (London), October 16, 2005, http://www.timesonline.co.uk/tol/news/article578853.ece (accessed February 3, 2009).

59. Ibid.

60. Ibid.

61. Ibid.

62. "Beaten Saudi Woman Speaks Out," *BBC News*, April 30, 2004, http://news.bbc.co.uk/2/hi/middle_east/3667349.stm (accessed February 3, 2009).

63. "Saudi Women Angered by Oprah Winfrey Show," Memri, July 20, 2005, http://www.memri.org/bin/articles.cgi?Page=archives&Area=sd&ID=SP93705#_ednref3 (accessed March 21, 2009).

64. Nimah Nawwab, "The Price of Abuse," *Arab News*, December 8, 2007, http://www.arabnews.com/?page=7&section=0&article=104409&d=8&m=12&y=2007 (accessed February 3, 2009).

65. Campbell, "Testimony of a Broken Face."

66. Maha Al-Hujailan, "The Nature of the Abaya," *Arab News*, November 6, 2006, http://www.arabnews.com/?page=7&section=0&article=77694&d=6&m=11&y=2006 (accessed February 4, 2009).

67. Maha Al-Hujailan, "The Intimidation of Women in Our Society," *Al-Watan* (Saudi Arabia), January 28, 2007, cited in "Saudi Women Columnists Protest against Oppression of Women in Saudi Arabia," Memri Special Dispatch Series, no. 1570, May 4, 2007, http://www.memri.org/bin/opener.cgi?Page=archives&ID=SP157007 (accessed February 4, 2009).

68. Al-Hujailan, "The Nature of the Abaya."

69. Ibid.

70. Ibid.

71. Ibid.

72. Ibid.

73. Ibid.

74. Ibid.

75. Ibid.

76. Ibid.

77. Ibid.

78. Ibid.

79. Rezgar.com, May 25, 2006, http://www.rezgar.com/debat/show.art.asp?aid=65733A, cited in A. Dankowitz, "Saudi Writer and Journalist Wajeha Al-Huwaider Fights for Women's Rights," Memri Inquiry and Analysis Series, no. 312, December 28, 2006, http://memri.org/bin/articles.cgi?Page=archives&Area=ia&ID=IA31206 (accessed March 22, 2009).

80. "The Arab Rosa Parks," Aafaq, November 1, 2007, http://www.aafaq.org/english/aafaq_today.aspx?id_news=60 as cited in "New Arab-English Reform

Website on 'The Arab Rosa Parks,'" Memri Special Dispatch–Reform Project, no. 1757, November 2, 2007, http://www.memri.org/bin/articles.cgi?Page=archives &Area=sd&ID=SP175707 (accessed February 4, 2009).

81. Wajeha Al-Huwaider, "The Upbringing of Males in Arabic Society," *Arab News*, August 15, 2003, http://www.arabnews.com/?page=9&section=0&article =30304&d=15&m=8&y=2003 (accessed March 21, 2009).

82. Wajeha Al-Huwaider, "When" (satirical poem), Aafaq, September 28, 2007, http://www.aafaq.org/english/pysk.aspx?id_alri=14 (accessed March 21, 2009).

83. Interview with Wajeha Al-Huwaider, Hurra TV, May 26, 2007, cited in "There Are Five Types of Shackles, or Jails, for the Woman—If She Manages to Escape One, She Might Enter Another," Memri Special Dispatch Series, no. 1604, June 1, 2007, http://www.memritv.org/search.asp?ACT=S9&P1=1465 (accessed February 4, 2009).

84. See http://www.metransparent.com/texts/wajeha_al_huwaider_5_percent .htm, July 15, 2006, cited in Dankowitz, "Saudi Writer and Journalist Wajeha Al-Huwaider Fights for Women's Rights."

85. "Saudi Arabia: Writer and Human Rights Activist Detained: Letter to Assistant Minister for Security Affairs HRH Mohammed bin Nayef bin Abdulaziz Al Saud," Human Rights Watch, October 20, 2006, http://hrw.org/english/docs/ 2006/10/20/saudia14461.htm (accessed February 4, 2009).

86. Omran Salman interview with Wajeha Al-Huwaider, Aafaq, http:// www.aafaq.org/english/search.aspx as cited in "Saudi Feminist Wajeha Al-Huwaider: The Campaign for Women's Right to Drive in Saudi Arabia Is Just the Beginning," Memri Special Dispatch–Saudi Arabia/Reform Project, no. 1722, September 21, 2007, http://memri.org/bin/articles.cgi?Page=archives&Area=sd&ID =SP172207 (accessed March 22, 2009).

87. Damien McElroy, "Saudi Arabia to Lift Ban on Women Drivers," *Telegraph* (London), January 21, 2008, http://www.telegraph.co.uk/news/main.jhtml?xml=/ news/2008/01/21/wsaudi121.xml (accessed March 22, 2009).

88. "The Arab Rosa Parks."

89. Metransparent.com, May 1, 2004, http://www.metransparent.com/texts/ wajeha_al_huwaider_alonousa.htm, cited in Dankowitz, "Saudi Writer and Journalist Wajeha Al-Huwaider Fights for Women's Rights."

90. "Saudi Human and Women's Rights Activist Wajeha Al-Huwaider Speaks Out against Honor Killings," Memri Special Dispatch Series, no. 1945, June 2, 2008, http://www.memri.org/bin/articles.cgi?Page=archives&Area=sd&ID =SP194508 (accessed March 22, 2009).

91. Dankowitz, "Saudi Writer and Journalist Wajeha Al-Huwaider Fights for Women's Rights."

92. Ibid.

93. Ibid.

94. Ibid.

95. In her defense, the Syrian woman, Khamisa Mohammed Sawadi, claimed one of the men was indeed related to her as a son "through breast-feeding." See chapter 28.

96. Mohammed Jamjoom and Saad Abedine, "Saudis Order 40 Lashes for Elderly Woman for Mingling," *CNN*, http://www.cnn.com/2009/WORLD/meast/03/09/saudi.arabia.lashes/index.html (accessed March 11, 2009).

97. Elaph.com, February 5, 2006, http://www.elaph.com/elaphweb/Elaph Writer/2005/2/38710.htm?KeyWords=vZjHNMUVQ+0S+WDM66+mqg, cited in Dankowitz, "Saudi Writer and Journalist Wajeha Al-Huwaider Fights for Women's Rights."

98. This refers to the Battle of the Camel in 656 CE.

99. Metransparent.com, August 26, 2006, http://www.metransparent.com/texts/wajeha_al_huwaider_i_am_afraid.htm, cited in Dankowitz, "Saudi Writer and Journalist Wajeha Al-Huwaider Fights for Women's Rights."

100. Elaph.com, March 7, 2005, http://www.elaph.com/ElaphWriter/2005/3/45862.htm, cited in "Arab Feminists on Women's Rights: Cats and Dogs in the Developed World Have More Rights Than Women in the Arab and Muslim World," Memri Special Dispatch Series, no. 890, April 12, 2005, http://memri.org/bin/articles.cgi?Page=archives&Area=sd&ID=SP89005 (accessed March 22, 2009).

101. Metransparent.com, July 15, 2006, http://www.metransparent.com/texts/wajeha_al_huwaider_5_percent.htm, as cited in Dankowitz, "Saudi Writer and Journalist Wajeha Al-Huwaider Fights for Women's Rights."

102. Elaph.com, March 7, 2005, http://www.elaph.com/ElaphWriter/2005/3/45862.htm, cited in Dankowitz, "Saudi Writer and Journalist Wajeha Al-Huwaider Fights for Women's Rights."

103. Ibid.

104. *Al-Riyadh* (Saudi Arabia), February 18, 2007, in "Saudi Women Columnists Protest against Oppression of Women in Saudi Arabia," Memri Special Dispatch Series, no. 1570, May 4, 2007, http://www.memri.org/bin/opener.cgi?Page=archives&ID=SP157007 (accessed March 22, 2009).

105. Ibid.

106. Ibid.

107. Ibid.

108. Ibid.

109. Ibid.

110. Ibid.

111. Ibid.

112. Ibid.

113. "Saudi Journalist: The Belgians Publish the Koran—And We Spread Horror," Memri Special Dispatch Series, no. 1530, April 3, 2007, http://memri .org/bin/latestnews.cgi?ID=SD153007 (February 4, 2009).

114. Ibid.

115. Ibid.

116. Ibid.

117. Ibid.

118. Raid Qusti, "Misconception the Root of Our Problems," March 14, 2005, http://www.arabnews.com/?page=6&section=0&article=60072&d=7&m=3&y =2005 (accessed February 4, 2009).

119. Ibid.

120. Javid Hassan and Hasan Hatrash, "Nadia Bakhurji Pledges to Back Women Engineers," *Arab News*, December 26, 2005, http://www.arabnews.com/?page=1& section=0&article=75263&d=268&m=12&y=2005 (accessed February 4, 2009).

121. Somayya Jabarti, "Engineers Council Poll: One More Step for Saudi Women," *Arab News*, December 28, 2005, http://www.arabnews.com/?page=1 &section =0&article=75393&d=28&m=12&y=2005 (accessed February 4, 2009).

122. Hassan and Hatrash, "Nadia Bakhurji Pledges to Back Women Engineers."

123. Bill Law, "Saudi Stories: Candidates," *BBC News*, July 4, 2005, http:// news.bbc.co.uk/2/hi/middle_east/4648087.stm (accessed February 4, 2009).

124. Ibid.

125. Qusti, "Misconception the Root of Our Problems."

126. Ibid.

127. Ibid.

128. Ibid.

129. Ibid.

130. Ibid.

131. Ibid.

132. Samar Fatany, "Education Reform Is the Pathway to the Future," *Arab News*, October 2, 2007.

133. Ibid.

134. Ibid.

135. Samar Fatany, "Women: Small Steps Taken Where Giant Strides Needed," *Arab News*, May 28, 2008.

136. Ibid.

137. Samar Fatany, "Women's Rights in Kingdom," *Arab News*, July 22, 2008.

138. Samar Fatany, "Plight of Women Gets Deserved Attention," *Arab News*, June 1, 2008.

139. Ibid.

140. Samar Fatany, *Saudi Women: Towards a New Era* (Ghainaa Publications, 2007), p. 56.

141. Samar Fatany, "Let's Embrace Moderation," *Arab News*, September 16, 2008.

142. Samar Fatany, "Let Us Codify Shariah Laws," *Arab News*, January 31, 2008.

143. Ibid.

144. Lubna Hussain, "Emancipating a Nation," *Arab News*, April 1, 2005, http://www.arabnews.com/?page=9&section=0&article=61400&d=1&m=4&y =2005 (accessed February 4, 2009).

145. Ibid.

146. Ibid.

147. Ibid.

148. Ibid.

149. Ibid.

150. Ibid.

151. Lubna Hussain, "A Slap in the Face of Justice," *Arab News*, November 21, 2007, http://www.arabnews.com/?page=7&section=0&article=103806&d=21&m =11&y=2007 (accessed February 4, 2009).

152. Ibid.

153. Ibid.

154. Halima Muzaffar, "What's Happening in the Girls' Schools?" *Al-Watan* (Saudi Arabia), January 8, 2008, cited in "Saudi Columnist Criticizes Preoccupation with Death in Saudi Girls' Schools," Memri Special Dispatch Series, No. 1831, January 31, 2008, http://www.memri.org/bin/articles.cgi?Page=archives&Area=sd&ID =SP183108 (accessed February 4, 2009).

155. Ibid. According to the Islamic faith, Allah sends the destroying angels Munkar and Nakir to question the deceased in his grave regarding his religion and beliefs. If his answers are unsatisfactory, the angels break his bones with their hammers.

156. Ibid.

CHAPTER 21: SOMALIA

1. "Somalia: Women Demand Greater Role in Government," November 28, 2004, UN Office for the Coordination of Humanitarian Affairs, http://www.irinnews .org/report.aspx?reportid=52243 (accessed February 8, 2009).

2. United Nations Development Programme (UNDP-POGAR), "Gender

and Citizenship, Somalia, Women in Public Life," http://gender.pogar.org/countries/country.asp?cid=17 (accessed February 8, 2009).

3. "Somalia: Women Demand Greater Role in Government," November 29, 2004, *IRIN News*, http://www.irinnews.org/report.aspx?reportid=52243 (accessed March 22, 2009).

4. Ibid.

5. United Nations Development Programme (UNDP–POGAR), "Gender and Citizenship."

6. Somalia: "UNICEF at Work in Somalia," http://www.unicef.org/somalia/about.html (accessed February 8, 2009).

7. United Nations Development Programme, "Gender and Citizenship."

8. Ibid.

9. Ibid.

10. *Nagaad* is a Somali word meaning "after hardship and difficulties, we have come to rest in peace."

11. United Nations Development Programme, "Gender and Citizenship."

12. David Cohen, "Violence Is Inherent in Islam—It Is a Cult of Death," *Evening Standard* (London), February 7, 2007, reprinted on the Lawyers Christian Fellowship Web site, http://www.lawcf.org/index.asp?page=Evening+Standard+article+on+Islam+in+Britain (accessed February 20, 2009).

13. Ayaan Hirsi Ali, *Infidel* (New York: Free Press, 2007), p. 17.

14. Ibid., p. 33.

15. Ibid.

16. Ibid., p. 118.

17. Ibid., p. 174.

18. Ibid., p. 246.

19. Ibid., p. 272.

20. Ibid., p. 285.

21. Ibid., p. 302.

22. Ibid., p. 296.

23. Ibid., p. 295.

24. Ibid., pp. 308–309.

25. Cohen, "Violence Is Inherent in Islam."

26. Hirsi Ali, *Infidel*, p. 304.

27. Fareena Alam, "Enemy of the Faith," *New Statesman*, July 24, 2006, http://www.newstatesman.com/200607240051 (accessed March 22, 2009).

28. Ayaan Hirsi Ali, "The Role of Journalism Today," speech given to the National Press Club (Washington), June 18, 2007, http://www.aei.org/publications/pubID.26367,filter.all/pub_detail.asp (accessed March 22, 2009).

29. "Submission Part 1 by Theo Van Gogh," http://www.submission.eu.tt (accessed March 22, 2009).

30. "Manifesto of Liberties," http://www.manifeste.org/article.php3?id _article=18 (accessed February 20, 2009).

31. "Ayaan Hirsi Ali Press Statement on Resignation from Parliament," May 16, 2006 http://www.pierre-van-paassen.com/files/resourcesmodule/@random4477 a2cfc8fb8/1148691274_Ayaan_Hirsi_Ali.pdf (accessed February 20, 2009).

32. Bill Steigerwald, "Defiant Infidel," *Front Page Magazine*, May 2, 2007, http://frontpagemag.com/articles/Read.aspx?GUID=FE2A4FFB-6AE6-4CD3 -BE81-3F57CDC1E569 (accessed February 20, 2009).

33. Anne Applebaum, "The Fight for Muslim Women," *Washington Post*, February 4, 2007.

34. Alam, "Enemy of the Faith."

35. Hirsi Ali, "The Role of Journalism Today."

36. Ibid.

37. Steigerwald, "Defiant Infidel."

38. Janet Albrechtsen, "Enlightened Spirit of Inquiry," *Australian*, August 6, 2008, http://www.theaustralian.news.com.au/story/0,25197,24134569-32522,00 .html (accessed February 20, 2009).

39. Jeppe Hirslund Wohlert, "Somalian Woman Honored for Work," *No Peace without Justice*, April 19, 2005, http://www.npwj.net/node/2299 (accessed February 8, 2009).

40. Ibid.

41. Ibid.

42. Ibid.

43. Amnesty International DC Women's Human Rights Action Team, http://dcwhrat.blogspot.com/2005/04/upcoming-event-discussion-with-hawa.html (accessed February 8, 2009).

44. Ibid.

45. "Somalia: Giving Somali Girls a Chance," May 30, 2007, *IRIN News*, http://www.irinnews.org/Report.aspx?ReportId=72452 (accessed March 22, 2008).

46. Ibid.

47. Hawa Aden Mohamed, Iranian Women's Network Association (SHABAKEH) http://www.shabakeh.de/en/archives/individual/000167.html (accessed February 8, 2009).

48. "Somalia: Giving Somali Girls a Chance,"

49. Wohlert, "Somalian Woman Honored for Work."

50. Ibid.

51. Ibid.

52. Hawa Aden Mohamed, Iranian Women's Network Association.

53. "Somalia: Giving Somali Girls a Chance."

54. Ibid.

55. Wells Dunbar, "Amnesty International Does Austin," *Austin Chronicle*, April 15, 2005, http://www.austinchronicle.com/gyrobase/Issue/story?oid=oid :266774 (accessed February 8, 2008).

CHAPTER 22: SUDAN

1. "Rebuilding Sudan . . . One Woman at a Time," Women for Women International, http://www.womenforwomen.org/global-initiatives-helping-women/ help-women-sudan.php (accessed February 7, 2009).

2. Ibid.

3. Ibid.

4. Wayne Ellwood, "Fatima Ahmed Ibrahim: . . . a Sudanese Activist Who Has Long Campaigned for Women's Rights in Her Country," *New Internationalist*, February 1996, http://findarticles.com/p/articles/mi_m0JQP/is_276/ai_30468449 (accessed March 22, 2009).

5. Dr. William F. Schulz, executive director of Amnesty International USA, cited by Lisa Alvy, in "Violence against Women in Sudan Reveals Common Weapon of War," National Organization for Women, December 3, 2004, http://www .now.org/issues/global/120304sudan.html?printable (accessed February 7, 2009).

6. Alvy, "Violence against Women in Sudan Reveals Common Weapon of War."

7. Ibid.

8. "Women to Women—DARFUR," May 30, 2006, http://hellonearth .wordpress.com/2006/05/30/women-to-women-darfur (accessed February 7, 2009).

9. United Nations Development Programme (UNDP–POGAR), "Gender, Sudan," http://www.pogar.org/countries/gender.asp?cid=18 (accessed March 22, 2009).

10. "Rebuilding Sudan . . . One Woman at a Time."

11. Ibid.

12. United Nations Development Programme, "Gender, Sudan."

13. "Sudan Blasted on Women's Ban," September 7, 2000, http://www.hrw .org/en/news/2000/09/07/sudan-blasted-womens-ban (accessed February 7, 2009).

14. Monika Hoegen, trans. from German by Mark Rossman, "Portrait Awatif Elageed," February 25, 2005, http://www.qantara.de/webcom/ show_article.php/ _c-478/_nr-245/i.html (accessed March 28, 2009).

15. "Weaving the Social Networks of Women Migrants in Sudan: The Case of Gezira, http://www.buchhandel.de/detailansicht.aspx?isbn=978-3-8258-1726-8 (accessed March 28, 2009).

16. Hoegen, "Portrait Awatif Elageed."

17. Ibid.

18. Ibid.

19. Wayne Ellwood, "The NI Interview, Fatima Ahmed Ibrahim," *New Internationalist*, no. 276, February 1996, http://www.newint.org/issue276/interview.htm (accessed February 7, 2009).

20. Fatima Ahmed Mohamed Ibrahim, "My Life: Personal Biography," http://www.ibn-rushd.org/pages/int/Awards/2006/documents/cv-long-en.html (accessed March 22, 2009).

21. Ibid.

22. Ibid.

23. Ibid.

24. "Sudanese Human Rights Activist Fatima Ibrahim Receives Ibn Rushd Award," http://www.arabworldbooks.com/News/newsitem2.htm (accessed February 7, 2009).

25. Ibid.

26. Ibrahim, "My Life: Personal Biography."

27. "Sudanese Human Rights Activist Fatima Ibrahim Receives Ibn Rushd Award."

28. Ibrahim, "My Life: Personal Biography."

29. Ibid.

30. Ibid.

31. "Sudanese Human Rights Activist Fatima Ibrahim Receives Ibn Rushd Award."

32. Ibid.

33. Ibid.

34. "Fatima Ahmed Retires from Sudanese Communist Party, Parliament," *Sudan Tribune*, March 19, 2007, http://www.sudantribune.com/spip.php?article20869 (accessed February 7, 2009).

35. Ibrahim, "My Life: Personal Biography."

36. Al-Arabiya TV, October 10, 2008, cited in "Sudan Liberation Movement Leader Abd Al-Wahed Al-Nur Supports Relations with Israel: An Israeli Embassy in Khartoum Will Serve Interests of the Sudanese People," Memri Special Dispatch Series, no. 2119, November 17, 2008, http://www.memri.org/bin/latestnews.cgi?ID=SD211908 (accessed March 28, 2009).

37. "Sudanese-Canadian Human Rights Activist Taraji Mustafa Talks about the Sudanese-Israeli Friendship Association She Founded," Al-Arabiya TV, De-

cember 1, 2006, Memri TV Clip no. 1331, http://www.memritv.org/clip/en/1331 .htm?auth=f45157b8f19af1c85050f2 0d14df8326 (accessed March 28 2009).

38. Ibid.

39. Ibid.

40. Ibid.

41. Brian Adeba, "Sudan-Israel Friendship Group Breaks Taboos," *Sudan Tribune*, January 18, 2007, http://www.sudantribune.com/spip.php?article19797 (accessed February 8, 2009).

42. Ibid.

43. Ibid.

44. "Sudanese-Canadian Human Rights Activist Taraji Mustafa Talks about the Sudanese-Israeli Friendship Association She Founded."

CHAPTER 23: SYRIA

1. US Department of State, "Syria," http://www.state.gov/g/drl/rls/hrrpt/ 2004/41732.htm (accessed February 8, 2009).

2. United Nations Development Programme (UNDP–POGAR), "Gender and Citizenship: Arab Countries," http://gender.pogar.org/countries/country .asp?cid=19 (accessed February 8, 2009).

3. World Bank Group GenderStats, http://go.worldbank.org/AETRQ5 QAC0 (accessed February 8, 2009).

4. United Nations Development Programme, "Gender and Citizenship: Arab Countries."

5. Ibid.

6. Ibid.

7. "Syrian Women's Union," http://www.mediterraneas.org/article.php3?id _article=201 (accessed February 8, 2009).

8. United Nations Development Programme, "Gender and Citizenship: Arab Countries."

9. "Syria, Events of 2008," Human Rights Watch, http://www.hrw.org/en/ world-report-2009/syria (accessed February 9, 2009).

10. US Department of State, "Syria."

11. Katherine Zoepf, "U.N. Finds That 25% of Married Syrian Women Have Been Beaten," *New York Times*, April 11, 2006, http://www.nytimes.com/2006/04/ 11/world/middleeast/11syria.html (accessed February 8, 2009).

12. "Profiles: For Bread and Democracy," *Syria Today*, August 2005, http:// www.syria-today.com (accessed February 9, 2009).

13. Ibid.

14. Ibid.

15. Interview with Syrian historian and author Dr. Georgette Attiyya, Syrian TV, June 15, 2005, in Memri TV Clip no. 715, June 15, 2005, http://www.memritv.org/clip_transcript/en/715.htm (accessed February 9, 2009).

16. Ruthie Blum Leibowitz, "One on One: A Woman's Work in Progress," *Jerusalem Post*, October 25, 2006.

17. Ibid.

18. Janet Albrechtsen, "Breakout from Islam's Mental Prison," *Australian*, August 22, 2007.

19. Blum Leibowitz, "One on One: A Woman's Work in Progress."

20. Ibid.

21. Asra Q. Nomani, "Wafa Sultan," *Time*, April 30, 2006.

22. John M. Broder, "For Muslim Who Says Violence Destroys Islam, Violent Threats," *New York Times*, March 11, 2006.

23. Jamie Glazov, "A Voice of Courage," *Front Page Magazine*, December 27, 2007, http://frontpagemag.com/Articles/Printable.aspx?GUID=985C80CF-FA08 -46D5-B696-E0B1A9E391A7 (accessed July 15, 2008).

24. "LA Psychologist Wafa Sultan Clashes with Algerian Islamist Ahmad bin Muhammad over Islamic Teachings and Terrorism," Memri TV Clip no. 783, Al Jazeera TV, July 26, 2005, http://www.memritv.org/clip/en/783.htm (accessed March 22, 2009).

25. Ibid.

26. "Arab-American Psychiatrist Wafa Sultan: There Is No Clash of Civilizations but a Clash between the Mentality of the Middle Ages and That of the 21st Century," Memri TV Clip no. 1050, Al Jazeera TV, February 21, 2006, http://www.memritv.org/clip_transcript/en/1050.htm (accessed March 22, 2009).

27. Broder, "For Muslim Who Says Violence Destroys Islam, Violent Threats."

28. Nomani, "Wafa Sultan."

29. "Panel: Women in Islam," http://www.youtube.com/watch?v=up3yu QDAWKQ (accessed March 23, 2009).

30. Blum Leibowitz, "One on One: A Woman's Work in Progress."

31. Interview with Wafa Sultan, Al-Hayat TV, December 4, 2008, cited in "Arab-American Psychiatrist Wafa Sultan: The Subjugation of Women Reduces Them to a Level Lower Than Beasts," Memri TV Clip no. 1993, February 4, 2009, http://www.memritv.org/clip/en/1993.htm (accessed February 17, 2009).

32. Stephen Julius Stein, "Islam's Ann Coulter: The Seductive and Blinkered Belligerence of Wafa Sultan," *Los Angeles Times*, July 16, 2008.

33. Broder, "For Muslim Who Says Violence Destroys Islam, Violent Threats."

34. "Dr. Wafa Sultan in Hiding," *Israel National News*, http://www.israel
nationalnews.com/News/Flash.aspx/144165 (accessed March 23, 2009).

35. Glazov, "A Voice of Courage."

36. Albrechtsen, "Breakout from Islam's Mental Prison."

37. Syrian Women Observatory, November 1, 2006, "Who Stabbed Syria . . .
in the Face?" http://nesasy.org/languages/index.php/En/2006/11 (accessed February
9, 2009).

38. Ibid.

39. Freedom House, "Syria," 2004, http://www.freedomhouse.org/template
.cfm?page=183 (accessed February 9, 2009).

40. Ibid.

41. United Nations Development Programme (UNDP–POGAR), "Gender
and Citizenship, Syria, Women in Public Life," http://gender.pogar.org/countries/
country.asp?cid=19 (accessed February 9, 2009).

42. Ibid.

43. Syrian Women Observatory, http://www.nesasy.org/languages/index.php/
En (accessed February 9, 2009).

44. Freedom House, "Syria."

45. "Syria, Events of 2008," Human Rights Watch, http://www.hrw.org/en/
world-report-2009/syria (accessed February 9, 2009).

46. "Honor Crimes, Stop Women Killing. . . . Stop Honor Crimes!" SWO,
October 5, 2006, http://nesasy.org/languages/index.php/En?s=stop+honor+crimes
&sentence=sentence&submit=Search (accessed February 9, 2009).

47. Bassam Al-Kadi, "The Knife of Honor Slices Zahra's Throat!!" trans.
Areej Shmaies, SWO, January 22, 2007, http://nesasy.org/languages/index.php/
En?cat=23 (accessed March 23, 2009).

48. Bassam Al-Kadi, "Killing Syrian Women Continues, a New 'Honor
Crime' in Edleb!" trans. Nawar El-Sabaa, SWO, January 5, 2008, http://nesasy.org/
languages/index.php/En?s=killing+syrian+women+continues&sentence=sentence
&submit=Search (accessed February 9, 2009).

49. Kinda Shammat, "Domestic Violence," trans. Basel Jbaily, SWO, October
21, 2008, http://www.nesasy.org/languages/index.php/En?blog=6&cat=22&page
=1&paged=3 (accessed February 9, 2009).

50. Dr. Bassam Al Mohammad, "Physical Harm against Women Caused by
Domestic Violence," trans. Diala Halloum, SWO, October 21, 2006, http://www
.nesasy.org/languages/index.php/En?blog=6&cat=22&page=1&paged=3 (accessed
February 9, 2009).

51. Katherine Zoepf, "Syria's First Study of Violence against Women Breaks
Taboo," *New York Times*, April 10, 2006, http://www.nytimes.com/2006/04/10/
world/middleeast/10cnd-syria.html (accessed February 9, 2009).

52. Abdullah Ali, "Sexual Coercion between the Right of Husband and the Freedom of Wife," trans. Angela Shoufi, SWO, March 22, 2008, http://nesasy.org/languages/index.php/En/2008/05/10/p198#more198 (accessed February 9, 2009).

53. Ahmad Manoha, "The Return of Slaves in the Modern Age: The Maids in Syria," trans. Diala Halloum, SWO, October 21, 2008, http://www.nesasy.org/languages/index.php/En?blog=6&cat=22&page=1&paged=3 (accessed February 9, 2009).

54. "Report on Application of the Convention on the Elimination of All Forms of Discrimination against Women in Syria (CEDAW)," trans. Angela Shoufi, SWO, May 20, 2007, http://www.nesasy.org/pdf/En/E-cedaw-report-SWO-05-2007.pdf (accessed February 9, 2009).

CHAPTER 24: TUNISIA

1. "Tunisia Gender Profile," *Afrol News*, http://www.afrol.com/features/13250 (accessed February 9, 2009).

2. Ibid.

3. World Bank Group GenderStats, http://go.worldbank.org/AETRQ5QAC0 (accessed March 23, 2009).

4. United Nations Development Programme (UNDP–POGAR), Gender and Citizenship Initiative, "Country Profiles: Tunisia," http://gender.pogar.org/countries/country.asp?cid=20 (accessed March 23, 2009).

5. Ibid.

6. "Tunisian Women: Effective Partners of Men," *North Africa Times*, August 26, 2007.

7. Ibid.

8. Ibid.

9. Ibid.

10. Mounira M. Charrad, *States and Women's Rights: The Making of Postcolonial Tunisia, Algeria and Morocco* (Berkeley: University of California Press, 2001). See http://ark.cdlib.org/ark:/13030/ft05800335 (accessed March 23, 2009).

11. Ibid., pp. 234–38.

12. Ibid.

13. Ibid.

14. See www.metransparent.com, March 13, 2005, cited in "Arab Feminists on Women's Rights: Cats and Dogs in the Developed World Have More Rights Than Women in the Arab and Muslim World," Memri Special Dispatch Series, no. 890, April 12, 2005, http://memri.org/bin/articles.cgi?Page=archives&Area=sd&ID=SP89005 (accessed February 9, 2009).

15. Ibid.

16. Ibid.

17. "Shari'a Must Not Be Implemented Today," www.metransparent.com, September 9, 2004, cited in "Tunisian University Lecturer: Shari'a Must Not Be Implemented Today," Memri Special Dispatch Series, no. 795, October 6, 2004, http://memri.org/bin/articles.cgi?Page=archives&Area=sd&ID=SP79504 (accessed March 14, 2009).

18. Ibid.

19. Ibid.

20. See www.metransparent.com, March 19, 2005, cited in "Arab Feminists on Women's Rights: Cats and Dogs in the Developed World Have More Rights Than Women in the Arab and Muslim World," Memri Special Dispatch Series, no. 890, April 12, 2005, http://memri.org/bin/articles.cgi?Page=archives&Area=sd&ID=SP89005 (accessed February 9, 2009). All other quotations in this section are taken from the same source.

21. See www.metransparent.com, February 2, 2005, cited in "Arab Feminists on Women's Rights: Cats and Dogs in the Developed World Have More Rights Than Women in the Arab and Muslim World," Memri Special Dispatch Series, no. 890, April 12, 2005, http://memri.org/bin/articles.cgi?Page=archives&Area=sd&ID=SP89005 (accessed February 9, 2009).

22. Samia Labidi, "A Nightmare in Tunisia," in *Leaving Islam: Apostates Speak Out*, ed. Ibn Warraq (Amherst, NY: Prometheus Books, 2003), p. 330.

23. Ibid. p. 321.

24. Ibid.

25. Ibid., p. 322.

26. Ibid.

27. Ibid., p. 324.

28. Ibid., p. 325.

29. Ibid., p. 327.

30. Ibid.

31. Samia Labidi, *Karim Mon Frère, Ex-intégriste et Terroriste* (Paris: Flammarion, 1998).

32. Labidi, "A Nightmare in Tunisia," p. 329.

33. Association d'Ailleurs Mais Ensemble (AIME), http://www.assoaime.net (accessed July 23, 2008).

34. Labidi, "A Nightmare in Tunisia," p. 330.

35. Samia Labidi, *D. Le Zéro Neutre* (Paris: Editions Publibook, 2001).

36. Labidi, "A Nightmare in Tunisia," p. 331.

37. Samia Labidi, *Mazel Azel* (Paris: Editions Publibook, 2000).

38. *Mazel Azel*, excerpt in review by Center for Inquiry, http://www.centerfor inquiry.net/isis/islamic_viewpoints/cdwrme_bulletin_13 (accessed February 9, 2009).

39. Labidi, "A Nightmare in Tunisia," pp. 331–32.

40. *Afrique Magazine* (France), August–September 2006, cited in "Tunisian Feminist Fawzia Zouari on 50th Anniversary of Tunis's Personal Status Code: 'In Tunisia, Women Have Become Just Like Any Other Man,'" http://memri.org/bin/ articles.cgi?Page=archives&Area=sd&ID=SP131406 (accessed March 31, 2009).

41. Ibid.

CHAPTER 25: TURKEY

1. Ayse Ozturk, "Turkey's Engagement with Women's Rights," *Studies in Global Media*, Spring 2007, http://www.media-studies.ca/globalmedia/ozturk/ women.htm (accessed February 10, 2009).

2. In most Western European countries, women were not granted suffrage until the end of World War II or later: France 1944; Italy 1945; Greece 1952; Belgium 1960; and Switzerland 1972. See Ozturk, "Turkey's Engagement with Women's Rights."

3. Ozturk, "Turkey's Engagement with Women's Rights."

4. Sarah Rainsford, "Women Condemn Turkey Constitution," *BBC News*, October 2, 2007, http://news.bbc.co.uk/go/pr/fr/-/2/hi/europe/7025294.stm (accessed February 10, 2009).

5. Yigal Schleifer, "Turkey's Political Tensions Weigh on Women's Heads," *Women's eNews*, March 17, 2008, http://www.womensenews.org/article.cfm/dyn/aid/ 3530/context/archive (accessed February 10, 2009).

6. "Turkey Fails to Protect Women," *BBC News*, June 2, 2004, http://news .bbc.co.uk/go/pr/fr/-/2/hi/europe/3768847.stm (accessed February 10, 2009).

7. Ibid.

8. Ozturk, "Turkey's Engagement with Women's Rights."

9. Rainsford, "Women Condemn Turkey Constitution."

10. Thomas Seibert, "Four Turkish Women in 10 Abused," *The National* (Abu Dhabi), February 17, 2009, http://www.thenational.ae/article/20090217/ FOREIGN/725388038/1002 (accessed March 19, 2009).

11. Nebahat Akkoç, "Imagining a New World," http://www.ciaonet.org/ journals/tpq/v6i1/0000378.pdf (accessed February 10, 2009).

12. Yigal Schleifer, "Women in Southeastern Turkey Now Have Own Oasis," *Women's eNews*, October 24, 2003, http://www.womensenews.org/article.cfm/dyn/ aid/1574/context/archive (accessed February 10, 2009).

13. Akkoç, "Imagining a New World."

14. Schleifer, "Women in Southeastern Turkey Now Have Own Oasis."

15. Seyhan Eksioglu, former president of KA-DER, quoted in Mariella Esvant, "No Moustache, No Place in Politics!" February 5, 2007, http://www.cafebabel.com/en/article.asp?T=T&Id=10799 (accessed January 16, 2009).

16. Seyhan Eksioglu, quoted in "Resulting Report on the International Congress on 'Women in the Alliance of Civilizations,'" January 28–29, 2006, in Ankara, p. 19, http://www.ksgm.gov.tr/congress_report.pdf (accessed January 19, 2009).

17. European Women's Lobby, Turkey, http://www.womenlobby.org/site/1Template1.asp?DocID=520&v1ID=&RevID=&namePage=&pageParent=&DocID_sousmenu= (accessed January 19, 2009).

18. CIA, "Turkey," in *The World Factbook*, http://www.cia.gov/library/publications/the-world-factbook/print/tu.html (accessed January 16, 2009).

19. Esvant, "No Moustache, No Place in Politics."

20. "Turkey—Women on the Rise?" http://www.qantara.de/webcom/show_article.php/_c-478/_nr-650/_p-1/i.html?PHPSESSID (accessed January 24, 2009).

21. "Mustache Goes a Long Way to Create Awareness," *Turkish Daily News*, March 26, 2007.

22. Dorian Jones, "Women Pushing for Increased Representation in Turkey," *VOA News*, July 16, 2007, http://www.voanews.com/english/archive/2007-07/2007-07-16-voa34.cfm?CFID=221855969&CFTOKEN=20028328 (accessed January 24, 2009).

23. "The Economics of Gender," World Economic Forum, http://www.weforum.org/en/knowledge/Events/2006/WorldEconomicForuminTurkey/KN_SESS_SUMM_18322?url=/en/knowledge/Events/2006/WorldEconomicForuminTurkey/KN_SESS_SUMM_18322 (accessed January 24, 2009).

24. "Women Aspiring to Top Candidates List," May 12, 2007, http://www.turks.us/article.php?story=20070512073637309 (accessed January 24, 2009).

25. "Turkey—Women on the Rise?"

26. Hülya Gülbahar, chairperson of KA-DER, quoted in "Women on the Rise?"

CHAPTER 26: USA

1. Mona Eltahawy, "Western Muslims and Terrorism Prevention," *Middle East Online*, October 29, 2007, http://www.middle-east-online.com/english/?id=22864 (accessed March 28, 2009).

2. Mona Eltahawy, http://www.monaeltahawy.com (accessed March 28, 2009).

3. Mona Eltahawy, "Shame on Egypt's Sexist Bullies," *Globe and Mail* (Toronto), August 5, 2008.

4. Mona Eltahawy, "Musawah—How Do You Say Equality?" *Jerusalem Post*, March 15, 2009.

5. Mona Eltahawy, "A Hymen, a Veil and France," Agence Global, July 21, 2008, http://agenceglobal.com/Article.asp?Id=1659 (accessed March 28, 2009).

6. "Detoxing the Lies of Mona Eltahawy," Dr. M's Analysis, February 2, 2006, http://drmaxtor.blogspot.com/2006/02/detoxing-lies-of-mona-eltahawy.html (accessed March 28, 2009).

7. Mona Eltahawy, "Iraq's Women Suicide Bombers," Agence Global, http://www.agenceglobal.com/Article.asp?Id=1514 (accessed March 28, 2009).

8. Mona Eltahawy, "Arab Bloggers Keep Watch Over Government—And Each Other," *PostGlobal*, May 22, 2008, http://newsweek.washingtonpost.com/post global/mona_eltahawy/2008/05/arab_bloggers_keep_watch_over.html (accessed March 28, 2009).

9. Jane Lampman, "Muslims Split over Gender Role: American Muslim Women Challenge the Tradition That Only Men Can Lead Ritual Prayers," *Christian Science Monitor*, March 28, 2005, http://www.csmonitor.com/2005/0328/p11s01 -wogi.html (accessed February 10, 2009).

10. Teresa Wiltz, "Her Vision of Islam Sees Women Praying Next to Men," *Seattle Times*, July 9, 2005, http://community.seattletimes.nwsource.com/archive/ ?date=20050709&slug=religionfeminist09m (accessed February 10, 2009).

11. "Women Face Curbs in Makka Mosque," Al-Jazeera, August 28, 2006, reproduced at Sweetness and Light blog, http://sweetness-light.com/archive/ muslim-women-faces-restrictions-in-mecca (accessed March 23, 2009).

12. Teresa Wiltz, "The Woman Who Went to the Front of the Mosque," *Washington Post*, June 5, 2005, http://www.washingtonpost.com/wp-dyn/content/ article/2005/06/04/AR2005060401646_pf.html (accessed March 23, 2009).

13. Asra Q. Nomani, "Struggle for the Soul of Islam," *Sojourners Magazine* 34, no. 1, January 2005, p. 9.

14. Ibid.

15. Wiltz, "The Woman Who Went to the Front of the Mosque."

16. Ibid.

17. Nomani, "Struggle for the Soul of Islam," p. 9.

18. Asma Gull Hasan, quoted in Wiltz, "The Woman Who Went to the Front of the Mosque."

19. Wiltz, "The Woman Who Went to the Front of the Mosque."

20. Asra Q. Nomani, "Tapping Islam's Feminist Roots," *Seattle Times*, December 14, 2005, http://seattletimes.nwsource.com/html/opinion/2s002674911 _sunislamwomen11.html (accessed February 10, 2009).

21. Ibid.

22. Amina Wadud, "A'ishah's Legacy," *New Internationalist*, no. 345, May 2002, http://www.newint.org/features/2002/05/01/aishahs-legacy/ (accessed February 12, 2009).

23. "Woman Leads US Muslims to Prayer," *BBC News*, March 18, 2005, http://news.bbc.co.uk/2/hi/americas/4361931.stm (accessed February 12, 2009).

24. Amina Wadud, *Qu'ran and Woman: Re-reading the Sacred Text from a Woman's Perspective* (New York: Oxford University Press, 1999).

25. Ibid.

26. Geneive Abdo, "When Islam Clashes with Women's Rights," *Boston Globe*, April 9, 2005.

27. Barbara Ferguson, "Woman Imam Raises Mixed Emotions," *Arab News*, March 20, 2005.

28. Luthfi Assyaukanie, "Amina Wadud's Breakthrough," August 10, 2005, http://www.quantara.de/webcom/show_article.php/_c-307/_nr-23/_p-1/i.html ?PHPSESSID=133099 (accessed February 12, 2009).

29. Ibid.

30. "Woman Leads Muslims in Prayers," *Daily News* (New York), March 19, 2005.

31. Amina Wadud, *Inside the Gender Jihad: Women's Reform in Islam* (Oxford: Oneworld Publications, 2006).

32. Interview with Amina Wadud, *Frontline*, http://www.pbs.org/wgbh/pages/frontline/shows/muslims/interviews/wadud.html (accessed February 12, 2009).

CHAPTER 27: YEMEN

1. See www.metransparent.com, April 4, 2006, excerpts cited in "Yemeni Reformist Writer Urges Muslim Women to Take Off the Veil," Memri Special Dispatch Series, no. 1144, April 24, 2006, http://www.memri.org/bin/articles.cgi ?Page=archives&Area=sd&ID=SP114406 (accessed February 12, 2009). All other quotations in this section are from the same source.

CHAPTER 28: MALE MUSLIM ACTIVISTS

1. Najah Alosaimi, "Saudi Arabia: Women's Rights Body in Pipeline," WLUML, January 28, 2008, http://www.wluml.org/english/newsfulltxt.shtml ?cmd[157]=x-157-560088 (accessed February 12, 2009).

2. Ibid.

3. Television debate, LBC TV, May 19, 2007, in "Saudi Intellectuals Discuss on LBC TV Whether Women Should Be Allowed to Drive," Memri Special Dispatch Series, no. 1613, June 7, 2007, http://memri.org/bin/latestnews.cgi?ID=SD161307 (accessed February 14, 2009).

4. Ibid.

5. Ibid.

6. Ibid.

7. Ibid.

8. "Editorial: Sleeping with a Devil in Islamic Clothing," *Awdalnews*, August 26, 2006, http://www.awdalnews.com/wmprint.php?ArtID=7794 (accessed March 25, 2009).

9. "Somali Muslim Journalist on the Detrimental Effects of Wahhabism on His Country," Memri Special Dispatch Series, no. 625, December 9, 2003, http://memri.org/bin/articles.cgi?Page=archives&Area=sd&ID=SP62503 (accessed August 24, 2008).

10. "Saudi Police 'Stopped' Fire Rescue," *BBC News*, March 15, 2002, http://news.bbc.co.uk/1/hi/world/middle_east/1874471.stm (accessed March 25, 2009). See also chapter 20, "Saudi Arabia," Background section.

11. "Somali Muslim Journalist on the Detrimental Effects of Wahhabism on His Country."

12. Ibid.

13. Abul Kasem, "Women in Islam: An Exegesis," Faith Freedom International, http://www.faithfreedom.org/Articles/abulkazem/Women_in_Islam.htm (accessed February 14, 2009).

14. Abul Kasem, "Islamic Women's Day," Faith Freedom International, http://www.faithfreedom.org/Articles/AbulKasem50315.htm (accessed March 25, 2009).

15. Jamie Glazov, "Abul Kasem in Interview: An 'Apostate' Speaks," *Front Page Magazine*, January 7, 2008, http://www.frontpagemag.com/Articles/Read.aspx?GUID=2297e37d-87c3-492e-8e5d-1808af77f703 (accessed February 14, 2009).

16. Abul Kasem, "Women's Paradise," http://www.islam-watch.org/Abul Kasem/womens_paradise.htm (accessed February 14, 2009).

17. Al-Hajj "Abdullah Yusuf" Ali CBE (1872–1953) was a South Asian Islamic scholar who translated the Koran into English. See http://www.masud.co.uk/ISLAM/bmh/BMH-IRO-famous_muslims.htm (accessed February 14, 2009).

18. Kasem, "Women's Paradise."

19. Ibid.

20. Kasem, "Women in Islam: An Exegesis."

21. Ibid.

22. Ibid.

23. Glazov, "Abul Kasem in Interview: An 'Apostate' Speaks."

24. Kasem, "Women in Islam: An Exegesis."

25. Lafif Lakhdar, interviewed by Professor M. Milson, Elaph.com, September 8, 2007, cited in "Tunisian Reformist Lafif Lakhdar: European Muslims Should Adopt Universal Values; There Is Only One Civilization; The Koranic Verse on Wife-Beating Should Be Abrogated; When Bourguiba Abolished Polygamy in Tunisia, the Majority of Women Were Opposed; Why?" Memri Special Dispatch—North African Reformist Thinkers Project, no. 1729, October 2, 2007, http://www.memri.org/bin/articles.cgi?Page=countries&Area=northafrica&ID=SP172907 (accessed February 14, 2009).

26. "Liberal Journalist Fired from *Al-Hayat*," Memri Special Dispatch Series, no. 439, November 13, 2002, http://memri.org/bin/articles.cgi?Page=archives&Area=sd&ID=SP43902 (accessed February 14, 2009).

27. Al-Jazeera TV (Qatar), May 21, 2001, cited in "Zionism and Nazism: A Discussion on the TV Channel Al-Jazeera," Memri Special Dispatch, no. 225, June 6, 2001, http://memri.org/bin/articles.cgi?Page=archives&Area=sd&ID=SP22501 (accessed March 26, 2009).

28. Lafif Lakhdar, interviewed by Professor M. Milson.

29. Ibid.

30. Elaph.com, April 24, 2005, cited in Aluma Dankowitz, "Tunisian Reformist Thinker: Secularism Is Vital for the Future of the Arab and Muslim World," Memri Inquiry and Analysis Series, no. 222, May 19, 2005, http://memri.org/bin/articles.cgi?Page=archives&Area=ia&ID=IA22205 (accessed February 14, 2009).

31. Ibid.

32. Ibid.

33. Lafif Lakhdar, interviewed by Professor M. Milson.

34. *Kol Ha'Ir* (Israel), March 19, 2004, cited in "Israeli Arab Intellectual and Poet on Illiteracy in the Arab World, 'Backward-Looking' Islam, and the Complex of Arab Secularists," Memri Special Dispatch, no. 688, March 31, 2004, http://memri.org/bin/articles.cgi?Page=archives&Area=sd&ID=SP68804 (accessed March 26, 2009).

35. A. Arazi and S. Masalha, *Six Early Arab Poets, New Edition and Concordance*, Max Schloessinger Memorial Series (Jerusalem: Institute of Asian and African Studies at the Hebrew University of Jerusalem, 1999).

36. Salman Masalha, Israel—Poetry International Web, June 26, 2006, http://israel.poetryinternationalweb.org/piw_cms/cms/cms_module/index.php?obj_id=3177 (accessed February 24, 2009).

37. Elaph.com, September 24, 2004, cited in "Israeli Arab Author: The Arab Man Is the Problem, the Arab Woman Is the Solution," Memri Special Dispatch, no.

807, October 28, 2004, http://memri.org/bin/articles.cgi?Page=archives&Area =sd&ID=SP80704 (accessed March 26, 2009).

38. Ibid.

39. Ibid.

40. *Arab News* (Saudi Arabia), September 17, 2003, cited in "The Writings of Liberal Saudi Journalist Raid Qusti," Memri Special Dispatch, no. 665, February 20, 2004, http://www.memri.org/bin/articles.cgi?Area=saudiarabia&ID=SP66504 (accessed March 26, 2009).

41. "Saudi Arabia: Should a Woman Cover Her Face?" WLUML, March 17, 2005, http://www.wluml.org/english/newsfulltxt.shtml?cmd%5B157%5D=x-157 -143167 (accessed March 26, 2009).

42. "The Writings of Liberal Saudi Journalist Raid Qusti."

43. Ibid.

44. Ibid.

45. Ibid.

46. Ibid.

47. Ibid.

48. "Tradition vs. Religion," in Memri Special Dispatch, no. 720, http:// memri.org/bin/articles.cgi?Page=countries&Area=saudiarabia&ID=SP72004 (accessed March 26, 2009).

49. "The Writings of Liberal Saudi Journalist Raid Qusti."

50. "Al-Ikhbariya Makes Waves," *Arab News*, January 13, 2004, http://arab news.com/services/print/print.asp?artid=89107&d=22&m=11&y=2006&hl =Women%20Asked%20to%20Leave%20Seminar (accessed March 26, 2009).

51. "Women Asked to Leave Seminar," *Arab News*, November 22, 2006, http://arabnews.com/services/print/print.asp?artid=89107&d=22&m=11&y=2006 &hl=Women%20Asked%20to%20Leave%20Seminar (accessed March 26, 2009).

52. "Coffee with Colleague Lands Woman in Trouble," *Arab News*, February 5, 2008, http://arabnews.com/?page=1&section=0&article=106499&d=5&m=2&y =2008 (accessed March 26, 2009).

53. "Nigerian Lands in Jail for Helping 60 Year Old Woman in Riyadh," *Arab News*, August 6, 2007, http://www.arabnews.com/?page=1&section=0&article =99378&d=6& (accessed March 26, 2009).

54. Ibid.

55. *Arab News* (Saudi Arabia), September 4, 2003, in "The Writings of Liberal Saudi Journalist Raid Qusti."

56. Ibid.

57. *Arab News* (Saudi Arabia), September 17, 2003, in "The Writings of Liberal Saudi Journalist Raid Qusti."

58. *Arab News* (Saudi Arabia), December 24, 2003, in "The Writings of Liberal Saudi Journalist Raid Qusti."

59. "Kingdom in 2007: The Year of the Human Rights," *Arab News*, December 30, 2007, http://www.arabnews.com/?page=9&d=1&m=1&y=2008 &pix=community.jpg&category=Features (accessed March 26, 2009).

CHAPTER 29: ORGANIZATIONS THAT SUPPORT MUSLIM WOMEN'S RIGHTS

1. "Plan of Action—Senegal 2006," January 2006, WLUML, http://www .wluml.org/english/publistype.shtml?cmd[72]=c-1-Other%20Publications (accessed February 16, 2009).

2. "Fundamentalisms—A Web Resource for Women's Human Rights," http://www.wluml.org/english/newsfulltxt.shtml?cmd[157]=x-157-28298 (accessed February 16, 2009).

3. WLUML, "The Global Campaign: 'Stop Stoning and Killing Women!'" November 26, 2007, http://www.wluml.org/english/news/campaign_concept _paper.pdf (accessed February 16, 2009).

4. See http://www.wluml.org/english/about.shtml (accessed March 29, 2009).

5. Ibid.

6. "Plan of Action—Senegal 2006."

7. Samar Fatany, "Saudi Arabia: Arab Women Can Power Peace, Progress," Arab View, cited in *WLUML News and Views*, March 28, 2006, http://www.wluml .org/english/newsfulltxt.shtml?cmd[157]=x-157-530134 (accessed February 15, 2009).

8. *Women's eNews* Staff, "Seven Who Hear the Voices of Women in Need," January 2, 2006, http://www.womensenews.org/Article.cfm/dyn/aid/2568 (accessed February 15, 2009).

9. "Saudi Arabia: Arab Women Can Power Peace, Progress."

10. Ibid.

11. Arab International Women's Forum, http://www.aiwfonline.co.uk (accessed March 26, 2009).

12. "Muslims and the West: Living Together—But How?" Conference held at the National Library, Vienna, October 18, 2007, http://www.frauen-ohne-grenzen .org/news/aktuell/99 (accessed February 15, 2009).

13. Arab International Women's Forum.

14. *Women's eNews* Staff, "Seven Who Hear the Voices of Women in Need."

15. Ibid.

16. Diana Nammi, "In Memoriam. In Memory of All Women Who Fall Victim to Honor Killings," ICAHK, September 2005, http://www.stophonour killings.com/?name=Content&pa=showpage&pid=2 (accessed February 16, 2009).

17. Afif Sarhan and Caroline Davies, "Mother Who Defied the Killers Is Gunned Down," *Observer* (London), June 1, 2008, http://www.guardian.co .uk/world/2008/jun/01/iraq (accessed February 16, 2009).

18. James Emery, "Reputation Is Everything. Honor Killing among the Palestinians," http://www.worldandi.com/newhome/public/2003/may/clpub.asp (accessed February 16, 2009).

19. Ibid.

20. "STOP! Honor Killings, International Campaign against Honor Killings," http://www.stophonourkillings.com (accessed February 16, 2009).

21. Damien McElroy, "Saudi Woman Killed for Chatting on Facebook," *Telegraph* (UK), April 1, 2008.

22. "International Women's Day: Remembering Our Dead," *STOP! Honor Killings*, March 2006, http://www.stophonourkillings.com/?name=Content&pid=13 (accessed February 16, 2009).

23. Dr. Hans-Peter Raddatz, quoted in Jamie Glazov, "Symposium: Killing Women for Honor," *Front Page Magazine*, June 10, 2005, http://www.front pagemag.com/readArticle.aspx?ARTID=8314 (accessed February 16, 2009).

24. H. Mahmoud, "Human Chattel," ICAHK 2007, http:// www.stophonour killings.com/index.php?name=News&file=article&sid=1609 (accessed February 16, 2009).

25. Mideast Youth: Ahmad, http://www.mideastyouth.com/author/ahmad (accessed February 15, 2009).

26. LAHA Web site, http://la-ha.org/about (accessed February 15, 2009).

27. "Young Jordanian Activist Mobilizes to Stop 'Honor Killings,'" CRIME Report, Civil Rights in the Middle East, August 14, 2007, http://www.hamsaweb .org/crime/3.html (accessed February 15, 2009).

28. Ahmad Ghashmary, "Let's Stop Othello and Save Desdemona (No More Honor Killings)," August 20, 2007, http://mideastyouth.com/2007/08/20/let%E2 %80%99s-stop-othello-and-save-desdemona-no-more-honor-killings (accessed February 15, 2009).

29. Ibid.

30. Ahmad Ghashmary, "An Update on the Issue of FGM in Egypt," December 14, 2007, http://la-ha.org/category/civil-rights (accessed February 15, 2009).

31. "Young Jordanian Activist Mobilizes to Stop 'Honor Killings.'"

32. Ibid.

33. Anisa de Jong and Suhraiya Jivraj, "Muslim Moral Instruction on Homosexuality," in *(Homo)Sexualities and Youth: An Encyclopedia*, 2004, Safra Project Publications, www.safraproject.org (accessed February 16, 2009).

34. Suhraiya and Anisa, "The Journey to Acceptance—Working with and for Lesbian and Gay Refugees from Muslim Countries.pdf," in *InExile Magazine*, Refugee Council, September/October 2002, www.safraproject.org (accessed February 16, 2009).

35. Al-Fatiha, http://www.al-fatiha.org (accessed March 28, 2009).

36. "Findings and Needs," *Safra Project Initial Findings January 2002*, http://www.safraproject.org (accessed February 16, 2009).

37. Ibid.

38. Ibid.

39. "Diversity as Strength," presentation at Confederation of Indian Organizations Conference on Sexuality and Mental Health," March 2006, Safra Project Publications, www.safraproject.org (accessed March 26, 2009).

40. *Safra Project Initial Findings January 2002*, http://www.safraproject.org (accessed March 26, 2009).

41. "Diversity as Strength."

42. De Jong and Jivraj, "Muslim Moral Instruction on Homosexuality."

APPENDIX

1. *Arab Human Development Report 2005 (AHDR): Towards the Rise of Women in the Arab World*, http://www.arab-hdr.org/contents/index.aspx (accessed March 26, 2009), p. vii.

2. Ibid., p. 34.

3. Ibid., p. 70.

4. Ibid., p. 71.

5. Ibid., p. 79.

6. Ibid., p. 80.

7. Ibid., p. 86.

8. Ibid., p. 96.

9. Ibid., p. 99.

10. Ibid., p. 119.

11. Ibid.

12. Ibid., p. 121.

13. Ibid., pp. 15–16.

14. Ibid., p. 146.

15. Ibid., p. 148.
16. Ibid., p. 168.
17. Ibid., p. 151.
18. Ibid., p. 219.
19. Ibid., p. 224.
20. Ibid., p. 225.
21. Ibid.
22. Ibid.
23. Ibid., p. 231.

GLOSSARY

Abaya (jilaabah, jilbab, pl.): A loose-fitting black robe/cloak worn by Muslim women, covering the body from head to toe. A variety of veiling (including the burka and headscarf), in accordance with *hijab*.

Burqa (burkha, burka, burqua): An outer garment that envelops the whole body and is commonly worn in Afghanistan.

Dhimmi: A non-Muslim subject of a Muslim country who was offered protection by the state but had social and legal restrictions and was required to pay a special tax (*jaziya*).

Diyya (diyeh, diya, dieh): Blood money. Financial compensation for bodily injury or murder in lieu of punishment. Allows for pardon if victim's family accepts blood money. Compensation for the death of a man is twice as much as that for a woman.

Fatwa: Religious edict, for example, the 1989 death sentence pronounced by Ayatollah Ruhollah Khomeini on Salman Rushdie, author of *The Satanic Verses*.

Fikh (Figh): Islamic jurisprudence. The Koran and the Sunnah are the two major sources of Islamic jurisprudence.

Fitna: Divisions and disagreements within Islam that could lead to chaos.

Hadith (*al-hadīth*): Oral traditions relating to the teachings and example of the Prophet Muhammad. Important sources for determining Muslim jurisprudence and way of life.

Haram: The Arabic word for that which is forbidden or sacred. *Haram* can also mean unclean, defiling, or sinful.

Hijab: Literally "curtain." Arabic term meaning to veil or cover, associated with women's modest dress in public, covering the whole body except for face and hands. In contemporary usage, the term *hijab* refers to the headscarf and is used to identify women who cover their hair (*muhajabat*).

Honor Killing: Refers to the murder of a woman by a family member who believes her behavior has brought shame on the family or clan through an unacceptable relationship or violation of dress codes.

Hudood (Hudud) Ordinances: Pakistani law instituted in 1979 by President Zia as part of an Islamization process and relating to theft, fornication, and consumption of alcohol.

Ijtihad: Independent critical approach to the interpretation of Islamic jurisprudence and a technique to produce a more liberal, reformed Islam.

Imam: Leader of an Islamic mosque and/or Muslim community.

Islamism/Islamist: Terms denoting movements and their adherents who promote Islam as a political movement and whose aims are the conquest of state power and rule by shari'ah law.

Jahaliya: Arabic word referring to the pre-Islamic time of ignorance.

Jihad: A term with both violent and nonviolent connotations meaning to strive and/or struggle, and in the West, commonly associated with war on behalf of Islam.

Jilbāb (jillbob): See *Abaya*.

Jirga (*jirgah*): An assembly of tribal elders formed to channel communications, resolve conflicts, and make decisions, particularly among the Pashtun in Afghanistan.

Kaaba: Arabic for "cube." A structure inside the al-Masjid al-Haram mosque in Mecca, Saudi Arabia, and the holiest place in Islam. According to Islamic tradition, the Kaaba was built by Abraham and his son Ishmael.

Koran (Qur'an): Arabic for "the recitation." The central, guiding religious text of Islam, as revealed to the Prophet Muhammad in the seventh century and believed to be God's final revelation to man.

Mabahith: Secret police agency of the Ministry of Interior, Saudi Arabia.

Madrassa: Islamic school or seminary.

Mahr (*mehr, meher, or mahrieh*): Mandatory bride price in Islamic cultures, given by a groom to his bride.

Mahram: Unmarriageable kin; commonly used to denote a guardian or chaperone.

Mesfar Marriage: Temporary marriage to a guardian (*mahram*) to allow women to travel abroad with a legal escort.

Misyar Marriage: A Sunni marriage contract in which the wife remains in her parent's home and gives up rights such as maintenance, housing, and dowry. A man may have a *misyar* wife in addition to traditional wives.

Mullah: Male Muslim theologian.

Muta Marriage (*mut'ah*): A temporary Shia marriage, contracted for a fixed time period ranging from hours to years, without commitment or financial responsibility. At the end of this period, the marriage is automatically dissolved and the wife considered divorced.

Mutaween (*muttawa, mutawa'ah, mutawwa*): Arabic for "volunteers." Government-authorized religious police who enforce shari'ah law and prohibit adherents of other religions from proselytizing. The Saudi Arabian Mutaween, composed of thousands of officers and volunteers, form part of the Committee for the Propagation of Virtue and the Prevention of Vice, assigned to enforce shari'ah, prevent homosexuality, proselytizing by other religions, and so forth.

Niqab: The full-face veil, often synonymous with the burqa.

Polygamy: The condition of having more than one spouse (usually referring to having more than one wife).

Polygyny: Having more than one wife at one time.

Repudiation of marriage (*talak*): Classic Islamic law allows for unilateral divorce by the husband.

Salafism: Arabic for "predecessors" or "early generations." Refers to a Sunni ideology that aims to revive Islam as practiced during the time of the Prophet.

Self-Immolation: The act of committing suicide by setting oneself on fire, often as a form of protest.

Shari'ah Law (shari'a, sharia): Arabic for "way" or "path to the water source." The body of rules and norms derived from the primary sources of Muslim law, the Koran, and hadith. Shari'ah refers to regulations covering worship, ritual, and judicial and political duties. Believed to reflect the divine will.

Shia Islam: The second-largest branch of Islam (after Sunni Islam) and the majority branch in Iran, Bahrain, and Iraq. Unlike Sunnis, Shia Muslims believe that Ali ibn Abi Talib, the Prophet Muhammad's cousin and son-in-law, was his true successor.

Shura: Arabic for "consultation." Consultative decision-making process. Village council of respected male tribal elders in Afghanistan.

Sunnah: Arabic for "trodden path." Religious actions of the Prophet Muhammad transmitted through the generations. In Shia Islam, the Sunnah also includes the deeds and sayings of the twelve imams considered to have been chosen by Muhammad to lead the Umma or the world community of Muslims.

Sunni Islam: The largest denomination in Islam, whose followers believe the successor to Muhammad was his father-in-law, Abu Bakr, who became the first caliph (leader of the *Umma*).

Takfir (*takfeer*): The practice of alleging that certain Muslims are heretics or nonbelievers in God.

Takiyya: Concealing one's faith.

Talaq (talak): An Arabic word meaning "to release" or "to divorce." Under Muslim law, *talaq* refers to divorce by means of articulating words. Triple *talaq* is a controversial Sunni method of divorce in which the husband says, "talaq, talaq, talaq" (I divorce you, I divorce you, I divorce you).

Ulama: A council of Islamic religious and legal scholars.

Umma: Arabic for "community" or "nation." Refers to the entire community of Muslims.

Wahhabism: (Wahabism, Wahabbism): A puritanical form of Islam based on the teachings of Muhammad ibn Abd-al-Wahhab and practiced primarily in Saudi Arabia. Wahhabi ideology aims to remove deviances and idolatries from religious practice. Practitioners see their role as rescuing Islam from what they perceive to be polytheism and consider other branches of Islam as heretical.

Wanasa ("platonic" or "fun company") Marriage: designed mainly for older men who or wish to marry young girls.

Zina: Extramarital sex. The offense could incur a punishment of stoning to death in the case of married women and one hundred lashes for unmarried women.

REFORM WEB SITES AND CONFERENCES

MUSLIM WOMEN'S REFORM WEB SITES

Afghan Women's Network (AWN)
Advocacy group that campaigns for women's empowerment and lobbies
    Afghan government and UN agencies.
http://www.afghanwomensnetwork.org

Al-Zahraa Palestinian Arab Women's Organization
Supports higher education for women and runs courses in economic
    management.
http://old.ittijah.org/member/alzahra.html

Arab International Women's Forum
UK-based organization that links Arab business and professional women in
    Arab countries and globally.
http://www.aiwfonline.co.uk

Arabs and Muslims against Honor Killings
http://www.nohonor.org

Asian-American Network against Abuse of Women (ANAA)
Volunteer human rights organization in Pakistan.
http://4anaa.org

Association for Women's Rights in Development (AWID)
Advances the rights of women internationally.
http://www.awid.org

Aurat Foundation
Pakistani activist women's rights NGO that promotes women's educational,
    advocacy, empowerment, legislation, and public policy programs.
http://www.af.org.pk/mainpage.htm

Center for Development and Population Activities (CEDPA)
Dedicated to improving the lives of women and girls in developing countries
    through programs in education, health, and leadership.
http://www.cedpa.org

Center for Women's Global Leadership (CWGL)
Develops leadership for women human rights activists.
http://www.cwgl.rutgers.edu

Change for Equality Campaign
Aims to collect a million signatures in support of changing Iran's discrimi-
    natory laws against women.
http://www.change4equality.com/english (has been intermittently blocked
    by Iranian government authorities)

Dr. Homa Darabi Foundation
Promotes the rights of women and children as defined by the Universal
    Declaration of the United Nations 1948 General Assembly.
http://www.homa.org

Defending Women Defending Rights
Defends women activists who work in the field of women's rights.
http://www.defendingwomen-defendingrights.org

Equality Now
Global activist campaign to end violence and discrimination against women.
    Driven internationally by Women's Action Network.
http://www.equalitynow.org

Fatema Mernissi
A Web site providing a selection of articles, books, and research by Fatema
    (Fatima) Mernissi.
http://www.mernissi.net

Female Genital Cutting Education and Networking Project (FGCENP)
Advocates the abolition of female genital mutilation (FGM) or female cir-
    cumcision. Library of material for sufferers, practitioners, activists,
    researchers, lawyers, and healthcare professionals.
http://www.fgmnetwork.org

Femin Ijtihad
Academic initiative for Muslim women's rights. Aims to produce a resource on *ijtihad* (critical thinking within Islam), a manual on gender equality and reform of the Afghan civil and criminal code.
http://feminijtihad.webs.com

Feminist Majority Foundation
Based in the United States. Projects include Campaign to Stop Gender Apartheid in Afghanistan, and support for Shirin Ebadi, defender of women's rights and Nobel laureate, whose human rights organization in Iran was forcibly closed.
http://feminist.org/welcome/index.html

Feminist Sexual Ethics Project
Academic exploration of sexual ethics and slavery in ancient religious texts and their transmission and relevance to contemporary women.
http://www.brandeis.edu/projects/fse

GAMS (French site)
Advocates the abolition of female genital mutilation.
http://pagesperso-orange.fr/associationgams/gamsiteeng/pages/presgams.html

Global Fund for Women
Provides grants to women's organizations that work toward freedom from poverty, violence, and discrimination.
http://www.globalfundforwomen.org

Heinrich Boell Foundation Feminist Institute, Berlin
Provides future-oriented research and exchange of information on women's policy issues.
http://www.glow-boell.de/en/rubrik_1/811_941.htm

Human Rights Service (HRS)
An independent Norwegian think tank focusing on violations of women's rights, for example, forced marriage, female genital mutilation, and honor killing.
http://www.rights.no

Intact-Network

Egyptian-based organization. Aims to eliminate FGM worldwide through social, epidemiological, and intervention research, education, and training. Organizes campaigns and seminars to increase public awareness. Utilizes research findings to guide local and government policies.

http://www.intact-network.net

International Campaign against Honor Killing (ICAHK)

Campaigns against "honor killings," stoning, and female genital mutilation. Provides confidential assistance to potential victims.

http://www.stophonourkillings.com

International Women's Rights Action Watch—Asia Pacific

Monitors implementation of the Convention on the Elimination of All Forms of Discrimination against Women (CEDAW) in order to reform laws and social policy. Significant presence in twelve countries, including Bangladesh, India, Nepal, Pakistan, Sri Lanka, Indonesia, and Malaysia.

http://www.iwraw-ap.org

Irshad Manji Blog and Official Web Site

Web site of courageous Muslim reformer and author of *The Trouble with Islam Today: A Muslim's Call for Reform in Her Faith*.

http://www.irshadmanji.com

Karamah: Muslim Women Lawyers for Human Rights

Educational human rights organization committed to Muslim women's liberation within Islamic law. Informs Muslims in the United States about their civil rights.

http://www.karamah.org/home.htm

KMG (Kembatta Women's Self-Help Center)

Ethiopian organization in Kembatta region that empowers women to confront gender-based violence and abuse, particularly female genital mutilation. Programs include HIV education, livelihood training, and protection of the environment.

http://www.kmgselfhelp.org

Madre
Works with women affected by human rights violations.
http://www.madre.org

Mehrangiz Kar
Promotes democracy, human rights, and women's rights within the framework of Islamic law in Iran.
http://www.mehrangizkar.net

Musawah: For Equality in the Family
Malaysian-based global movement advocating equality in the family consistent with Islam and universal human rights principles.
http://www.musawah.org

Revolutionary Association of the Women of Afghanistan (RAWA)
Oldest political/social organization in Afghanistan, promoting women's
rights, democracy, peace, and freedom.
http://www.rawa.org

Saudi Amber
Aims to raise women's awareness of their rights, with the objective of creating a Saudi women's news forum and "mainstream."
http://saudiamber.blogspot.com

Sisters in Islam (SIS)
Malaysian activist organization striving for women's rights and human rights
by revealing diverse interpretations within Islam. Campaigns include
targeting Islamic Family Law 2005 amendments and opposition to
gender violence, polygamy, moral policing, and book banning.
http://www.sistersinislam.org.my

The South Asia Women and Islam Virtual Network Project
Collaborative Internet-based project dealing with the challenges facing
Muslim women in five countries: Afghanistan, Bangladesh, Nepal, Pakistan, and Sri Lanka. Promotes tolerance, diversity, democratic institutions, and opposition to Islamist extremism. Features news, research, and
symposia. Includes Muslim Women's Research and Action Forum

(MWRAF), Sri Lanka, and Organization for Research and Education (ORE), Pakistan.
http://www.womenandislam.net

UNIFEM (United Nations Development Fund for Women)
Its programs advance women's rights around the world.
http://www.unifem.org

Vital Voices Global Partnership
Identifies and trains women leaders around the globe.
http://www.vitalvoices.org

Voice of Women Organization
Runs a women's shelter and educational projects in Afghanistan to counter gender violence, self-immolation, and substance abuse, improve hygiene, and generate employment.
http://www.vwo.org.af

Womankind Worldwide
Funding, training, and networking for women in developing countries.
http://www.womankind.org.uk

Women against Shariah
Aims to enable women to oppose shari'ah law worldwide and prevent the application of shari'ah in the United States by informing the American public about shari'ah-related honor killings, and human rights and gender rights violations.
http://www.womenagainstshariah.com

Women for Women International
Provides assistance to women survivors of war.
http://www.womenforwomen.org

Women for Women's Human Rights (WWHR)—New Ways (Turkish site)
Turkey and worldwide. Incorporates women's rights, domestic violence, sexual rights, and rights of girls. Combines research, training, lobbying, and outreach.
http://www.wwhr.org

Women Living under Muslim Law (WLUML)
International network for information, support, alerts, and Muslim women's
    rights campaigns.
http://www.wluml.org/english

The Women of Islam
News and article resource aimed to raise awareness of Muslim women's
    plight.
http://thewomenofislam.info/index.html

Women's eNews
Promotes women's freedom of speech and defends against gender-based
    censorship.
http://womensenews.org

Women's Forum against Fundamentalism in Iran
Provides news and research on human rights and women's rights violations.
    US-based.
http://www.wfafi.org

Women's Freedom Forum (WFF)
US-based organization. Activist group and resource for misogyny, violence
    against women, combating Islamic fundamentalism, human trafficking,
    and child abuse. Runs annual WFF event.
http://womenfreedomforum.com

Women's Initiatives for Gender Justice
International women's human rights organization working toward an effec-
    tive and independent International Criminal Court (ICC). Based in The
    Hague.
http://www.iccwomen.org

Women's International League for Peace and Freedom
Promotes the full implementation of United Nations Security Council Res-
    olution 1325 on women, peace, and security.
http://www.peacewomen.org

Women's Islamic Initiative in Spirituality and Equity (WISE)

Global Muslim women leaders' initiative working to change negative views of Muslim women and advance women's rights in accordance with Islamic law. List of participants includes many reformers and like-minded women living in the West. Sponsored by the ASMA society and Cordoba Initiative.

http://www.asmasociety.org/wise/news.html

Women's Learning Partnership (WLP)

Promotes feminist movements in Muslim-majority societies.

http://www.learningpartnership.org

Women without Borders

International advocacy, public relations, and lobbying organization that stands for peaceful conflict resolution and offers a forum for women in politics and civil society.

http://www.women-without-borders.org

ISLAMIC REFORM WEB SITES

AAFAQ

Independent, nongovernmental Arabic news Web site based in the United States. Committed to reform, liberalism, and democracy as opposed to Islamism and dictatorship in the Middle East.

http://www.aafaq.org/english/Index.aspx

American Islamic Forum for Democracy

Voice of Muslim Americans who support the citizenship pledge, American domestic and foreign interests, and the separation of state and religion.

http://www.aifdemocracy.org

American Muslim Congress

Secular civil rights organization that promotes tolerance and exchange of ideas among Muslims and the wider community. Advocates responsible civic leadership and interfaith understanding.

http://www.aicongress.org

ASMA Society

Founded in 1997 by Imam Feisal Abdul Rauf, in New York City. Committed to advancing American-Muslim identity in a pluralistic society and improving understanding between American Muslims and non-Muslims.

http://www.asmasociety.org

Center for Democracy and Human Rights in Saudi Arabia

Promotes a variety of reforms in Saudi Arabia: political and religious freedom, women's rights, minority rights, economic reform, and US legislation to support reforms in Saudi Arabia.

http://www.cdhr.info

Center for Islamic Pluralism

Think tank that opposes politicized Islam and promotes moderate Islam through publications, media activism, conferences, and outreach to Muslim communities internationally.

http://www.islamicpluralism.org

Faith Freedom International

Forum for ex-Muslims and those who want to leave Islam. Provides factual information about the negative aspects of Islamic texts and history. Holds the belief that Islam cannot be reformed.

www.faithfreedom.org

Free Muslim Coalition (FMC)

Supports reform within Islam. Challenges Islamic terrorism. Believes women's rights are integral to the defeat of Islamic extremism and terrorism.

http://www.freemuslims.org

The Initiative for an Open Arab Internet

Enterprise of the Arabic Network for Human Rights Information (ANHRI). Advocates online freedom without censorship, blocking, or spying. Reports on Arab governments' handling of the Internet. Defends Internet writers, Web designers, and users by means of legal and media campaigns.

http://www.openarab.net/en

Institute for the Secularization of Islamic Society (ISIS)
Promotes rationalism, secularism, democracy, and human rights within
    Islamic societies. Highlights the plight and achievements of Muslim
    women.
http://www.centerforinquiry.net/isis

International Centre for Islamic Pluralism (ICIP)
Disseminates Islamic texts supporting pluralism, human rights, and democ-
    racy by Indonesian and international moderate and progressive Muslims.
    Supports gender equality within Islamic discourse and critical inter-
    change between the Muslim world and the West.
http://www.icipglobal.org/index.php

International Quranic Center
Committed to an interpretation of the Koran consistent with the principles
    of American democracy, human rights, and interfaith dialogue.
http://www.ahl-alquran.com/English/main.php

Islam and Human Rights
Fellowship program at Emory University that explores tensions between
    Islamic and Western perspectives on human rights. Provides a collection
    of academic articles. Advocates human rights in Muslim societies.
http://www.law.emory.edu/ihr

Islamic Reform
Web site featuring a theological exposé of Islam.
http://www.islamicreform.org

Jaringan Islam Liberal (Liberal Islam Network)
Indonesian network promoting a liberal interpretation of Islamic texts, plu-
    ralism, and separation of religion and state. Activities include book pub-
    lishing, articles, advertisements, and seminars.
http://islamlib.com

Manifesto of Liberties
Paris-based organization advocating reform for Muslims worldwide,
    including democracy and secular politics. Condemns misogyny, homo-

phobia, and anti-Semitism perpetuated by Islamists. The founding document, published on February 16, 2004, was signed by 1,800 Muslim men and women and concluded with an appeal for other interested parties to sign the manifesto.

http://www.manifeste.org

English-language: http://www.manifeste.org/article.php3?id_article=18

Muslim Reform Movement Organization

Seeks to guide progressive Muslims by restating the revelations of the Prophet Muhammad for the contemporary world.

http://www.mrmo.org

Muslims against Sharia

Committed to reform of Islam by educating Muslims about the dangers of Islamism and non-Muslims about the difference between moderates and Islamists.

http://www.reformislam.org

Muslim Wake Up! (MWU!)

Promotes reformist ideas within Islam, publishes articles by regular and guest columnists, maintains a discussion forum, and organizes special events.

http://www.muslimwakeup.com

No to Political Islam Petition

Umbrella organization of fourteen groups united in a campaign to oppose political Islam by gathering signatures for a petition. Web site features exposé of political Islam.

http://www.ntpi.org

Quilliam Foundation

Counter-Islamist think tank based in London and founded by former Islamists. Seeks to reform extremists and develop a Western Islam free of radicalism.

http://www.quilliamfoundation.org

Radical Islam
Activist Web site offering educational resources and tools to counter violent
    Islamic extremism.
http://www.radicalislam.org

Rooz online
News Web site in Farsi and English. Contributing journalists come from
    within and outside Iran.
http://www.roozonline.com/english

The White Path
Mustafa Akyol, Turkish writer. Articles, analysis, and debates about Islam.
http://www.thewhitepath.com

CONFERENCES: MUSLIM WOMEN'S REFORM

Association for Women's Rights in Development (AWID)
International Forum conferences bring together women's rights activists
    from around the world every three years.
http://www.awid.org

Cordoba Initiative
Multifaith organization founded in 2002 by the ASMA Society. Third Inter-
    national Conference, "Islam and the West: Bridging the Gap," was held
    in June 2007 in Kuala Lumpur.
http://www.cordobainitiative.org

International Congress on Islamic Feminism
Three conferences in Barcelona since 2005 under the auspices of the Catalan
    Islamic Board. Third congress took place in October 2008. Aims are to
    improve women's rights from within Islam by challenging patriarchal
    culture and religious interpretations. Focus on Islamic feminism in rela-
    tion to global feminism and the antiglobalization movement.
http://www.feminismeislamic.org/eng

Sisters in Islam (SIS)
International meeting, Malaysia, February 13–17, 2009, to launch Musawah,
    global movement for "equality and justice in the Muslim Family."
http://www.sistersinislam.org.my

Women without Borders
Conferences: "Muslims and the West: Living Together—But How?" Vienna,
    October 2007; "SAVE Israel-Palestine: We Must Give Peace a Chance.
    Voices from the Israeli-Palestinian Frontline," March 15, 2009.
http://www.women-without-borders.org